Robert Steele, T. Henderson

Three Prose Versions of the Secreta Secretorum

Vol. I

Robert Steele, T. Henderson

Three Prose Versions of the Secreta Secretorum
Vol. I

ISBN/EAN: 9783744686211

Printed in Europe, USA, Canada, Australia, Japan

Cover: Foto ©Thomas Meinert / pixelio.de

More available books at **www.hansebooks.com**

Three Prose Versions

of the

Secreta Secretorum.

EDITED

WITH INTRODUCTION AND NOTES

BY

ROBERT STEELE.

AND

A GLOSSARY BY T. HENDERSON, M.A.

VOL. I.

Text and Glossary.

LONDON:

PUBLISHED FOR THE EARLY ENGLISH TEXT SOCIETY
BY KEGAN PAUL, TRENCH, TRÜBNER & Co.,
PATERNOSTER HOUSE, CHARING-CROSS ROAD, W.C.
1898.

Extra Series, LXXIV.

R. CLAY & SONS, LIMITED, LONDON & BUNGAY.

NOTE.

THE present volume contains three versions of the *Secreta Secretorum*, the first from a shortened French source, the second from a Latin source. The third text, perhaps the only lengthy work known written in the English of the Pale early in the fifteenth century, is so important, linguistically and historically, that Dr. Furnivall wishes it to be in the hands of students as soon as possible. I have therefore postponed my Introduction and Notes. In the meantime some account of the originals may be found in my Introduction to Lydgate and Burgh's *Secrees*. As the work is being issued I discover that the greater portion of this text is a direct translation of the French version made by Jofroi of Waterford.

R. S.

THE SECRETE OF SECRETES.

TRANSLATED FROM THE FRENCH.

(MS. Reg. 18 A. vij. B.M.)

4   t his is the book of the governaunce of kyngis and of Pryncis, callid the Secrete of Secretes, whiche that Aristotille made to kyng Alexandre forth, with the ordinaunce of the Chapitris in ordir: and a Prologe of a gret
8   doctoure recomendyng Aristotille.

			PAGE
	1 The epistille that Alexandre sent to Aristotille. ...	4
	2 The answer of the same epistille.	4
	3 The prologe of him that translatid þis book into latyne.	4
12	4 Of the largenes of a kyng.	7
	5 Of largenes and avarice of a kyng.	8
	6 Of vertues and vicis, and doctrine of Aristotille. ...	9
	7 Of entendement, which is vndirstondyng.	9
16	8 Of the entencioun that longith to a kyng.	10
	9 Of yvelis that cometh of flesshely desires.	10
	10 Of wisdome and ordinaunce of a kyng.	11
	11 Of a kyngis goodnes and holynes.	11
20	12 Of the purveaunce of a kyng.	12
	13 Of clothyng of a kyng.	12
	14 Of the countenaunce of a kyng.	12
	15 Of the rightwisnes of a kyng.	14
24	16 Of worldly desires of a kyng.	14
	17 Of the chastite of a kyng.	14
	18 Of the pleiyng of a kyng.	15
	19 Of the discrecioun of a kyng.	15
28	20 Of the reuerence of a kyng.	16
	21 How a kyng shalle make sugetis.	17
	22 Of the mercy of a kyng.	17
	23 Of the peynes and vengeaunce of god.	18

[1] These page- and chapter-numbers are not in the MS.

SECRETE.   B

			PAGE	
24	Of knowleche of the same peynes.		18	
25	fforto kepe the feith.		18	
26	Of studies and scolis.		19	
27	Of kepyng of a kyng.	[fol. 1 b]	20	4
28	Of the difference of Astronomye.		21	
29	Of kepyng of helthe.		21	
30	Of gouernaunce in seeknes.		22	
31	In how many maners a man may kepe helthe.		22	8
32	Of dyuerse metis.		23	
33	Of the stomak.		23	
34	Signes to knowe the stomak.		23	
35	A pistille of gret price.		23	12
36	The maner of trauayle.		24	
37	Of abstinence.		25	
38	Nought to drynke pure watir.		25	
39	The maner forto slepe.		25	16
40	Of kepyng of Custome.		26	
41	How a man owith to chaunge custome.		26	
42	Of foure tymes of the yere.		27	
43	Of prime temps, what it is.		27	20
44	Of somer tyme.		27	
45	Of hervest tyme.		28	
46	Of wyntir tyme.		29	
47	Of naturalle hete.		29	24
48	Of thing that fattith the body.		29	
49	Of thing that leneth the body.		30	
50	Of the first parti of the body.		30	
51	Of the secund parti of the body.		31	28
52	Of the thridde parti of the body.		31	
53	Of the fourthe parti of the body.		31	
54	Of the maner of fisshis.		32	
55	Of nature of watris.[1]		33	32
56	Of nature of wyne.[1]		33	
57	Of sowre Syrupe.		33	
58	Of foure maner of rightwisnesse.	[fol. 2 a]	33	
59	Of a kyngis secretarie.		35	36
60	Of a kyngis messangeres.		36	
61	Of governaunce of the peple.		36	
62	Of ffisnomye of ffolke.		38	

[1] Chap. 55 and 56 were missing in the MS. from which this copy is printed.

The Prologe of a gret doctour recomendyng Aristotille.

Od almyghty kepe oure kyng and conferme his Rewmc
in the lawe of god, and make him regne in gladnes, in
lovyng, and in worshipe of god. I that am servitoure of
the kyng, haue put in execucioun his comaundement, and
travaylid forto gete the book of good thewes to him; whiche is
callid the secrete of secretis of the makyng of Aristotille, prince *Aristotle, son of Mahomet*
of philesofris, sone of Machomete of macedonye, which was sent *(Nichomachus).*
to his discipille as in governaunce Alexandre the emperoure,
sone of kyng Philip of Grece, the whiche Alexaundre had two
Crownes. This book made this forseyd Aristotille in his gret
age, whan he myght not travayle ne done the nedis that he had
in charge of Alexandre. ffor Alexandre had made him governoure
and maystir aboue alle othir, for the excellent witt þat he had in
clergie and sotille vndirstondyng, for euyr he was stodiyng in *The good qualities of*
good and gracious thewes, charitabille, spirituelle and contem- *Aristotle.*
platyf; and also he was so wys & meke, and lovyd resoun and
rightwisnes; and euyr reportid trouthe and lewte. Therfore
oold Philesofres seyne by him, that they haue founden in Greke
bokis that god hath sent his excellent Aungille and seyde to *An angel sent to him from*
him, "y shalle do the to be namyd thorugh alle the world more *God.*
for Aungille than for man." And witith welle that Aristotille
made in his lyvyng many wondres, of the whiche [1]some be right [¹ fol. 2 b.]
meruelous to telle; and in his diyng fille many mervelous
thingis. Wherfore a certeyne Religioun helde an opynyon that
Aristotille was mountid vp to hevene in lyknes to a dowue of
fyre. And as long as Aristotille lyvid, Alexandre bi his coun- *Alexander conquered*
selle helde alle londis vndir foote and conquerid alle lordshipes *the world by following his*
of the world, and thorugh alle londis went his fame and his *advice.*
renome. Alle nacions were putt vndir his imperialite and
comaundement, and specially they of perce and of Arabie, and
no lond durste withstond him in word nor dede. And Aristotille
made many fayre Epistolis for the gret loue that he had
to Alexandre, forto make him knowe alle secretis that bilongith
any erthely man to knowe or vndirstond. And on of his
Epistelis is here vndir writene, which he sent to Alexandre. ffor *The reason for the follow-*
whan Alexandre had put hem of Perce in subieccioun, and the *ing letter.*
grettist men of Romaynes had in his prisone, he sent an Epistille
to Aristotille in these wordes folowyng.

The Epistille that Alexandre sent to Aristotille the gret clerke. Ca^m primum.

What is to be done with the wise men of Persia?

o Doctoure of gret rightwisnes and nobille gouernour, we signifie to thi gret wisdom that we haue founden in the lond of Perce many men the which habound gretly in wisdome, resoun, and vndirstondyng, welle sotille and perceyvyng, and hope forto haue lordship aboue alle othir, and forto gete Rewmes. Wherfore we purpose to putt hem alle to deth. But only thou certifie vs bi thi lettres, as thou semest most spedfulle vnto vs, for therbi wolle we worche, and noon othir wise.

The answer of the same Epistille ayen to Alexandre. Capitulum ij^m.

[¹ fol. 3 a.]
Govern them with kindness, and they will be meek subjects.

a nd thou mowe chaunge the eyre of the lond, and the watris, and the ordinaunce of Citees, than do as thou hast purposid, and ellis nought. But gouerne þat ¹pepille in goodnes, and enhaunce them in thi benygnyte. And if thou do thus, y truste in god, alle they shulle be þi meeke subiectis, And obeye alle thi likyngis and comaundementis. And for the loue that they shalle haue to þe, thou shalt regne on them pesibly with gret victory. And whan Alexandre had red this epistille, he did aftir the counselle of them of Perce, and found hem more lowly and obeyshaunt to him than any othir were.

The prologe of him that translatid this book into latyne. Ca^m iij^m.

His search for secrets.

Philip, interpretour and vndirstondere of alle langagis. y haue knowe no stede, ne place, ne temple where philesofres haue customyd to make or vnmake alle werkis and secretis, that y ne haue sought hem. Ne y haue herd told of no wise mane þat had knowleche in scriptures of philesofris, that y ne haue visitid

He finds a hermit in the Temple of the Sun:

him vnto þe tyme y come to the knowleche of the [temple of the] sone that made Esculapideos: there y fond a man solitarie, fulle of gret abstinence and right wijs in philosofie, to whom y lowid me diligently, And bisought him that he wold shewe me

who teaches him with good will.

the scriptures of the knowleche of the sone, the which he yaf me with good wille. And wite ye welle y fond alle that, that y desirid, and alle that y went fore to the forseid place, and alle that that y so moche desirid. I retornyd home with gret ioye,

and yeldid many gracis and worshipis to my makere. And
sithen at the request of the nobille kyng Alexandre, in gret
studie and moche laboure, y translatid this book, out of Greke *He translates the book from Greek into*
into the langage of Caldee, and aftir into the tonge of Arabike, *Syriac, and thence into Arabic.*
the which book made the right wijs Aristotille, that answerid
euyr to alle the questiones of kyng Alexandre, as ye shalle se
more pleynlier sewyng bi ordre.

¹Ight glorious sone and emperoure rightwis, god comfort the [¹ fol. 3 b.]
in the wey of trouthe and of vertues, and refrayne the from *Aristotle's preface.*
flesshely and bestly desires, and conferme thi Rewme to his
seruice and his worshipe. Wite welle, dere sone, that y haue
rescevyd thyn epistille reuerently and honourably as it to me
bilongith, and y haue fully vndirstond the gret desire that thou
hast that y were personally with the; and thou merveylist þat y
may holde me so long fro the, and also thou vndirtakist me
gretly, and seist that me rekkith but litille of alle thi gret nede,
and therfore y haue hastid me and ordeynyd me to make a book *His reasons for not coming to Alexander.*
for the, the which shalle conteyne alle thi nedes, and it shalle
fulfille myn absence and my defaut, and it shalle be rewle and
doctrine ayens alle adversitees. But, dere sone, thou owist not
repreue me ne put me in blame, for thou wost welle that ther is
no thing that myght lette me to come to thee, but only as thou
knowist welle that y may not bistere my silf, y am so gretly in
age and febille of persone, not able to go ne to ride. And wite
thou wel thou hast axid me, and so moch desirid to knowe of
suche secretis, of whiche mannys thoughtis may not comprehende
ne susteyne, how myght than eny hert of dedly man vndirstond
that, þat longith not to be knowe. But euermore bi right y am
holde to answere to that that thou axist of me. And so be thou *Cautions respecting these secrets.*
holde bi wisdom neuyr to axe me thing othir þan is contenyd
therin. ffor without dout thou shalt fynde þerin alle thing
worldly that is nedfulle or spedfulle to thyn estate. ffor god
hath yevene suche grace to thee of vndirstondyng and subtilite *Alexander's natural abilities.*
of witt, and bi the doctryne that y haue oft tymes yove thee,
that bi thy silf thou maist conceyve, ²vndirstonde, and wite alle [² fol. 4 a.]
thingis that thou desirist or axist. ffor the desire of the wille
that thou hast shalle opene the the wey to fynde thi purpos, with
the myght of god. And wite thou welle that the cause wherfore
y shewe my secretes figuratifly & derkly, and bi derke ensamplis: It is for y dowte me, that if this book come vnto the

hondis of vntrewe men, and prowd, whiche were not worthi nor able forto knowe the secretis of god almyghti, for they are not worthi therto. And wite thou welle þat y putt me in gret dowte and indignacioun of god, forto shewe thee his secretis, as he of his excellent goodnes hath shewid hem to me. And therfore and thou discouere hem vnto eny at eny tyme, wite welle that sone aftir thou shalt haue y-nowe of yville fortunes, and þou shalt not eschewe the grete disesis that are hastily to come, fro the whiche god kepe the euermore, amen. And loke in alle thing that thou haue in mynde this profitabille techyng that y haue ordeynyd to the, and am in purpos forto expowne, and bi the leue of god thi nobille hert enforme, and þat shalle be to the gret solace and myrroure of helthe. It bihovith, dere sone, þat eche kyng haue two thingis to susteyne him and his Rewme, but he may not haue hem but he be stedfast in gouernaunce, so that alle tho that ben vndir his regne ben of oon obeyshaunce, and in on subieccioun of trewe ligeaunce vnto her liege kyng, for disobeyshaunce of subiectis is most enfleccioun and enfeblisshyng of euery lord. ffor if the subiectis regne, the lordis myght is litill or ellis nought, and y shalle shewe yow cause whi. The subiectis ben mevid in corage forto obeye her lord, and þat is for two causis; the on cause is within, the othir cause without. The cause without [1] is whene the lord wisely dispendith his goodis and his ricchessis among his subiectis, And that he yeue yeftis largely to euery man aftir that he is worthi: and this is a gret poynt of wisdome, forto enforce him silf to haue the hertis of his subiectis thorugh good werkis. and this is the first degre and principalle foundacioun of his prosperite. And that he mayntene rightwisnes and euen iustice, as welle to poore as to riche, and that his rightwisnes be medlid with pite and mercy. The cause within is, that his philesofris and grete wisemen of clergie be had in worshipe and high recomendacioun: ffor god hath recomendid to hem a part of his high science. And y recomende to the this science and secrete of wisdome, forthwith the othir that thou shalt fynde in dyuerse partis of this book, in the whiche thou shalt fynde high doctryne, for thou shalt fynde the cause fynalle of thi principalle purpos. ffor whan thou hast vndirstond the sothe of the significacions of the wordis, and þe derknes of the examples, than shalt thou haue fully and perfitly alle that thou desirist. Thus pray y god,

rightwis and glorious kyng, that he enlumyne thi resoun and *May God make him know these secretis.*
thyn vndirstondyng, so that thou may come and parceyve the
secretis of this science, that thou may be therin myn heyr and
4 myn only successoure, and that graunt the god, that his ricchesse
enlargisshith and habundauntly yefith vnto lijf of wys men;
And yefith grace to do [to those] þat stodien forto knowe that is
straunge and hard in kynde, for without specialle grace of god
8 no thing may be doone vnto any good purpos.

Of the largenes of a kyng. Ca^m 4^m

t   Her are foure condiciones of kyngis. ther is a kyng that *Four kinds of kings.*
is large to him silf and large to his ^{1}sugetis. Ther is a [^{1} fol. 5 a.]
12 kyng that is skars to him silf and large to his sugetis. Ther is
a kyng that is larg to him silf, and skars to his sugetis. And
ther is a kyng that is both skars to him silf, and to his sugetis
also. Men of ytalie seyne, that ther is no vice in that kyng *Italian,*
16 that is skars to him silf, and large to his sugetis. The Iew *Indian, and Persian views.*
saith, that kyng is good that is skars to him silf and to his
sugetis bothe. The parisien saith, that kyng that is large to
him silf and to his sugetis bothe, he is not worthi to be in no
20 preysyng, but werst of alle othir. And if he be skars to him
silf and to his sugetis bothe, his Rewme may not stonde longe
in prosperite but sone come to distruccioun. Than it nedith
wisely to enquere of vertues and of vicis, what is largesse and
24 what is skarsnes, and wherin stondith the erroure of largesse,
and what disese cometh of skarsnes. It is clere thing, that þe
qualitees arne forto be reprovid, whan they aliene them from
ther meene. And wite ye welle that it is hard thing forto kepe *It is hard to keep the just mean of largesse.*
28 largesse, and light thing forto passe it. And it is a light thing
a man to be skars or foole large. And if thou wille gete larges,
biholde and considir thi power and thi ricches, and also the tyme
of nede and the deservyngis of thi men. And than owist thou
32 forto yeue mesurably vnto hem that haue nede therto, and best
haue deseruyd it, and he that yevith othir wise passith the
rewle of largesse. ffor he that yevith his good to suche as be
not worthi, [it] is but lost, and he þat spendith his good out of
36 mesure shalle sone be poore, and this makith her enemyes to
haue maystrie ouyr hem. Than he that yevith his good in *Wise largesse.*
tyme of nede to suche as haue nede therto, and principally to
suche as haue deservid ^{2}it, suche a kyng is large to him silf and [^{2} fol. 5b.]

to his sugetis bothe, and his rewme shalle stonde in gret prosperite, and his comaundementis shul be fulfillid. And he that
Foolish largesse. dispendith the goodis of his Rewme out of ordir and discrecioun,
and yevith suche as be not worthi, ne haue no nede þerto, that 4
kyng distroyeth his peple and the comoun good of the Rewme,
and is not worthi forto regne, for he is fool large. The name of
skarste is vnconvenient to a kyng, and yville bicometh to his
royalle maieste. Than if a kyng wolle regne worshipfully, it 8
bihouyth him neyþer to haue that on ne that othir of two
vicis, skarste ne fool large. And this may not welle be doon
Advantage of having a wise treasurer. without counselle. Therfore it nedith with gret diligence to
haue an Inwijs man and a discrete to counselle, the which must 12
be choscne among many othir, and suche a man must be com-
myttid to suche a charge bi the kyng and his wys counselle,
forto governe the ricches of the Rewme as it owith best to be
disposid, to the worshipe of god principally and worshipe of the 16
kyng, and thus shalle thi Rewme stonde in gret prosperite.

Of largenes and skarsnes, and many oþir vertues. Cap^m 5^m

Don't spend more than you receive. k Yng Alexandre, y telle the in certeyne that what kyng
makith gretter dispences than the profites conteyne that 20
longen to the crowne, he enclyneth him to fool largesse and
nought to skarsnes. That kyng without dowt shalle sone be
distroyed. And if he enclyne him to worshipfulle largesse, he
shall haue perpetualle ioye of his Regne. And wite welle, dere 24
sone, that y haue founde in techyngis and comaundementis of
the gret doctour Hermogenes, that the grete souereyne clerte of
vndirstondyng is plente of lawe, and konnyng is a signe of
[¹ fol. 6 a.] perfeccioun of a kyng, and þat previth whan ¹he withdrawith 28
Covetous kings have destroyed many realms. forto take the goodis and possessiones of his sugetis, for that
hath ben the cause of distruccioun of many Remes. ffor kyngis
that haue made so outrage dispenses, that the Rentis and
profetis that longid to him myght not susteyne ne mayntene 32
ther outrage dispenses, And forto mayntene it, they took the
goodis and possessiones from her sugetis, for which cause the
pepille cried to god, and god herde hem and sent on hem kyngis
Their exactions cause rebellion. of vengeaunce. The pepille rebellid ayens hem and were 36
distroyed of alle, and alle her name putt to nought. And ne
were the grace of glorious god, that susteneth and helpith the
Innocent peple, alle shuld go to distruccioun and into the

domynacioun of Alienes for euyr. And þerfore kepe the fro *Be temperate in all things.*
outrageous expenses and yeftis. And kepe euyr temperaunce
in largete, and stodie not abowt derke prophecies, ne secretis
that passith thi witt, ne neuer repreue thi yeftis with ayen- *Don't take back gifts.*
takyng, for it longith not to the condicioun of a gentille kyng.

Of vicis and vertues, and of þe doctrine of Aristotille.
Ca^m. 6^m.

He substaunce of alle vertues of a kyngis regne is forto *A summary of kingly*
yeue to good men, and to foryeue wrongis, and worshipe *virtues.*
hem that owen to be worshipid, and to do reuerence to hem that
are worthi, and to thynke on meke deth, and to kepe hem fro
ouermoche speche, and to lete passe wrongis into a tyme, and
forto feyne him that he kan not bere the foly of foolis. Dere
sone, y haue told the and shalle teche the many thingis whiche
thou shalt witholde in thyn hert, and y haue stedfast trust, that
as long as thou gouernest the as it is rehersid, thou shalt euyr
haue shynyng clernes and sufficient konnyng to thi gouernaunce
alle the tyme of þi lyf. And y shalle teche the the science of
phisik abreggid, [1] the which y had not purposid to haue spokene [¹ fol. 6 b.]
of, but for that science with the techyng that cometh therof,
may suffice the in alle werkis in this world and in that othir.

Of entendement, that is vndirstondyng. Cap^m 7^m.

Ite thou welle, right dere sone, that vndirstondyng is cheef *Praise of understand-*
of the gouernaunce of man and helthe of thi sowle, and *ing.*
keper of vertues, and flemer of vicis, for vndirstondyng shewith
vs what we owen to fleme, and what we owen to chese and
folowe. It is the keye of vertues and roote of alle louabille
goodnes and worshipe, and þe first instrument therof is desire
forto haue good renowne. ffor he that desirith to haue good *Desire to be of good re-*
renowne, shalle be ouir alle glorious and worshipfulle, and he *nown.*
that desirith it feynyngly and ypocritly, that is to say without
deseruyng, he shalle in the ende be confoundid by yville renowne
as he is worthi. A kyng owith principally forto gete and haue
good renowne, more for the gouernyng of his Rewme than for
him silf.

Of entencioun fynable of a kyng. Ca^m 8^m.

Good fortune and bad fame bring on envy.

He bigynnyng of wisdoom and vndirstondyng is forto haue good renowne, bi the whiche remes and lordshipes are conquerid and getene. And if thou seke to conquere remes or lordshipes, and thou haue no good renowne, thou shalt fynde that the ende is and shalle be but envye. And envie is neuyr without lesyngis, the which is roote and mater of alle vicis.

Envy brings on strife.

Envye engendrith yville spekyng, and of yville speche cometh hatrede: Hatrede engendrith vylenye, vylenye engendrith rankoure: Rankoure engendrith contrariete: Contrariete engendrith vnrightwisnes, vnrightwisnes engendrith batayle: Batayle yevith vp alle lawes and distroyeth citees, and is contrary to kynde and distroyeþ mannys body. And therfore, dere sone,

[¹ fol. 7 a.] *Desire good fame and truth.*

bithynke the and ¹sett thi desire as thou maist haue good renowne, for of gret desire that thou shalt haue to haue good renowne, thou shalt drawe to the the trouthe of alle thing. And wite welle that trouthe is roote of alle thingis that owen to be bilouyd, and trouthe is matere of alle goodnes, for it is contrary to lesyngis, the which is roote and mater of all vicis. And vndirstonde that trouthe engendrith desire; desire engendrith

Truth brings on friendship.

Iustice. Iustice engendrith good feith. Good feith engendrith largesse; largesse engendrith famulyarite, that is homelynes. ffamulyarite engendrith frendshipe. ffrendshipe engendrith counselle and helpe, and bi these thingis rehersid was alle the world ordeynyd and the lawes made, and they are accordyng to reson and to kynde; than semeth it welle that desire to haue good renowne, is long lastyng lyf and worshipfulle.

Of yvelys that cometh of bestly desires. Ca^m 9^m.

a Lexandre, dere sone, leve bestly desires and flesshely, for they ben corruptible. fflesshely desires bowith the hert of mane to delitis, which are corrupcioun to the sowle, and it is bestialle without discreccioun. And he that ioyneth him to bodily corrupcioun, he corruptith the vndirstondyng of man.

The evils arising from animal desires.

And wite welle þat suche desires engendrith flesshely loue: And flesshely loue engendrith avarice: Auarice engendrith desiris of ricchesse: Desiris of ricchesse makith a man without shame: Man without shame is prowd and without feith: Man without feith drawith to thefte: Thefte bryngith a man to endles shame, and so cometh a man to kaytifnes and to fynalle distruccioun of his body.

Of the wysdome and ordinaunce of a kyng. Ca⫯ 10⫯

4 It is convenabille thing and rightfulle Iustice that good renowne of a kyng be in lovable konnyng and good manhode, and þat shalle make his name ¹sprede thorugh alle parties of his rewme; and that he haue parlement and wys counselle oft 8 tymes; and so shalle he be preysid and worshipid and dowtid of his sugetis whan they here him speke and done his thingis wisely. ffor in suche wise may fully be knowene the wisdome or ellis the folie of a kyng. Whan he governyth him wisely 12 ayens god, he is worthi to regne, and worthily to holde lordis estate. But he that settith his Rewme in servitute and yville customes, he ouyr passith the wey of trouthe, he settith at nought good lyvyng and goddis lawe: And he shalle at the 16 ende be sett at nought of god and alle worldly good men.

[¹ fol. 7 b.]

Justice makes a king praised.

A tyrant wins for himself evil fame.

Of a kyngis goodnes and holynes. Ca⫯ 11⫯

I Prey the foryete not þe lernyng that wijs philesofres haue spoken of, and that they seyde that it is fittyng that the 20 royalle maieste be governyd aftir the rightis and the lawes, nought bi feynt semyng but in dede doyng, so that eche mane se and knowe the goodnes of the kyng and that he dredith god, and that he wolle governe him aftir goddis plesaunce; than 24 shalle the kyng be worshipid and dred whan men seyne that he dredith god. And if he feyne him good man and holy, and is yville to his sugetis, he shalle be sett at nought of god, and be diffamyd of alle men, and his doughti deedis shulle cese, and 28 the worship of the crowne shalle fayle, for yville werke may not long be hidde. What may y sey þe more, there is no tresoure ne othir thing in this world that is comperable to good renowne. And on that othir side, dere sone, it longith that thou do 32 worshipe to clerkis and reuerence good men of Religioun, and avaunce wijs men that be of good lyvyng, and speke oft with hem, and axe ²hem questiones and dowtes of diuerse thingis, and also answere wisely to her axyngis, and lete alle thi Rewlis 36 be goode. And worshipe euery man as he is worthi, nought aftir estate, but aftir hir goodnes, and so wold god.

Fear God, and men will fear thee.

Reverence clerks and religious men.

[² fol. 8 a.]

Of the purvyaunce of a kyng. Capitulum 12ᵐ

Prepare for the future.

It is nedfulle that the wijs kyng thinke oft of thingis that arne to come, so that he may wisely purveye and make contrary ordynaunce ayens hem, and þat he may the more lightly bere and susteyne þe contrarye aduersitees and aduen-

Be not hasty, but pitiful.

tures; and also a kyng owith to be pitevous, and his yre and malice wisely to cover and refreyne, so that without good and discrete avisement he do nought that he thought to done in his male talent; and so may he knowe with resoun erroure, and with excellent discreciou*n* repelle it. ffor the most sovereyne vertu of wisdome that a kyng may haue it is to governe him

Do all things with discretion.

wisely, and nought do without discreciou*n*; and whan he saith a thing þat is good and profitable to be done, lete him do it diligently wisely and gladly with discreciou*n*, and so shalle he be cuyr obeyd and dred in loue-drede of alle his lieges, and that is an high signe þat he is bilouyd of god.

Of clothyng of a kyng. Caᵐ 13ᵐ

A king should be the best dressed man in the country;

It is right welle semyng vnto a royalle maieste of a kyng, þat he be royalle and excellent in his array, so that euyr he shewe him in riche and precious clothyng, and þat his clothyng be of the most straunge cloth þat may oughwhere be founde; and þat is a gret prerogatif and an high dignyte þat he sur-mounte alle othir lordis, and royallis of his rewme in his royalle array; and therby his dignyte shalle be the more worshipid, and

[¹ fol. 8 b.]

his my3t ¹the more enhauncid, and the gretter reuerence to him shalle be yoven of alle men. And also it bicometh to a kyng

And very sweet-spoken.

to be a fayre and a swete spekere with amyable and gracious wordis, and specially in tyme of warres and batayles.

Of the countenaunce of a kyng. Caᵐ 14ᵐ

Better too little talk than too much.

Dere sone Alexandre, it is a precious and an honurabille thing to a kyng forto kepe sylence and speke but litille but if it be nede, for it were bettir that the eeris of the peple were brennyng in desire to here the speche of her kyng than the pepille wofulle and wery in the listenyng of hir kyng, and the hertis envenymyd of his presence and his sight. And also a kyng owith not to shewe him ouer oftene to his peple, ne ouer oft haunte the company of his sugetis, and specially of chorlis

Ch. 14.] *Of the Countenance of a King.* 13

and rurall*e* folke, for bi ouyr moche homelynes he shalle be the
lasse honourid. And þerfore the Iewes had a fayre custome in
the observaunce of her kyng, for they ordeynyd that her kyng *Kings should only be seen*
4 shulde not shewe him openly to alle the peple but at on tyme of *once a year;*
þe yere, and than he shulde shewe him in the most royalle
apparayle, and þe barones and knyghtis of his Rewme shul ben
abowt him alle in bright armoure, and the kyng most royally
8 sett on a stede wi*th* his septre in his hond, and the Crowne on *and then in their royal*
his hed, and on his body his cote Armure of his royalle armes, *array.*
and alle þe peple aftir and bifore him. Then speken they and
tretene with the kyng of alle þe nedis of the Rewme, and tellen
12 of diuerse aventures that haue fallen in that yere bifore. In
the whiche he and his counselle must ordeyne remedy and *They should hold Parlia-*
ordeyne governau*n*ce, and there the kyng yevith grete and riche *ment:*
yeftis, and also foryevith men dyue*r*se trespacis that han de-
16 servid to be deed, and there they loke if it [1]be nede forto [1 fol. 9 a.]
abregge grete chargis that the peple were wont to bere. And
forto make ordinau*n*ce of suche thingis as ben nedfulle and
spedfulle for the comou*n* profit of the Rewme. And whan this
20 emparlyng is doone, than risith on of the wisist lordis and *and then a great lord*
reportith to the peple gret recomendaciou*n* and preysyng of the *should speak to the people,*
kyng, and of þe good governau*n*ce, and done gret thankyng vnto *praising the king:*
god þat hath sent so excellent a witt vnto the kyng of Iewes to
24 goue*r*ne hem in suche wise, and also they preyen god that they
may be obeyshaunt to him that holdith hem in suche governa*u*nce. And whan that this worthi lord hath þus reportid and
spokene, then alle the peple enforcith hem forto enhaunce the
28 preysyng of þe kyng, recomendyng his goode werkis, and preyen
to god for him, and þus thorugh alle þe lond in Citees of name
þe good werkis of hir kyng are publisshid and comendid, and
thus the children of her childrene ben taught and norisshid vnto *and the people will*
32 love, worshipe, and reuerence and obeyshaunce of her kyng. *reverence him.*
And at that time are punysshid and Iustified alle tho that
mysdone, so that alle tho þat stonde in any wille forto forfete,
they withdrawen hem and bicome good men; and also the kyng
36 doth grace and allegeaunce to marchauntis of the tribute that *He should forgive the*
they owe to the kyng, and maynteneth the marchaundise and *merchants their tribute,*
þe ricches diligently to be kept and diffendid, and þat is þe
cause that the cuntre of Iewes is fulle of pepille, and of mar-
40 chaundise, and of alle ricches, for of alle þe partis of þe world

and thus attract them to his country.

marchauntis approchen to them, for in hem men fynde grete wynnyngis. And in þat cuntre straungers riche and pore are sustenyd and holpene. Wherfore þe tribute of þat lond, and þe rentis of the kyng ben cuermore growyng ¹and encresyng. 4

[¹ fol. 9 b.]

Of the rightwisnes of a kyng. Ca^m 15^m

Merchants can spread his fame.

a kyng owith not to do no vyleny ne hyndryng to Marchauntis, but forto done hem right gret worshipe, for they go thorugh alle þe world bi see and londe, and þey wol report as 8 they fynde, good or yville. And the kyng owith eythir bi him silf or bi his trewe depute to done even Iustice in yeldyng to every man that is his of right, and than shalle the worshipe and the ioye of the kyng encrese, and [he shall be] the more dowtid 12 of his enemyes, and lyve and regne in prosperite and pees, and shall haue at his wille alle his desires.

A king should be just to all.

Of worldly desires of a kyng. Ca^m 16^m

a lexandre, dere sone, desire nought worldly thingis that are 16 passyng and corruptible, but thynke that thou must leve alle and go hens nakid. Caste than thi desiris vnto tho thingis that euer shulle laste, that is, the lijf of the world perdurable, where that euyr is myrthe and ioye without ende. leue þe 20 noughti lyf of bestis that euyr lyve in filthis; trowe not lightly alle that that men wille telle the, ne be nought ouyr hasty in yevyng mercy vnto them that thou hast conquered, and evir thynke afore of thingis that are possible to come. Sett not thi 24 desire to gretly in excesse of metis and drynkis, for it wolle norisshe the in slepe and slouthe, and stere the vnto lecherie, which is most destruccioun to mannys body.

Desire things that will last.

Do not eat or drink too much.

Of þe chastite of a kyng. Ca^m 17^m 28

Evils of unchaste life.

n obille emperoure, sett nought thyn hert in lecherie of women, for þat is the lyf of swyne. Ioy and worshipe shalt thou noon haue, while thou governyst the aftir that lijf and aftir the lijf of vnresonable bestis. Dere sone, lecherie is 32 destruccioun of body abreggyng of lijf and corrupcioun of vertues; Enemy to conscience, and makith a man oft femy- ²nyne. In whiche is oft tyme found cowardnes, and þat is the grettist poynt of repreef that may be vnto Chyvalrie. 36

[² fol. 10 a.]

Of pleiying of a kyng. Capi*tu*lum 18ᵐ·¹

it is semely to a kyng sumtyme wi*th* his pryncis lordis and othir that ben honest gentiles, forto delite him in honest pleyes and myrthis, and forto haue many dyverse mynstralcies in his audience, and dauncyng and syngyng, for whan the kynde of man is reioysid· in myrthe of kyndely nature, the talent of man takith therof gret strengthe and corage in all*e* manhode. Than if thou delite the in suche myrthe, loke that it be doone in honeste and pryvy place, and whan thou art in þi most myrthe kepe the wel from ouermoche drynke, but lete othir haue drynke at wille, and than shall*e* þou here many pryvy thingis discoverid, than take to the tho that thou lovist best, that they may reporte to the an othir day of that men seyne and tellen in here dronkenshipe; Onys or twyes ayere suffisith to haue suche maner myrthis. And euyrmore loke that thou holde all*e* thi lordis in gret worshipe as they ben of estate, and diu*er*se tymys make them ete wi*th* the on aftir an oþ*ir*, and yeue hem rewardis of Iewellis or of riche clothyng after that they ben of estate and worthi; and loke þat ther be no man of thi counselle ne famulier wi*th* the, but if he be rewardid wi*th* yeftis of thi largesse, for ellis makist thou not ther hertis toward the in trusty loue, nor savist not thyn estat.

A king should enjoy himself now and then:

privately:

and make his nobles drunk, so as to hear what they say.

Do not make favourites among your lords:

And see that no one is neglected.

Of discreciou*n* of a kyng. Ca*m* 19ᵐ

dere sone, haue euyr thi countenau*n*ce in sadnesse and vse not to laughe ouermoche, for bi ouermoche laughyng men that be wise chesen a foole, or ellis a man without sadnesse. And a kyng owith to do more ²worshipe to men of his counselle than to othir. And if any violence be done in thi court or in thi presence, lete it not skape vnpunysshid that othir mowe be ware. And regarde owith to be take in punysshyng, for sum ma*n*nys persone is more worthi than sum othir is, and sum tyme must be doon rigoure of lawe, and sum tyme it must be abreggid aftir that the persone be of estate. Itt is writen in the book of Macabeus that a kyng owith to be louyd and preysid, that is like to the Egle, which hath lordshipe aboue all*e* fowles, and noon to the owle, whiche that is suget and aferde of all*e* fowlis.

Be sober of cheer,

[² fol. 10 *b*.]

and have regard to persons in punishing crime.

Maccabees says a king should be like an eagle, not an owl.

---

¹ Numbered 17 in MS., so that from this point the numeration of the chapters is not in accord with that of the MS., being one in advance.

And therfore if any man do violence in the presence of thi royalle maieste, thou must considir if it be don by pley to make othir forto laughe and be glad, or if it be don in dispite and reprefe of thi presence; for vnto the first longith correccioun, and to that othir longith nought but deth.

Of reuerence of a kyng. Ca^m 20^m

Have no violence done in thy presence.

A king is revered for four reasons.

a lexandre, dere sone, the obeyshaunce of a kyng cometh thorugh foure thingis: for goodnes of þe kyng, for gentilnes, and for worshipe that he vsith, and for reuerence that he doth to hem that are worthi. Dere sone, vse these condiciones, and thou shalt turne the coragis of thi sugetis at thyn owen desire; and loke that no wrongis ne Iniuries be doon to thi peple, that thou yeve hem no mater to speke ayens the, ne do neythir, for oft the voys of the peple doth harme, if it be in malicious wille, and wite thou welle that the wisdome of þe kyng is the ioy of his dignyte, and of his reuerence, and is enhaunsyng of his rewme. Than reuerence and souereyne wisdome is aftir þat love be in the hertis of his sugetis. It is

A king is like the rain. [^{1} fol. 11 a.]

founden in bookis that a kyng is among his sugetis as is the reyne in ^{1}erthe. And of alle creaturis lyvyng, for of reyne cometh first the wey that ledith marchauntis into alle londis, whiche marchaundise is helper to alle biggeris. And alle though

If rain does harm, it does much good.

in Reynes cometh some thondris and dissesoun wederis with lightenyng and othir tempestis, whereby man and beste is oft perrishid, and yet alle though suche accidentis ben yville, it makith men & women crye for fere, that wolde but litille thynke on god or on his myghti power, and so it makith folke forto thynk and considir that þe Rayne cometh of goddis grace and of his endles mercy; and suche ensampil thou mayst take

So with the wind.

of the wynd þat cometh also of the tresoure of goddis mercy, for bi the wynde men be mevid on the watir to alle londis to fecche and brynge thyngis that ben helpeliche to mannys kynde, and yet by the wyndis comen many perellis and lettyngis in watir and londe, and gret ricchesse is cast in the see, and by the wyndis are engendrid many corrupcions in the eyre, of whiche cometh many venemous pestilencis and othir diuerse diseses, and then folke pray god and requyren him that he take fro them tho

God allows the planets to hold their course.

diseses. Neuyrtheles god suffrith the planetis forto make and holde her cours in the rewle and ordir as he ordeynyd hem, for

[Ch. 21, 22.] *How a King shall make Subjects, &c.*

the wisdome of god peysith euenly, and ordeyneth alle thingis
forto serve to his creaturis, and that did he of his high goodnes
benygnyte and mercy. And this same ensampille may thou *So with winter and summer.*
4 fynde in wyntir and in somer, in whiche the souereyne wisdome
of god hath ordeynyd the coldes and the hetis for the engen-
dryng and encresyng of alle naturalle thingis, and evyr many
diseses comen to mankynde bi gret rigoure of colde and also of
8 hete. And þus ¹it farith, dere sone, sumtyme of a kyng whan [¹ fol. 11 b.]
he doth many greves and disesis to his sugetis, for than they
beren it welle grevously ayens him and ayens hert; but whan
the peple seene and knowene that bi the grace of god and good *The good from kings*
12 governaunce of þe kyng that they arne in pees and welle *makes the evil forgotten.*
governyd, they foryetene the yvelis and disesis above seide, and
thanken glorious god that he hath purveyde hem so wijs a kyng
in governaunce.

16 How a kyng shalle make Sugetis. Capi*tul*um 21ᵐ

i Prey the, dere sone, that thou oft enquere of þe necessite
of thi sugetis, and bi thi power thou helpe hem at her *Help your subjects in their need.*
nede. Also thou must chese a man þat is good and trewe, and
20 that louyth god and rightwisnes, and kan the langage of thi
sugetis, to whom thou co*m*mytte thi governaunce of thi sugetis,
and that he governe hem pitously and in loue; and if thou do *Choose a good viceroy.*
þus, thou shalt plese thi creatoure, and he shalle kepe thi
24 Rewme, and the gladnes of the sugetis is kept þoruȝ mercy of
the kyng.

Of the mercy of a kyng. Caᵐ 22ᵐ

d Ere sone, y counselle the that thou gete gret purvyaunce of *Have great store of food ready to distribute in famine.*
28 cornes and of alle othir vytaylis that the cuntre haue
habundaunce therof, so that whan the tyme of derthe cometh
thou maist wi*th* thi purveau*n*ce and forsight helpe thi sugetis in
her nede, and do crie and make knowe whan tyme is of thi
32 vytaylis, and thi refresshyng thorugh thi Rewme in alle citees
and borowes, that it may be fette of thi folke at nede, and this
shalle be gret preysyng to thi name, that so kanst ordeyne for
the sauacioun of thi peple; than shalle þi sugetis wi*th* gret
36 corage done alle thi comau*n*dementis wi*th* fre hert and good
wille, than shalle thi deedis falle (falle)² to gret prospe*r*ite, and [² fol. 12 a.]

² falle repeated in MS.

SECRETE.   C

Then men will praise your foresight;

euery man shalle merveyle of thi gret wisdome, and thus shalle thi wisdome be seen and knowe of alle men, and alle men shalle knowe and speke of thi forsight, and holde the gracious and

and praise you.

worthi to ben a governour, and thus shalle þou stonde in love and preysing, and euery man loth to do the offence.

Of peynes and vengeaunce of god. Capitulum 23m

Don't shed blood.

a Lexandre, dere sone, among alle othir thingis kepe the wel fro shedyng of mennys blood, for that longith only to god, for he knowith þe hertis of alle men, and wot what euery man is worthi to haue. Therfore take not vpon the goddis myght but if thou haddist his knowyng therwith. The doctour Hermogenes saith that he that slethe the creature that is like to

The vertues of heaven cry to God for vengeance,

god, alle the vertues of hevene cesse neuer of criyng to the maieste of god, saiyng, "lord, thi servaunt wolle be like to thee, takyng on him hasty and sodeyne vengeaunce," and wite this wel that who so sleth any man without cause resonabille, god

and He promises to avenge it,

wol avenge the blood, for god saith him silf vnto the vertues of hevene, "lete be, lete be, for in me is the vengeaunce, and y shalle quyte it." And wite þou welle that the vertues of

to still their cry.

hevene leue neuer of criyng of vengeaunce for mannys deth, vnto the tyme that god hath herde hem and done his iustificacioun in vengeaunce doyng.

Of knowleche of þe same peynes. Cam 24m

d Ere sone, wite welle that y haue had knowleche of moche disese in my tyme, and therfore haue oft in memorie the dedis of thi forne fadris, and thynke how they haue lyvid, and so maist thou se and knowe bi many goode examplis how þou

[¹ fol. 12 b.]

shalt done in thi governaunce in tyme comyng of tho ¹dedis

Don't wrong simple men,

that are passid; and loke thou haue no dispite, ne greue nought him that is lesse of myght than thou arte, for often it is sene

for they oft become great.

that god encresith sympille men, and makith hem riche, and so cometh the pore man to power to quite that is done to him afore tyme, good othir yville.

fforto kepe þe ffeith. Cam 25m

Keep your word in all cases.

a Iso kepe wel thi feith and thi word euermore, and alle thi hestis that thou hast made and false neuer thi tonge, for

Ch. 26.]   *Of Study and Wisdom.*   19

that bilongith to no man þat coueytith to haue worshipe; it is a
poynt þat perteyneth only to folke that be feithles, Strumpetis
and thefes; and alle that it vsith comen to yville ende, alle
4 though it seme þat it doth good for a tyme. And what good
cometh therof þou maist vndirstonde in many weyes, for bi feith   The land is kept by good faith.
are citees and castellis holden, and gret worshipe vnto hem þat
so trewe are founden in here feith; and tho that are false of her
8 feith bitraye her lord and hem silf bothe, and comen vnto a
shamefulle deth, and that is her ende. Also bi feith and bi
heste men kepe the comaundementis of god, and haue euer
lastyng lijf for her rewarde; and tho that breken her feith, ther
12 is no man kan deme hem iustly, but only god aboue. And
vndirstonde þat euery man hath two spiritis folowyng him, that   Two spirits accompany man:
on drawith him to yville and wikkidnes, and alle the yville he   one evil, who
kan he drawith him to, and yet he is þe same that shalle recorde records all his sins against
16 and reherse alle his defautis at the day of dome in shame and   the day of doom.
shenshipe of him þat haþ wrought hem thorugh his entisement.
This mater shuld make the aferd forto do any yville there as
þou myghtist do good; kepe the also fro sweryng, for þou owist   Don't swear, for fear you
20 neuyr to swere, but if necessite axe it, as that he be highly   break your oath.
requyrid therto. ffor the destruccioun that was of þe Assiryenes,
it was bicause her kyng made many othis in disseyt ¹of the   [¹ fol. 13 a.]
citees that were next to him, and brake allyaunce of his hestis The Assyrians did so, and were
24 þat he had made vnto hem, and god sygh the falsnes of þe kyng destroyed.
and his counselle, and wold suffir it no lenger, but made her
sugetis put hem into thraldome: dere sone, do so, that thi
goodnes, thi lewte and thi curtesie be knowen and kid alle
28 abowt, and þat shalle be kepyng of thi rentis and distruccioun
of thyn enemyes.

Of studie and wijsdome.   Capitulum 26ᵐ

d   ere sone, loke that ther be stodies and skolys in thi Citees;   Have compulsory edu-
32   and comaunde alle men that þey sette her children vnto   cation.
lettrure, and make hem be studyauntis in the nobille sciencis;
and it longith to the to helpe and socoure alle, that haue nede
and haue noȝ frendshipe, and thou must yeve sum prerogatif   Help students.
36 vnto studiauntȝ forto susteyne and helpe them in her stodiyng.
And avaunce hem that are konnyng, be they pore or riche;
preyse hem that are worthi, and worshipe hem that are wor-

shipfulle; yeve thi yeftis often vnto them that are worthi, thus shalle þou stere hem and excite hem to preyse the, and to cronycle alle þi nobille dedis, the whiche owen perpetuelly to be in recomendyng.   4

Of the kepyng of a kyng. Capi*tul*u*m* 27ᵐ

Never trust a woman;

a lexandre, dere sone, trust neuyr in wome*n*, in her werkis, in her service, ne in her company, ne dwelle thou nought wi*th* hem; and if þou must nede haue company of sum woman, 8 loke that thou preve hir welle and longe, and in diue*r*se wise, or thou trust to moche in her, for a man þ*a*t is in the possessiou*n*

if you do she can sell you if she likes:

of a woman, he stondith as do iewelis in the hondis of a marchaunt, whiche that hath power to selle or to yeve tho 12

[¹ fol. 13 *b*.] Iewellis to whom him lust; right so doth ¹a man that puttith him in the hondis and power of a woman, he puttith his lyf

many kings have been poisoned:

and his deth in gret aventure: þou hast herd tolde that kyngis, dukis, and many othir worthi men haue ben dede thorugh 16

a woman's hate is the worst poison.

venyme. Now the most violent venyme that any man kan deuyse or thynke is the yville wille of a woman, for ayens þat venyme is no leche that kan make tryacle, ne ordeyne medicyne or remedy, but only to fle the dampnaciou*n* of hem. And also 20

Don't trust one doctor: have a lot.

truste thou neuyr in oon sool ffisicia*n*e, ne take neue*r* medicyne [from] on allone, but if gret nede make it, but lete many ffisiciens come togidre, and lete hem trete of that mater, and as they alle accorde, so is best to truste, for it is well p*er*ilous whan the lyf 24

Remember the girl who was sent from India.

of a man stondith in the wille of oo pe*r*sone. And thynke also, dere sone, whan thou were in Inde how thou haddist ben disceyvid thorugh thyn owen lust þat thou haddist to a maydene that was norisshyd wi*th* venyme, and had not y ben there and 28

I saved your life,

thorugh the craft that y knewe of phisnomye and of othir natures, thou haddist ben ded bi her; and therfore haue euyr

so always keep a doctor near you.

abowt the good phisiciens and wise philesofris, that mowe telle the of suche accidentalle maters, and so maist thou kepe thyn 32 helthe thorugh good governau*n*ce; and thynke on thyn owen prosperite, the whiche is yovene vnto the of the excellent power of goddis maieste, and be suche i*n* goue*r*nau*n*ce that þou maist be glorified and magnyfied in the nombre of wijs men.   36

Of the difference of Astronomye. Ca^m 28^m

d　Ere sone, y prey the and it may be done, that þou rise ne sitte, ete ne drynke, but if it be bi counselle of sum wijs mane that knowi*th* the constellacions and þe course of the planetis; and vndirstond that glorious god hath made no thing without cause, but all*e* thyng with [1]passyng resou*n* of his excellent and vnknowe science.　The nobill*e* Plato he stodied in the science of Astronomye, and fond and compassid foure qualitees and humoures contrarious, bi the which he had that nobill*e* science and gret knowyng in alle thingis visible that god made.　And haue noon affecciou*n* in folys þat seyne the science of Astronomy is nought to stodie ynne for hardnes therof, trewly they wote nought what they mene, for god made no thyng visible that it ne is able and possible to ma*n*nys witt forto vndirstonde.　He that is a parfit studiaunt in that science, he may knowe and se pereylis and disesis that are to come of werres, pestilencis, famyne and othir accidentall*e* thingis the whiche he may vndirstond and ordeyne remedye: thus maist thou se and knowe þat it is good to konne þe arte and the cours of the planetis, and if thou kanst fynde no remedy, it is good that thou prey hertily to god that he ordeyne remedy, for as he wol so it shalle be, and no thing may with*s*tonde him.　for what disese the planetis shewe in her worchy*n*g good men mowe so preye vnto god, by orisones, bi fastyng, bi sacrifice, bi almes dede doyng, and penau*n*ce for her synnys, that god will*e* turne, revolue, and reuoke all*e* that men dowte.　Nowe to oure first mater and purpose, it is to wite, that Astronomye is dividid in foure parties, þa*t* is to wite, In the ordinau*n*ce of the sterres; In disposiciou*n* of þe signes and ther alyenyng and mevyng fro þe sonne; and this party is called Astronomye; that othir part is of qualitees, and also for to knowe the mevyng of þe firmame*n*t, and the degrees of þe risyng of þe signes that are vndir the firmame*n*t of þe mone, and this is the most worthi part of Astronomye, for þe*r*in is the cheef knowyng of þat science.　[2]and there are 100028 planetis that ben fixe and meve not, of the whiche we shulle speke aftirward more playnly.

Marginalia:
- Don't do any thing without your astrologer's advice.
- [1 fol. 14 *a*.]
- Plato was a great astrologer.
- Don't believe fools who say Astrology is a hard science.
- By it you can predict wars, famine and pestilence, and prepare a remedy.
- If you pray and fast God may order it otherwise.
- Four parts of Astronomy.
- [2 fol. 14 *b*.]
- There are 1028 fixed stars.

Of the kepyng of helthe. Ca^m 29^m

d　Ere sone, helthe is the most precious thing that longith to man, for it passith all*e* ricchesse, and all*e* helthe is [no] more

Marginalia:
- Health is the most precious thing.

but this governau*n*ce evenly conioynyd bi attempe*r*aunce of
humoures; and evir glorious god ordeyneth þe world, and yevith
many remedies to the attempe*r*aunce, and shewid to his holy
profetis the writyngis and sciencis of secretis, for in her writyng 4
is founde all*e* thing come*n*dable, and no reprefe ne foly as it is
alday previd bi most wijs men; glorious god, worshipid he be in
alle his werkis. Amen.

Of governau*n*ce in seeknes. Ca*m* 30*m*. 8

d Ere sone, have in mynde that all*e* wijs men and naturall*e*

Man is made of 4 humours.
philesofris seyn*e* that man is made of foure elem*e*ntis, and
foure contrary humoures, the whiche haue eue*r* nede to be sus-
teynyd bi etyng and drynkyng, and ellis þe substaunce shulde 12
fayle, and if a man ete and drynke out of tyme or ouyr moche
it makith him febille, and to falle into dyuerse seeknes and many
othir i*n*co*n*venientis, and if a ma*n* ete and drynke moderatly
and tempe*r*atly he shalle fynde helthe to his lyf, strengthe to 16
his body, and helthe of alle his lymes. The philesofres seyn*e*

If a man passes the mean of eating, &c., he may not fail of sickness.
that if a ma*n* trespace the god of nature in good lyvyng, be it
in ouyr moche etyng or in ouyr moche drynkyng, in slepyng,
wakyng, traveylyng or restyng, in letyng of blood or liyng, And 20
he outrage in eny of these, he may not fayle of gret seeknes,
wherof y shall*e* shewe my doctryne and remedie. These delicate
men seyne that all*e* that men don is forto lyve, be it in etyng or
drynkyng, in gaderyng of worldly ricches, or in flesshely lykyng, 24

[1 fol. 15 a.]
it is nought done but forto [1]lyue and last long, and y sey but if
he iustifie him wit*h* tempe*r*aunce as longith vnto lastyng of
long lyf he shalle fayle or he be ware. And he that wille [not]
do ayens his owen wille, and refrayne him from oui*r*moche etyng 28
and drynkyng, but caste mele vpon mele, he is not abill*e* to

Hippocrates dieted himself, and lived long.
haue long lijf, for Ipocras kepte the observau*n*ce of dyetyng
forto lyve long, and enforcid him nought to ete and drynke.
And also it is a grete helthe a man to be purgid at certeyne 32
tymes in resonabil manere.

In how many maners a man may kepe helthe. Cap*itulum* 31*m*.

Eat accustomed food.
i prey the, dere sone, that thou wille kepe in mynde this
trewe and certeyn tretis, and knowe that helthe stondeth 36
in two thingis; the first is, that he vse and kepe to ete and

drynke suche as he hath ben norisshid in his youthe. The
secund is, that he purge him of yville humoures and corrupcions *Purge evil humours.*
that greve him.

4 ### Of dyuerse metys. Ca^m. 32^m.

W   Han the body is hoot and fulle of vapoures than are grete *Gross food, when suitable:*
metis goode and profitabille, and that that shalle be diffied
of that body shalle be of gret quantite, for the grete hete and
8 vapoure of the body. And whan the body is smalle and drie,
smale metis are goode and norisshaunt, and that that shalle be *small meats.*
diffied of that body shalle be of litille qua*n*tite for the conditis
that are strayte; and this is to take hede of, that a man vse
12 metis and drynkis that longe to his complexiou*n*, for and he be *Eat according to complexion.*
of hoot complexiou*n* he shalle vse hoot metis tempe*r*atly, for and
the hete eu*ir* growe and inflawme the body within bi surfete of
ouyr stronge metis or drynkis, or bi any othir accident case, than
16 contrary metis and drynkis are most helpeliche to his helthe;
that is to sayne, colde metis and colde drynkis till that ¹he be [¹ fol. 15 b.]
ayen in his good estate.

Of the stomake. Cap^m. 33^m.

20 W   han the stomak is hoot and good, than alle metis arne good *Suit your food to the state of your stomach.*
for them that arne hote and grete, for suche a stomak is
like vnto a fire that brenneth thorugh gret habundau*n*ce of
woode; but whan the stomak is cold and febille, than is
24 bettir esy metis and drynkis tille that he be stronger and in
more hete.

Signes to knowe þe stomak. Ca^m. 34^m.

S   Ignes of an yville stomak is yville digestiou*n*, and that *Signs of disorder of the stomach.*
28   makith the body hevy and sluggy, and the visage bolnyd,
and suche a ma*n* yeneth often, and hath sumtime disese in his
eyen, and he rowtith moche in his slepe, and hath the mylte
soure and bittir and fulle of stynkyng wat*ir*, and so is engendrid
32 ventositees and swellyng of the wombe, and þat makith noon
appetite to ete; kepe the then, dere sone, from metis and drynkis
that are contrary to the or thou maist not recover.

Of a pistille of gret price. Ca^m. 35^m.

36 D   Ere sone, what is the cause that ma*n*nys bodie is corrupte?
it is for dyuerse complexiones and humoures contrary that

are in him, and therfore y purpose to make and write in this present Epistille thingis that shalle be necessary, the whiche y haue drawe out of þe secretis of medicynes, for sum tyme come to a kyng diseses that are not honest no lechis to knowe; but 4 the grettir nede were / and vndirstonde welle this lore, and thou shalt neuir haue nede to phisiciane outake the case of batayle. Alexandre, dere sone, whan thou risist fro slepe, goo a litille and that shalle strengthe þi membris, and strecche hem evenly, than 8 kembe þi hed, for that dryuyth away the vapoure that cometh into thyn hed in slepyng, and dryvith hem fro þe stomak. [1]In somer wasshe thyn hed with cold watir, and that shalle holde in the hete of þe hed and cause appetit of mete, than do on honest 12 clothyng, for the hert of man reioyceith gretly in precious clothyng and honeste: þan frete thi teeth with barke or with sum thing that is of drie and hoot complexioun and of bittir savoure, for þat makith the teeth clene, and distroyeth the yville savoure 16 of the mouthe, and also it makith the voyce clere, and yevith appetite to mete; than frote welle thyn heed, for it openyth the shettyngis of þi brayne and comfortith the nekke, and makith the face clere, and amendith the blood, and lettith moche the 20 horyng of the heere; than anoynt the with precious oynementis aftir that þe sesoun askith, for good odoure is gret plesyng to mannys lijf and norisshyng to the hert, and whan the spirit hath take refeccioun in good odoures, the blood renneth the more 24 gladlier in euery parti of the body. Take than of a tre that is callid aloes, and of Rubarbe the weight of iiij d., and it wille take awey the flewme of þi mouthe and of thi stomak, and yevith hete to the body, and dryvith away ventosite, and makith good 28 taste, and also that thou be oft tyme with the noblees, and wijs men of þi Rewme, and haue emparlement with them of the nedis of thi Rewme, and mayntene alle goode customes.

Of the maner of travayle. Capitulum 36ᵐ.

W han thyn houre of custome cometh that thi talent hath take the, haue a litille travayle or thou ete, in ridyng or goyng, or sum othir maner of laboure, and that helpith moche þe body, and dryvith away alle ventositees, and makith the body 36 more light and stronge, and alayeth the hete of þe stomak, and [2]wastith the yville humoures of thi body, and makith the flewme

of thi stomak forto descende; whan þi mete is come afore the,
ete first of that thou desirist most, with bred that is welle bake, {Eat first what you like best.}
and if þou haue diuersite of metes, ete first of that that is most
light to diffie and most digestable, for at the bottome of thi
stomak is the most hete to make digestioun, for as moche as it is
next the hete of the lyver, þe which diffieth the mete bi sethyng
in the stomak.

Of Abstinence. Ca^m 37^m

W han thou etist be nought to hasty, but ete with leyser and {Eat slowly.}
good masticacioun, or thou take it downe alle though thou
haue gret appetite, for and thou ete to sone or ouyr hastily, the
yville humoures multiplien in the stomak, and the stomak is
ouyr chargid, þe body grevid, and þe hert hurte, and that mete
dwellith vndefied in þe bottom of the stomak.

Nought to drynke pure watir. Ca^m 38^m

A lso, loke that thou drynke not pure watir whan thou hast {Don't drink water:}
eten thi mete, but if þou haue vsid it; for þe cold watir put
upon thi mete coldith thi stomak and quenchith the hete of þi
digestioun, and confoundith and grevith the body. and if þou
muste drynke watir for þe grete hete of þi body or of þi stomak, {or, at most, a very little}
take it attemperatly, and not ouirmoche attones ne to ofte. {of it.}

Of the maner of slepyng. Capitulum 39^m

W han thou hast take thi refeccioun ley the to slepe on a soft {Sleep on the right side}
bed on thi right side þe tyme of an houre, and than turne {for an hour: then turn}
the and slepe on þat oþir side as the thynketh good is, for the {over.}
left side is cold, and hath nede to be chafid, and if þou fele
any disese in thi wombe or in thi stomak, lete hete an hoot
cloth, ¹and ley it on thi stomak, or ellis take a fayre yong [¹ fol. 17 a.]
mayde and lete hir slepe in thyn armes, and that is the best
hete for it is naturelle. Traveylyng afore mete yevith hete
to thi stomak, but aftir mete it doth harme, and slepe before
mete is not good for it drieth þe humiditees, but aftir mete it
yevith norisshyng to the body, for whan a man slepith, than the
kyndely hete drawith into the stomak alle that the which was
spredde into alle the membris, and goth to the bottome of þi
stomak on the refeccioun, and makith good digestioun, for the
vertu naturelle makith good reste. And some philesofres seyne

Reasons for eating late rather than early. that the refecciou*n* at morowe is werse than is that at eve, for the etyng at morowe grevith the stomak, for the hete of the day spryngith, and therbi is the body more travaylid, and on þat othir side a man chatith him silf wit*h* dyuerse bisynesse, in goyng, in 4
spekyng, and othir occupacio*n*s that longith to man þat cometh by the hete of þe day, and enfeblisshith the naturelle hete within and doth harme to the stomak, and makith it of lesse myght to diffie that in him is, but at eve is all*e* contrary, for the body is 8
more restid and lesse grevid of naturell*e* hete, and the hete of all*e* oþi*r* membres are more at reste, than cometh þe coldenes of þe nyght, and alayeth the supe*r*fluitees of hete, and doth the stomak moche good, for than hath he nought but of nature. 12

Of kepyng of Custome. Cap^m 40^m

Don't break through your habits. t Hou owist forto knowe that he that hath in custome forto ete twies a day, and he vse to ete but ones, it grevith him for that he vsith not his custome, for þe stomak is out of his 16
wone. ffor he þat usith him to ete at a certeyne houre, and he
[¹ fol. 17 b.] bigyn*n*e ¹to chaunge that houre, he shall parceyve in short tyme þa*t* it doth him harme, for chaunging of custome chaungith nature. 20

How a man owith to chaunge Custome. Cap^m 41^m

Or, if you must, do it little by little. a nd necessite constrayne the to chaunge custome, thou muste done it wisely, that is to say, litill*e* and litill*e*, and thus wit*h* helpe of god shall*e* thi mutaciou*n* be good; but be ware 24
that thou ete no tyme, but þou wite that thi stomak be voyde, and hath made digestion of his first mete, and this shall*e* thou
Don't eat till your stomach is empty: knowe bi thyn appetite; and if thou ete and haue noon appetite, þe hete of thi stomak shall*e* kele, and if þou haue good appetite 28
it shall*e* hete of nature and make good digestiou*n*, and beware that thou ete anoon as thyn appetite is come, and ellis it shall*e* resceyue yvill*e* humoures, the whiche shall*e* turne þi brayne, and
and don't wait long after it is. disese thyn hed; for who þat abitith ouyr longe aftir that his 32
appetite is comen, his stomak enfeblisshith, and his mete profitith nought to his body; and if it falle so, þat þou maist haue no mete whan þou hast appetit to eat, and thi stomak fille so by resceyvyng of yvill*e* humoures, than loke that þou caste or thou 36
ete, and sone afti*r* thou maist take thi refecciou*n* in sauf manere.

Of foure tymes of the yere. Ca. 42.

h   Ere mayst thou see the foure tymes of the yere, and her *The four seasons.*
    foure qualitees, and her prosperite and difference, and con-
4   trarietees. The foure tymes of the yere are devidid thus. In
    ver, In somer, In hervest, and in wyntir. Ver bigynneth whan
    þe sonne entrith into the signe of þe Ram, and dewrith foure *Spring lasts 93 days, 18½ hours.*
    skore dayes and xiij, and xvijj howres, and the fourthe part of
8   an houre, that is, from the xiij day of marche vnto the xiij daye
    of Iune. In veer the tyme is so hote, þe wyndis risen, [1]the snowe [¹ fol. 18 a.]
    meltith. Ryvers aforsen hem to renne and wexen hoote, the *The effect of Spring on Nature.*
    humydite of the erthe mountith into the croppe of alle growyng
12 thingis, and makith trees and herbes to leve and flowre, þe medis
    wexen grene, the sedis risen, and cornes wexen, and flouris taken
    coloure; fowlis clothen them alle newe and bigynne to synge,
    trees are fulle of leves and floures, and the erthe alle grene;
16 bestis engendre, and alle thingis take myght, the lond is in beute
    clad with flouris of diuerse coloures, and alle growyng thingis are
    than in her bewte.

Of prime temps, what it is .I. ver. ca. 43.

20 p Rime temps, that is, veer, is hoot and moyste; in this time *Its qualities.*
    sterith mannys blood and spredith into alle the membris
    of þe body, and the body makith it intemperate complexioun.
    In this tyme shulde chykenys be ete, and kydes and eggis, soure *Suitable food.*
24 letuse þat men calle carlokis, and getis mylke. In this tyme is
    best to be lete blood, for onys than is bettir than thre tymes an *Be bled, and well purged.*
    othir tyme; and it is good to travayle and to haue thi wombe
    soluble, and than it is good to swete, to bathe, and to goo, and
28 to ete things that are laxatijf, for alle thing that amendith bi
    digestioun or by blood letyng it shalle sone retorne and amend
    in this prime temps .i. veer.

Of somer tyme, what it is. Cap. 44.

32 s Omer bigynneth whan þe sonne entrith into the signe of the *Summer lasts 4 score and twelve (92) days, 18 hours, and 20 minutes.*
    Crabbe, and lastith iiij^xx dayes and xij, and xvijj howres, and
    the thridde part of an houre, that is, fro þe xiij day of Iune vnto
    the xiij day of septembre; in þis tyme are the dayes longe and
36 þe nyghtis shorte. In alle cuntrees growe the hetis, and wyndis

aslake, þe see ¹softe, and the eyre clere and swete, cornes growen, and serpentis caste her venyme, the vertues of þe body are strengthid, and the world is fulle of goodnes. the tyme of somer is hoot and drie, and in this tyme sterith the Colre, and it bihovith a man in this tyme to kepe him fro alle tho thingis that are hoot and drie of complexioun, for they stere colre, and kepe the fro ouyrmoche etyng and drynkyng, for therbi shalt þou quenche þi naturalle hete. In this tyme ete metis þat arne of cold and moist complexioun, as welle mylke with vinegre as potage made with barly mele and ripe frute of soure savoure as pome Granate, and drynke litille wyne, and haunte no company of women; in this tyme lete no blood, but if greet necessite cause it; make no travayle but litille, and vse no bathes.

Of hervest, what it is. Capitulum 45ᵐ

h Ervest entrith whan the sonne entrith into the first degre of þe signe of the balaunce, and durith .iij^{xx 2} dayes and on, that is to say from the xiij day of septembre vnto the xiij day of Novembre. In þat tyme are the dayes and the nyghtis evene, and aftir þe nyght growith more, and the day lesse; the eyre wexith trobely, and þe wyndis entren into the Region of Septentrione, tymes chaungen and Ryvers discresen, and wellis wexen litille, the erthe and the trees wexen drie, and the beute of þe erthe and of þe ground fadith, and birdes sechen hoot cuntrees. Wilde bestis drawen to Cavernes, and serpentis sechen the hoolis where they may assemble and kepe her lyvyng; for wyntir is like an oold bareyne woman fro whom youthe is depertid. This tyme of hervest is cold and drie, in whiche risith þe black colre, than it bihovith to ete hot metes ³and drynkes, as chekenys, lambe, and oold wyne, and swete reysynges; and vse not moche goyng ne moche reste in liyng with women more than in somer, and kepe þe fro bathes, but it be for nede, and if þou wille do it, caste the to do it in the houre of none, for that is the hotist houre of þe day, and in suche houres þe superfluytees arisen and gaderen in mannys body. Also it is goode to purge þe wombe for an yville that men calle Asmon and Asmaton, and for alle othir thingis þat engendrith blak colre and refreyne þe humoures.

² iiij^{xx} in MS.

Of wyntir tyme, and what it is. Ca. 46ᵐ

w Yntir bigynneth whan the sonne entrith into the first degre *Winter lasts 6 score (120) days.*
of þe signe that men callen Motou*n*, and dureth vj^{xx} dayes,
4 that is, from the xiij day of novembre vnto the xiij day of
marche. In this tyme þe nyghtis are longe, and þe dayes shorte, *Its properties.*
the colde is gret, þe wynde is sharpe, leves fallen, and alle
thingis lesen her grennes for þe more party. Alle bestis drawen
8 to her resortes into diches and Caves of mounteynes for colde,
þe eyre and the tyme is blake; and þe erthe as an oold woman
broken wit*h* age and nere deed; wyntir is cold and moyste, and
therfore it nedith to ete hoote metis, as chekenys, hennes, *Suitable diet and manner*
12 motou*n*, and othir hoot metes, and fatte ffiges, notes, and reed *of life.*
wyne, and be ware that thou be not laxatijf, and lete no blood,
but it were the gretter nede, and enfebille not þi stomak with
excesse of mete ne of drynke. Ne companye thou nought moche
16 wit*h* women, but it be attemp*er*atly. And bathis are goode to
be vsid in tyme of colde. þe hete naturall*e* gederith togidre in
the body, and there good digestioun is bettir in wyntir, and in
ver than in hervest or in somer, ffor in hervest and in somer
20 the wombe is colde, and þat ¹tyme be the pores open, for hete of [¹ fol. 19 b.]
that tyme and nature spredith it through alle parties of the body,
and therfore the stomak hath litille part of þe hete, and þat
lettith the digestiou*n* and the humoures gaderen.

Of naturall*e* hete. Cap*itulum* 47ᵐ

24
a lexandre, dere sone, aboue alle thingis kepe thi naturall*e*
hete, for as long as naturall*e* hete is attemporat in thi body,
thou shalt haue good hele and vndirstondyng. And vndirstonde
28 þat in two thingis and maners deyeth a ma*n*, that on mane*r* is *The two causes why*
naturall*e*, as age þat ou*ir*cometh man and distroyeth þe body; *men die.*
that othir is bi accident maner, as bi seeknes take thorugh mys-
gou*er*naunce, or hurtyng of egge tole, and many othir happis of
32 aventure.

Of thingis that fattith the body. Ca*m* 48ᵐ

d Ere sone, there are thingis that makith the body fatte and *Things that fatten the*
moyste, that is, reste and replevisshyng of dyuerse metis *body.*
36 and swete drynkis, as wyn that is dowsett, mede, and mylke,
and slepe aft*ir* mete, soft liyng, and alle good odoures, bathes of

fresshe watir; and if thou bathe the, dwelle not longe therin, for
it wille make þe more feble, and haue in thi bath thingis welle
savouryng, and drynke no wyn but it be allayed with watir of
a floure callid Alchymyng, and put of þat watir in thi wyne for 4
it is hoot of natur. And in somer vse þe flouris of violett and
malowe, and othir thingis of cold nature, and haue ones in þe
moneth a vomete, and namely in somer tyme for castyng
clensith the body, and purgith it of yville humoures þat are 8
within the body; and though ther be litille humoures in the
stomak yet it comfortith the naturalle hete, and whan thou hast
welle caste, than fille him with humydite and good grennesse,

[1 fol. 20 a.] and than þi stomak is in good disposicioun [1]forto make digest- 12
ioun. And if thou governe the thus, þou shalt haue ioy in thyn
hert and gladnes, good hele, resoun and good vndirstondyng,

Reasonable pleasures for a king. glorye and worship of thyn enemyes. Also sumtyme þou must
delyte the in pleyes, in biholdyng of fayre men and fayre 16
women, and redyng delectable bookis, and in aray, and weryng
of royalle clothyng after the tyme of the yere.

Of thingis that makith þe body lene. Cap[m] 49[m]

Things that harm the body. t Hese thingis are they that makith þe body lene. Excesse 20
of mete and drynke, ouyr moche travayle, moche stondyng
in the sonne, moche goyng, moche slepyng afore mete, moche
wrath, moche fere, and bathyng in watris þat be of Sulphure
nature. Etyng of salt metes, drynkyng of oold wyn, ouirmoche 24
to vse chambir worke. Ipocras seith that who so bathe him
with fulle wombe shalle haue seeknes in the bowelis, and also he
that lythe with women wombe fulle. And also he þat etith oft
tymes hoot fisshe, or that drynketh mylke and wyne medlid, 28
is able forto be a lepre, þus saith ypocras.

Of the first party of þe body. Capitulum. 50[m]

t he body is divided in foure partes, the first party is the
Troubles in the head: hed. Whan superfluytees assemblen into þe hed and yville 32
humoures, thou shalt fayle and knowe bi þese signes, thyn eyen
shalle be trobille, thi browes shalle wexe grete, thyn eyen betene,
thi nose thrilles wexe strayte, þan and thou fele this in the,
their cure. take wormode, and do it in swete wyne, and lete it boyle with 36
the Rote þat is callid Pollygony, so that by boylyng the wyne

be half wastid, than put it in þi mouthe and holde it longe, and
wasshe welle þi mouth therwith, and ete thi mete with þe grayne
of whijt mustard made into powdir, and it shalle profite [1]the, [1 fol. 20 b.]
4 and if thou do not thus, thou shalt haue gret disese in thyn
eyen and in thi brayne, and in many othir partis of thi body.

Of þe secund parti of þe body. Ca^m 51^m

t   He breste is the secund parti of þe body, and if seeknes *Troubles in*
8   come therin thus shalle thou knowe, þi tunge shalle be *the chest:*
pricchid, þi mouth shalle be bittir, and þe mouth of þi stomak
shalle be soure, and thi membres shalle ake, than it bihovith
that thou ete but litille, than take a vomyte, and aftir þi cast- *their cure.*
12 yng, take sugir rosett with aloe, and mastyk and chewe alle
harde, and than mayst thou ete a good soule aftir as thyn appetit
takith the. And aftir mete take an electuarie that is callid
dyonysion, and if thou do not thus þi membres wolle ake, disese
16 cometh in thi Reynes, and so folowith the axcesse and enpech-
yng of þi tonge, þe whiche wolle lette the to speke, and many
othir seeknessis.

Of the thridde party of þe body. Ca^m 52.

20 t   he thridde parti of þe body is þe wombe, many yville *Troubles of*
humoures cometh therin. And thus shalle thou knowe, *the belly:*
thi wombe shalle swelle, and thou shalt ake of stiffenes þat
cometh therin, þe knees wexe grete, and thou shalt go hevily
24 and with disese. It bihovith the then to be purgid with sum *their cure.*
light medicyne, as y haue seid aboue. And if þou do it not þou
shalt haue akyng of thyn haunchis and of thi mylte, and in thi
bak, and in thi ioyntis, and disese of þe flixe, and disese of thi
28 lyvir, and yville digestioun.

Of the fourthe party of þe body. Ca^m 53^m

t   he fourthe parti of þe body be the Ballokis, where super- *Troubles of*
fluytees and yville humoures engendren, and thus thou shalt *the genitals:*
32 knowe, thyn appetit shalle wexe cold, and þou shalt wexe
roynous on the ballokis, and on þe share. Take than mugwede,
[2]the herbe with the Rote, and put it in good whijte wyne, and [2 fol. 21 a.]
of that wyne drynke a litille euery day at morowe, with a litille *their cure.*
36 watir or hony, and ete not ouyr moche. And if þou do not
thus, thou shalt haue disese in the bleddre, and thou shalt not

mowe pisse, and also thi ballokis wolle ake, and in thi bowellis thou shalt be disesid, and also in thi lunges; and there may engendir the, the stone.

A king once sought for the best medicine.

I haue redde that ther was a kyng, and [he] made a gret assemble of alle the beste phisiciens in Inde, and in Grece, and comaunded hem to make him such a medicyn so nobil and profitable that ther shulde nede noon othir helpe to mannys hele. The

The Greeks advise him to drink two mouthfuls of warm water.

Grekis seiden that who so euyr dranke euery morowe twies his mouth fulle of hoot watir þat it shulde make a man hoole, and þat him shulde nede noon othir medicyne. The phisiciens of

The Indians advise millet and water cress.

ynde seiden that who so ete the graynes of whijt mylle fastyng with watir cresses it profitith moche, or who so ete eche morowe of alibi Amei 7 dragmes, and of swete grapis and Reysynes, he shalle haue no dowte of flewme, and he shalle haue the bettir vndirstondyng, and he shalle haue no quarteyne, and who so etith notes or ffygis with loves of Rewe, that day him thar drede

Keep natural heat,

of no venyme. And euyr peyne the to kepe the naturalle hete of thi body, for the distruccioun of thi body cometh of two thingis and two causis, that on is naturelle and þat othir is ayens kynde. The naturalle distruccioun is for the contrariete of complexioun of man, for whan age surmounteth, the body it must

for then you need only fear accidents.

nedis noye. And that that is ayens kynde, it cometh of accident aduenture as by swerd, spere, ston, or any case that cometh of secknes, by yville governaunce, and excesse of metis and

[¹ fol. 21 b.]

¹drynkes, for some metes are smale, and some metes are grete,

Foods which make good blood.

and some are mene. Smale metis engendren good and clere blood, as bred of good whete, Chekenys, Eggis, hennes. Grete metis ben goode for hoot men that travaylen, and namely aftir mete. The mene metis ben goode, for they engendren no swellyng, no superfluytees, noon yville humoures as kedis, lambis, and geldid shepe, for they are hote and moyste, alle though they ben harde whan they ben rostid and hoot in the wombe.

Of kyndis of ffisshis. Ca^m 54^m

Which fish may be eaten.

t he fisshis that ben of thynne skyn, and norisshid in fresshe watir Rennyng is bettir and more holsome than any othir. Kepe the fro fische þat is hard skynned, for þat is werst, for it is norshyng of wynde, whiche is cause of moche disese.

Ch. 55-58.]   *Of Nature of Water and Wine, and of Sour Syrup.*   33

Of nature of watris, Of nature of wyne, Of soure Syrupe. Ca^m 55, Ca^m 56, Ca^m 57.[1]

   a   lexandre, dere sone, it is holsome to take sowre Syrepe   <small>Sour syrups are good.</small>
4   fastyng for flewme and yville humors that habounde gretly,
and that Syrepe is an excellent remedy ayens flewme. And y
haue merveyle þat man may deye þat etith bred of good whete   <small>Good bread and good</small>
and fresshe, and drynketh clene wyne of grape attemperatly,   <small>wine should keep a man</small>
8   and kepith him fro ouirmoche etyng and drynkyng and travayle, <small>alive.</small>
and if seeknes come to suche a man, it is nedfulle to worche
wisely and do to him as to a dronken man. Wasshe him with <small>A cure for drunken men.</small>
hoot watir, and aftir sett him on a Rennyng Ryver, so that he
12 haue grene leves of wylowe about him, and anoynte his stomak
with an oynement that men calle Triasendale, and lete him
haue savor of encence and othir good spicis among. And if a
man wolde leve the drynkyng of wyne that hath [2]cuyr be <small>[² fol. 22 a.]</small>
16 norisshyd therin, he may not leve it attones, but litille and litille, <small>Do not leave off drinking</small>
and make him drynke of verious and watir, and thus may he <small>suddenly.</small>
kepe his helthe and his complexioun.

Of the forme and maner of rightwisnes.   Ca^m 58^m

20 d   Ere sone, rightwisnes may not ben ouyr preysid, for it is
of þe propir nature of glorious god, and it is made to sus-
tene all Rewmes for helpe of his servauntis, and rightwisnes <small>The praise of righteous-</small>
owith to kepe the royalle blood, and the richesse of the posses- <small>ness.</small>
24 sioun of sugetis, and governe hem in alle her nedes; and what
lord doth thus, he is in that case like vnto god. Rightwisnes
is forme and vndirstondyng, whiche god made and sent to his
creaturis. and bi rightwisnes was þe erthe bildid, and kyngis
28 made to mayntene it, for it makith sugetis obeyshaunte, and
prowde men meke, and savith the persones from harme, and
therfore seyne men of ynde that Iustice of a good lord is bettir <small>The Indian opinion.</small>
to þe pepille than the habundaunce of goodis of the erthe, and
32 bettir than the reyne that fallith from hevene. Onys it was
founde writen in a stone of þe tunge of Caldee, that a kyng and <small>The stone of witness.</small>
rightwisnes are bretheryn, and that þe which on hath nede of an
othir hath nede of þe same, and þat on may nought do without
36 þat othir. ffor alle kyngis were made to mayntene Iustice and
rightwisnes, for it is the helthe of sugetis. Dere sone, whan

---

[1] The text is but a part of Cap. 57.

SECRETE.   D

Hear all men's counsel before you give your doom.

[¹ fol. 22 b.]

Don't scorn good advice from young men.

A story of a child born in India,

who became great;

while the king's son would not learn,

[² fol. 23 a.]

because of the stars.

Therefore never despise a poor wise man.

Take counsel.

þou hast oughte to do be governyd bi counselle, for þou art but on sool man, ne telle nought alle þi thought of thyn owen cast to thi counselle, but here what eche man wolle say, and than maist þou deme in thyn owen witt þe best of hir witt, and of þyn owen witt, and þus shalt ¹thou be holden wijs and worshipfulle for thi governaunce. Shewe not thi thought vnto tyme thou performe thi wille of the which thou hast take thi counselle. But considir welle which persone counselid the beste, and haue him in cherte. And if he be a yong man þat yevith the good counselle haue him not in dispite for his youthe, ffor it happith many a tyme and often þat a man is borne in suche a constellacioun þat good counselle is yeue to him of god. As it bifelle in a tyme in þe cuntre of ynde, ther was borne a child in an hous there as a wys man was herbrowid, whiche man fond by the planetis þat that child þat was borne in that constellacioun and signe shuld be wys, curteys, and of good counselle, and shulde be louyd of kyngis and grete lordis, and yet he wolde not telle it to his fadir, for he was but a poore wever. So it fell that whan this child was of age, they wold haue sett him to a craft, but for betyng or fayre speche that they kouthe do he wolde neuir lerne, and than they lete him do his owen wille, and than he yaf him alle to the science of Astronomye, and aboue alle thingis on erthe vnto the governaunce of a kyng. And at laste he was the governour of a kyng and of alle his rewme. Alle the contrary fille of a kyng of ynde þat had two childrene; whan þat on child was woxe the kyng sett him to lerne science in the grettist vnyuersite of alle ynde, and had the beste maystir of þat lond, and was taught most diligently, as it ought to a kyngis sone. And yet the gret wille of þe fadir, and the gret bisynes of the doctoure myght not festene no witt vpon him, ne he wold not enclyne his hert to no science. Wherfore þe kyng in gret wrath lete assemble alle þe philosofris of ²his lond to wite wheron it was long, and they seide he was borne in suche a constellacioun that he had noon othir grace. And therfore, dere sone, dispise neuir a man of poore birthe, ne of litille havyng, ne bi his persone, and thou se in him science and good counselle, for god wolle yeve his grace as him likith, and shewe his myght as welle in poore as in riche. A wijs man of mede wrote to his son on this wise, "Dere sone, in euery nede take counselle to thee, for thou art but oo man as on othir is, on that othir

Of the Secretary of a King. [Ch. 59.]

side y amonisshe thee, that thou ne make oo soole man thi leef *Don't trust to one man in all things.*
tenaunte forto yeve him thi power, for he myght with a cawtele
distroye thee, and alle thi Rewme. Truste nevyr in him þat
4 settith alle his bisynesse to make tresoure and gadir money, for *Don't trust covetous men:*
he wolle serve the nought for love, but for gaderyng of gold,
and suche men wolle slouthe thi worshipe, and suche men mowe
welle be liknyd to helle, for helle hath no grounde. And the
8 more a man growith in ricches, the hyer encresith his covetise
in good. And wite it welle that suche officers abowt a lord or
a kyng are but distroyers of his worshipe in many casis, for it *they may betray you.*
myght happe that for covetise he shuld bitraye the or consent
12 vnto thi deth. Therfore, dere sone, thou shalt loue that creature
that is in office with the, and bisieth him to save thi worship, for *Whom to trust.*
þat is the grettist tokene of loue." God made man, dere sone,
creature resonable, and he made neuyr in beste oþir than is
16 founden in man. ffor a man is hardy as a lyone, fferd as an *The twenty-three animals whose nature is found in man.*
hare, skars as an hound, harde and sharpe as Ravene or Crowe.
Meek as a turtille, dispitous as lyonesse, chaste as a dowve.
Malicious and angry as a ffoxe, lowe as a lambe, light as a
20 Goot, and lijk to a Got in many condiciones, hevy and slowe as
a bere, precious and dere ¹as an Olyfaunt, ffool and rude as an [¹ fol. 23 b.]
asse. Rebelle as a litille kyng, obeyshaunt as a pecok, gret
speker without profit. Profitable as a bee, vnbounden as a boore,
24 strong as a bole. Smytyng bihynde as a mule. Resonabille and
chast as aungille, lecherous as swyne, ffowle as an Owle. ffayrist
of alle creaturis, and shortly to say that ther is no condicioun in
best, ne in planet of heuene, ne in erthe that it ne is founden in *He is the microcosm.*
28 man, and therfore the philcsofre callith man the litille world.

Of þe secretary of a kyng. Cap^m 59^m.

d   Ere sone, it bihovith the to haue a secrete man to yefe *The need for a secretary.*
attendaunce to thi privat writyngis, and to conceyve thyn
32 entendement, and he must be a fayre speker, and on that kan
comprehende thi wille in dewe ordir, and enditt fayre langage;
for as a fayre Robe is worshipfulle to a kyng, so is fayre endit-
yngis, emblisshyng of his maieste of lettris vndir his seele. And
36 also he owith to be a man of good feith and trewe, and wijs to *His qualities.*
knowe thyn entendement, and take souereynly hede of þi
worshipe, and þat no man be so prive with him, forto se þe
lettris of thi secretȝ, and loke þat alle officers be welle rewardid

He should be rewarded. for her bisynesse, eche man in his degre, and enhaunce hem so in avauncementis, to whom euery man hath hool hert to, and doth thee dewe and trewe service, for in trewe servauntis is alle the glorie and high worshipe of thi lijf and thi distinccioun.   4

Of a kyngis messangeris. Cap^m 60^m

d   Ere sone, messangeres shewen the wisdome of hem that senden hem, and a messangere is the eye, the ere, and the
The properties of a messenger.
tunge of the lord; than it bihovith a messangere to ben the   8
most sufficient and cherfulle speker, wijs, honourable and lele,
[² fol. 24 a.] and that he loue þi¹ ²worship and thyn honure, and hate alle thi dishonoure, vnto suche on discouer thi counselle, and in case thou may not fynde such on, enquere the on that wolle trewly 12 bere thi lettris, and kan report an answer. And if thou fynde
Who are not to be chosen.
thi messangere be couctous forto take yeftis of them that they are sent to, truste not in hem, but refuse hem for euyr. And make neu*ir* thi messangere of man that is dronkelew, for bi him 16 shalle be seid and tolde alle that he know*ith*. And also make
Don't send a great man,
not thi messangere of no gret officer, ne lete noon suche go fro the, for that myght be distrucciou*n* of the and thyne and of thi
for fear of treason.
rewme also. And if thou myght perceyve that þi messangeres 20 did to the any tresou*n* thorugh takyng of gret mede, deme thou than as the thynkith they are worthi, for trewly y kan not.

Of governau*n*ce of the peple. Cap*itu*l*u*m 61^m

Your people is your treasury and your garden.
d   Ere sone, the peple and thi sugetis is the hous of thi 24 memorie, and þi tresore by the whiche thi reme is conformyd, thi sugetis are thi gardyne, in the whiche are many trees, heryng diue*r*se frutes, on these trees are many braunchis, beryng frutis and sedis, and multiplien in many maners, 28 and diffence and durabille tresoure of þi rewme. It nedith
Govern your subjects by
the than þ*a*t thi sugetis be welle governyd, and thou to haue in hert alle that is profitable vnto hem, and that no vylenye ne extorcion be done vnto hem, and that they be 32
their ancient laws,
gouernyd aftir þe maners and oold customes of her cuntrees, and yofe hem such officers that entende not to ther distrucciou*n*, but
have good officers
forto governe hem welle and iustly, and þat tho officers be of good condiciones, wijs, lele, and pacient, and if he be contrary, 36

¹ thi repeated in MS.

Ch. 61.]   *Of Government of the People.*

the sugetis that first were goode shulle wexen rebelle to hem
and the bothe, [1] supposyng that it be mayntenaunce. On that [1 fol. 24 b.]
othir side loke that thi Iustices be wijs and Iuste men, for þat *and just Judges.*
is thi worshipe and ende of thi name, and perpetuelle fame to
thi Rewme. And that thi Iuges haue trewe notories, so that *and Appeal Courts.*
thi Iuges be not corrupte with false covetise and yeftis as they
ben oft tymes. And, dere sone, y amonysshe the that thou vse
chyvalrie in dedis of armes, bi good governaunce and good coun- *Be careful in battle.*
selle and trewe. And avie not him þat puttith him into batayle,
for envye or foly or covetise, ne presumpcioun. And haue no
dispite of a good man of armys though he be poore, for often
tymes it happith a poor man to doo as good a dede of armes or
feete of werre as a lord. Norshe alle men with comfortable *Encourage your soldiers.*
wordis and goodly, and bihote hem yeftis and worshipe, and
loke thou lakke no thyng that is nedefulle vnto armes. And
whan thou sest thyn enemy Renne, Renne nought on him
sodeynly vnavisid, and loke thou haue goode waytes and aspies
in thyn oste. And euyrmore, and thou mowe, logge nere a *Choose good camping ground;*
mounteyne or an hille, for the valey wantith nothir watir ne
woode, and haue euyrmore plente of vytayles, and aboue alle
þingis haue plente of trompis and trumpetis, and othir dyuerse *plenty of trumpets,*
mynstrelsies, for þat makith gret vertu in mannys corage, and
gretly discomfortith enemyes, and puttith hem to divisioun and
drede, and be not alwey armed in on armes, but in dyverse. And
loke thou be welle stuffid of good Archers and Arblasteres, and *archers and arblasteers.*
sett in good governaunce and ordinaunce, some to renne, and
some to stonde and abide batayle. And whan thou entrist to
fighte comforte thi meyne with fayre wordis, and that shalle
yeve hem hert and hardynesse forto abide in batayle, and [2] euyr [2 fol. 25 a.]
kepe the wel from tresoun. And euyr be wel purveyde of good *Have a good horse, in case*
horse and wel rennyng, so that nede were that thorugh tresoun *of defeat.*
or any othir adventure it nedid thee to fle, than thou maist bi
thi swyft horse save thyn owen persone. And if þou see thyn
enemyes fle, chase hem nought to hastily, but holde thi folke
togidere on þe best maner thou kanst, for oft tyme in chasyng of
enemyes a man is disseyvid and deed. And if þou assayle
castelle or towne, loke that thou haue Engynes and Gonnes gret *In sieges cut oƭ the*
plente to breke the wallis and the yatis, and good crafty myn- *water from the city,*
oures, and by any wey that thou mayst bireve hem her water,
for that is the most confusioun in any holde. And if thou

or at least poison it;
and don't make war, if you can get your purpose otherwise.

maiste not reve hem her watir, loke that thou ordeyne forto envenyme it, and haue to the two or three of that othir side, forto telle the her castis and her counselle. And if thou mayst haue thi purpos othirwise than bi batayle, y redo thee take it, or ellis do thi worste vnto thyn enemyes, and on alle wise worche by counselle.

Of ffysnomye of folke. Capi*tul*um 62ᵐ

Physiognomy is most useful to you.
Physiognomus found it out.

A monge alle othir thingis caste the to knowe the mervelous science of ffysnomye, for therbi thou shalt knowe the natures and the condiciones of alle folke. And this science fonde a gret clerke that hight, ffysnomyas, the which serchid the qualitees and the natures of alle folke. In the tyme of this ffysnomyas reynyd the nobille and excellent doctoure ypocras. And for this ffisonomyas bare such a name of wisdome the disciplis of ypocras portreweden the liknes of her maystir, and bare it vnto fisnomyas, and bade him "Iuge the nature of him that that figure was lijk to"; and than he seide, "that man

[¹ fol. 25 b.]

Hippocrates' disciples tried him:

that is lijk to this figure, or þat þis figure ¹ is lijk to, is lecherous, and baratous, and boystous"; than they that had brought this figure to him, they seidene, "O fole, this is the figure of wijs ypocras, the best man and the wisist that lyvith." Than seide phisnomyas, "I knowe welle this is the figure of wijs ypocras, and y haue seid and Iugid the sothe theron, but of his wijsdome and resou*n* he refreyneth him silff from these vicis that nature shew*ith* in him." These disciples come home to her maystir, and

but Hippocrates confirmed his judgment.

tolde him of her doyng; than seide ypocras, "y haue herde tolde moche of the wijsdome of phisnomyas, but it is previd in doyng now, so that y shalle holde him eui*r* a passyng wijs man; for trewly he hath iugid þe trouthe." Therfore y haue writen to thee, dere sone, the rewlys abreggid of this science of ffisnomye,

Washy-looking men are bad.

in whiche þou shalt fynde greet loore. And thou se a man that is of febille coloure, fle his companye, for he is lecherous, and enclyned to many yvelis. And thou se a man that is glad

Signs of a man that loves you.

laughyng, and whan he lokith on the is dredy and ashamyd, and his visage wexith ·reed and sigheth, and the teeres fallen in his eyene whan thou blamyst him, wite welle that he doutith and lovith moche thi pe*r*sone. And kepe the welle from him

Avoid the maimed or crippled.

þat hath not alle his [membirs] fulfilled of byrthe, or is markid in the visage, and from alle tho that are of yville forme and

shappe. The beste forme is in mene men that haue the eyen and the heere blak, the visage rounde, coloure whijt, reed, and browne medlid togidere, these haue hool hert and trewe, they that haue the hed meene, not to litille ne to moche, and speken litille but if it be nede, and the voyce swete, suche complexiou*n* is good, and suche men take nere the. And the heer be fulle and softe, that man is deboner . . . .
. . . . ¹coloure, bitwix whijt and reed, wi*th* soft heere and playne, and eyen menely grete and rounde, þe heed wel made of good mesure, good nekke and sufficient longe, and hath not the leggis ne the knees ouyr flesshy, þe shuldris a litille goyng downeward, the palmes, þe fyngris sufficient longe and nought ouyr grete, and laugheth litille, and skorneth no man, and hath laughyng visage and glad, this man is good in alle nature. Dere sone, it is not lefulle to Iuge of oon signe in a man. But thou muste considir alle þe signes in him, and than take hede on the signes that most habounde in man, and deme þe beste and most naturalle party.

Best colour of men.

[¹ fol. 26 a.]

Signs of a good man.

Take all the signs into consideration.

This is the tretys that Aristotill*e* made to Kyng Alexandre, callid Secreta secretor*um* of goui*r*naunce of Kyngis in worship*e*, wijsdome, and gret helthe, of whiche lougher men in degre mowe lerne gret and bihoueful doctryne.

¹ One leaf had gone from here before the MS. was bound.

THE GOVERNANCE OF LORDSCHIPES.

MS. Lambeth 501.

A 15th Century Translation of the Secreta Secretorum.

(Soon after 1400.)

[Epistle dedicatory.]

¹To his lord most hegh and in worschippynge of Cristes religioun most noble Guy sothely of Valence of þe Citee of
4 Tripol glorious Bisshop, Phelip þe lest of his clerks hym and trew seruice of deuocioun recomendys. As mikel as þe mone ys more shinynge þan þe oþer sterrys, and as þe beni of þe sonne ys moor bryght þan þe light of the mone, As mekyl þe clernesse of
8 ʒoure wyt & þe depnesse of ʒoure conynge passys aH men þat now er on any syde þe see, as wel Barbarys as Latyns yn litterure. No-þer ys non of hool mynde þat may stryf aʒeyn þis sentence, ffor where þe Gyuer of graces, fro whom aH goodis
12 passys forth, to ilke man his goodis deles, It semys he has gyuen to þe oon þe gyftes of graces & of conynge, ffor yn þe er founden aH þe graces of halowes, þe clennesse of Noe, þe strenth of abraham, þe faith of ysaak, þe longe lastynge of Iacob, þe soffer-
16 ynge of Moyse, þe stabilnesse of Iosue, þe deuocioun of hely, þe perfeccioun of helise, þe Benignite of dauid, þe wit of Salamon, þe pacience of Iob, þe chastite of daniel, þe ffaconde of ysae, þe perseuerance of Ieremi with aH oþer vertuʒ of halowes yn þi
20 halynes most fully dwelles; ʒit yn aH fre conynges þou ys best lettridd, yn decretals of haly chirche & lawes wysest, In diuinite & moralite beste taught. Wher-fore worthy ys þat ʒoure swet-nesse haue þe booke of thys werke, yn þe whilk some profitable
24 þinges negh of aH sciences ys contend. When y was with ʒow at Antyoche, and þis precious margarite of Philosophye ffounden, it likyd to ʒoure lordschip þat it were translatyd out of þe tonge of arabye yn to latyn. Sothely y coueytynge mekly to bowe to
28 ʒoure biddynge & to ʒoure wyl as y am holdyn to serue, þys booke þat latyns wantyd and ys founden with fewe arabyes I haue translatyd with greet trauaille ynto opyn vnderstandynge of latyn out of þe langage of araby, to ʒoure heghnesse and

¹ Fol. 1 a.
Dedicated to Guy de Vere of Valence, Bishop of Tripoli.

His fame;

his virtues.

The book was found at Antioch, and translated from Arabic into Latin.

worschipe som tyme expounande letter of letter, and som tyme vndirstandynge of vndirstondynge, ffor other maner of spekynge ys with arabys & oþer with Latyns. ¹Þe wilke booke Aristotel þe wyseste Prynce of Philosofers made at þe askynge of kynge Alexander his disciple þat askyd of him þat he sholde come to him or elles þat he sholde shewe to him þe preuyteȝ of diuers craftes, þat ys to say þe sterynge of wirkynges and power of sternes in astronomy, þe craft of alkenamy in kynde, and þe craft of kennynge kyndes & of wirkynge eschauntementȝ in [piromancye]² & gewmatry, þe whilke Aristotel for elde eldand, and henynes of body myght nought goo, and yf all he hadde purposyd in all manere to hide þe preuytes of þes craftes forsayd, Nopeles he durste nought ne sholde nought aȝeyn say þe wyl and þe askynge of swylke a lord. He willand in party to make asseth to þe Emperour, & in party þe preuytes of þe craftes to hide, he made þis booke, spekand by tokyns & ensamples, & lyke spekyngges techand outward by lettre philosofre techinge falland to lordlynes of lordes, to hele of body to be kepyd, & to profyt þat may nought be nombred of kennynge of heuenly bodis to be had. Inward he shewys to þe margh by toknys & preuyly to Alexander þe principal purpos þat he askyd him with greet praiere, departand þis booke yn distinccons or bokes, ten of the whilke ylkon yn hym contentys, Chapytrys, and partyes termynd. And I yn þe begynnynge of þys booke haues gedird to gedyr & wretyn þe bigynnynge of þe bokes and all þe Chapitres of the titles, so þat þat ys askyd may mor redily be founden yn certeyns tetlys. GOODLY ffader, þys werke y haue translatid to ȝoure glorye and worschipe þat þe mynde of me with ȝow more fast dwelle, and my deuociown to ȝoure seruice mekly shewe hym, prayand denoutly, þat yn þys werke is founden profitable & acceptable, be hit assigned to his gyft þat gaf me grace to translate it, and to Aristotyl þat made it ; And if þer be ought founden nought right or nought conable sette, be it attornyd to myn vnconynge & vnwyt mor þan to my malyce. ³And ouer ȝoure ffaconde þat I wele knowe in enterpretaciown in wordes and yn properte of abundaunce of blisful spekynge do to amende þat ys to amende, þe mercy of god safe & hale longe kepe ȝow to þe glorye & worschipe of criste and Cristyn men, & after greet lengh of tyme he make ȝow blysfully to come to euer lastynge ioye.

² Blank in MS.

THE CHAPTERS OF THE BOOK.[1]

		PAGE
Cap. 1.	Of aforspekynge of louynge of Aristotel ...	47
Cap. 2.	Of a Epistyl fro Alexander to Aristotel....	48
Cap. 3.	[The answer of the same]	48
4 Cap. 4.	Of aforspekynge of þe translatour of þis booke ...	48
Cap. 5.	Of Aristotel epistel to Alexander	49
Cap. 6.	Of kynges & þer maners yn largesse & aueryce ...	51 Book I.
Cap. 7.	Of largesse and oþer vertue3. [Of þe evels þat	
8	comes of ffole largesse]	52
Cap. 8.	Of teching of Aristotel yn vertue3 and vices	53
Cap. 9.	Of þe endly entente þat kynges awe to haue	53
Cap. 10.	Of euels þat seuen flesshly apetit...	54
12 Cap. 11.	Of þe wyt of a kynge	54 Book II.
Cap. 12.	Of þe religiouste of a kynge	55
Cap. 13.	Of his purueyance & his sleghte ...	55
Cap. 14.	Of þe costome of a kynge.[2] [Of ornament cleþ-	
16	inge of a kynge.]	55
Cap. 15.	Of þe contynance of a kynge. [To eschewe	
	mekyl Spekynge]	56
Cap. 16.	Of þe ryght of a kynge	57
20 Cap. 17.	Of his fynale entente	57
Cap. 18.	Of þe chastite of a kynge...	58
Cap. 19.	Of þe solace of a kynge	58
Cap. 20.	[Of the descrecioun of a kynge]	58
24 Cap. 21.	[Of obedyence]	59
Cap. 22.	Of þe similitude of a kynge	59
Cap. 23.	Of þe socour and þe help of a kynge	60
Cap. 24.	[Of þe purueyance of a kynge]	61

[1] The pages, chapter numbers, and headings in brackets are not in the MS.
[2] After 15 in MS.

The Chapters of the Book.

		PAGE
Cap. 25.	Of þe mercy of a kynge	61
Cap. 26.	[To kepe fayth and othes sworne]	62
Cap. 27.	Of his kepynge	62
Cap. 28.	Of auauncement of study yn his londe ...	63 4
Cap. 29.	Of þe kepynge of his Body [from women] ...	63
Cap. 30.	[Of trysting noght only yn oon leche]	64
¹ Fol. 26. Cap. 31.	¹Of þe sight of oures in Astronomy	64
Cap. 32.	Of þe profyt to kepe hele	66 8
Cap. 33.	[Of þe composition of man of foure humours] ...	66
Cap. 34.	Of kepynge of helthe	67
Cap. 35.	[Of þe tokens of þe stomak]	68
Cap. 36.	Of maners to kepe helthe	69 12
Cap. 37.	Of kepynge of helth and manere of lyuynge ...	69
Cap. 38.	[Of contynance afore mete]	70
Cap. 39.	Of manere of slepynge	71
Cap. 40.	[Of slepynge aftyr mete]	71 16
Cap. 41.	Of kepynge of costome	72
Cap. 42.	[To eschewe Engrutynge]	72
Cap. 43.	Of þe ffoure tymes of þe ȝere; Of þer qualite and diuersite; Of veir	72 20
Cap. 44.	Of Somer	73
Cap. 45.	Of Heruest	74
Cap. 46.	Of Wynter	74
Cap. 47.	[Thynges that fattith the body]	75 24
Cap. 48.	[Thynges þat feblys and dryes þe Body] ...	76
Cap. 49.	[The Reule of Ypocraas]	76
Cap. 50.	Of knowynge of ffoure principaly Membrys; Of þe euyle of þe heued and þe remedy ...	76 28
Cap. 51.	Of þe euyle of þe brest and þe remedy	77
Cap. 52.	Of þe euyle of þe pryue membrys & þe remedy ...	77
Cap. 53.	[Opynyounus of dyuers ffesisyens]	77
Cap. 54.	[Of þe kepyng of kyndly hete]	78 32
Cap. 55.	Of knowynge of Metys	78
Cap. 56.	[Of ffisshes]	78
Cap. 57.	Of knowynge of waters	79
Cap. 58.	Of knowynge of alle manere of wynes	79 36
Cap. 59.	[Of þe euelys þat folwyn to mekyll of wyn] ...	80
Cap. 60.	[Of venegre, and þe beste medicyn for dronkenesse]	81
Cap. 61.	Of thinges þat strynghes þe body	82 40

The Chapters of the Book.

		PAGE
Cap. 62. Of thinges þat wastys & enfeblys þe body	...	
Cap. 63. Of Bathes ; Of ordinance of stuynge	...	82
Cap. 64. [Techyng to lyf hool withoute leche]	...	83
Cap. 65. [Of þe greet medicyne]	...	84
Cap. 66. Of makynge of hony to medecyns	...	84
Cap. 67. Of þe ffrste medecyne	...	84
Cap. 68. Of þe secounde	...	85
Cap. 69. Of þe þridde	...	85
Cap. 70. Off þe ferthe	...	
Cap. 71. Of þe ffyft	...	
Cap. 72. þe sext	...	Caps. 70-75, though indexed, are not translated in the MS.
Cap. 73. þe seuend	...	
Cap. 74. þe eght	...	
Cap. 75. Of þe greet medecyne, last and fynale	...	
Cap. 76. Of latyng of blood, and of oures þerto	...	85
Cap. 77. [Off takynge of medicyn laxatyue]	...	86
Cap. 78. [Of doctryne of tokenynges]	...	86
Cap. 79. Off propertes of herbes and stones	...	87
Cap. 80. [Off þe stoon, þe Eye of Philosophers.]	...	87
Cap. 81. Off þe Oppynyoun of Hermogenes	...	88
Cap. 82. [Off þe vertu of precious stoones]	...	89
Cap. 83. [Off þinges vegetable]	...	89
Cap. 84. [Off þe trees þat hauyn kyndly vertu·]	...	91
Cap. 85. Off right	...	92 Book III.
Cap. 86. [Off þe makyng of þinges in order]	...	94
Cap. 87. [Off þe steryng of heuens]	...	95
Cap. 88. Knowynge of Sawle.	...	96
Cap. 89. [Off þe makyng of man]	...	97 Book IV.
Cap. 90. [Of sight]. Off þe V wyttes	...	97
Cap. 91. [Off harkenyng]	...	97
Cap. 92. [Off tastynge]	...	97
Cap. 93. [Off touch]	...	98
Cap. 94. [Off werkyng of wyttes]	...	98
Cap. 95. [Off perfeccioun of ffyue wyttes]	...	98
Cap. 96. [Off conseillers]	...	98
Cap. 97. [Off byholding engenderures]	...	99
Cap. 98. [To dyspys noght lytyll stature]	...	100
Cap. 99. [How þe kyng awe to ask conseyll]	...	101
Cap. 100. [Off putting vpberers in þe kyngs stede]	...	101
Cap. 101. Off Prudence to assaye a Conseller	...	102

The Chapters of the Book.

		PAGE
	Cap. 102. ffyuetene Vertueȝ off a good Consoiller	... 103
	Cap. 103. [þat man ys þe lesse werld]	... 104
	Cap. 104. [Noght to haue trist yn man þat trowys noght þy lawe]	... 104 4
Book V.	Cap. 105. To chese a Qweynte Scryueyn and Pryue	... 106
Book VI.	Cap. 106. To teche a Messagere	... 107
Book VII.	Cap. 107. To gouerne þy self	... 108
	Cap. 108. [Of expendours]...	... 108 8
Book VIII.	Cap. 109. Off ledcres off ostes and here ordinaunce	... 108
	Cap. 110. [Of the horn of battle]	... 109
Book IX.	Cap. 111. Off auenture off Bataylles	... 110
Book X.	Cap. 112. Knowynge by diuers tokenynges	... 112 12
	Cap. 113. [Off colour]	... 114
	Cap. 114. [Off byholdyng]	... 114
	Cap. 115. [Off þe mysauentrous] ...	... 114
	Cap. 116. [Off attemprance]	... 114 16
	Cap. 117. Of heer of men ...	... 114
	Cap. 118. Of eghen ...	... 115
	Cap. 119. Of browes	... 115
	Cap. 120. Of nees	... 115 20
	Cap. 121. Of face. Of mouth	... 115
	Cap. 122. Of þe temples ...	... 116
	Cap. 123. [Of þe eeres] ...	... 116
	Cap. 124. Of voyces	... 116 24
	Cap. 125. Of Mouynge of body ...	... 116
	Cap. 126. Of þe Throte	... 116
	Cap. 127. Of þe wombe. Of þe sholders ...	... 116
	Cap. 128. Of þe armes	... 117 28
	Cap. 129. Of þe palmes of þe hondes ...	... 117
	Cap. 130. Of knees, Of þe soles of þe feet ...	... 117
	Cap. 131. Of þe paas of men, & manere of goynge	... 117
	Cap. 132. [Of þe tokenynges of good kynde] ...	... 117 32
	Cap. 133. [Of oon wytnesse in Iugement] ...	... 118

Cap. 1. [Of aforspekynge of louynge of Aristotel.]

¹God almy3ty kepe oure kynge to ioye of his ligeys, and make
fast his kyngdome to defende þe lawe of god, and make hym
4 dwellynge to enhye þe worschipe & louynge of gode men. I
3oure seruant to þe comandement þat 3e enioynyd me haues put
myn entent to enserche þe book of maners of gouernance of
lordschipes, þat is sayd preuyte3 of preuyte3 or consaiH of con-
8 sailles, þe whilke þe Prynce of Philosophers Aristotel, þe sone of
Nichomake of Macidoyne, made and wrate to his disciple þe
greete Emperour Alexander, þe sone of Phelippe kynge of grece,
þe whilke Alexander two hornes ys sayde to haue had. þys book
12 mad Aristotel yn his elde, & in his wayknesse of bodely vertue3
þat he myght nought goo, no to vse & gefe entent to þe kynges
nedes; ffor Alexander had mad him cheefe gouernour of his
londes, and set him byfore oþer als hym þat he had chosen &
16 mekyl louyd, ffor he was a man of greet conseyle & letterure, &
of persand vndirstandynge, and yn trew stody wakand, and yn
gracious maners & spiritualy conynges, and yn charitables con-
templacions descreet and meke; wharfore many of þe philoso-
20 phers hold hym als of þe nombre of prophetes, And men fyndes
wretyn yn old writynge of Gregeis þat souerayn god sent his
Angel to hym sayand, "I saH name þe bettir Angel þan man."
Many ar þe takenyngys of hym and greet meruailles & straunge
24 wirkynges þat longe wer to me by ordre to telle. Bot of his
dede er diuers oppynyons, for oon sect þat er namyd ypatetiks
affermes þat he steigh to þe emperien heuene yn þe semynge of
fir. Als longe als he leuyd was Alexander valiant by kepynge of
28 his hale counseil, folowand his biddyngys; and for þat he con-
querd Citce3, and hadde victory of aH kyngdomes, and of aH þe
world he oon hadde chefe gouernaunce, Whare fore þe name of
his renoun) spredde hym þourgh alle londys of þe ffoure partyes
32 of þe world, so þat alle naciouns putte hem vndir his empir and

Marginalia:
¹ Fol. 3 a.
The dedication of the Arabic author.
The name of the book.
Aristotle's honours.
He is honoured by God.
The Peripatetics.
Aristotle was taken up to heaven.

comaundementʒ, Arabies & Perseis, so þat no man ne dorste in sawe no yn dede aʒeyn-stond his lordschipe. He made many morales epistels to Aristotel [1] of greet delyt to haue his secree fynal, of þe whilke þys ys oon part. Alexander sente to his techere Aristotel whanne he hadde ouer-comen þe Perseis in þys ffourme.

All men obeyed Alexander.
[1] Fol. 3 b.

Cap. 2. [Of a Epistyl fro Alexander to Aristotel.]

"O Noble doctour, gouernour of right, y do to vnderstonde to ʒoure conynge þat y haue foundyn yn þe lond of Perse a ffolk þat is abundand of resoun and of persand vnderstondynge, & þay stody to haue lordschipe of oþer, whar-fore we purpos to slaa þam alle; but þat semys to ʒow yn þys matere ʒe sende vs by ʒoure letters."

How am I to deal with the Persians?

Cap. 3. [The answer of the same.]

And Aristotel answerd yn þis manere. "If þou may chaunge þe eir and þe watir of þat lond, and also þe ordinanceʒ of Citeeʒ, do þy purpos, and ellys gouerne hem wyth goodnesse, And vnderstonde hem wyth debonertee, and yf þou so doo, be þou seker with þe helpe of god þay all shall be subgitʒ to þy likynges & biddynges, and be loue þou shall reigne vp-on hem pesabely with victorye." þis Epistel ressayued, Alexander did after his consaill, & þey of Perse were most obeisaunt to hym of alle Naciouns.

Behave well to them.

Cap. 4. [Of aforspekynge of þe translatour of þis booke.] Howe this Book was ffirst ffounden.

Iohan þat translatyd þis book Patrik sone ful wys, & leel enterpretour of langages sayd, "I haue noght left vnsoght no stede no temple whare Philosophers vsyd to wryte & þaire pryue wirkynges to make, no no wys man þat y trowyd þat vnderstood þe wrytynge of Philosophie, þat y ne soght hym, to þe tyme þat y cam to þe Oracle of þe sone þat Esculapides mad for hym, where y fand oon solitarye man abstinente ful wys of Philosophie, and of greet conynge, to whom y mekyd me, and yn als mekel as y coude I seruyd and ful deuoutly y requerd hym þat he wolde shewe me þe secreteʒ wretyn yn þat oracle; and he will- and did hyt, And omonge oþer doynges þe werke desird I ffand þere, and of greet trauaylle and longe tyme [2] I trauayled and

The prolog of John, son of Patrick.
I found this book at an Oracle of the Sun.
[2] Fol. 4 a.

hadde hit; & wit̄ ioye y wente hoome ȝeldand to oure creatour
gret þankynges in many maneres; And at þe requeste of oon
worthy kyng y trauaillyd, studyd, and translatyd hit out of þe *I translated from Greek*
langage of grew yn to Calden & out Calden to þe langage of *into Chaldee, and thence*
arabye; And yn þe bigynnyge y fand þis book of wys Aristotyl, *into Arabic.*
and translatyd hit; In the whilke book he answers to þe request
of Alexander yn þys fourme.

Cap. 5. Þe Epistle of Aristotel to Alexander.

Oune most glorious, most rigȟtful Emperour, god make þe *God help and keep thee.*
fast in way of knowynge and felynge of þreut̄ & vertues, &
restreyn yn þe bestials apetites, & þi wyte ligȟten to his seruice
and his worschipe, I haue ressayuid to worschippe þat fallys
þerto, And fully y haue vnderstonde how greet desir þat ȝe haue
of my persone þat y were with ȝow; ȝe meruaille how y may
absteyne me fro ȝow, And chalangys me þat y haue no þougȟt of
ȝoure besynes, wharefore y haue besyed me & hastyd me for þat *I donot forget your wishes.*
cause to make a wrytynge to ȝowre heigȟnes, & it shal be a
balaunce to aH ȝoure werkys dressand righ̄t myn absence fulfill-
and, And it shal be a certeyn reule to ȝow to what ȝe wille as y
sholde shewe ȝow if y were present with ȝow; ȝe sholde nogȟt
haue chalangid me sithen ȝe woot and sholde wete, þat I leue
nogȟt to to come to ȝoure most cleer worschippynge for dispyt,
But þat heuynesse of age and feblenesse of body hauys so *I would come to you if I*
vmbylappyd me, þat þey make me heuy and nogȟt able to goo; *could.*
And ouer þat þat ȝe equere and coueytis to wete, it is swilk a
secre þat vnnethis mannys brest may it vnderstonde, how may
it þanne be wrete in dedly skyns? To þat þat fallis to ȝow to
enquere, and ys leful to me to trete me byhoues and of dette ys
holden to answere, Als ȝe of dette of discrecioun is ¹ys holdyn to ¹ *Fol. 4b.*
enquere no more of me of þis secret þan y deliuere ȝow yn þis *It is a great secret.*
book, ffor yf ȝe besely study it, rede hit, and fully vnderstond
yt þat is content þer ynne, I trowe with outen doute þat non
obstacle shal be by twen ȝow and þat þat ȝe desire, ffor god
hauys geuyn to þe so mekyl grace of vnderstondynge and righ̄t- *But you can understand*
ful wyt in letterure of sciences be my techinge byfore tagȟt þat *my teaching.*
by oure seluyn ȝe mowe comprend & by fygurs vnderstonde aH
þat ȝe aske to be tagȟt of, ffor þe desir of ȝoure brynnand wyl
shal opyn a way to gete ȝoure purpos, & shaH lede ȝow to þe *You will attain your*
ende desiryd by þe graunt of oure lord. *end.*

SECRETE.   E

þe cause ys þat y wiłł shewe to ȝow þis secree by liknes
spekand to ȝow by ensamples, signifiaunces, and tokenynges; ffor
y doute mekyl þat þis book come nought to þe hondes of vntrew
men and ynto power of proude men, And so shulde þis laste good 4
and secree of lordschipes to swilk come þat souereyn god iugys
vnworthi & enemys, And so y shulde be a trespasour to goddys
grace, and breker of heuenly secree & of þe pryue shewynge.
And þarefore vndir coniurisoun of ˙goddis Iugement y haue dis- 8
couerd to ȝow þis sacrament after þe manere þat it ys shewyd to
me, And wete wel þat he þat secreetȝ discouers & shewys preuyteȝ,
myshappe shal sone sewe him, wherfore ȝif ȝe do it þe same com-
ynges ȝe ¹shal lightly ryn in. But god fro ałł euelys, and swilke 12
wirkes, & fro ałł vnhoneste by his mercy kepe ȝow, And after ałł
swylke oþer þinges brynge to ȝoure mynde þat sauand techinge
þat y ofte sithes was wont to shewe to ȝow, and ȝoure noble saule
to enfourme, and þat shal be ȝoure solas and mirrour of hele. 16

²Sustentement of kynges.

It most nede be of force þat ilk a kyng haue two helpes to
susteyn his kyngdome, þe oon ys strenght of men to defende
him and make his kyngdome stalworth, and þat may he noght 20
but whenne he is gouernour in right and lord yn his subgitȝ,
and þat his subgitȝ of oon accord obeisse hem to his lordschipe.
As for inobedience of subgitȝ is þe myght of lord put vndir and
mad feble, & subgetȝ regnys, I haue shewyd cause þat subgitȝ 24
sholde be steryd to þaire lord to be obeisaunt, þe cause ys
double, on ynward a-noþer outward; þe outward y haue declared
before, þat ys to say þat þou despend þy good and Rychesse
wysly, & make þy largesse after þe desert of ilk oon. And it 28
byhoues þat kynges haue a-noþer queyntise, but þerof y shal
make mencioun after yn þe chapitre of riches & helpes; þe
seconde þinge is to drawe þe wil of his subgitȝ to wirkynge, and
þat awe to go before yn þe firste degree, And þe seconde helpe 32
awe to haue two causes, oon ynward and a-noþer outward, and
þat ynward ys þat kynges awe holde and do right of poscessiouns, riches & purches þat right heir be maad þerof, and trewe
successours. ³A cause ys foreyn þat ys to say sparand þe riches 36
of subgitȝ.

---

² This is not a separate chapter in the Latin.
³ This paragraph follows in the MS. after 'lord,' on p. 49.

Of Liberality and Avarice.

And þe inward cause ys þe secree of olde Philosopheres and of rightful men þat glorious god before chose and his knowynge gaf hem, And if y gif ȝow þis secree with oþer þinges þat ȝe shall 4 fynde yn dyuers titles of þis book yn þe whilk ȝe shal fynde greet Philosophie and conynge, ffor with Inne ys foundyn þe fynal cause of ȝoure entent and ȝoure purpos, principal & fynal, when ȝe haue fully þe vnderstondynges of þe sentences, and of 8 þe ensamples, þanne shal ȝe pursewe fully & perfitely ȝoure purpos desiryd. God þat ys most wys & glorious, he light ȝoure resoun, and make cleer ȝoure vnderstondynge to persayue þe sacrament of þis science þat ȝe mowe se þer in. Þe toþer ys þat 12 he make his riches to abounde largely in the soules of wyse men, & gif graces to vnderstondantȝ & studiauntȝ, to whom no þinge ys inpossible, and with oute whom no possessioun is possible.

[marginalia: This book contains all you desire.]

Cap. 6. Of maners of kynges.

16 ¹Kynges er ffoure, large to him and large to subgitȝ, and kynge auers to hym and auers to subgitȝ, And kynge auers to hym and large to subgitȝ, And kyng large to hym & auers to subgitȝ. Þe ytailes sayen it ys no vice to a kynge if he be auers to hym 20 seluen, so þat he be large to ²his subgitȝ. Þe Indyes sayen þe same of a kynge þat ys auers to hym seluyn, and to his subgitȝ good; þe perseyens affermen aȝeyn þat a kynge is noght worth þat ys noght large to hym seluyn.

[marginalia: There are four kinds of kings.]
[marginalia: ² Fol. 5 b.]

24 Of largesse and Auarice.

Ws byhoues now sotely enquere of þes vertues and vices, and for to shewe what ys largesse & what auarice, and what errour ys yn largesse, & what euyl suys withdrawynge of largesse. ffor 28 opyn þinge ys þat qualytes er to be despysed whenne þey disacord fro þeir mein; And we woot wel þat þe kepynge of largesse ys right herd, and his brekynge right light. If þow wylt gete þe vertu of largesse, behold þy power, þe tyme of 32 mester, and þe desertes of men, And þanne shalt þow after þy pouere with mesure gif þy godes to þeym that hauys myster and er worthy. He þat oþer wyse gyues, synnes, and trespasys þe rule of largesse; ffor he þat gyues his good to hem þat hauys 36 no myster, he purchases no louynge þerof, And whanne þay er gyuen to vnworthy þay er louyd; And he þat spendys his good

[marginalia: What are largesse and avarice?]
[marginalia: Give to poor and deserving.]
[marginalia: If men are not poor, they do not thank you.]

¹ þ in MS.

ouyr mesure shal sone come to þe better riuale of[1] pouert, and he
ys likynd to hym þat geuys victorye to his enemys vpon him.
He þat gyues of his godes in tyme of nede to nedful men, swylk
a kynge ys large to him and to his subgitȝ, and he shal reigne in
prosperite, and his comaundemente shal be holdyn. Olde men
louyn swylk a kynge, and he ys sayd vertuous, large and attempre. And he þat geuys þe giftys of his kyngdome out of
ordre to vnworthy and to hem þat has non nede, he is a wastour
of his goodys, & distruour of his kyngdome and vnmyghty to
reigne, & he ys callyd a prodegaleous man þat is ffole large; ffor
his forseynge ys farre fro his reygnynge. But certys þe name of
oon Auers mys fallys to a kynge, and mys semys to his real
mageste; þerfore ȝif a kynge haue þe oon or þe oþer vice, þat ys
to say aueryce or [2]folee largesse, if him self can noght conseill
hym, It aweþ to be purueyd to him with greet besynesse a trew
discret man chosen), to whom he may trowe to ordeyne þe besynesse of his godys, and his richesse to gouerne.

margin: The king who gives proper largesse.
margin: The waster and destroyer.
margin: [2] Fol. 6 a.
margin: A king ought to have a prudent counsellor.

Cap. 7. Of þe euels þat comes of ffole largesse.

Alexander, y say stedfastly to þe, what kyng þat wille continue giftys yn surfaytes ouer þat his kyngdom wyl suffyse to
hym, That kynge with outen doute shal be destroyed. Ouer þat
y say to þe þat y neuer sesyd to say to þy heighnes, þat for to
eschewe Auerice and ffole largesse is ioye of kynges and longe
lastynge of kyngdomes, and þat ys namly whanne kynges withholdys hem & withdrawes her hondys frome þe goodys and
poscessiouns of her subgitȝ, wher of it ys founden) in þe book of
þe greet doctour Hermogenes, þat souerayn and verray goodnes,
nobeley, and vnderstondynge, & fulfyllyng of lawe & tokenynge
of perfeccioun are yn a kynge þat withdrawys hym from þe
siluer and poscessiouns of his subgitȝ. **What was þe cause
þat þe distruccion of þe kyngdom of Ingelond.[3]** Whenne
þat þe superfluyte of despensȝ ouer passyd þe rente of citeeȝ,
& þer rentys fallyþ hem and despensez, þo þe kynge extendyd
his hondys to oþer menys goodys and rentys, and þe subgitȝ
for þe wronge cried to hye god and glorious, and sente hem
an hote wende, and torment hem stalworthly, and þe poeple
dressyd hem aȝeyn hem, and þer names for euer dyd out of þe
lond. And but yf glorious god had so ordeyned, þis lond hadde

margin: A king may destroy himself and his kingdom by prodigal gifts.
margin: Hermogenes' teaching.
margin: Prodigal kings are tempted to spoil their subjects.

[1] 'of' repeated in MS.   [3] Made a separate heading in the MS.

Of Understanding and Good Fame. 53

vtterly ben destruyd. And wete þat richesse er þe lastynge of saule bestfuH & a party þerof, and þe saule may noȝht last yf
4 þat cause be destruyd; wherfore man awe gretly eschewe ouer-doynge and ouerabundance of despens3, And þat largesse be attemprance be getyn, & þat foly and ouerdoon gyftys be eschewyd.

<small>Riches and the 'anima animalis.'</small>

Cap. 8. [Of teching of Aristotel yn vertue3 and vices.]

8 [1] þe maners and þe goodis sustinance3 of vertues er to guerdon olde trauailles, to reles wrongys, honurable men to worschippe, to helpe simple men, to vpbere þe defautes of Innocent3, to faire speke to hem of gretys, to restreyne þe tonge, to suffre
12 wronge ffor a tyme, to leue and flee foly. Ȝyt y lere þe þat y was wont to lere þe and sawe yn þy brest, And y trist þat þis techinge shaH be yn aH þy wayes and werkys surtee and sufficiante to þy gouernaille alle þe tymes of þy lyf. I shal say
16 þe trewly þe conynge of Philosophye abreggyd, And yf y hadde neuer sayd to þe but þis folowand techinge, it sholde suffise to þe in alle þy werkys touchand þis werld & þe oþer.

<small>[1] Fol. 6 b. The kingly virtues are these.</small>

<small>All the results of Philosophy are here.</small>

Cap. 9. [Of þe endly entente þat kynges awe to haue.]
20   Of vndirstondynge.

Wete þou þat vndirstondyng ys heued of gouernance, hele of saule, keper of vertue3, Mirrour of vices; ffor we byholde yn hit þat þat ys to flee, and we knowe by it þat þat ys to be chosen.
24 It ys growyng of vertu3 & rote of alle goodes loucables & worschipfuH, And þe firste teching of vndirstondynge is coueyng of good lose, ffor he þat coueys trewly good lose he shaH haue good name and glorious. And he þat coueytis yt fayntly, by shame
28 he shal be confoundyd.

<small>The praise of understanding.</small>

Of goode lose.

Goode lose ys principaly by hym self to be coueyted, ffor kyngdome awe noȝht to be coueyted bot for good lose, And
32 þerfore bigynny of wyt and vndirstondynge ys desir of good lose þat ys purchasyd by good gouernance and to wele lorde; and þerfore if gouernance or lordschipe for oþer cause be coueyted, it ys no purchas of no good lose, but of enuye. Enuye en-
36 gendres lesynge, þat ys rote of alle euelys, & ys matir of vices. Lesynges engendrys detraccioun; detraccioun engenders haatredyn; haatredyn engendrys wronges; wronges engendrys vn-

<small>The value of a good name.</small>

<small>It is what kings should desire.</small>

<small>The tree of evil.</small>

reuerence; vnreuerence engendrys Ire; Ire engendrys aȝein-
stryuynge; aȝeinstryuyng engendrys enmyte; enmyte bataiłł;
bataiłł destroys lawys and sitceȝ, and þat ys aȝeyn rigħt and
kynde, and þat þat disaccordys to kynd destruys alle wirkynges. 4

The root of all good things.
Stody and loue, desir of good lose in treuthe & sothfastnesse,
þat ys rote of alle þynges loueables & Moder of alle goodis, ffor

[1] Fol. 7 a.
How one good thing engenders another.
it ys [1]contrarie to lesynge, And desir of right engendrys right;
rigħt engendris Trist; trist engendrys largesse; largesse engen- 8
drys ffamiliarite, þat ys trew seruice; trew seruice engendrys
frendschipe; ffrendschipe engendrys conseil and helpe; by þes
þinges ys al þe werld stablissyd, and lawes set to men; þes
accordes to resoun and kynde, wherfore it semes þat desir to 12
gouerne fore good lose ys good þinge and lastynge.

Cap. 10. [Of euels þat seuen flesshly apetit.]
To eschewe fflesshly delytes.

The evils of lust,
Alexander, bowe þy wyl fro bestials delices, fro fflesshly 16
appetitȝ makes þe corages of men lyk to þe willys of bestys,
wyth outyn resoun and discrecioun; and hit destruys the body,
& makys heuy þy wyttes and þyn vnderstondynge. It ys to

and their consequences.
knowe þat flesshly delyces engendrys fleschly loue, and flesshly 20
loue Aueryce; Aueryce desir of richesse; desyr of richesse
dredys no shame; to drede nogħt shame makys foly takynge;
ffoly takynge makys vntreuthe; vntrewthe theft; theft repreef,
wherof comes cheitifty and takyng, þat brynges a man to shame 24
and his distruccioun.

BOOK II. Cap. 11. [Of þe wyt of a kynge.]
Of vertues þat kynges awe to haue.

First and principaly it is nedful to a kynge, þat touchand his 28
owen persoun, þat good lose of his name sprede of his lowable
wyt, and þat he wysly conten hym with his folk, and þerof he
shal be louyd and worschipyd, and he shal be doutyd whanne
þey seen hym in wyt eloquent and yn his werkys wysly doand. 32

You can easily tell whether a king is wise. Does he honour the Divine law?
And a man may ligħtly knowe, and by tokenynges perseyue
whether wyt or no wyt be yn a kynge lordand; ffor what kynge
þat puttys his kyngdom vndirlout to þe lawes of god, he reignes
rigħtfully and worschipfully to his lordschype. And he þat 36

Book II. *Of the Virtues a King should have.*

puttys his lawe in seruage and vndirlout yn his kyngdom and
empir, he is a trespasour to treuth and despisour of his awene
lawe; And he þat dispyses his lawe of alle men, he shal be *If not, he is to be con-*
4 dispysed and dampnyd in lawe. *demned.*

Cap. 12. [Of þe religiouste of a kynge.]

Ȝyt y say als wys Philosophers and spekers of þe myghts *All Philoso-phers agree*
of god sayen, þat first soueraynly it fallys to a kynge þat he *that he ought to be reli-*
8 attempre hym with trewe stablementȝ & lawes noght in fenyd *gious.*
semynge but in opyn shewynge of dede, þat alle þe folk wete
þat he doutys god myghtful, and þat ¹he ys subgyt to þe hegh ¹ Fol. 7 b.
myght of god; ffor þanne men was wont to worschippe and
12 doute a kynge whenne þey se hym worschippe and doute god;
and if he oonly shew hym semand religious, and yn his werkys
be an euyl doere, And euyll wirkynges may noght hyd hem, *Hypocrisy will not im-*
but ȝif folk wete hem, he shal be refusyd of god and of þe folk *pose on the people.*
16 despysed, his dedys shall be dyfamed, and his empir lessyd, and
þe heght of his glorie and mageste shal be without outen worschipe.
And ouer þat þer is no pryce ne no tresour þat may aȝeyn bye
his good fame. Ouer alle þinges it fallys to a kynge to wor-
20 schipe trew men, to forthbere religious men, wys men to enhye *Kings ought to talk much*
and ofte sithes speke wyth, to stirre doutablys questions, honestly *with religious men.*
to aske hem, and discretly answore hem; þe most wys and most
noble most to worschippe aftir her states.

24 Cap. 13. [Of his purueyance and his sleghte.]

and yt ys nedfull to a kynge to þynk on auentures to *A king should exercise fore-*
come, and so ordeyne þat he suffre more lightly aduersytes. *thought:*
Also it fals him to be pytous, & namly restreyne hym fro
28 inordinat sterynges, and he do noght yn dede with outen
deliberacioun, and þat he sone and resonably knowe his errour
and wysly repele hit, ffor it ys souerayn wyt yn a kynge to wel
gouerne hym seluyn. Whanne a kynge sees any good or profit
32 to doo, with discrecion do he hit noght ouer latly ne ouer hastly, *be neither too fast nor*
þat he be noght sen hastyf ne slowe. *too slow.*

Cap. 14. Of ornement cleþinge of a kynge.

It mckyl byhoues and semes to a kynges dignite worschype- *A king should wear the*
36 fully be cled, and euyr more yn fayr apparell to apper & passe *finest clothes in his coun-*
oþer in fayrhede; þerfore a kynge sholde vse cleþynge and *try.*

ornementȝ dere, fayre, and straunge, ffor it semes to a kynges prorogatyue to passe oþer, so þat his dignite þerby be maad fairer, and his myght be nought empeyred, and þat due reuerence be ȝolden to hym. It semes a kyng to haue fair faconde, and þat he be fair spekand, and þat he haue a cleer voyce þat mekyl profytes yn tyme of Bataill.

He should have a good voice.

Cap. 15. [Of þe contynance of a kynge.]
To eschewe mekyl Spekynge.

¹ Fol. 8 a.
Kings should not talk too much,

¹Alexander, fayr þing and worschipful ys to a kyng þat he withdrawe hym fro mekyl spekynge but whenne nede askys, ffor it semys bettir þat þe eres of þe folk be thristy to þe wordes of þe kyng þanne þay be fillyd of his talys, ffor whanne þe eres and þe sawles er so fillyd, þey here nought bleghtly þe kyng. It semes also a kyng þat he haunte noght mekyl þe company of his subgitȝ, & namly of vnhonest persouns, ffor ouer mekyl familiarite among þe poepyl brynges in despyt and contempt of worschipe, and þerfore þay of Inde hauen a ful fayr costome yn disposisioun and ordynance of hir kyng and kyngdome; ffor þey haue ordeyned þat hir kyng onys yn þe ȝeer appere yn his real apparel byfore his poeple sittand on a stede enourned of his armes, and he nobley armed, & his comune poeple shall be maad to remue aferre from him, and his noble Barouns negh and aboute hym alle; And þanne ys it costome þat he spede greet nedys, and to shewe diuers þinges þat ar fallyn, and do besynesse and entent to ordeyne for the comyn profyt, þat day he ys wont to geue gyftes, and þey þat ar lytel gylty to delyuere out of prisoun, and to allege his poeple of gret charges, and to do dyuers werkys of pytee; And at þe sermon endyd þe kyng shal sitte, and þanne shal rise oon of his princes þat ys next hym, þat ys haldyn most wys and most best spekand of oþer, and he shal speke honour louynge and goodnesse of þe kyng, ȝeldand þankynges to glorious god, þat so wel haues enourned þe kyngdome and þe contree of Inde with so wys a kyng, þat yn vnite and obedience haþ confermed and fastyd þe louable poeple of Inde; And aftyr þe louynges and praysynges of here kyng he shal turne hym to þe poeple to prayse hem and loue hem, and remeue & recomend her gode maneres, and styr þayre goode willes, and shew by ensamples and resouns of meknesse and of obedience to loue & reuerence of þe kyng. And after þat þe

or their subjects will lose respect for them.

Do like the Indians.

The king shows himself once a year,

and gives gifts, and releases prisoners.

Then a great lord praises his rule.

poeple shal afforce hem to enhye and loue þe kyng and his *And the people pray for him, and love him.*
goode dedes, to prayse and to pray for his lyf, and in citeȝ and
greet assembleȝ hys wyt ¹and his gode werkes telle, and þerfore ¹ Fol. 8 b.
4 þay lere þaire children yn þaire ȝouthe and enfourmes hem to
loue, honoure, obeisse, and doute þe kynge. In þys manere
pryncipaly ys shewyd and grewys þe gode name of a kynge
boþe pryuely and openly.   And þe forsayd kyng of Inde vsyd *Then the king punishes misdoers,*
8 þat tyme to ponysse mysdoers and trespasours, þat þe way of
wrong be put away fro rightwyse lyuyeres, And brekers of þe
lawes be chastysed. And also he vsys þat tyme to alegge
trowages and for to dispense wyth marchauntȝ, and for to reles
12 party of rentys, and Marchauntȝ with alle here Marchaundise *and rewards merchants.*
besely defende and helpe. And þat ys þe cause þat Inde ys so
ful of poeple, ffor þedyr Marchauntȝ trauaille on alle sydes, and
faire and wel er resceyued, and þere wynnes ryche & pore
16 Citeȝeyns and fforeyns, And þerfore trowages and þe kynges
rentys encresys.

Cap. 16. [Of þe ryght of a kynge.]

It ys gretly to eschewe to offende Marchauntȝ and do hem *Merchants should never be injured.*
20 wronge, ffor þay er berers of louynges and gode name of kynges
and kyngdomes þurgh þe world. It ys to ȝelde to ilk man þat
his ys, ffor so er citeeȝ warmstoryd and rentys gyuen. So
grewys kyngdomes, & glorye and worschipe to kynges; So
24 dredys hem enemys, and er agayn standyd. So lyuys kynges
peseabely and sekirly, and haue desir of her wylles.

Cap. 17. [Of his fynale entente.]
Þat kynges be noght coueytous ne cruell.

28   Alexander, coueyte noght þinges coruptibles & passant, þat *Do not desire worldly things.*
þou most sone forsake. But gete þe stabyl richesse, a lyf þat
may noght be chaungyd, a kyngdome ay lastand dilatable.
Euer ordeyn þi þoughtes in goodnesse; ȝeld þy seluyn glorious
32 & vygerous; fflegh þe folowyng of bestys and lyouns, and hir
fylthes. Be noght cruel, but bonand to spare hem of whom
þou hauys victorye; þink of auentures and cases to falle, ffor
þou woot noght what day to-morwe sal falle þe. Wille þou *Avoid mere bodily pleasures.*
36 noght folowe þy delyces yn etynge and drynkynge, in lichery
ne longe slepynge.

Cap. 18. [Of þe chastite of a kynge.]
To eschewe licherye.

These are the evils of lechery.

Worthy Emperour, bowe noght þe to þe vse of women, ffor swylk a vse ys a properte to swyne. What ioye ys to þe to vse þe vyce of bestys þat hauen no resoun, and folwyn her dedys? trowe me wyth outen drede, þat lychery ys distruccioun of body, shortynge of lyf, corypcioun of vertueȝ, trespas of þe lawe; And hit engendrys women maners, and at þe laste yt ledys man to þat euyll þat we haue be-fore sayd.

Cap. 19. [Of þe solace of a kynge.]
Of Instrumentȝ of Menstralcye.

[1] Fol. 9 a.
Kings should delight in Music.

[1]Hit fals to emperiale magestee to haue with hym pryue men and trewe, with whom he mowe delyt hym wyth Instrumentȝ and maners of Organes whanne he ys ennoyed, ffor man sawle kyndly in swilke þinges delytes, Wyttes restyn hem, Curiosyteȝ vanysshes away, and al þe body ressayues strynght. Whenne þou wylt delyte þe with swylk þynges, at þe moste dwelle yn swylk lyf þre dayes or ffoure after þou sees hit profyt, and euer-more wyth þe beste and most honestely, and þat yt be pryue.

Take solace three or four days at a time.

And whenne þou ert yn swylke solaces, wythdrawe þe fro mekyl drynkynge, and lat oþer drynkyn þat wille, And feyne þe as þou were eschaufyd wyth wyn, ffor þanne shalt þou persayue many pryue þynges, and here also, but do noght þat ofte but twyes or thryes yn þe ȝeer; and þe awe to haue aboute þe specyal meynee, þat mowe telle þe what er doon and sayd by þi kyngdome. When þou ert amonge þy Barouns, worschippe þe wyse and þayme þat þou seeȝ þat doon to be worschipped, and hold ylkon in his staat,

Make your companions drink.

Do not favour one more than another.

And calle to þe solace oon today, a-noþer to morwe. And after it fallys to ilke degree worschipe hem, and lat noon of þi nobles be, but if he fele þy worschipe and largesse yn þe swetnesse of þi mageste; and þe nobleye of þy free wyl shewe it to ylkoon.

Cap. 20. [Of the descrecioun of a kynge.]
Of reddour attempred.

A king should make himself and his Court respected.

It semes a kynge to haue discrescioun, and þat he content hym and hold hym fro mekyl laghynge, ffor oft laghynge takys away reuerence and engendirs elde. Also þou awe to wete þat a man ys more holden to worschipe þe kynge yn his court and yn his constory þan yn oþer place, ffor þare hymself awe of dette if

any doo wronge to do ponysshe hym after þe qualyte of his persoun, so þat oþer be war and lere and abstene hem to do wronge. It ys to punyssh þe most nobles on oþer wyse þan oþer
4 heigh men, And oþer wyse hym þat commes among þe folk þan oþer subgitȝ, wharfore good þinge ys to kepe reddour and ¹continence togedre, þat bytwyx þe kyng and his subgitȝ be distinccioun of persones, ffor it ys wretyn yn þe book of Esculabicis
8 þat þat kyng ys to be enheighed and loued þat holdes þe semblance of þe Egle, þat ys manisand & dred omange þe foulys, & noght he þat ys lykned to oþer subgitȝ ffowles. þarfore if any yn þe presence of þe real mageste takys on honde or profres to do
12 wronge, it ys to se on what wyl he did hit, whethir to plese þe kynge and to glade men, or in contempt and dishonour of þe kynges dignite; after þe firste manere him awe to be chastysed, and after þe oþer manere to be ded.

Marginalia: Punish offenders with respect to their persons. ¹ Fol. 9 b. A king is likened to an eagle. Examine the motives of offenders.

16   Cap. 21. **Of obedyence.**

Alexander, obedience of lordschipe we vnderstonde in foure maners, þat ys to say [in] religiousite, in ffrendschipe, in Curtasye, and reuerence. O Alexander, draw to þe þe good wylles of þy
20 subgitȝ, and putte away þaire vnryghtys and wronges. Gyf noght matere to þe people to mysspeke of þe, ffor þat þe poeple may say, þay may som tyme lightly doo; perfore contene þe so, þat men may noght say aȝeyn the. And þerby þou shalt eschewe
24 here doinges. And ouer all þynge wete þat discrescioun of meknesse is ioye of dignite, reuerence of lordschipe and enhansynge of a kynge. It ys a souerayn wysdom þat þou make more þy reuerence dwelle yn þe hertys of þy subgitȝ þan loue.

Marginalia: The four groundis of Obedience. Let men say no evil of thee. Rather be reverenced than loved.

28   Cap. 22. **Of lyknes of kynges.**

Men redys þat kynges ar yn kyngdomes as rayn yn erthe, þat ys þe grace of god, þe benysoun of heuene, strengh of þe erþe, and helpe to alle þat leuyn; ffor by rayn ys way maad to
32 merchantȝ & helpe gyuen to biggers; And noþeles yn rayns fallys thondres & leuenynges, & ouer-drownynges þurgh flodes, and greet tempestes yn þe see, and oþer many euelys comyn, þurgh whilk many leuand creatures ar perschyd. Noþeles þes auentures
36 disturbes noght þe poeple to loue god yn his mageste, byhaldand þe tokenynges of his grace, & þe gyftes of his mercy, þat he ²by rayne what þinge þat is makys whik, dede þinges reburgones, and

Marginalia: Kings are likened to rain. It does good and harm. ² Fol. 10 a.

But its good is more than its harm.

Kings are likened to winds.

Their good and their evil.

Nevertheless they cannot be altered, and must be borne with.

he geuys hys benysoun in alle vertuʒ. And þerfore þe poeple louys hit, and forgetys alle þe euelys byforepassyd. Also a kynge ys ensamplyd to þe wyndes þat heiʒh god sendys out and ordeynes of þe tresour of his mercy, by whom he sendys out 4 moysturres to make cornes to waxe, frutes of trees to come swete, and Esperiteʒ taken hir strynghe, and water desired ys ressayued; and to hem þat sailyn yn þe see opnys way, and many oþer goodys folwys of þe wyndes. And noþeles of wynd comys 8 diuers perils and lettynges als wel yn þe see as yn þe land, and brynges ynward sorwys to mannys hertys. Richessys of men þurgh tempestys it losys and takys away. By þe wyndes comes corrupcions of þe eyr and norschiʒht dedly venyms, and many 12 oþer vnacordand þinges comes þerof; wher fore foreyns creatures prays þe mercy of her makere to take swylk euelys fro hem. Noþeles he suffres þe wyndes to lede and hold her cours þat he hauys stabillyd hem; ffor he hauys ordeyned by his wyt alle 16 þinges yn euyn weiʒht and certeyn nombre and ordre, and he hauys stabelyd hem to seruyn his seruantʒ, and þat passys out of his greet mercy and of his goodnesse þat may noʒht be Nombred. 20

Ensample of þe same of somer and wyntyr.

Kings are likened to summer and winter.

þis same lyknesse ys of wynter and somer þat God hauys lastandly stabyled of cold and hete by his souerayne forsyʒht to engendrure and norshynge for lastynge of temporel þynges and 24 kyndly. If alle þat vnaccordandʒ and dedly perils commen of coold of þe wynter and of hete of somer, yn þe same manere it fals in a kynge of whom many goodnesses commen ofte sythes, þat to his subgitʒ dysplesys and heuys, and ʒyt yt ys to hem 28 greet profyt.

Cap. 23. [Of þe socour and þe help of a kynge.]
To helpe Meseyes.

[1] Fol. 10 b.

Kings should help all those in evil case.

[1]Alexander, enquere of þe dysese & enuye of þe pouere and 32 feble, and helpe hem yn here desease of þy pitee; And puruey a man knawand þaire langage, fair spekand, and louand riʒht, þat mowe take entent to hem on ʒowre half, and loue hem and gouerne hem mercyably. þys ys a good obseruance of a kynge, 36 and gladnesse to þe poeple and plesaunce to oure makere.

Of the Forethought and Mercy of Kings.

Cap. 24. Of þe purueyance of a kynge.

Alexander, puruey þe yn tresour of cornes and greynes pro- *Kings should get together corn and grain against time of scarcity.*
fitable to be eten, þat mowe suffyse in þy land yn tyme of
4 hunger and nede; So þat whanne swilk a ȝeer as it has costomed
fullys, þy mercyful purueyance may helpe þy poeple and socour
þy nedfull Citeeȝ; ffor þat tyme þow awe opyn þy garners and
selers, & make opyn by þy kyngdom) whete and oþer manere
8 of cornes; þat ys a greet forwyt and a greet purueyaunce, þe
warmstore of þe kyngdome, þe hele of þe poeple, and kepynge of
Citeeȝ. þanne shal þy comandementȝ be wel keped, þy dedes *So their subjects will praise their name.*
louyd, and þy fayre purueyance be yn perpetuel mynde, ffor it
12 helpys þe poeple by þy wys forsyght. And þanne shal alle men
wete þy forsyght of þyn eyen, and by þat þay shal fully prayse
þy myghtes and pytee, and doon to write þy heigh Magestee.

Cap. 25. [Of þe mercy of a kynge.]
16   To eschewe Manslaghter.

Alexander, ofte y haue warnyd] þe, and ȝit y warne þe, þat *Kings should not shed blood.*
þow kepe my techinge; for if þow kepe hit, þy purpos shal wel
chefe, and þy kyngdome be lastand, þat ys to wete þat þou eschewe
20 to sheede mannys blood, ffor þat fallys al oonly to god þat vndir- *God alone should slay.*
stondys þe priuyteeȝ of hertes and secretȝ of ffolk. Tak nought
on þe godys offyce, ffor it ys noght gyuen to þe to knowe his
secrete; þarfore eschewe þou yn so mekyl as þou may to sheede
24 mannys blood. ffor as þe noble doctour hermogenes wrytes,
whanne þat a creature slees a creature lyk to hym, þe heigh *The Virtues of Heauen cry for vengeance on the manslayer,*
vertueȝ of heuene cryen to goddys mageste and sayen, "lord,
lord, þy seruantȝ wille be lyk to þe;" And if he wyth wronge
28 haue slayn hym, þe he makere shall answere, "suffre þat he sla,
ffor he shall be slayn. ¹To me ys þe vengaunce, and y shal ȝelde ¹ Fol. 11 a.
hit;" and as ofte sithes þe vertuȝ of heuene shal represent þe þe
deth of hym þat ys slayn, to vengance be takyn of hym þat slow *till vengeance is done.*
32 hym, þat shal be oon of hem þat shal dwelle yn euer-lastand
payne.

To haue ensample of antecessours.

Alexander, yn alle peynes haue knowyng; many maners of *Call to your mind the deeds of your ancestors.*
36 euelys þou hauys lered in assay, draw to þy mynde þe dedys of
þyn ancestres; þou may þer-out drawe goode ensamples, And
alle þynges passyd sal gyue þe certeyn techynge of swylk þynges
command; dyspyse noght a lesse man þan þi seluyn, þat a man

Despise not little men. þat now ys of litel value and poure, to richesse and worschipe amountys, And þanne ys of mor stryngh and power to doo euyll.

Cap. 26. To kepe ffayth and othes sworne.

Keep faith with all men, Kepe þe þat þow broke noght þy fayth gyuyn no Alliance 4 confermed, ffor it ffallis noght but for vntrewe men and light women of body. Hold trewly þy fayth hyght, ffor euer moor to *whatever gain may come by faith-breaking.* all vntreuthe folwys euyl ende, And if al falle som tyme any good in alliance brokyn, Noþeles þe kynde þerof ys wyckyd in it 8 seluyn and þe maner of wykkyd men, And wete þow wel þurgh trew alliance dwellys folk togedre, and þerby ys inhabitacioun *Society exists by faith-keeping.* in citeeȝ, comunynge to-gedre of ffolke. Þe lordschype of a kynge ys worschippyd þerby, þurgh þat er Castels holdyn, citeeȝ 12 kepyd and kynges lordes. If þou take away fayth, þe folke tornys aȝeyn to hir olde staat, þat ys to say to þe lyknes of Bestys with-outen resoun. O kynge, kepe þe so trewly þat þou broke noght þy fayth gyuen ne oth ne oþer alliance, if al it greue 16 *Two spirits tell of each man's deeds.* þe; wost þou noght what Heremogenes wytnessyth—"Two espirytes er þat kepys þe, oon on þe right syde, anoþer on þe left syde, þat knowyn & representyn to þy makere trewly euerylke þinge þat þou doos." Þys sholde with drawe þe & eueriche man 20 fro alle vnhonest wirkynges. Who destreyns þe to swere ofte? *Swear not but for great need.* Þou shold noght swere but for greet mester; A kynge, but he were mekyl and ofte requeryd, he ne sholde noght swere. Ne [1] *Fol. 11 b.* wost þou noght þat yt mysseinys þi dignite [1] and þat þou trespasys 24 to þy worschipe whanne þou swerys; it ys to subgitȝ and seruantȝ *vide vindicta iuramentis* to swere, but noght to a kynge. If þou aske me of þe distruccioun of þe kyngdomes of Ambayens & citeeȝ, I answere þe for othys þat hir kynges vsyd yn fraude and desceyt of þe folk, and 28 *The ruined kingdoms often broke faith.* of negh Citeeȝ, brekand allyance stabyl ffor welfare and profyt of men, ffor wyckedly and vntrewly þay brake here othes in disceyt of hir neghburs, þe ryghwys euenhede of god almyghty of godys Iustyse wolde suffre no lenger. 32

Cap. 27. [Of the kepynge of a kynge.]

There are special teachings to govern a king's private following. Alexander, y wille þat þow wete yat yn þe ordinance of a kyngdom & of a empire þer ben techinges ful specyals and manerlys þat falles to þe to þe gouernance of þyn owyn meynee 36 and of þe commyn poeple, but þay haue noght hir stede here. Noþeles y shal deliuere hem to þe yn a certeyn stede of þis book,

How a King should help Students.

And þay shal be helful techinges abbreggyd and gretly profyt- *Keep my counsels,*
ables, And yn her kepynge þou shalt ressayue greet welfare *and don't*
þurgh þe helpe of god. Repent þe noght of þinges passyd, for *worry over*
4 þat ys a propirte to feble women). Kepe apert manhode, mayn- *things past.*
tene curtasy, and vse goodnesse, ffor yn þes þinges a kyngdome
ys defendyd and enemys destruyd.

Cap. 28. [Of auancement of study yn his londe.]
8   To fforþer studiantʒ.

Ordeyne to þe wel lettryd men, and stable studyes yn Citeeʒ *Make your subjects send*
of þy kyngdome. Byhote and comaunde þy liege men þat þay *their children to school.*
make her sones lere sciences and letterure, and make hem to
12 study in fre & nobles sciences, and þy purueyance awe helpe
hem in sustynaunce. Do some auantage of good to hem þat pro-
fytabely studys, þat þou gyf þerby ensample and manere to oþer
scolers to study; here her requestys, ressayue her epistles, And *Encourage students in*
16 take entent to loue hem þat er to be louyd, and to reward hem *every way.*
þat er to be rewardyd; þer-by þou shalt drawe to þe lettryd men)
to enheye þi louynge, and þy dedys to make ay to laste in
scripture. þys manere ys to be praysyd, and þys queyntyse ys
20 to be louyd; yn þis oon empyr shal be honured & a kyngdom
worschippyd; yn þys ¹a court² shal be lightyd, and ʒers and ¹ Fol. 12 a.
reals dedys shal bettir come to a kynges mynde whon enhyed.
þe kyngdom of grece, who maad opyn hir dedes to ouerlaste *What made the kingdom*
24 þurgh alle þe world? wyth-outyn doute þe diligence of studiantʒ *of Greece so great?*
dyd þys, and þe clen wyt of wyse men, þat hooly loued sciences
& folwyd hit, yn so mekyl þat a mayden) yn hir fadir hous *Why, even a girl was*
knewe þurgh her greet study þe cours of þe ʒere and þe monthys, *learned.*
28 and þe cours of þe planetys, and þe cause of þe abregynge of þe
day and þe nyʒt, and þe aʒeynturnynges of · þe planetys, þe
abreggement of þe day serclys, þe tokenyng of sterrys, þe shew-
ynges of þinges þat wer to come, and oþer þynges wyth-outen
32 nombre of tokenynges of þinges to come.

Cap. 29. To tryste noght in women.

Alexander, haue þou neuer trist in wirkynges no in seruice *Never put any confi-*
of women, ne gyf þou no credence to no wymmen), and yf þe *dence in women.*
36 nedys of a woman, drawe to þe to here þat þow trowys trewe,
and þat þou demys good; ffor yf a woman reule þy persone, þou

          ² 'sourt' in MS.

The Tale of the Poison Maiden.

If you do, you will soon regret it.

ert als a þinge þat ys layd yn her bandoun), and þy lyf ys al yn
here hondys[1]; eschewe þe dedly venyms of women þat not[2] of
newe bygynnes to venym; kynde þat ys, þat gret multitude of
kynges and of lordys er perschyd and deed byfore her tyme 4
stablyd, þurgh drynkes of dedly venyms.

Cap. 30. Tryst noght only yn oon leche.

Never put your confidence in one physician.

Alexander, yn a oonly leche trist þou noght, for he may
harme, and lightly he may order vndirtake to brynge manys 8
deth to effect. If it may be, be þay ten[3] at þe leste, & make
hem alle to accorde too oon purpos. And yf þow take a

Have a lot.

medecyne do it by þe conseil of many; And haue a trew man
þat konnys þe maners of spyces and þaire qualiteeȝ. and whenne 12

[4] Fol. 12 b.

þou hauys mester, gedir þe by þe consaill of [4]þy leches yn certeyn
weght and mesure alle þat nedys to þe composicioun, and þat he
knowe to make it als it awe to be. Alexander, þynk of þe

Remember the Queen of India's daughter.

doynge of þe Queue of Inde whenne she sente to þe, by cause to 16
haue þy frendschipe, many presentes and noble gyftes, amonge þe
whilke a ful fair mayden) was sent to þe, þat of her childhood
drank and was norschyd with venyms, yn-so-mekyl þat her
kynde was turned to þe kynde of serpentys; And but yf y moor 20
besely by þe craft magyk hadde persayued here, she by here
assiduell and hoge lokynge yn þe faces of men, hadde slayn

If it hadn't been for me, you would have died.

hem: þat þy seluyn by assay preued. And certanly, but þou
hadde ben warnyd by me þare-of, þy seluyn hadde takyn deed, 24
þurgh þe hete of fleschly kennynge with here.

Cap. 31. Of þe conseyl of Astronomye.

Watch yourself, and do nothing but by counsel of Astronomy.

Alexander, kepe þy most noble saule hegh, and to angeles
pereugale, þat ys geuyn to þe, noght to be maad vnhonest by þe, 28
but to be enhyed and glorifyed, so þat it be noght of condicions
and maners of foles, but of þe wyse. O kynge debonure, if it
mowe be, noþer ryse no syt, ete no drynk, no no-þyng doo with-
outen þe conseyl of a wys man in þe craft of Astronomy. ffor 32
wete certaynly þat glorious god hauys maad no þynge yn vayn,
no ydell yn kyndes. But alle þynges er maad yn certayn
enchesoun and resoun, And by þys way vnderstood oure wys

Plato.

doctour Plato þe kyndes of partyes maad to-gedir of dyuers 36
qualytes and colours and complexiouns in engendrure, by þe

---

[1] 'bondys' in MS.   [2] 'now' in MS.   [3] MS. x.

lyknes of þynges maad to-gedyr, and herby hadde he knowynge
of sterrys and þynges formed; and I pray þe gyf no faytħ to þe *Do not believe those who scorn Astrology.*
sawys of vnwysmen þat sayen þat men mowe noght come to
4 science of þe Planetys, ffor þay wat noght what þay say; ffor no-
þyng ys hard to þe power of vndirstondyng, ffor aH þynges mowe
be knowe by þe way of resoun. Þere ben oþer, no lesse þan fols,
sayn þat god haues purueyd and ordeyned alle þynges at þe *Some say it is useless to know the future: we cannot alter it.*
8 ferste bygynynge, wherfore þay say it profites noght to knowe
þynges to come, sithen þay nedys moste come. And þerfore þay
say, what ys þe science of þe sterres worth? Þese er, as þe firste
er, in gret errour, wharfore y say if aH some þinges of force er to
12 come, Noþeles if þay be wyten byfore þay [1] er moor lightly suffred, [1] Fol. 13 a.
moor wysly passand, and so in manere eschewed; ffor yn als
mekyl als þey ar forsey yn oure knowynge, we take hem mor
discretly to passe withoutyn heuynesse and most harme. Als by
16 ensample, whanne men trowyn wynter þat it is cold, men ordeyns *When we know winter is coming, we prepare for it.*
herbergage and cloþing, and warmstores of cole and woode, and
of many oþer þynges; And þerfore whanne þe wynter comes, þay
er noght harmyd of þe cold. And yn somer of þe same maner
20 þurgh cold metys and dyuers spyses þay kepe hem fro þe hete of
somer; and yn þe same maner, when men knowyn byfore ȝeres *If we know of famine, we lay up wheat.*
of nede and hunger, þurgh kepynge and holdynge of whete and
of oþer þynges, men suffren þe tyme mor lightly. Wherfore yt
24 ys mekyl worth to knowe þingys before, ffor men mowe bettyr
thole hem, and eschewe hem whenne þey knowe hem to come.
Wherfore men oghte wyth byse prayers bysek þe heghe desty- *So if the stars tell of evil, we may pray for God's pity.*
nour, þat he by his mercy torne þe euyls þat er to come, and
28 þat he wille oþerwyse ordeyne, and for þat men awe to praye to
goddys pitee in orysouns, deuociouns, prayers, fastynge, seruices,
and almesse, and oþer goode dedys, bysekand forgyfnesse of hir
trespas, and be repandant of hir synnes, And so þay shal mowe
32 sothly trowe, þat god almyghty shal turne fro hem þat þat
þey drede.

Of þe partyes of Astronomye departyd in two[2] partyes.

Torne we to þe word bygoon; It ys to wete þat Astoronomye *The parts of Astronomy: (1) The ordinance of the heavens and stars.*
36 ys departyd yn þre partys, þat ys to wete yn ordynance of þe
heuens and of þe speres, and þe disposicioun of þe planetes and
departynge of signes, and of þair aloigenementȝ and of þair

[2] 'þre' in MS.

SECRETE. F

sterynges. And of þys party of Astronomye ys clepyd science.

(2) The knowledge of the rising and setting of signs:

þe seconde partye ys of þe qualyte & of þe manere to knowe þe sterynge of þe firmament and þe firste risynge or spryngynge of þe signes opon þinges able to falle byfore þay abouyn þe firma- 4 ment of þe moone. And þis seconde partye ys clepyd Astrologie or science of Iugementʒ. And þe worthyeste partye of Astronomye ys þe science of þre þinges, þat ys to wete of speres,

Astrology.

There are 1029 fixed stars.

planetys, & signes. Wete also þat stablyd planetys vnmooable 8 ar a þousand twenty and nyne, or thus M¹xxix, of whom in a party of þys book I shall delyure to þe þe full mery teching.

Cap. 32. [Of þe profyt to kepe hele.] Of Medicynes. 12

¹ Fol. 13 b.

¹Now first y wyl delyure to þe techinge Medicynal, and conseilys þat shal suffyce þe in kepyng of hele, þat þow shalt noght nede oþer leche, ffor kepyng of hele ys mor bettir and mor precious þan any medicyne; and wete wel þay er right 16 needful to þe gouernance of þys werld. It ys to wete þat no way ys to do by any þynge, or any cause to be had, but by myth, And myght ys noght but by hele, and no hele ys but by equalyte of complexiouns, and non equalyte of complexiouns ys but by 20 temperance of þe humours; And glorious god has ordeyned maner and remedye for attemperance of þe humours and kepyng of hele, and no oþer þynges to be getyn, and þaym has opynly shewyd to haly profetys and seruantʒ & rightwys philosophers 24 & oþer rightwys his chosen, lightend with godys spryt of wyt. Of whom of philosophers þe bigynynge of Philosophye hadden Indes, Grecys, Percys and Latyns, And in þayre secretʒ and writynges no fals þynge ne repreuable ys founden, but of wys 28 men apperoued and loued. But he þat ys to hymself a cause of losse and perdicioun, mor lightly he shal geue to oþer cause of perdicioun, ffor þat we chese þat we loue, and þat we vndirstonde trewe. Noþeles with þat, heigh god hath most enlightend 32 Gregeys amonge alle oþer philosophers to enserche sciences, and to perfitly knowe alle manere of Naturels þinges; And þarefore aftir hem we purpos to procede, god grantand.

Keeping of health is more precious than medicine.

Health comes from equality of complexions or temperance of humours.

The ancient philosophers found out remedies to keep health:

and especially the Greek philosophers.

Cap. 33. Of þe [composition of man of] ffoure humours. 36

Man is made of four humours.

Þe wyse philosophers accorden yn oon þat man ys mad of dyuers elymentʒ and of ffoure contrarious humours þat euer

hauyn myster to fode and drynke to be sustenyd by: and if a *His food nourishes these humours.* man want hem his substance fayles, And if he out*ra*gously vse hem or ouer scarsly, he may falle yn-to syknes, ffebylnes, and
4 ynto oþer vnabiltes. And if he vse hem attemperally and mesurly he shal fynde helpe of lyf, stryngh of body, and hele of al his substance. Also þay accorden) þat who so ouerpassys yn ful or voyd, yn slepynge or wakynge, [1]in rist or sterynge, in out- [1] Fol. 14 a.
8 passynge or wythholdynge of þe wombe, yn witholdynge of *If he overpasses the mean, he shall fall into sickness.* blood, or latynge ouer mekyl blood, he mowe noght eschewe maladyes and heuynesse of siknesse; of alle swilke maters y shal determyn a couenable abregement, shewynge a certayn
12 techynge of alle mauere of syknes and þe remedyes. Also þay accordyn, þat who so kepys hym fro superfluyte and also fro *If he keeps the mean, he shall have good health and long life.* defaute, and holdes him yn euenhed and attemperance, þat he shal haue good hele and longe lyfe. I haue founden) no philo- sopher þat disacordys to þis sentence, þat all delitable þinges of
16 þys world, Ryches, delyces, or worschippes, þat þay ben alle for longlastynge of durabilyte: And þarfore he þat coueytes to leue and endure, putte his force to purchace þe þynges þat accorden)
20 to durabilte and kepys þe lyfe, And lette his owene wyl, þat he putte noght etynge abouyn etynge. I haue herd of ypocraas, þat *Hippocrates told his disciples,* he kepyd him so mekyll yn abstynence, þat he hadde gret febyl- nesse of body; wharfore oon of his discyples sayde to hym,
24 "ffair Mayster, yf þow wolde wel ete, þow shold noght haue so mekyl febylnesse of body." And ypocraas answerde, "ffair sone, I will ete so þat y leue, and noght lyf þat y ete; lyflode for *"I eat to live, not live to eat."* lastynge ys to be had, and noght durabilite for liflode." I haue
28 knowyn many þat withdrew hem froo etynges of surfaytȝ, and her appetitȝ with-drawand froo glotonye, lyuand mesurably by *Men who give up gluttony, and live temperately, are better in health.* dyetes, And þerfore hauyn ben elder of body, of bettir trauail- lynge, of lenger lyf, of good appetyt, and of mor light sterynge;
32 and þat shewys wel yn lanternys, and yn men) þat trauaillen by desertys and longe wayes. And þerfore yt ys oon opyn preue þat abstynence fro mekyl etynge, and to clense a man of super- fluytes, ys A souerayn medycyne.

Cap. 34. Off kepynge of hele.

36 [2]Alexander, a certayn and trew techynge ys content yn *Two things preserue* medicyn þat kepys hele, and þat ys princypaly yn two þinges; þe firste ys þat a man ete metes couenable to his elde, and yn þe helthe. [2] Fol. 14 b.

What Things preserve Health.

(1) A man should eat food suitable to his age and custom.
tyme acostomyd to his kynde; þat ys to wete þat he vse mete and drynke þat he was costomed to [be] byfore norisshed by, & þat has festnyd his substance. þe secunde ys þat he clense hym of

(2) He should cleanse his body of corrupt humours.
þat þat ys engendryd yn his body of surfaytes and of corumpyd 4 humours. It ys to wete þat mannys body, þat ys takynge mete and drynke, continuely er dimunisshed and resoluyn aȝeyn, als wel þe bodyes þat ressayuen als þe mete and þe drynke ressayued; ffirst þay ar resoluyd by kyndly hete, þat makes drye þe moystnes 8 of þe body, and is norisshed and fedde with þe same moystnesse.

Natural heat dries up and resolves the food.
Also by þe hete of þe sonne and dryenesse of þe wynd, þat makys drye þe moystnesse of alle bodyly þinges, & þay er fed with moystnesse of bodely þinges & of fflodes. Whenne a body 12

Hot and moist bodies require gross meats.
is hoot & moyst, þanne gret metys er good þerto; ffor þat þat ys defyed & passys fro swylk a body ys of greet quantite and of greet substance for þe grete hete of þe body. And whenne a

Thick and dry bodies require soft and moist foods.
body ys þicke and drye, softe metys and moyste er goode þerto, 16 ffor þat þat passys fro þat body ys of lytel quantyte for his streyt issuys. Also it ys a certayn techinge for hele to be keped, þat a

A man must use food of his own complexion.
man vse metys þat accordyn to his complexioun and nature yn his hele, Als yf a man be of hote nature, þanne hote metys 20 atempred accorden to hym; And if he be of cold nature, þanne colde attempred metys accordyn to hym; And oþer-wyse y say outerly of a moyst body and drye. þarfore yf hete be mad more wyth ouer mekyl hete, or by hote metys and stalworthe, or for 24 oon oute hete þat maystres and ouercomes, þanne contrarious

To a strong stomach, strong meats.
metys helpyn, þat ys to say, colde metys. And whanne a stomake ys hoot, stalworthe, and good, þanne profitys most grete metys and stalworthe, ffor swylke a stomake ys a gret ffyr, myghty to 28 brenne grete trees; And whenne a stomake ys cold and feble,

To a weak stomach, delicate meats.
þerto er best sotel metys and light, ffor þat stomake ys lykned to a wayk & feble feer, þat vnnethes may to-brenne rosels and smal chippys. 32

Cap. 35. [Of þe tokenys of þe stomak.]

The tokens of a good and of an evil stomach.
þes er þe tokenys of a good stomak—lightnes of body, clernes of vnderstondynge, styrynge appetyt. Of oon euyl stomak and wayk, þes er þe tokenys ỵ heuynesse of body, sleuthe, bolnynge 36 of þe vesage, ofte openynge of þe mouth, heuynesse of þe eighen,

[1] Fol. 15 a.
[1] a foul and euyl belkynge, þat ys to wete whenne it ys vnsauery, bitter, or watery, or stynkand; and þerby er engendryd wyndes

Rules of Diet to keep good Health.

and bolnyng of wombys, and appetyt ys lessys; And if þes þynges be in greet quantite, þarof comes excercitaciouns, and þat lettys þe strechynge and ageynbowynge of þe membres, ffilth of body, openynge of mouth, and oþer euyles þat er contrarye to hele of man & destrues nature. And þerfore þe awe kepe þy seluyn fro alle swylk euelys, and fro þe vncouenable þinge afore sayd. *[margin: The ills that come from an evil stomach.]*

Cap. 36. [Of maners to kepe helthe.]
A lernyng to kepe hele.

For þe body of man coruptible ressayues his corupcioun of contrariouste of complexiouns & humours þat er yn him, I am auysed to wryte to þe in þis werk profitable þinges and necessarye, of þe conseils of þe craft of medicyns þat shal suffys to þe, ffor It ys vnhonest þat all maladyes of a kynge be shewyd to a leche; wharfore yf þow wele byhold þys techinge, and after þis precious ordre lyue, þou shalt haue no myster of leche, But it falle yn auentures of batailles, or oþer þynges þat a man mowe noght eschewe. *[margin: Since no leech should know all the secrets of a king, he must be able to cure himself.]*

Cap. 37. [Of kepynge of helth and maner of lyunge.]
Of contynance after slepe.

Alexander, whenne þou risys fro slepe þou salt goo a lytyl, & euenly streight out þy membres, and kembe þy heued, ffor forth-strechynge of þe membres makys stalworth þe body, & kembyng of þe heued latys out þe smoke of þe stomake þat comes vp to hit yn tyme of slepyng. In somer, wassh þy feet with cold water, ffor hit restrenys and holdys þe hete yn þe body, and it shal make desire to etynge. After, cleth þe yn good clepynge and ordeyn þe yn good aparayll, ffor þy wyl kyndely shal delyt yn þe byholdynge and ffayrhed þerof, And þe vertu of þy shynynge lyf shal be comfortyd and gladyd þerby. After þou shalt frote þi teth and þy gomes with þe barke of oon hoote tree, and of drye kynde and of bitter sauour, for þat helpys mekyl to clense þe teth, & makys þe mouth moyst, and clensys þe tonge, and claryfys þe speche, and sterys desir of etynge. Aftir þat stewe þe with stewynge couenable to þe tyme, for þat mekyl profytes. It opyns þe closynges of þe brayn, it makys þe necke gretterre & þe armes fattere, þe face and þe sight clerer, shaarpys þe wittes, and kepys a man þat he hore noght sone. After *[margin: To kembe thi hew. to wasshe thi legges in colde water in somer. goodd to chafe thi gomes with the bytter barke of a tre. stewe in stewis holsome.]*

enoynt þe wíth precious oynementȝ wel sauorand, couenable to
þe tyme þat þou ert ynne, [1] ffor þe sawle ys noght with-outen⁾
good sauour, and ilk-a swet sauour ys a fulfillynge to þe sawle;
And whenne þe saule ys filled safe and delytable, þanne þe herte 4
enioyes, and þe blood for gladnesse rynnys yn þe veynys. After
þou shalt take a-latred, þat ys to say of þe electuary of the tree
of Aloes þat ys foundyn yn bokes of medicynes, and after of
exrohand, þat ys reubard, foure peny weght, ffor þat ys mekyl 8
worth, and withdrawys þe fleume fro þe mouth of þe stomake, it
sterys hete to þe body, and destroyes wyndes, and geuys good
sauour. After with þy worthy and wyse men sytte and spek
after þe custome of kynges and worthymen⁾ þat þat þe fallys and 12
semys to speke.

^{margin:} [1] Fol. 15 b. Anoint thyself after bathing.

^{margin:} Take some aloes and rhubarb. It is good for you.

^{margin:} Then have some pleasant chat.

Cap. 38. Of contynance afore mete.

Whenne þou hauys wyl to ete, aftir þe oure of þy costome, vse
a lytel trauaiħ yn ridynge, yn goynge, or som-þinge doynge, ffor 16
þat helpys þe body, it dryues out wyndys, comfortys þe body and
makys hit souple; yt kyndels hete of þe stomake, hit constreyns
þe ioyntures, and makes þe superfluous humours to melte, and it
makys þe fleume to falle yn-to þe stomake, hoote and drye. 20
Many metys be sette afore þe, and after þy desyr ete whilke þe
lykes wíth breed euenly raysed and perfitly thersyd. And take
first þo þat þe awe first to take, As if a man ressayue yn oon mete a
potage nesshe and laxatyue to þe wombe and anoþer holdand, If 24
þe nesshe be first take, hit shal make more light digestioun,
And ȝyf þe holdynge be first etyn, and after þe nesshe, bothe
shal be wastyd. Also ȝyf a man take many potages nesshe and
laxatyfe, yt nedys þat he take first a holdynge mete yn þe ground 28
of þe stomake, þat ys mor stalworthe and more hoot to defye,
ffor þat party ys moor fleshly and next to þe lyure, þurgh whilk
hete þe metys sethyn. And in þy etynge þow shalt reule þy
hond, þat ys to say, to leue etynge whenne þy wyl and desir 32
lastys ȝyt to etynge; ffor of superfluyte of mete þe stomak ys
maad strayt, þe body ys greued, and þe wyl ys hurt, and þe mete
þat dwellys yn þe ground of þe stomak ys heuy & noyous. Also
withdrawe þy wyl to drynke watir vpon þy mete, [2] but þou haue 36
it of custome, ffor þe drynke of cold water vpon mete makys
cold þe stomak, it slekyns defying, and shendys þe mete, and yt
engendrys greet impedymentȝ yf mekyl be drunkyn, ffor þer ys

^{margin:} Take a little exercise before your meals.

^{margin:} Take some bread with your meat.

^{margin:} Think about the order of your meals.

^{margin:} Leave off while you have an appetite left.

^{margin:} [2] Fol. 16 a. Don't drink much cold water at meals.

no þing mor noynge to þe body; but yf þou haue nede, for hete of þe tyme or of þe stomak, or of metys, to drynke water, tak but lytel, and leet it be wel cold. *unless you are used to it, and want it.*

Cap. 39. [Of manere of slepynge.]

Whanne þou hast wel etyn, goo lye vpon a nesshe bed, and slepe atemprely, and reste an hour vpon þy right syde, & after turne þe vpon þy left syde, and fulfylle þy sleepe vpon þat syde; ffor hit ys cold and nedith to be het. And yf þou fele þanne greuance yn þy stomake or in þy wombe, or any heuynesse, þis ys þanne þe medicyne; ley vpon þy wombe an hoot sherte and weyand, or ellys halfe to þe a hoot mayden; if þou fele a bitter balchinge yt is tokenyng of coldnesse of stomak, and þe medicyn ys þys, to drynke cler watir with a sope of vynegre, and spewe, ffor in-prisonynge of corupt mete yn þe wombe ys a greet distruccioun of þe body. And stirynge before þe mete sterith þe hete of þe stomak, but after þe mete þat ys noyous, ffor þe mete falleth doun er it be defyed in-to þe ynnere partyes of þe stomak, And þeroffe growyn wyndes withinne lokyn, costyfnesses and oþer euelys. *After meals, take a nap, one hour on the right, and the rest on the left side. If you feel ill, apply heat to your womb. a bitter belching is a token of cold etc Don't move much after meat.*

Cap. 40. Of slepynge aftyr mete.

And wetith þat slepyng byfore mete makyth a mannys body lene and dryes his moystures, but after mete it filleth him, stryngthes hym, and norscheth hym. ffor whanne a man sleepeth þe herte restyth, and þanne þe kendly hete ys y-drawe þerto and spredforth by al þe body to þe stomak & to þe Innere partyes of þe stomak; þanne ys þe stomak mad stalworthy to defye mete, And þanne kendly vertu & resonable askyth his reste, And þerfore some philosophers seyen þat mete at euen more profyteth þan of þe mydday; ffor þe mete ¹of þe mydday resceyueth þe hete of þe day, whanne þe wyt werketh and þe wyl ys trauaylled, ffor þo þinges þat hit hereth and spekyth, and for þoughtes and many oþer vnprofitable þynges þat assayleth þe hetes and sterynges; And þerfore yn þe hour of þe mydday þe kendely hete spredeth him out to þe vttere partyes of þe body, wherfore þe stomak comeþ feble and losyth his strengthe to fully sethe þe mete. But þe soper at euyn ys al contrarye, ffor þanne fallyth to þe body reste of trauaille, and restynge to þe wyttes, and þanne comeþ þe cold of þe nyght, and ʒeuyth hete to þe Inward of þe stomak. *sleping afore meate etc In sleep the natural heat is withdrawn from the extremities. Food at even better than at noon. ¹ Fol. 16 b. Why the stomach is too feeble at noon to digest food.*

Cap. 41. [Of kepynge of costome.]
Off þe costome of etynge.

naughte to breake dyete

Wete þou wel, þat he þat vsys him to ete twyes þe day, and he holde him to oon meel, yn certeyn yt shal harme hym. And 4 also yn þe selue manere to hym þat hauys vsyd to ete but oon meel, and he begynne to ete twyes; ffor he shal wante defyinge of stomak, and so his mete dwellys nought defyed. And he þat has vsyd to ete at oon certayn hour, and tarys his etynge to oon 8 oþer hour, he shal take þat profytes noght to his kynde, and mekyll greuys his kynde, ffor costome ys þe oþer kynde. And

howe to vse custome

þerfore 3if any nede make þe chaunge þy costom, do hit discretly and wisly, þat it be lityl and litil, oon tyme chaungyd after 12 anoþer, And so it shal be wel þourgh þe helpe of god.

Cap. 42. To eschewe Engrutynge.

Naught to eate till the fyrste etinge be clensed.

Kepe þe wel þat þou ete noght anoþer tyme, vnto þou vnderstonde certanly þy stomak voyde, þat ys to wete, þat it be 16 clensyd of þe ferste etynge, and þat shalt þow knowe by appetyt of etynge and by þy spatill remnand to þy mouth; ffor he þat takys mete wyth oute myster, he shal fynde hys kyndly hete right cold and engelyd, And whenne he takys his mete yn þe 20 tyme of aptyd, he shal fynde his kyndly hete hoot as fyr. And

goode to eate as sone as thie appetyte covetith

whenne þou hauys apetyd of etynge, ete þou sone; ffor but þou þanne ete soone, þy stomak shal fille hym with euyl humours þat he drawys to hym of superfluytes of þy body, and þat shall 24 trobbyl þy brayn with euyll fumosyte, so þat after whanne þou shalt ete, þy stomak ys but leukwarme, and þy mete shal be lytel of profyt.

Cap. 43. [Of Veir.] 28
¹Off þe ffoure seysouns of þe 3ere.

¹ Fol. 17 a.

Purpos ys in þis stede shortly determyn þe ffoure seysouns of þe 3eer, and of þe qualyte & quantyte, and of þe properte of ilk oon seysoun, and of þaire variance. ffour tymes er of þe 3eer, 32

Spring begins when the sun enters Aries: it lasts 89 d. 23 h. 15 m., from March 10th to June 24th.

þat þus er departyd. Veir bigynnes whenne þe sonne entres yn to þe toknynge of þe sheepe, and it lastys iiij & ix dayes, xxiij houres & þe ferthe part of oon hour, þat ys fro þe xᵉ day of March out passand to þe xxiiijᵉ day of Iuyn. In þis tyme þe 36 day and þe nyght ys of oon length, the body of man waxis hard, þe eyr waxys feyr, þe wyndes blowyn, þe snow resoluys, waters

rynneƿ among hilles, wellys ouerflueƿ, moistures styen vp to þe *The effects of Spring on all things.*
croppys of trees and to þe heuedys of braunches, cornys bygynnes
to grewe, Medwes waxen grene, ffloures waxen fayre and beres
4 flourys: Trees er cled with newe leuys, þe erthe ys fair wyth
spirynges: Bestes engendres, Pastours waxen, alle þynges takeƿ
strynghe, Bryddes syngeƿ, þe nyghtyngale souƿ, and þe erthe
holy takys his worschippe and fairhede, and bycomes as a fair
8 damoysele, a spouse semly dighte of ryche ornements and dyuers
colours, to be shewyd to men yn þe feste of weddynge. Veyr *Its qualities.*
ys hoot and moyst, and atempre, and ys lyke to þe eyr, And
þerynne newys þe blood, and spredys alle þe membrys to profyt
12 of him, þat ys of euene complexiouƿ, and þerynne sholde men
vsyn, þat ys to say, henchekyns, surlens, eyren, but noght ouer vj, *Suitable food.*
nesshe to be suppyd, wylde letus þat feldmen clepyn skarioles,
and gotys mylk þann drynke. No tyme ys bettir to latyng of *springe tyme*
16 blood, and vse stirynge of þy body, lousynge of wombe, vse of
bathynge and swetynge, drynkes of spices for digestiouƿ, & to
ressayue purgaciouƿ þanne er profitable, ffor þat þat wanys by *Suitable medicine.*
dygestiouƿ or bloodlate, þat tyme by his moysture he restorys.

20   Cap. 44. Off Somer.

[1]Somer begynnes þanne whenne þe sonne entrys yn to þe [1] Fol. 17 b.
firste tokenynge of þe crabbe, and it lastys lxxij dayes, and xxiij *Summer begins when the sun enters Cancer, and lasts 72 d. 23 h. 20 m., from June 23rd to Sept. 24th.*
houres and þe þrydde party of oon hour, þat ys to wete fro þe
24 xxiij^e day of Iuyn to þe xxiiij^te day of Septembre; þat tyme
haueth longe dayes and shorte ny3tes; hete sprynges þanne yn
alle kyngdomes, þe wyndes litel blowyn, þe see ys paisyble, yn *Its effects.*
þe heyr ys cleernesse, cornys waxen drye, Neddrys er born and
28 etyn venym, þe vertu3 of bodys er stalworthe, And so þe world
ys as a spouse of perfyt elde, with hete wel colourd. Somer
tyme ys hoot and drye, and þanne þe rede colere ys steryd. *Its qualities.*
Wherfore it nedys þanne to absteue fro what þing ys of hoot
32 and drye complexiouƿ, and to abstene to mekyll ete and drynke,
and fro greet saule, þat kendly hete failleth noght. Ete in þat
tyme þat ys cold and moyst complexiouƿ, As veel with venegre, *Suitable food.*
and briddys þat er clepyd Cucurbit3, and ffatte chekyns, and
36 potages of barly mele, and frutys of egre sauouryng, and egre
appelys; vse lytel flesshly likyng, and with-holde þe from
latynge of blood, But yf gret myster aske it; sterynge of body,
ne bathes vse but latly.

Cap. 45. Off Heruest.

Autumn begins when the sun enters Libra, and lasts 88 d. 22 h. 12 m., from Sept. 24th to Nov. 23rd.

Heruest bygynnes whenne þe sonne entrys þe firste degree of þe tokenynge of weighes, and it lastys lxxxviij dayes and houres xxij^ty, & thre xv of oon hour, þat ys fro þe xxiiij^ty day of septembre to þe xxiij day of Nouembre. In þis tyme ys also þe day and þe nyght euyne, and yn þis tyme þe nyght bygynnes to

Its effects.

grewe and waxe lenger, and takys of þe day; þe heyr coldeth, þe wyndes blawen out of þe north, þe tymes er chaunged; 8 ffodes decresys, fflodys waxen lytel, alle gren thynges faillen, ffrutys sesyn, and þe erthe losys his beaute; Bryddes drawan toward hote kyngdomes, and alle Bestes drawyn to her resset, and neddrys to her holys; þe Ampte getys litlode for wynter; 12

Its qualities.

þanne þe world ys lyk to a woman of full elde, nedand cloping. Heruest ys cold and drye, yn whilk rysys þe blak colere; and it

¹ Fol. 18 a.

nedys þat ¹a man vse yn þat seysoun hote þinges a[nd moist as

Suitable food.

chekyns] lambren old wyn and swete raysyns; [And þat a man 16 kepe hym] fro alle þynges þat norsshe Mala[ncoly / Steryng of body & flessh-]lykyng more vse þan yn so[mer. Bathes & purgacions, if nede] be, þat tyme be doon, A[nd if a man nede to cast, be it in þe] mydouernone, or yn þe [last houre of þe day: 20 ffor in þo houres] superfluytes er ged[eryd to-gedre in a man.

Suitable medicine.

Purgacion of þe] wombe awe to [be mad þat tyme, by a symoun & aggrauacion,] and by alle þi[nges þat in-drawes malancoly & aȝeynletys] humours.   24

Cap. 46. Of Wynter.

Winter begins when the sun enters Sagittarius, and lasts 79 d. 23 h., from Nov. 23rd to March 21st.

W[ynter bygynnes when þe sonne entres þe first de-gree of Archer, & it lastes lxxix days & xxiij^te houres.] þat [is, fro þe xxiij^te day of Nouembre, to þe xxj^te day of Marcȝ.] In [þat tyme 28 þe nyght lenghthys, þe days shorten, Coldenes waxes] g[ret, þe wyndes waxen scharp, þe leues of þe trees dryen & dyen: And for þe more party all þat was gren dyen & hardene as ston. þe gretter party of Bestes for mykyl cold & moistnes [flee] to þe 32

Its effects.

wombe of þe erth / and to holes of hylles; & [for] coldnes & water þe heyr waxes dyrke, & þe tymes blake. Bestes trembles, þe vertuȝ of þe bodys waxis feble, and þe world is as oon olde wyfe, a-cremet for eld, nakyd of cloþinge, neghand to þe deth. 36

Its qualities.

Wyntyr is cold & moist, in þe whylk¹ it nedes man lyuyng to be bowit, þat is to wyt, to torne aȝeyn to hote meites, & to hote maters, as puletys, & motoun, & fruturs, & rostyd mallerdes, &

aH maner hote pyment3 & hote potages, figes, & nottys, & good <small>Suitable food.</small>
red wyn, & to vse good hote electuary3, & to with-drawe hym
fro solucion of wombe, & fro latyng of blod, bot if mistir aske
4 it, & chaung þe eir for eschaufynge ; þan shold noght a man eyte
mykyl for febelyng of þe stomak, Onoynt þi body with good & <small>Suitable medicine.</small>
hote onyment3, &. vse Bathes attempre3. A man to styr &
knowe hys wyfe, & to eyte mykyl, it is noght so noyant as in
8 oon oþer tyme. ffor þe gret cold gedrys to-gedre þe kyndely
hct]¹es, and entrys þe Inner partyes of þe [body : and þarefore <small>¹ Fol. 18 b.</small>
bettyr diges]tioun ys yn wynter and yn Veer, & in [Somer is þe <small>The theory as to natural heat and digestion.</small>
wombe cold : ffor] yn þe tymes þe lytel holes of þe [body are
12 opyn, & þe kyndely hete] ys ȝit out of þe stomak, and [so þe
diffying is lettyd, & þe humours] stiryd; þerfore know þes
[þinges, & God by thes shaH susteyn þe.
    Alexander, þis precious diet þat I haue t]aght þe, kepe [it
16 wele vp-on aH þinges, with kyndely hete,] ffor als [long as
atempre hete dweH in a man, hele las]tys, & long [tyme is
kepyd. ffor in two maners a man waxes olde] & faylys : [þe <small>Two causes why men die.</small>
first kyndely, þat oone due maner destrues & ouercomes k]ynde <small>Natural : accidental.</small>
20 [of body with elde, & þe oþer is accident, þat comes of seke-
ne]sse [& oþer euyl enchesouns.

Cap. 47. [Thynges that fattith & moistes the body.] To Preserve Health.

24 THes fattyth & moistes þe body, Rist, sture, ettyng of swete <small>Things that fatten the body.</small>
meites, & dryngkyng of swete mylke, & hote wynes & mad
swete, & slepyng aftyr eityng vpon soft beddes & wele sauorand,
in steydes & tymes couenable, & to entyr in-to Bathes of Swet
28 watyr, & lytiH dwellyng þar-in; ffor long dwellyng in Bathes
makys þe body feble, And in þe Bathes be sothen herbes wele <small>Herbs for use in baths.</small>
sauorand, or oþer þinges of good sauor, after þe tyme : In
wynter, alchitimum, or alloigne, þat is þe spyce of oon manere of
32 floure of hote kynd : In somer, Rosys, violet3, & what so is cold.
kastyng be vsyd in ilke moneth oonys at þe lest, & most in <small>The use of vomits.</small>
somer : ffor out-kastyng wasshis þe body, & clensis þe stomake
of roten & euyl humours, and if few humours ben in þe stomake
36 it shaH be comfortyd & fulfyllid of moisture & grece. And it <small>Pleasure is a good medicine.</small>
is mykyl bettyr if a man haue with disposicion ioy, gladnes,

---

¹ These pages (fol. 18 a & b) are supplied from Laud 685, the whole of the leaf being torn off except a corner.

Those Things that injure the Body.

margin: ¹ Fol. 19 a.
margin: Suitable pleasures for a king.

resoun, louyng, & worshippe, & ouer-comyng of enemyes, hope, & triste in his folke & haue delyt in playnge, & to] ¹byholde fair ffaces, to rede or here delytable bokes, to laugh with ffrendys, softe songes and delytables to here, In goode clopes & riche of dyuers colours lettyd to be cled, and yn couenable tymes wyth goode oynementȝ to be enoynted.

Cap. 48. Thynges þat ffeblys and dryes þe Body.

margin: Things that harm the body.

In þe contrarye manere, þes þynges dryes and feblys þe body; to ete litell and drynke mekyll; To trauaill besily, and stond yn þe sonne; to goo ouer mesure, to slepe byfore mete vpon a hard bed; to þynk mekyl, and to drede, and to entir yn bathis of vnclene water, and to drynke mekyl old wyn, and to ete salt metys; mekyll out-passynge out of þe wombe; to lete blood and passe mesure þerof; to haue euyl and drery þoughtes.

Cap. 49. The Reule off Ypocraas.

margin: Don't bathe on a full stomach: nor swive.
margin: Don't eat flesh and milk together.

Who-so engrutyd of mete, or costyf of body, entrys Bathes, may sone renne yn euyl of fflank, and of his entrailles. Who-so, his wombe full, knowys a woman, lightly he rynnys yn-to perlesy. And also it noyeth mekyl, to renne after mete, or ryde mekyll. Who-so etys mekyl togeder mylk and fflesch, þay rynne yn lepre; Wyn & mylk on þe same manere wirketh.

Cap. 50. [Of þe euyle of þe heued and þe remedy.] Off foure partyes of þe Body.

margin: Tokens of sickness of the head.
margin: Suitable medicines.
margin: What evils are to be feared.
margin: ² Fol. 19 b.

Mannys body ys departyd in ffoure partyes; þe firste partye ys þe heued. And whenne superfluyteȝ ouer mekyll surhabundys to þe heued, þou shalt persayue it by þese tokyns, þat ys to wete, derknesse of þe eyghen, heuynesse of þe browys, greet sterynge of þe temples of þe heued, dynnynge of þe eres, stop- pynge of þe nosestrylles. Whenne any felys yn him þes þinges com, tak effuentim, þat ys Eufrasy, with þe rotys of Pulegye, þat ys pulyol, and sethe hem yn swete wyn, to þe half wastyd, and hold ilke morwe of þis licour yn þy mouth, tyl þou fynde hele; And vse in his metys, mostard seed sothen, þe weight of a peny, with þe poudre dictamm, maad of twelf oynementȝ, & þat at his slepynge. And yf he leue & dispyse þis, he mowe drede perilous sykuesse, þat ²ys to wete corupcioun of sight, werkynge of þe brayn, and oþer many euelys, fro þe whilk god defende þe.

Cap. 51. Off þe Brest.

Brest ys þe secunde partye; if superfluyteȝ be gedryd [1] þere- *Tokens of sickness of the breast.*
yn, þes tokyns folwyn; þe tonge ys maad heuy, þe mouth salt,
and he felys his mete bitter in his brest, and werkyng of þe
koghe; þerfore hym byhoues ete lesse, and vse kastynge, and
after þe kastynge to take ȝugere roset, and chewe of þe tree of *Suitable medicines.*
Aloes, or som oþer perfyt aromatyke, after þe takyng of þe sugre
Roset, with water of rosys, or perfyt wyn, or with a syrupe
confortyf, and after ete with appetit; And after þe etynge take þe
gretnesse of oon .3. of electuarye Anisoun, þat ys maad of þe tree
of Aloes, and Tansey. And he þat doth noght þys, lightly may *What evils may come.*
renne yn Werkynge of his sydes, and Reynes, and many oþer
euelys.

Cap. 52. Off þe Ballokys.

The ballockys er þe fferthe party of a manys body. Whenne *Tokens of trouble in the*
superfluytes waxen in hem, þes tokenynges sewen; þe appetyt *genitals.*
of etynge waxes feble, with oþer eueles; he þat felys þat hauys
mester to take þe herbe þat ys clepyd Ache, and Aueng, þat y *Suitable medicines.*
vnderstonde Auence, and of þaire Rotys, and put þe herbys and
þe Rotys yn whit wyn of good odour, and tak ilke morwe þerof,
so þat yt be tempryd with water and hony, and withdrawe hym
fro mekyll etynge. He þat leuys þys medicyn may drede werk- *What evils are to be*
ynge of his genitalȝ and of þe longys, and of peryl of þe stoon. *feared.*

Cap. 53. Opynyouns of dyuers ffesisyens.

Men redyn yn olde storys þat a kynge [gathered together] *A king once sought for a*
alle þe beste leches of Inde, and of Mede, and of Grece, And he *universal medicine.*
enioyned hem to make a medicyn, þat yf a man vsyd hit, he
sholde fele hit so profitable to nede noon oþer. And oon old
Gregeys of hem shewyd and sayde, þat a mouth-full of hoot *The Greek's advice.*
water, ilk morwe twyes ressayued, sholde make a man so hool
þat he ne sholde haue no mester to non oþer medicyne. On-
oþer of Mede affermyd mekyl profyt to vse greynes melyens *The Mede's advice.*
fastyng, þat er Gromell sedes; And y [2] say, þat he, þat so [2] Fol. 20 a.
mekyl slepys, þat he hauys no heuynesse yn his wombe, he
shall noght drede goutys; And he þat vche day etys seuyn *The best diet.*
dragmes of pressyd rasynges of good swetnes, he shal noght
doute of no manere fleumatyke siknesses; By þe whilk a
Mannys memory ys amendyd, and his vnderstondynge enlight-

[1] 'þore' in MS.

How to avoid poison. end; And he þat yn couenable tyme to his complexioun can purge his wombe, he shall noght doute þe ffeure quarteyn). And he þat etys ffyges, with notes, and a fewe leuys of Rue, þat day venom shall noght dere hym.   4

Cap. 54. [Of þe kepyng of kyndly hete.]

Keep your natural heat. Souerayn kyng, study in alle þe maners to kepe and witholde kyndly hete; ffor whenne hete and moysture ys attempre yn man, kyndly hete ys attempre and maade stalworthe, ffor hele 8 stondys yn þes two þynges. It ys to wete yn þis place, þat corupcioun and distruccioun of body commyth yn two þinges; On ys kyndly, þe oþer ys aȝeyn kynde. þe kyndly comyth of repugnance of contrarious qualyteȝ and contradiccioun, þat ys to 12 *Then you need only fear accidents.* wete, whenne drynesse haues lordschipe of þe body; corupcioun aȝeyn kynde commys of chaunce, as of bataille, or of hurtynge to a stoon), or any oþer auenterous caas, or of seeknesse, or of euyl conseyll.   16

Cap. 55. Off knowynge off Metys.

Kinds of food. Of metys some er sotyl, some greet, and some menee; some sotyl metys engendre sotyl blood cleer and good, as whete, *Gross foods.* chykenes wel fed, and eyren. Greet metys er good to stalworth 20 men and hoote, and trauelynge men in fastynge, and to men þat vse to slepe after mete. Meene metys engendrys noght boln- *Delicate food.* ynges ne superfluytes, as lombe fflessh, motoun and Capouns, and alle ffleschys þat er hote and moyst. But it fayls in þes flesches, 24 whenne þey er rostyd, ffor þerby þay bycomes hard, hoot, and drye; But whenne swylk fleschis ar rostyd, be þay sone etyn *Foods which cause melancholy.* with softe spyces, and þanne er þey profitable. Som flesch engendres malancoly, as boef, kyen, and greet fleschs drye and 28 [1] Fol. 20 b. sharpe; but some of hem hauyn softe fflesch, þat er [1] born and norsshyd yn moyst stedys, and wateri, and shadwy, And of hem þe flessh ys bettir and more helefull.

Cap. 56. Of fisshes.   32

Which fish may be eaten. In þe selue manere, It ys to wete of ffisshes of lytyll substance, of thyn skyn, and of light chewyng, of waters þat ebbyn and flowyn, as yn Ryuers, þay er moor light and beter þan þay *Which to avoid.* of þe see or of oþer swete waters. But eschewe fisches þat ben 36 of greet quantyte, for þay er wont to be venemous, þo of hard skynes. Þys sayinge suffyse þe of ffysshes, ffor yn þe book

Of the Knowledge of Waters.

þat y made of Potages and medicyns, þou shalt fynde suffysant determinacioun of þys matere.

Cap. 57. Off knowynge of Waters.

4 Hit ys to wete þat watirs ben profytable as wel to bestys as to man; And þenk how y taughte þe suffyciently of waters, And y shewe yt þe, þat alle watrys, as wel swete as bytter, drawyn þer first beynge of þe see; And þerof y maade þe oon
8 opyn shewynge. Now it ys to wete þat most light and most heelfull watrys er þo þat er rynnand watres negh Citeeȝ, whenn þe erthe ys clene with-oute roche, and with-oute reke, þe water of þat stede ys light, ful good, and to be praysed; And waters
12 þat spryngyn yn stony lond, and ys reky Abundandly, er heuy & noyant, yn þe whilk er frosshyn, and serpentys, and oþer venym, And þay ar vnhelfull, as þes stondyng waters; þe toknyng of goode waters er lightnes, clernes, good colour, and
16 good sauour, and whenne þay will sone be hoot and sone cold: And yn swych water kynde hath delyt. And yn þe contrary manere, salt water, and bitter, and rekand, ar euyl, ffor þay drye þe wombe and corumpys it; hoote waters er heuy, ffor þay
20 stonde and may noght stire, And þarfore þe sonne dwellys long yn hem, And þerfore þay engendre þe blake colere, and þey make [þe] splen to waxe and þe longys. Waters þat of betyn to two londys er hote and vnhelfull, ffor þey holde yn hem partys of
24 þo erth. Drynkyng of cold water fastynge, byfore mete, ys noyant þe body, & slekyns þe kendly hete of þe stomake, And drynkyng þerof after mete, makys hoot þe body, and engendres fleume; And yf mekyll be dronkyn, it corumpys þe mete yn þe
28 stomak. But noþeles þe awe drynke cold [1] water in somer, and hoot yn wynter, and noght aȝeynward, ffor hoot water dronkyn in somer makys nesshe and feblys þe stomak, and destruys þe appetit: And also cold water dronkyn yn wynter slekyns þe
32 naturell hete, and destruys þe Instrumentȝ of þe brest, & harmys þe longys, and engendrys many oþer euelys.

All waters come from the sea.
Which are the best.
Which are unhealthy.
Tokens of good water.
Tokens of bad water.
Drinking when fasting is evil.
[1] Fol. 21 a.
Drink cold water in summer and warm in winter.

Cap. 58. Off kynde of wyns.

Hit ys to wete of kynde of wynes, þat þat wyn whos grape
36 growys in hellys aȝeyn þe sonne, ys of moor drye kynde þan þat growys in playn and moyst valeyes, and stedys shadwyd; þe firste wyns er gode to olde men and to hem þat abounden in

The two sorts of wine.

Dry wine is good for old men.   humours of flume, and þey ennoye ȝonge men and hoote men;
And þe olde man and þe ffleumatyke it hetys, and delyueres
hem of ffumosyteȝ greet and colde. And þe redder wyn and
thickere mor heuys þe blood; But whenne it ys stalworth and 4
Redder and thicker wine. of a strong tast, þanne ys hit sayd þe firste blood, and þe firste
norisshynge, And it hauys kynde of drynke and medicyne, and
mekyll ressayuyd, mekyll harmys. Whenne wyn of þis kynde
ys swete, it harmys þe stomak, and it engendrys wyndes & 8
The best wine of all. bolnynges. Þe moste heelfull & þe moste louable wyn to alle
complexiouns ys it þat grewys yn lond þat spredys hym bytwen
Where it grows: hellys & valeys, whos grape ys of a good swetnesse and of a
perfyt tast, and of a sotyl eyre, þat ys noght cuttyd and gedryd 12
or þe force of þe substaunce be fully sprongyn out, and þe
moystnesse of his stok sty vp to þe crope and þe braunches,
its qualities: whos colour ys gold, lyk þat ys meen bytwen reed and ȝalwe, þe
sauour sharpe and dilitable, & his leghes pressed to þe botme, 16
and his partys sutyl and clere. Whenne þou fyndest swylk
wyn, tak þarof attemprely, aftyr þe elde of þy body, and þe
its properties. qualyte of þe tyme, for it comfortys þe stomak, & afforcys þy
kendly hete, it helpys to difye, it kepys fro corupcioun, it ledys 20
þe mete, & sethis it yn-to þe membrys, to hit be turned in-to
It comforts the brain, substanciale and softe blood, And þanne it wendys vp to þe
haterell with attempre hete, and holdys þe heued sekyr fro
and glads the heart of man. vnhappy chauncys. Ouer þat it gladys þe herte, and makys þe 24
[1 Fol. 21 b.] colour reed, and þe tonge spedfull, and delyures a man [1] of euyl
þoughtes and besynes, makys a man hardy; it sturrys appetyt,
and doth many oþer goodys.

Cap. 59. [Of þe euelys þat folwyn to mekyll of wyn.] 28
But if you take too much But of wyn þat ys takyn abundanly in greet quantyte, þes
euelys folwyn: þe wytte waxis derk, it lettys þe vnderstond-
ynge, it troblys þe brayn, and it makys wayk þe vertuȝ of þe
it hurts the wits; sawle, and kyndly vertuȝ; it engendrys forgetynge, hit hurtys 32
alle þe fyue wyttes þat sholde gouerne and dispose alle þe
It feebles the body: wyrkynges of þe body; it away-chasys appetyt, it makys feble
alle þe Ioyntures of þe body, it engendrys bolnynge of membrys
and blerynge of eyen, it kyndels þe colere, it destruys þe lyure, 36
ffor it engrosys his blood, and it makys þe herte-blood blake.
And þerof comys bolnynge, tremblyng, drede, hydousnesse,
ouermekyll slepynge, syghtys of ffantasyes yn þe sleepe, cor-

Of the best Cure for Drunkenness. 81

upcioun of mannys colour, ffebylyng of his priue hernoys, {it causes all sicknesses;}
distruccioun of his sede, abominacioun of þe stomak, mysattemperance of þe complexiouns; it norsshes gretnes of body,
4 and þat worst ys, it brynges yn lepre, and þanne ys he of kynde {and causes lepra.}
venemous; and herfore it ys to eschewe to drynk to mekyll
of wyn, þat ys to wete, ouer mesure. Wete þou þat wyn
folowys þe kynde and þe complexioun of Reubarb, þat is þe {It is like rhubarb:}
8 lyf to þe lyuer, and it hauys noble profitȝ, as it ys foundyn in
bokes of medicyns. But som-tyme þis Reubarb is venomous, {sometimes good, some-}
and inbrynges doth to hem þat takys hit ouer manere, and {times bad:}
passys certeyn quantite and mesure. And wyn ys lyk þe kynde
12 of serpentȝ, of þe whilk Antidotum ys maad, And most hurt- {or like antidote.}
ynges and harmes by þe medicyns þerof er put away, And ȝit it
ys knowyn, þat it berys dedly venym yn it.

Cap. 60. [Of venegre, and þe beste medicyn for dronkenesse.]

16

Alexander, no tyme be it noyous to þe, at morwyn fastyng, {Take a sup of vinegar}
to take a soupyng of venegre, but noght yn Iuyn, whenne {fasting.}
humours surhabunden, and þe fleucme hauys lordschipe, for it
20 ys helfull. And with þat, ypocras þe wyse commendyd merueil- {Hippocrates praised good}
lously good wyn, and sayd: "It ys meruail of a man how he may {wine and good bread.}
be syke or dye, whos mete ys ¹breed of good whete, and his {¹ Fol. 22 a.}
drynkyng drynke of þe good grape." And flesch ys to be com-
24 mendyd if it be vsyd attemprely. And how þat syknesse
growys on hym þat abstenys hym fro surfaytes of mete and
drynke, and fro haunte of women & greet trauaill. It nedys to {If any one is drunk}
him þat ys dronkyn of wyn by outrage takyn, þat he [be] wasshid
28 with hote water, and sitte by a Rennand Ryuere-syd, and þat he
haue weleyghes and myrt, and with sandell confyt ennoynt his {use this cure.}
body, rockyd with reek of ensens, cold and wel sauorand; þys
ys þe beste medicyn for dronkenesse. If any purpos hym al {If any will become a}
32 holy forsake wyn, he shal noght vtterly abstene hym fro þe vse {total ab-stainer,}
of wyn, But lytyll and lytill froo a draghte of wyn to þe
quantyte of oon pressyd grape, and after þat it be alayed with {do it by easy stages.}
water oon tyme moor þan oon-oþer, to it come to clene water,
36 ffor by þis ordre complexioun of kynde ys kepyd froo greuous
syknesseȝ.

SECRETE. G

Cap. 61. **Thynges þat strynghtes and makys fat þe body.**

Some things strengthen the body, some weaken it.

It ys to wete þat some þing strynghys and fattys þe body, some makys it megre and feble; some moystes, and some dryes þe body; and some þat genys strengthe and fayrhecd, and some þat engendryn sleuthe and lachesse. þay þat genyn strynghe

These are the things that strengthen it.

ar liȝht metys and softe, and accordand to þe kynde, whenne þay er at couenable tyme and at mestir takyn, as it ys forsayd; þose fattys and moystes, Rest of body, gladnesse of wyl, lykynge companye, hote metys and moyste, drynkes of swete wyn, and ressayt of hony moyst, þat ys gadryd and norsshyd in Caulegedel; And no þinge ys so mekil worth þerto, as to slepe on softe beddys after mete yn cold.

4

8

12

Cap. 63. **[Of ordinance of stuynge.]**

¹ Fol. 22 b.

Baths are housed like the four seasons.

¹Bathes er on of þe merueylles of þys werld, ffor yt ys housyd after þe ffoure tymes of þe ȝeer, ffor cold accordes to wynter, leuk-warme to Veer, hoot to somer, drye to heruest.

They have four houses.

Greet wyt ys it to make ffoure dwellynges by ordre yn bathes, þe firste be cold, þe seconde leuk-warme, þe þrydde hoot, þe ferthe drye; And whenne a man entrys first yn-to þe bathes,

Bathers stay a short time in each.

he sholde be a lytyl while yn þe firste; and after yn þe seconde, and þere dwelle a lytil; And after yn-to þe þridde, & þere dwell a lityll; And after in to þe ferth entre, & so doo in þe selue manere. And whenne he wyl passe out, kepe he þe self manere, makynge a litill dwellynge yn ilke chambret so þat he passe noȝht fro ouer greet hete to ouer greet cold, no fro ouer

Build baths in a high site.

greet cold to ouer greet hete; and be þe bathes biggyd [in²] heye stede and wyndy, & haue it ffurnays, gyffand flammes, and hote water; And it ys to vse þare-ynne odoures couenables

Use suitable odours.

to þe tyme þanne beand, þat is to wete, to vse in Veer and in somer, treble or quatreblee, In heruest and yn wynter to vse double. After, him awe to sitte on setys wete with water of Roses, and do wype hym with a fair towaille of lyn, onys and eft; And whenne al þys ys doon, and he deliciously wasshyd, passe he sone to oþer houses, and vse þe techinges and oynementȝ

When one is overcome by heat, comb his head.

folwand. If he be ouercome with hete, kembe his heued, and vse he oynement clensyd, couenable to þe tyme; ffor yn Veer and in somer, he sholde vse oynement sesaryn, maad of sendall and emlege. In heruest and wynter, he sholde vse oynement

16

20

24

28

32

36

² '&' in MS.

How a Man should enjoy a Bath.

maad of myrre, and of þe iuwys of þe herbe þat ys clepyd And use ointments.
bletes, and to caste vp-on his heued wroȝht waters attempred;
And after he sholde wasshe his body, and rubbe it with þe self
4 waters, to he be wel wasshyd and clene. After, enoynt his body
of oynementȝ couenables to þe tyme, And after, passe he þennes
¹by þe orde byfore tauȝht, and vse hit to þe tyme he be allegyd. ¹ Fol. 23 a.
If he haue þrist, drynke he a syrupe of roses, and etc electuary What to drink in a
8 with musk, and after, reche out his armes a lityll. And a litel bath.
ouer after take he his mete, þat ys diȝht to him, with pees, and
drynke good wyn attempred with water, after þat he was Drink wine and water:
costomyd to drynke; and take he noȝht mekyll, but attemperly,
12 and after smoke him with ensens couenable to þe tyme, and use incense:
riste he yn a likyng bedde, and take of slepe a good party, ffor
þat shall profyte hym Mekyll. After, he shall contenu þe spend the rest of the day
remenant of þe day in ioye and riste. Þys is þe ordre of hele & pleasantly.
16 norsshyng of þe body; And he þat ys olde, or cold and moyst, Old people should not
dwelle noȝht longe in þe bathe. Noþeles he shall sytte þare- stay too long in the bath.
yn, to his body be moyst of þe bathe, and water be cast on
hym ofte sithes attemperly, and all so sone as he wille. Hit
20 ys noȝht couenable for a flleumatyk man to entre yn Bathes
but fastynge, and þat he enoynt hym with hote oynementȝ.
And he þat ys of hote kynde, kepe þe techynge byfore taȝht.

Cap. 64. [Teching to lyf hool with-oute leche.]

24 O Alexander, whenne þou hauys vnderstond þe teching þat y If you learn of me you
haue geuyn to þe, & in werke it fulfilled, It shall make þe lyf shall need no leech.
hool al þy lyfe with-oute leche, by þe helpe of god. It ys to
wete þat greuous syknesse þat commen of hete or of peryodis, and Watch the periods:
28 of þe cours of þe mone, er kennyd whether þey be sshort or long,
or ellys by þe tokenynges afore-goone, a man mowe knowe to
what ende þay shal come; And y haue trewly leryd þe, and
shortly shewyd þe, diuysyouns and þe knowynges of syknesse,
32 Also yn watir ys a proued tokenyng in swylk þinges. But þe attend to my book of
tokenynge byfore er moor profytable, mor sothfull and bettyr, waters:
Als y haue determynd to þe yn þe book of waters; And þes
tokenynges er suffysantȝ to hym þat holdys wel yn mynde þe
36 techinge of þis book, And also as it ys continuyd [in the boke] and to the book of
þat y made of maad medicyns, and of wroȝht waters, and oyne- medicines.
ment confitȝ, and Emplastres, aftyr þe ordre and þe craft of
gregoys, of yndoys, & of hem of Perse, en whom none esperience

¹ Fol. 23 b. was disceyuable. And ¹for-thy þat þes secretez were profytable,
Though these and were as hyde, and were so worthy, I aingyd þat þey sholde
secrets are
hid, I reveal noȝht be vnkennyd to þy worthy myȝhtynesse, ffor it ys worthy
them to thee.
and riȝhtfuH þat þou knowe þe greete medicyne, þat ys a louynge 4
þat may noȝht be thoȝht, and ys clepyd þe tresour of Philosophers.

Cap. 65. [Of þe greete medicyne.]

I neuere persayued, no y neuer sothly knewe who fonde it,
These men But some sayn þat Adam was fyndere þeroffe, And some sayen 8
are said to be
the finders of þat Esculapydes, and leche Hermogenes, and Hirsos, & Sonasties,
it.
& Vatileos, and ebreos, & Diorys, and Taranour, glorious Philosophers þat er eȝhte, to whom ys genyn þe knowynge of secretez of
sciencez, þat were hyd to alle men. Thes er tho þat out soȝht, 12
an[d] disputyd of þinges þat er ouer kynde, of fuH, of voyde, of
endyd, of vnendyd, and accordandly, & assemblyd to-gedir yn þe
And they confeccioun of þis medicyn, þat may noȝht be hopyd, and þay
divided it
into eight departyd it yn eȝht partyes. Nopeles, some affermyn þat ennoch 16
parts.
Some say knew þys secret by a uisioun, And þay wiH say, þat þis Ennoch
Enoch was
Hermogenes. was þe greet hermogenes, þat þe Gregeys praysen) so mekyH, and
louen), And þay gyf hym þe prys of alle science, secre and
heuenly.   20

Cap. 66. [Of makynge of hony to medecyns.]
Off þe Receytes off Medicynes.

A honey or   Wyth þe benisoun of god, take þe iowse of þe poume-garnet
vehicle for
medicines. swete, xxv Rotes, and of þe Iowse of swet appelys, x Rotes, And 24
of þe Iowse of clere Albamet, x Rotes, And aH þese þynges be
puttyd yn a vesseH, so þat it be to þe half, and with discrecioun,
of a softe fir withoute any reke, be þay sothen); AH þe scome
put away, to it be þicke becomen), And þis ys þe precious hony 28
wherof Medicynes er maad, And þou shalt vse hit as it byfore
ys sayd.

Cap. 67. [Of þe ffirste medecyne.]

² Fol. 24 a. ²Take with Goddys blyssynge and His helpe, of rede roses a 32
The first
medicine. Rote, and of violettys, þe fferthe party of a Rote, and put aH in
x Rotes of swete water, And after, put in of water elcorenge,
half a Rote, And of water Maȝafegys, þe fferthe part of a Rote,
And of water of lange de boef, a Rote; þus alle þes þynges be 36
gaddryd, and sothen with oon vnce of Elegantria de bariofilo,
And alle þes þinges shal be vpon þe fyr aH a nyȝht and a day,
vnto aH þayre stryngh be out passyd; And after be it put vpon

Some Medicines of great Worth.

a softe fyr, to þe þrydde party be lytild away, And þanne late it clere, And after put þer-ynne of þe forsayd digħtyd hony, thre Rotes, and sethe it so longe, to it be picke comen), And after put þar-ynne a dragme and a half of good Muske, & a dragme of dambre, and þre dragmes of þe tree of aloes, tryed and moyst; þys ys þe firste medicyn, ore porcioun), And his effect is properly to comforte þe brayn, þe herte, and þe stomak.

The effect of the first medicine.

Cap. 68. [Of þe secounde medecyne.]

Take of Merabole, galengan, Cabeli, þe bark put away, a Rote, of þe Meoule Carroble de babilone, þe ferthe part of a Rote, & of goode lycoryse witħ-outen) þe barke of ȝalowe colour, Two vnces, and of greynes Meures, virocis sayd, yn her tyme, two vnces, And alle þes þinges be wel stampyd or brysyd, and put yn x Rotes of swete water, a day and a nygħt, and sethe hem softly to þe half, and after lat þe sethinge be steryd and strenyd to it bycome cleer; And þanne put þar-yn after of þe firste hony two Rotes, & lat it eft sethe to yt bycome þykke, And after put yn of poudre of Mastyk, oon vnce, And of reubarbe, þe ferthe part of a vnce, And þis ys þe seconde medicyn; and his properte ys, to make stalworthe þe stomak, & destreyne & purge þe euyl and rotyn humours þat er in þe stomak witħ outen) abhominacioun or violence, And with outen) any hurtyng; And ouer þat, it comfortys þe brest, þe hernys, and al þe body.

The second medicine.

The effect of the second medicine.

Cap. 69. [Of þe þridde medecyne.]

Tak of Emlege, Rote & half, & delilege of Inde, half a Rote, ¹and of darseim, cariele, and of kalengera, galengal, & of nottys muschet, oon vnce, And aH þys be put to-gedre, and stampyd nogħt ouer smaH; And putte yn x arcul of swete water, and dwelle þerinne a day and a nygħt, and after sethe it softly witħ a softe fyr vnto þe half be wastyd, Aftyr be it mellyd & strenyd, to it be cleer; And þanne make it vp witħ thre Rotes of wrogħt hony, and after boille it, to it be þykke: þys ys þe þrydde medicyne, his properte ys to efforce þe pryue, and namly þe pryncypales.

The third medicine.
¹ Fol. 24 b.

Its effect.

Cap. 76. Off takynge of Medicynes of Bloodlate.

Alexander, kepe þe þat þou take no medicyn, no opyn no veyn, but of licence of þe science of Astronomy, ffor þe profyt of

The other chapters [70—75] are not translated in the MS.

Of Planets which govern Blood-letting.

Be not let blood in the new moon. þe science medicynable ys þare-yn enhyed and praysed. If þou wille late þe blood, do it noȝht to þe newe mone encrece so mekyll þat he part hym fro þe sonne; And loke þat þe mone be

Astrological advice. noȝht yn þe tokenynges of þe Bull or of ffisshes; And loke of þe 4 lokynge aȝeyn of þe sonne to þe mone vp-styand, And also in þe Coniunctioun, whenne þe mone ys yn þe watery tokenynges.

Watch Mercury. Loke also þat þe planet Mercurius be noȝht in constellacioun vpstyand or to him contrary, And þe self y say of Saturne; þe 8

Be bled in the third quarter. moste profytable to opyn veyne, ys yn þe laste half of þe Monthe of þe Mone, So þat þe mone be lessnyd of his ligligt, and þat he be yn þe tokenynge of þe balance or of þe scorpyoun: & whenne þe nusant sterres loke noȝht aȝeyn, ffor þanne ys þe mone yn 12 clen staat, whenne it ys yn þe secunde repreuable or noyant. In

In case of scarification follow these rules. latynge of blood, noȝht by openynge of veynes, but by scarificacioun of flleschi, whenne þe mone ys grewyng yn light, and þat noyant sterrys lokys noȝht him to, but þat it ys ynens Mercury, 16 And þat þe mone be with Venus, or ellys þat Venus or Mercury loke þarto. Whenne þe mone ys yn oon constellacioun vpstyand þanne haues he myght and lordschipe vp-on þe self stede yn þe body. 20

Cap. 77. [Off takynge of medicyn laxatyue.]

[1] Fol. 25 a. *When you take laxative medicine,* Whenne þou wille take a medicyn laxatyue [1] be þou certein þat þe mone be in þe scorpioun, or in balaunce, or in fisshes, but be-war þat þe mone be noȝht negh saturne, ffor þanne it makys 24 þe humours to engele, and þe medicyn yn þe body; And ay þe

follow these rules. more farre it ys fro Saturne, so mekyll it ys þe better; And it ys noȝht to doute, whenne it ys yn Mercury, And be þe bygynyng of þy werke after good constellacioun of þe mone, & his remuynge 28 fro nusant sterrys, and his prosperyte of his vpstiyng.

Cap. 78. [Of doctryne of tokenynges.]

Watch the signs of the zodiac. And whenne þou wyl gyf medicyn, wete þou yn what tokenynge þe sonne ys, and þat may þou kenne by þe moneth þat ys 32 present, if þou besily beholde þe tokenynges put yn þe present spere and writen; ffor if it be yn tokenynge coleryk, It byhouys þanne to make more scharpe þe medicyn; And yn þe tokenynge malencolien mekyll more. If it be yn tokenynge ffleumetyke, a 36

And watch the sun and moon. lityll after þe qualyte & resoun of þe tokenynge: whenne þe sonne ys colurge O kynde of þe wombe ys costyf or laxatyue; Ouer þat it ys besily to loke whether þe mone be in tokenynge coleryke,

or fleumatyke, or malencolien; If bothe þe lighthes in þe coleryk
tokenynge be sette or byholde it, a medicyn þat þat tyme gyuen
shall lityll profyt a man or styrre, And if þay be yn tokenynge
4 malencolien, it shall make þe takere right noght solyble, or ellys
ful litell; And yf þe sonne and þe mone bothe be yn tokenynge
fleumatyk, lightly þe medicyn takere shal forth lede, And most
whenne þe mone ys yn waxynge; ffor as Plinius seith, "þe mone
8 waxynge, þe humours of all þe body waxen, And also al moyst
þynge & [harmful] & superfluiteȝ of egestioun; And whenne þe
mone wanys all þes þinges wanys." Þes priuiteȝ of kynde þat we
haue compyled to-gedir, ilk-a man may knowe hem with-outen
12 doute, þat wyl preue hem expertly yn hym-self.

For the position of them in the sign is very important.

streatus
nota

nota

Cap. 79. Off propertes of herbes and stones.

¹ We shhall determyn after by a short trete, of properteȝ &
vertuȝ of herbes, and hir profitȝ. We haue maad a cleer sheu-
16 ynge yn oure oþer bokes, of properteȝ of stones, and of vertuȝ of
herbes, and þe kyndes of þe planytes, But now it ys to say of
planetȝ, and of stones, als mekyll as sufficeth to þis present werk.
But, alexander, þe awe to wete right as yn þe planetys er dyuers
20 kyndes, and dyuers stryngthes, set of god, so yn stones er founden
diuers spyces and vertuȝ, of whem þe fayrheed and profyt er of
prys, þat may noght be hopyd to a kynges mageste: And namly
and principaly, þay seme to a kynges dyademe to be ahournyd by
24 in fayrhede, of whilke fayrhede þe sight ys helpyd, and mannys
corage delytys þerynne, and þe dignite maad fayr; And by þaire
vertuȝ greuous siknesse of þe body er aȝeyn-put, with-outen
whom medicyn lityll profytes, And þarfore, leches vsen hem in
28 medycynes, to caste out greuous syknesses. Gret and merueillous
vertu ys gyuen of god, to planetes, and to stones, if all it be hyd
en greet party to man. But we haue fully expounyd yn þe
bokes of planetes and of stones, þaire properteeȝ and her vertuȝ.

¹ Fol. 25 b.
We shall now treat of the virtues of herbs and stones.

The use of these stones:

for ornament:

for physicians.

32   Cap. 80. [Of þe stoon, þe Eye of Philosophers.]

O Alexander, now at þe bygynnynge I wille delyure to þe,
most greet secreet of secreetȝ, & þe myght of god helpe þe to
fulfyll þe purpos, & to layne þe secreet. Tak þanne þe stoon
36 hauynge soule, thriuynge, and fallynge to myn, that ys noght a
stoon, ne haues noght kynde of stoon, But it ys lyk in manere to
stoones of mynyd hilles, and of planetȝ, and of þinges hauynge

This is the great secret.

This stone is found everywhere.

soule : And it ys foundyn yn ilke stede, and yn ilke tyme, and yn ilke man : and it may be turnyd to eueryche colour, and it holdys yn him alle þe clymentȝ, and it ys callyd þe lesse world ; And y shaH nemyn þe þe nome as þe comyn folk clepyth it, þat ys þe terme of þe Eyrn, þat ys to say þe Eye of Philosophers. Now depart it yn ffoure partyes, & euery partye ¹hauys oon kynde.

The philosopher's egg.
¹ Fol. 26 a.

After ordeyn it euenly in euyn porciouns, so þat þare be no diuisioun, no noon aȝeynfeghtynge, þanne shaH þou haue by þe helpe of god þi purpos. þys manere ys vniuersele, But y shaH departe hit in specials wirkynges. It ys partable in ffoure, and he hauys hym wel yn two maners with outen) corupcioun ; þanne whenne þou hauys water of eyre, and eyre of fyre, and fyre of erthe, þanne shalt þou fully haue þis craft. Ordeyne now þanne þe substance of þe eyre by discrecioun, and þe substance of þe erthe by moysture and hete, to þai assemble and ioyne to-gedre, and þat þay disacorde noght, no noght departe ; And þanne put to hem twoo vertuȝ wirkand, water and fyre, And þanne shaH þe werke be fulfyllyd, ffor if þou leue þe water aloon, it shal make whit, and if þow ioynge to ffyre by þe gyft of god it shal wel fare.

It can be divided into four.

Pure the elements,

and join them together in due proportion.

4

8

12

16

20

Cap. 81. Off þe Oppynyoun of Hermogenes.

This is the Emerald Table of Hermes.

Oure ffader Hermogenes, þat ys fuH fayr in Philosophic and wel faire Philosophiant, says, " Sothfastnesse hauys him so, þat it ys no doute þat þinges by-negh answeres to þinges abown, And þinges abown to þinges byneth. And þe werkere of meruaylles ys oon god, ffro whom ilke meruey1ouse werk descendys, And so alle þinges er maad of oon aH-oon substance, of oon aH-oon ordinance, whos ffadyr ys þe sonne, and þe mone þe modyr, þat baar hym yn þe wombe consayued by þe Ere, þat ys þe pryue erthe. Of þys ys þe fader of enchantementȝ, þe tresour of myracles, þe geuer of vertuȝ. Of fire ys maad þe erthe, of suaille erthly þinge, ffor delye þinge ys more worth þan greet, and þynne more worth þan þycke, and þat done wysly and discretly, ffor it assendys vp fro þe erthe to þe heuen), and it fallys doun) fro þe heuen) into þe erthe, and þare it slas þe souerayn vertu, and foreyn. So þanne ys lordschipe in fforeynteȝ & souerayn teȝ, and so shal þou be lord heye and lawe, ffor with ȝow ys ²þe lyght of lightes, And þerfore alle derknesse shal flee ȝow. þe souerayn vertu maynteignes alle þinges, ffor it geues

If one understands it, it contains all wisdom.

² Fol. 26 b.

24

28

32

36

latnesse, and it makys swyftnesse, and þat after þe ordinance of
þe gret world shortys þo werk," And þarfore hermogenes is callyd
full feyr yn Philosophy.

4   Cap. 82. [Off þe vertu of precious stoones.]

And [this stoon ys[1]] of þe merueilles of þe werld þat with *This is an account of an enchanted stone.*
waters and wyndes fightes; ffor þou seeȝ [it] vprys vpon waterys
whenne þay rynne with þe wyndes, and it bygynnys yn þe see
8 sayd mediterreyne, whos properte ys þys:—If þou take þis
stoon and put it yn oon oþer stoon, and bere it with þe, it
may noght be þat any hoste mowe laste aȝeyn þe, or aȝeyn- *No enemy can stand against its bearer.*
stande þe, but it shall faill fallynge byfore þe. And þar er
12 two precious stoones of merueillous vertu þat er founden yn derk
stedes, yn oon ys whit, þe oþer Reed, þat men fynden yn
rynnand waters, of whom þe wyrkynges er swylk; þe whyt *Magic white and red stones.*
bygynnes to appere at þe settynge of þe sonne abown þe waters,
16 and it dwellys on hem to mydnyght, and þanne it bygynnys to
falle donward, And at þe risyng of þe sonne he comys to þe
ground. Þe rede wirkes all þe contrary, ffor at þe sonne risynge *Contrary to each other.*
he bygynnes to shewe hym to þe hour of mydday, and þanne he
20 ys fallynge to þe doungate of þe sonne. And þe propertes of þes
stoones er þes: If þou hynge of þe rede þe weght of a moote
vpon a hors of þin host, alle þe hors of þyn ost shal noght cesse *Their effect on horses:*
to henny to þou doo awey þe stoon. And þe white werkys al þe
24 contrary, ffor a hors shal neuer henny where he dwellys. And
þer stones er mekyll worth in vsynge of wachis, and to þe vse of
ostys; And also þes ar þer properte; If two men stryuen togedir, *and on men in strife.*
put þe whit stoon yn oon of here mouthes, or of þe toþer, and if
28 right falle to him he shall sone speke, if he haue noght þe right
he shall be doume, to whilys þo stoon ys yn his mouth. And þe
rede stoon wirkys all þe contrary. Now y shal determyn þe
properteȝ and vertuȝ of stoones in eschauntementȝ, and oþer
32 þinges y shal after trete.

Cap. 83. [Off þinges vegetable.]

[O Alexander] ffor þou hauys knowynge full by myn oþer
tretys afore, where y haue tretyd þe of þe kyndes and secretȝ
36 of creatures, þat ys of degreeȝ and ordinance of þe planetys, and
after þe degrees and ordynaunce of [2]science of myne, after þaire [a] Fol. 27 a.

---

[1] 'he ys fader' in MS.

Of the Governance of Herbs by the Planets.

beynge, and þaire proper ffourme, þat þey ressayue after þaire
firste growyng, and þe kynde of kyndes abown, þat ys to wete
ouercomand and lordschype purchesand in it; ouercomand in
watery planetys Of nature, and of stoones of myne ouercomand
ys þe kynde of þe erthe, þanne þe kynde of þe planetys ressayues
þe kynde of out-spredyng of waterys, Als it-self ressayues water
be outputtynge of wyndes yn his stede, And als water ys of
dyuers lyknesse, ffor many lyknesse er in hit, so it fallys of
planetys, ffor all lyknesse er founden þerynne. And whenne
water ys ouercomand in Planetys, and staunches noght but by
doun-shedyng, and as þe wirkere of dissoluciou̇n of waters ys with
outen reles, oon ay-lastand wirkere in his heuen, þat ys to say,
Mercury; ffor with-outyn doute it ys soth, þat euryche planet
ys gouernyd and ordeynyd yn accordance of his kynde; as þou
may see here, Saturn haldys þe erthe, Mercury þe water, Iubiter
þe eyr, þe sonne þe ffyre. And no disconuenyent þing ys founden
in wirkynge of þe Planetes þat þay haue contynuell and ay lastyng, by þe hyeste vertu & vniuersele, þat ys abouen alle vertuȝ
of swylk wirkyng. But here ys no stede to shewe of so hard
and streyt science, And noþeles y haue maad mencioun þarof,
ffor it ys necessary and profitable to þe, ffor the tretee folwand
in þe whilk we sall determyn of singuleryte, And vndepartyng
of some planetis vegetableȝ: wherof þe knowynge of swylk þinges
fallys to Philosophers, And þe knowynge of wirkynges of naturele
þinges fallys to leches. And y will noght, þat it be hyd to ȝowre
knowynge, þat what þinge wantys light of þe nombre of þinges
vegetable, þat er to be sustenyd, Saturn gouernys hem, and to
hym it ys apropird; And what þing þat floryssheth and shynyth
of þinges vegetable, of Mercury is gouernyd, and to him attournyd.
And what þinge vegetable þat florschys and makys fruyt, to þe
sonne ys apropird, and by hym gouernyd. After ordeyne and
ioyne to-geder þese diuisiouns, and say all þinge vegetable þat
berys fruyt and noght florysshis, as porret and palm, ys assignyd
to Saturn and to þe sonne, And ilk þinge florysshand þat berys
noght fruyt ys attityld to Mercury, and to Mars. Also some
þinges [1] vegetables or sustenables er by [cuttings], oþer by sedys,
& with-outen plantyng [grown]. þanne it shewys opynly by þat
þat ys afore sayd, þat euerylk kende of vegetabiliteȝ haues a propre
ordre, þat ys, complexioun, & it folwys þe vertu of a plancte, and
ys assignyd and apropryd to hym, and som tyme apropred to his

Of Trees which have magical Powers.

felawe, and it ys atturnyd to þe vertu of two planytes, or of moo *And by virtue of this gov-*
after þat it mowe ressayue, And ilke vertu helpys of his pro- *ernance by the planets*
perte þat ys assignyd to hym, þat ys to wete þat kyndly vertu *it has its properties.*
4 þat his kynde ordeynes, As in colour, in sauour, in odour, and
in lyknes; And þe kendly sowel gedyrs to-gedyr aH þes propertes, & kyndly vertuȝ þat comeþ þarof and folwys it, and makys
it laste by as mekyH tyme, as þei determyn hit of þaire vertu,
8 ffor þar ys no wirkynge but it come of sterynge, no noon wirkynge with-outen terme. And so þou saH persayue oon kynde
vegetable noyant, And anoþer kynde wyrkand hele, And some *And these*
engendrys gladnesse and ioye, some loue & some hatredyn, and *properties are diverse and strange.*
12 some vpberyng reuerence and honour, & some vilte and despyt,
some gyfnesse auysiouns of fantasye and falshede, & oþer certeyn
and trewe auisiouns; some engendrys pruesse & stryngh, and
some sleuthe and febelnesse; some sauys þe body fro dedly
16 venyms, and some corumpys þe body and brynges it to þe deth.
And y shal make þe a certeynesse vpon aH þes kyndes with
opyn argumentȝ and preuys.

Cap. 84. [Of þe trees þat hauyn kyndly vertuȝ.]

20   þat portable kynde, þat engendrys reuerence and honour, ys *A plant which brings*
a tree whos leuys er lappyd to-gedir, his shape ys round, and his *reuerence and honour*
fruytes round, also his branches er moyst & [his odour most *to its wearer.*
sweet]. he þanne, þat yn his name racys hit, and berys it with
24 hym clanly, he shal purchace reuerence and honour. Þare ys
anoþer tree, þat bers longe leuys and moyst, þat hauyn whit *Another brings exalt-*
lynys yn hem; he þat bers of þe substance of þat tree shal be *ation.*
enheyed. Also þare ys a tree þat hauys leuys ¹of vygour, and ¹ Fol. 28 a.
28 his braunches spredyn hem on þe erthe, and ys of good sauour; *Another brings valour*
he þat berys it with hym shal be prowous and hardy. It is *and success in strife.*
noght good to stryue with þat man or fight, ffor euer-more his
aduersary shaH falle afore hym, And he shal euer ouercome yn
32 aH his wirkynges. And of þe kyndes of trees ys oon kynde þat
haues long leuys, and it losys hem or þat he bere ffloures; and
he haues three ffloures longe and rede, of delycat sauour; he þat
etys þo ffloures, ioye and laghenge shal come to hym; and he þat *Another makes all*
36 racys it vp by þe rote, and etys þe flour þynkand of any woman *women in love with its*
persone, sho shaH bycome brynnand yn his loue. Þare ys anoþer *bearer.*
herbe þat ys clepyd androsinoun þat grewys yn þe lond of syn, &
ys entrikyd; it hauys drye leuys and right lityH, and his seed

The seed of androsinon makes a man obedient to thee.

ys lityll and round, whit with-ynne. If þou take seuen graynes of þat seed, yn þe name of any persone, and broke hem yn þe vpsryngynge of lucyfer and venus, so þat þayre bemys touche hem, and gyf hem to hym to ete or drynke, þe drede of þe shal dwell yn his herte, And alle his lyf he shall be obeysant to þe.

Another plant causes languor.

And of þe kynde of plauntouns ys oon þat engendrys langour, whos rote plauntyd, and þe branches spredyn hem by oon arme, whos floures er whit, ouerpassant þe leuys, but it berys noght fruyt; his properte ys of Mars and Mercury, & his kynde of ffyre and eyr. He þat berys þis herbe with hym, he shall noght be with-outen langour to he caste it away. Anoþer ys of

Another cures various sicknesses.

þe maner of plantouns þat ys helefull, whos seed er soone sawen, whos braunche ys quarre, whos leuys er round, and his flour of heuenly colour; his seed ys reed, his odour softe, of good effect; he þat drynkys it, with þe sauour þeroff he shall fele hele, and he shal be sauf of catarre, of Malencoly, of curiousite, of drede, of ffrenesye, and of many oþer syknes. Anoþer plantisoun ys

Fertilidon causes hate. ¹ Fol. 28 b.

sayd for collodioun ¹þat engendrys [hate and contempt]. Anoþer

Nathason causes love.

is Matifoun clepyd, and þat ys of greet value to conquere loue and reuerence. O Alexander, y haue fully maad þe tretee to þe,

Now you know this, be virtuous.

þat y behight þe, And y haue fully shewed þe of playn solucioun. Be þou euer-more vertuous and glorious; God þe susteyne, þe dresse, and þe kepe, ffor hys bounte ilk-a creature takyth.

4

8

12

16

20

Book III. Cap. 85. **Off Right.** 24

What justice is.

Right ys a louable praysynge of propertes of þe heye simple glorious, wharefore swilk oon shulde reygne þat god hauys chosyn and stabyld on his seruantʒ, to whom þe nedes and gouernance vpon subgitʒ fallys to, þat awe to purueye and defende þaire poscessiouns, richesse, and blood, and alle þaire

28

It is like to God.

wirkynges als þaire god, ffor yn þat he ys lyk to god; And forþy it byhoues resemble and folwe þe heighenesse yn all his werkys. God ys wys and conynge, his louynges and his name er glorious yn hym, And þe gretnesse of his lordschipe ys gretter þanne alle tongys suffissent to determyn; þanne it ys to wete þat contrary

32

The praise of justice.

of his right ys vnright; In right dwellys þe heuens, and er stablyd abouen) þe erthe; In ryght was þe holy prophetys sent forth; Right ys þe shappe of vnderstondynge þat þe heye god makyd, and þare by² alle creatures hauys dwellynge; ffor by

36

² "and þare by" repeated in MS.

right ys þe erthe byggyd, and kynges er stabyld, and[1] [terrible] subgitȝ er obeissant & tame, And aH þare-by is vnderstandant, and neghys negh, þat þat ys remued of farre; þarby sawles er
4 sauyd and delyueryd of alle vyces, and of aH corupciouns ynens þayre gouernours; And þerfore þay of Inde sayen, þe right of hym þat reygnyth ys more profitable to subgitȝ þan plente of good tyme; And also þai sayd þat right of a lord ys [2]mor better
8 þan rayn wel norsshant. And it was founden wretyn yn a stoon yn þe langage of Caldee þat kynges and vnderstandynge er brether, and þat þe oon suffyce noght with-outyn þe oþer, and þat aH þinges al haly er termyned by right. And vnder-
12 standynge ys þe enchesoun þat puttys yn werk aH hys beinges and werkes, ffor it ys his Makynge, It ys his rightwys Iuge: and by þe consequent þe beynge of ryght, þat ys rote of [it, is] vnderstondyng, & it ys wirkand, and þerto ledand; It ys
16 his myght, & wherby he wirkys; It is his entent, and it waytys science; It ys Iuge wirkand and withhaldand þat þat vndoynge by-comes, and ressayues þat þat ledys to ryght, ffor it ys opyn þinge þat right ys double, þat ys to wete opyn and hyd, opyn
20 whanne he shewys hym yn dede wroght. And a pesable right & mesuryd ys, to byholde vpon statys by þe self vnderstondyng: and Iugement ressayues his hide name of hym. Certeynesse & confirmaciouns of saynges is yn þe faith or trowynge of þe Iuge
24 wirkand his werkys. Wherfore it semys, as we byfore haue sayd, þat a kynge holdys a resemlance in right to þe simple hyest; And þarfore it nedys þat he be fast and stable, yn aH his wirk- ynges propres & comouns. He þanne þat bowys fro his awen
28 right & þe comoun's, In part he tynys þe frendschipe of god, Iuge most he, & passys fro his wyl, & leuys faith, and suys þe lawe aȝeyn perfeccioun of lordshipe; als it shal shewe by his werkys, he schaH ryue þe hert of his subgitȝ, þat ys to say, so as
32 his werkys shewyn, his subgitȝ shaH fele hym at þaire hertes. And rightes er propre & comoun in dyuers degrees; And in trespasyng of right er greet difference, and þe names of right er relatyf, or aȝeynledynge to some þinges sayd, & amendyng of
36 wronge, and adressynge of stature, & shape of mesure; And it ys a name colectyf, or gederand togeder, byholdyng curtasye, and maners of larges, & wirkynge of goodnesse. And right is departyd [3]in diuisiouns, ffor oon right ys, þat byholdys Iuge-

The Indian saying.

[2] Fol. 20 a.

The saying of the Chaldees.

Understanding is the first cause of a king's deeds.

A king is likened to the Most High.

If a king forsakes Justice his subjects will fail him at need.

Justice is relative.

[3] Fol. 29 b.

1. A space left in MS. here filled by "terrible."

The justice of judges. mentʒ, þat ys to say domes, and þat fallys to doomysmen. Anoþer right ys, þat fallys to vche man to lede hym-self by
The justice of all men. resoun yn alle þinges þat er bytwen him & his creatour; þarfore make þou right stable yn þinges þat er bytwen þe & þe people, 4 þat ys to wete, mesure of thewes, and setynges of tokenynges, of þe whylk I goue þe a full fayre shappe, to be praysed of þe worthy knowynge of Philosophie by ensample. And y shall all
A likeness of Justice. holy [show thee by a form] al þat ys in man þat takyth on him 8 gouernance of subgitʒ, & shewe þe, þaire degrees and þaire qualiteʒ, & þe rotys þat þe moste haue of right in vche degree; þarfore it ys departyd in two diuisiouns of cerculers and speres, And vche diuision is oon degree. Bygynne þanne, of whether 12 þow wylt say, and it shall gif þe þat, þat no þinge ys moor
The sphere of the firmament. precious, þat ys to wete, þe sercle of þe firmament, and þe ceyte of all ordinance, and of all gouernance, of þinges bynethe and abowen, to þe kepynge of þis world. Thanne þinkyth me, þat 16 it ys þus to begynne touchand þe werld, and þis ys þe profyt of
The world compared to a garden. þis booke, And þis ys þe lyknesse. þe world ys a gardyn, his cloþinge or his echynge ys dome, doomesmen er gounours knowynge þe lawe; Lawe ys þe kyng, dome þat gouernys a kynge, 20 kynge ys þe Pastour of Barouns, Barouns er soudeours, susteyned of hauynge; hauynge ys a auenture, gedryd of subgitʒ; subgytʒ
Definition of Justice. er seruantʒ, þat er vndyr-put by ryght. Right ys, þat a man ʒelde to vche man þat his ys, [per se][1] it ys sayd, be it-seluyn, 24 ffor yn it ys þe hele of subgitʒ.

Cap. 86. [Off þe makyng of þinges in order.]

The Most High first created intelligence; And wete þat it ys þe firste þinge þat þe glorious hyest maade, a simple substance spirytuell yn þe ende of perfeccioun, 28 yn spedynge of goodnesse, yn þe whilk þinge, vndirstandynge
then the anima universalis; vpon all þinges ys first namyd, And after of þat substance [came another], lesse yn his degree, þat ys clepyd þe sawle; And
then the yle; of þe saule commys anoþer substance, þat ys clepyd þe yle, 32 before þe mesurynge, þat ys vndirstondyd, in lenghe, in brede,
[2] Fol. 30 a. [2]in heghnesse, yn depnesse, yn þe whilk a body ys maad symple;
then matter without shape. and after, þe body be, ffor þe moste noble lyknesse þat ouer passys all oþer lyknes, and ys most sothfast yn comparyson, 36 And þe moste [ancient, & it][3] dwellys yn a stede of þe speres, and of þe planetes. And þe spere þat enuirouns to þe terme of

---

[1] "purthy" in MS.   [3] A blank in MS.

þe spere of þe mone, is most clene and most symple, and þat ys þe firste of þe speres.

Cap. 87. [Off þe steryng of heuens.]

And þer ar nyne heuens, oon in erthe, þe oþer amonge hem scluyn, ilk oon amonge oþer; þe firste & þe souerayne of þe speres, is þe spere couerant, and þanne with-ynne þat þe spere of þe sterrys; after þat þe spere of Saturne, and so to þe spere of þe mone, vnder whom ys þe spere of þe clemenȝ, þat er fyre, Eyre, water, and erthe. þe Erthe þanne ys yn þe myddyl stede of þe oþer clementȝ, and it ys most thyk substance, a hool body & most thyk yn beynge; and þes speres wer ordeyned, some yn oþer and oþer yn hem self, as it ys sayd, after þe wit & þe ordynance of god symple, most glorious; yn ordinance of meruaill, and of ffayrheede ahournyd; And þes speres er steryd by sercles in þaire partys, And þe planetys, vpon þe ffoure elementȝ aftyr þaire body, nyght and day, wynter & somer, hoot and cold; & oon er mellyd in oþer, And þe thyne tempred togedir with þe thykke, and heuy with light, & hoote with cold, and moyst with drye; And þanne of hem ys maad by lengthe of tyme all maner of kynde of composisiouns þat originals, minerals, vegitables, & bestyals. And originals er what þyng ys engelyd yn þe entrailles of þe erthe, and yn þe depnesse of þe sees, & in Cauees of hilles, & in[1] fumositeȝ stoppyd & [from vapours] vpsteyinge, and moystures engelyd, and in concauacion of Cauernes, In whom erthly Eyre hauys most lordschipe, as gold, syluer, Bras, Iryn, leed, and tynne; and stones, Margarites, Corale, Tuty, and alany, and swylk lyk, to hem þat er seene and knowyn, hauynge sawle. And all þys manere of engendrynge stirres hem, and felys, and passys fro stede to stede by hem seluyn, as þe strengthe of þe Eyre hauys yn hem more [2]lordschipe. þe composision vegitable þat is sustinable is mor noble þan þe originale, [and almaill ys moor noble þan vegitable], And [man's] sawle ys moor noble in composicion þan all manere of almaill, And ffyre yn his properte hauys most lordschipe, and all þinges accorden yn his composiscion þat er founden yn symple eldys, and contrarious, ffor man ys maad of body þyke, togedyr mesuryd, and of saule simple, and substance spirituell.

[1] A blank in MS.

Cap. 88. **Knowynge of Sawle.**

If you wish to be wise, learn to know your own soul.

Now þe nedys if þow be knowynge vpon sciences and sothfastnes of þinges þat er & be dwellynge, þat first þou begynne at þe knawynge of þyn owen) sawle, þat is nest to þe and after to haue þe science of oþer þinges. Wete þanne, þat vche sawle is a spirituell stryngthe, growynge of vnderstondyng at godys wylle,

The soul has two strengths.

and it hauys two stryngthes ronnynge to-gedre yn þe body, right as þe light of þe sonne yn þe partyes of þe Eyre; oon of þe stryngthes is a tokenynge, þe oþer ys wirkand, þat glorious god

The seven virtues of the cis operans.

hauys inlightyd of vij strenghes; of stryngthe attractyue, and retractyf, of stryngthe digestyf, and purgatyf, of strengthe nutrityf, and infirmatyf, and sustantyf. Þe wirkynge of þis last,

The virtue vegetative lasts for 7 months after conception,

(þat þe Auctour clepys vegetatyf, & I here strenght sustantyf), yn composicion) of Mannys body, ys yn þe receyte of þe seed in þe mariȝ, And it lastys in his ordenyng seuen Monthys, and after

when the child gets the anima sensibilis.

þat tyme fortward it ys mesurid of þe hyest glorious souerayn, & so spedde, þat god þanne puttys þerynne a leuyng saule & feling, fro þat stede to hys outpassynge to hys dwellyng place,

At 4 he gets reason.

and he folwys a gouernance to ffoure ȝeer fulfillyd. And after he geuys hym to resonable vertu, þat þe name of sencibilite ledys

At 15 he gets understanding.

him to, And þanne he ressayues anoþer gouernance to xv ȝeer fulfillyd, and þanne he ressayues a stryngthe of vndirstandynge þat ys renunciatyf of ffygures and semblance, & of temptacions sensibles, to þe fulfyllynge of xiiij ȝer, And þanne comes to him a strengh shewable, or Philosophable, þat byholdys shappys

At 30 he gets judgment.
At 40 he gets kingly virtues.
At 60 he gets legal powers.

vndirstandable, & þanne he getys anoþer gouernance to þe fullilynge of xxx ȝeer, And þanne fallys to hym a reale willy vertu, and he ressayues anoþer gouernance to fulfillen) xl ȝeer, and þanne comes to him a lele sett vertu of originals, wharof he

[1] Fol. 31 a.

ressayues another gouernance aH þe tyme [1] of his lyf. If þe sawle

If the soul is made perfect, it is raised to highest perfection;

be þanne perfyt and fulfillyd byfore his departynge fro þe body, it shaH þanne be ressayued of aH sawly vertu, and þerby be enhyed, to þe heye perfeccion) be ledde, And þanne it purchasys anoþer gouernance, to it come to þe sercle or to þe firmament of

If not it is sunk to hell.

vnderstondynge, whore it shaH wel lyk; And if it be noght wel perfyt þe sawle shaH plunche into þe depnes of helle, and þare he shaH take a gouernance of kaytefnesse with-outyn hope of lykynge.

Book IV. Cap. 89. [Off þe makyng of man.]

Whenne god þe hieste made man, & made hym most noble of alle creatures, he comanded him, and defendyd hym, wherof he hauys failyng & mede, and he hauys stabyld his body riȝt as a Citee, and he hauys put vnderstondyng yn hym, as a kyng sette yn þe moste noble and most souerayn stede of man, þat ys yn þe heued. And ouer þat he hauys sette v. portours to gouerne it, and to presente to him what þing ys myster to him, & whareby he mowe helpe hym, & to kepe him fro what þing may be noyous to him. And he hauys no perfeccion ne dwellynge but by hem; And he hauys stabyld to vche of þe v. portours, his wyt as his awen arbytour or Iuge, in whom he hauys auantage, and is disseuyrd fro oþer faytours, and hauys his owen propre maners, & some common to oþer. And of þe gederynge & accordance of þe Iugementȝ, er þe substance and þe perfeccion of his werkys Engendryd.

When God made man, He gave him laws as a city: and made understandyng his governour; and gave him five chamberlaine to help him.

Each of them has his own sense.

Cap. 90. Off þe V wyttes. [Of sight.]

Þes v. portours byfore-sayd er þe v. wyttes, þat dwellys yn þe eighen, yn þe eryn, yn þe nese, yn þe tonge, and yn þe hondes. Þer ar x maners of þe wyt of þe eighen, ablenesse of siȝt; liȝt, and derknesse, colour, and body, lyknesse, setynge, remuynge, & neȝhcomyng, sterynge, & rest.

Where the senses dwell.

The ten species of the sense of sight.

Cap. 91. [Off harkenyng.]

Þe sensibiliteȝ of þe Eres er harkenyng of souns, and þerof er two maners, of sawle, and noȝht of sawle; soun of sawle ys double, oon resonable, fallyng to man spekyng, anoþer vnreasonabl, as hyneyinge of hors, chaterynge of bryddes, and swylk lyk souns. Soun noȝht of sawle ys a rappyngge togedre of stones, hewynge of wode, and swylk lyk, þat hauen no lyf, as of þe thoner, of tympans, and oþer Instrumentȝ; and wete þat vche voys yn his ordre ys al hool whenne it ys stiryd yn þe Eyre þat berys it, & þat self noble spiritalte stirrys þerwith, so þat part mellys noȝht with part, to at þe laste it come to wyt and herynge, þanne er þey brouȝht to-geder [1] to a vertu ymagynary.

Two kinds of sounds, animate and inanimate. Two of animate sounds, rational and irrational. Inanimate sound.

Cap. 92. [Off tastynge.]

[1] Þe sensibilyte of þe tonge ys by way of tastynge & sauour, And þarof er ix maneres; Swetnesse, bitternesse, saltnesse, &

[1] Fol. 31 b.
The nine species of the sense of taste.

SECRETE. H

Of the Perfections of the Number 5.

vnctuosite, Egrenesse & vnsauournesse, ponticite, stipticite, & acuement.

Cap. 93. [Off touch.]

The objects of the sense of touch.

Þe wyttys þat er yn þe hondes ys in atouchable & tastable stryngh, and his cours ys yn hete, yn cold, and in sharpe þing, and softe; And it ys content but bytwen) two skynnes, þe oon yn shewyng of þe body, þe oþer yn þat, þat it kepys to þe flesch. 4

Cap. 94. [Off werkyng of wyttes.] 8

Light skins run from the root of the brain.

Þanne whenne any of þes wittes er getyn þat god genys; of þe rote of þe harne, þare growyn light thynne skynnes as arayne webbys, & þey ar as a coueryinge & a curtyn to þe gouernour. And whenne þat vche a wyt hauys in hym his represent, & 12

The traces of the sensations are gathered by the virtue imaginative, they go to the virtue cogitative, in the midst of the brain.

commys to þo skynnes þat er yn þat substance of þe harnes, þanne gedirs togeder þe folwynges of þe sensibiliteȝ of man to a vertu ymaginatyf, þat representys hem to vertu pensyfe, þat ys yn myddes of þe harnes to byholde hem, And þanne it gedyrs 16 hem to-gedre, & stodys yn þaire ffygures & ensamples, and knowith what þing in hem er helpynge, and what þinge noyand, & what comys in wirkynge after þe mesurynge of hem.

Cap. 95. [Off perfeccioun of ffyue wyttes.] 20

The excellence of the number five.

Þanne þe stabylnesse and þe fullastyng of þe body dwellys yn þe v. wyttes afore-sayd: and þe perfeccioun of all þinges ar yn ffyue þinges: þe speres by whom þe planetys sterys hem

5 kinds of beasts:

after her sercles er fyue; And maners of Bestes er fyue, þat ys 24 to wete, man), and volatille, ffyssh of þe water, þat gooþ on

5 parts of trees:

ffoure feet, & þat stirrys vpon wombe; And ffyue þinges er, with-outen whom) no plauntyd þinge þat growiþ on þe erthe is perfyt, And er þes fyue, stoke, braunches, leuys, fruytes, and 28

5 tones of music:
5 best days in the year.

rotys; And fyue tones er of Musyke, and if þei ne were, no songe were accordant or perfyt. And ffyue dayes er most noble of all of þe ȝeer, In þe laste ȝate of May.

Cap. 96. [Off conseillers.] 32

So you have five counsellors.

Be þanne þy porters and þy conseillers ffyue, yn þe doynge of all þi werkys, and vche of hem be seueryd by hym-self. Withholde þanne þi conseill, and bigyn noght to say to þy conseillers þat þat þou hauys in herte, and say noght to hem[1] 36

---

[1] "þat" repeated in MS.

Of Counsellors and their Properties.

þat þou wille amende hire conseiH, ffor þanne þay shaH despyse *Listen to what they advise.*
þe. Attempre þanne yn þy sawle þaire wyl, as þe brayne doiþ
of þat þat commys to hym of wyt, And bowe fro þaire conseiH *Do what you think best.*
4 ¹in þat, þat þey be contrarye to þy wyl; And þarfore Hermo- ¹ Fol. 32 a.
genes sayde, whenne he was askyd, whether was better, þe doom
of hym þat geuys conseiH or askys conseiH, And he answerde,
" þe dom of þe Askand conseiH ys a spye of þe wyl," and þis ys *Hermogene's advice on*
8 a soth word; þarefore whenne þou assemblys hem to gyf a *asking counsel.*
conseil in þy presence, meH noght with hem anoþer conseiH, But
here whare-ynne þay accordeþ to-gedir; If þey answere þe hastly *Do not let your coun-*
& þay acorde sone to-gedyr, arrest hem yn þat and shewe hem *sellors decide too hastily.*
12 þe contrary, þat þayre þoght be maad lenger & taryed to þe
laste þynkynge of þe conseiH. Whenne þou hauys persayued
þe ryghtwysnesse of conseiH yn here wordys, or ellys yn þe
wordes of any of hem, make it be holdyn hool, and shewe hem *Don't let*
16 noght where-ynne þy wyl ys sett to it be shewyd yn dede & in *them guess your mind.*
preue; And byholde sotilly who ledys most euyn to rightwyse
conseiH, and þat after þe mesure of loue þat he hauys to ȝowe,
and to þe desyr of ȝowre welfare ressayue his conseiH, so noþeles
20 þat þou sette noght oon afore anoþer, But make hem oon yn *Don't make them jealous*
gyftes & in degres, and yn aH hir wyrkynges; ffor what ys moor *of one another.*
distrucciou) of werkys of a kynge in lengh of dayes & of tyme,
þan to shewe to some of his vpberers more worschipe þan to þe
24 oþer? And it ys noght inconuenient þinge hole conseiH of a *Don't despise the counsel of*
ȝonge man). And y say þe, þat Iugement folwys þe body, ffor *young men.*
whenne a body ys feble, þe Iugement ys feble.

Cap. 97. [Off byholding engenderures.]

28 Also, and it is to byholde, in some engenderures & lyu, ffor *You should look at the*
ofte-sithes he, þat ys engendryd, ys disposed or ordeyned after þe *planetary schemes of*
kynde of planetys þat er yn his engendrure, And yf it faH, *your coun- sellors.*
by auenture, þat þe engenderours of þe engendre lere hym any
32 craft, þe kynde of þe þinges abown) shaH drawe hym) soueraynly
to þe craft þat accordes to hem; ffor so it byfeH a semblable
þinge to some þat assemblyd yn a toune, & herberd hem yn a *The tale of the weaver's*
webbe hous, to whom þat nyght a child was born), And vpon *son:*
36 his engendrure þey took and ordeyned his planetys, and þey
fand him engendryd yn þe planetys of Venus & Mars, yn þe
degre of Gemeals with Balance, and he hadde no sterre vpsprongyn þat was euyl no contrary; so his engendrure shewyd hem

¹ Fol. 32 b.
Born to be wise and courtly:

who would learn:

and became a great counsellor.

The King's Son of India:

Who would be a Smith.

þat þe ¹child sholde be wys, & curteys, of² [swift] honde & of
wys consciħ, And þat he sholde be wel belouyd of kynges. But
þai layned it to his ffader. þe child wax yn prosperite, And his
fadyr and his modir pyned hem to lere hym som craft of here 4
wyrkynges, But þay myghte lere hym no-þing at aH; wharfore
þey bet him, and skowryd hym grevously, and at þe laste þai
leet hym goo at his wille, And he 3ons put him to folk of dis-
ceplyne, and he gat sciences, & knew cours and tyme vpon) 8
heuenly þinges, & maners and gouernaiH of kynges, and after
bycome a greet conseyller. AH þe contrary byfeH of þe merueyl-
lous werkynges and ordinance of þe planetys and her kyndes,
þat byfeH to two sones of þe kyng of Inde born) on oon day to 12
þe comparison of þe engendrynge; But it was laynyd to his
ffadyr. And whenne þe oon was waxyn, þe kyng thothte to do
lere him vpon) sciences, and sende hym þourgh Inde and oþer
contrec3 worschipfully, as it byfeH to þe sone of swylk a kyng. 16
But it profyted noght, ffor he myghte noght bowe hys kynde
but to þe craft of fforgynge; Wharof þe kyng was mekyH
drobyld, and assemblyd aH þe wyse men of his kyngdom, and
whanne þey were aHe aresonyd herof, þay accordyd in oon, þat 20
kynde ledde so þe chyld. So ofte sithes yn þe self manere it
fallys, as ofte it preuyd.

Cap. 98. [To dyspys noght lytyll stature.]

Despise not wise men of small stature.

Treat all such equally well.

Counsel is sight of things that are to come.

And þarefore dyspys noght lytyH stature of men) whom þou 24
sees lone sciences, and er habundant yn wayes of wyt, & thewes,
and eschewes þe fylth of vyces. Loue swylk, and holde hem
negħ to þe, whenne þou persayues hem coragous yn swylk vertus,
ffor swylk er customyd to be wel spekyng, wel taght, curteys, and 28
good storyers, knowyng of þy predycessours. Sette none byfore
no byhynde anoþer with-outen) conseyH, But drawe þe company
of hym to þe, þat louys treuthe, & þat þat fallys to a real magestee,
þat er fast of wyl, stabyld of herte, trewe to þe, and rightwys to 32
þy subgit3; ffor wete þou, þat þys conseiH adressys þy vpberers,
and ordeynes þy kyngdom, and þey þat er contrary to þys, put
hem away. Put noght byfore þat sholde be byhynde, ne be-
hynde þat sholde be byfore, ne do no þinge withoute þe consceyH 36
of Philosophye, ffor ffylosophers sayen) þat conseiH is sight³ of
þinges þat er to come.

² A blank here in MS.   ³ "caght" in MS.

Cap. 99. [How þe kyng awe to ask conseyll.]

¹And it ys foundenꝺ yn þe wrytinges of Persyens, þat oon of her kynges askyd conseyll of his vpberers of right a pryue þyng, and it was shewyd to hem þat he louyd mekyll, And he was answerd þus of oon of hem: "It nedys noght þat a kyng aske conseyll of vs, of any of his pryue doynges, But þat he aske seuerally of some his conseill, ffor yn pryue conseils er swyk þinges shewed to oon, þat byfore many or mo shold noght be shewyd"; þarfore y say, It nedys noght þat þys be doon yn alle doynges, But it nedys be doon with consideracion, and þat þay be callyd to þy presence yn þaire propertes, yn byndynge, & vnbyndynge, as byfore ys sayd. ffor oon olde ffhilosopher seith, þat þe wyt of a kynge ys helpyd by his vpberers, as þe see waxis by þe receyt of fflodes and waters; And þat he may conquere many þinges by queyntyse and conseill, þat he sholde noght haue by myght of bataill. It is sent yn þis wordes yn a Book of Mede to his sone: "Sone, greet myster ys to þe, to haue conseill, þat ys oon amonge men. Conseill þanne with hym þat of myght may deliuere þe, & spare noght þyn enemy. But yn eueryche tyme þat þou mowe shewe þy victorye yn hym, kepe þe out of þe myght of þy enemy."

Marginalia: ʳ Fol. 33 a. A King asked counsel concerning the deeds of a favourite queen; and was reproved by one of his counsellors. A king's wisdom is increased by the counsel of his servants. The Mede's counsel to his son.

Cap. 100. [Off putting vpberers in þe kyngs stede.]

And þat þe abundance of þy wyt, in þy hopynge, no þe hynesse of þy state disturbe þe noght in þy self, But all dayes putte oþer conseill to þyn, ffor some oþer conseill ys profitable, & embrace it yf þe lyke it, and þyn awen conseill dwelle ay to þy self. And if it disacorde to þy demynge, þanne it ys to þe to loke whether it be helpand and profytable, and after þy deuys enbrace it, & if it be noght profytable, leue it vterly. Besily and vnderstandandly y amonest þe, and gyues þe good conseill, þat þou putte noght any of þyne vpberers gouernour yn þi stede, ffor þanne myght his conseill destrue & putte to meschef þy kyngdom, & both hegh and lawgh, & to gyf entent to his awen profyt, and to study on þy vndoynge. If þou fynde noght ffyue vpberers þat be lykynge to þe yn þe manere afore-sayd, Puruey þe of thre worthy and no lesse, ffor greet good shal come þareof, þat ys to say of tho thre, ffor yf mor certeyn þing nowere it sholde noght be knowyn. ²Þe firste þing vpon whom alle þinges dwellys is trinite, and by ffyue er ledde, & by scuen full maad,

Marginalia: Always have other people's advice, no matter whether you take it or no. Do not put any of your counsellors in your own place. If you cannot find five, do not have less than three. ˢ Fol. 33 b.

The excellences of the number seven.

ffor seuen) heuens er, and seuen) planctys, & seuen) dayes, and þe cercuyt of þe moone ys seuen), and dayes of drynkynge or of medicyn er seuen), & dayes Periodies er seuen), and many oþer þinges bylonges to þe nombre of seuen), þat were longe to telle. 4

Cap. 101. ¹Off Prudence to assaye a Conseller.

This is how to test your counsellor.

Oon þinge ys wherby þou mowe assay þy consciller; If þou shewe þat þou hauys defaute of hauynge, And if he conseille þe to lytelynge of þi þinges þat þou hauys in tresour, & he say þat þat nedys þe, wete þou þat he puttys yn þe no good lernynge. And if he lede þe to take þe hauynge of þy subgit3, þat shal be a corupcion) of þy gouernance, And þay shaH hate þe as dys- 8

If he offers to give up his own goods, he is trustworthy.

mesure. And if he profre þe þat he hauys, and says, "þis ys þat y haue of þy grace and of þy lordschipe getyn, & here y offre it to 3ow," and geuys 3ow yt; He þis ys by right to be praysed, and worthy of greet prys, As he þat chesys his confu- sion) for þy glorye. Þou shall assay þy porteours in gyftes & 12

Don't trust the proud and covetous.

rewardes, And him þat þou sees stout and prowd ouer mesure, trowe neuer good yn him, þat þinkes to gedyr mekyH hauynge, and to kepe tresour; haue neuer trist on him, ffor he seruys but for gold aH-oon, And he latys hauynge ryn with wyttes of men). 20 And also he ys as a wele withouten) grounde, and also yn him ys noþer terme ne ende; ffor þe more hauyng þat grewys on hym, þe more ys his besynesse and his entent to gete more. 16

They often bring a realm to ruin.

And swilk þing ys vndoynge of a kyngdome by many skyls; ffor it myghte byfaH þat þe loue and þe brynnynge to his hauynge myghte cause þy deth, or to anoþer to whom he geuys his entent þerto; And þerfore it ys a nedfuH þinge þat þy porteour be 24

Don't let your counsellor deal with other kings.

noght farre out of þy presence, & bydde hym þat he drawe noght to oþer kynges, and þat he rede hem no sende hem no letters ne tydinges; And if þou persayue any swylk þing yn him, remewe him withoute taryinge, ffor corages er swyft to euyl, & lightly bowen) to contrarious willes. And loke þat þy 28

See that they consult your interest and honour.

porteours be couenable, & þat þey loue þy lyf, & be obedient to þe, ffor þis ys þe þinge þat moost ledys subgit3 to loue þe, & puttys his persone, & his goodes to þi aboundon), & plesaunce, & þat haues þe vertu3 & þe maners þat y shaH neuen) þe. 36

¹ This is at the top of fol. 33 *b* in MS.

Cap. 102. [1]**ffyuetene Vertueȝ off a good Conseiller.** [1] Fol. 34 a.

At þe firste þat he haue perfeccion̄ of his membrys, þat hym nedys to werkys ffor whom, & to whilk, he ys chosyn. On þe oþer syde, þat he be goodly to withholde, and willed to vnder-stonde, þat men sayen to hym; þe þridde, þat he be of good mynde to holde þat he herys, and þat he be noȝht forȝetfull; þe fferthe, þat he loke to, and be persayuant, whenne nede shal fall, as y afore haue sayd; þe ffyfte, þat he be curtays, and of fayr speche, and of swet tonge, acordant to þe hert and þe þouȝht, and þat he be of renable speche; þe sext part, þat he be knowynge yn all sciences, and namely in arsmetyk, þat is ful soth and shewable; wharof of kynde ys drawyn þe seuent part, þat he be sothfast of wordes, and louyng treuth, and fle lesynge, and þat he be wel ordeyned, of softe maners, & debonere, and tretable. Þe viij⁰ part, þat he be with-outen þe tecch of en-grotury, and dronkynnesse, & leccherye, bowynge fro playes and delyces. Þe ix⁰ part, þat he be of greet corage yn purpos, and louynge honurabilite. Þe x⁰, þat gold, and siluer, and all swylk accident þinges of þe world, be dispysable to hym, And þat his purpos and his entent be noȝht put in þinges, þat fallys to worthynesse and gouernaill, and þat he euen deme negh & ferre. Þe xj⁰, þat he deme and enbrace riȝhtwysse, and riȝht-wysnesse, and þat he hate wronges & trespas, ȝeldand to vche man þat ys his, helpynge to hem þat suffren disease and wronges, and þat he remewe alle Iniurys, and þat he make no difference in þe persones, no in þe degreeȝ of men þat god hauys maad euen. Þe xij⁰, þat he be of stalworth and lastyng purpos yn þinges þat he seeȝ to be doon, and hardy with-outen drede and fayntnesse of corage. Þe xiij⁰, þat he knowe alle þe issues of þi despensȝ, and þat no þinge be hidde to hym þat fallys to þe kyngdome, and þat þe subgitȝ pleyne hem noȝht in þat, þat he mowe auaille, But in cas sufferable. Þe xv⁰, is þat he be no Iangelour, no ouer mekyll laghenge, [2]ffor attemprance plesys mekyll þe folk; But þat he shewe hym curteys to men, & debonerly tretand. Þe laste, þat he be of þe nombre of hem þat eschewen synnys and vyces, And þat his court be opyn to all suruenantȝ, and þat he be entendant to enquere tidynges of all þinges þat mowe comforte subgitȝ, & to adresse þaire werkys, &

(1) He must be perfect in body:
(2) clear of apprehension:
(3) of good memory:
(4) thoughtful:
(5) courtly and affable:
(6) skilled in sciences, especially arithmetic:
(7) truthful:
(8) sober:
(9) courageous:
(10) not covetous:
(11) a lover of justice:
(12) strong and persevering:
(13) careful and economical:
(14) taciturn:
(15) accessible and kind, &c.

[2] Fol. 34 b.

do hem solas in aduersyte, and som tyme vpberand and sufferand
þaire symplenesse.

Cap. 103. [Þat man ys þe lesse werld.]

Wete þat god hauys maad no creature mor wys þan man,
and þat he gedrys in no þing þat sawle hauys, þat he gedyrs yn
him, ffor þou shaH fynde yn no beste, costom no maner, þat þou
ne shaH fynde yn him, ffor man ys hardy as a lyoṅ, dredful as
a hare, large as a Cokke, auerous as hounde, hard and feH as a
krowe, pytous as turtyH, malicious as lyons, ptyue and hamely
as douve, queynte & trecherous as ffox, symple and softe as
lombe, swyft and stirrand as goote, wayk and sleuthfuH as Bere,
Precious and dere as Elyfaunt, vyleyns and boystous as asse,
rebeH as a rambe, obedient and meke as Poo, ffoltisch as
[ostrich], profitable as a Bee, and vnstable as Goot, Proud as
Bole, sterrand as fyssh, Resonable as Angelee, leccherous as
swyn, cuyltaght as Owle, Conable as hors, noyand as Mouse; &
haly to speke, þer ys no best, no thynge vegetable, no originale,
no noumbrable, no heuene, no Planete, no tokenyng, no non
oþer þinge beynge, of alle þinges þat ere, þat some properte of
hem er founden in man. Wherfore man ys callyd þe lesse
world.

Man unites in himself all the qualities of a lion, hare, cock, dog, crow, turtle, lioness, dove, fox, lamb, kid, bear, elephant, ass, wren, peacock, ostrich, bee, goat, bull, fish, angel, swine, owl, horse, mouse.

Cap. 104. [Noght to haue trist yn man þat trowys noght þy lawe.]

And neuer haue trist yn man þat trowys noght þy lawe, þat
it faH noght to þe as it fille to twoo men þat felawschipped
hem to gedre in a way, of whom oon was oon enchauntere of þe
orient, þe oþer a Iewe; þe enchauntere rade on his Mule, þat he
hadde taght at his likynge, þat bar him whanne him mysteryd
by þe way; þe Iew wente on foote, and hadde nother mete ne
drynke, no oþer þinge þat hym neded, with him; And as þey
wente spekynge to-geder by þe way, þe Enchantere sayde to þe
Iew, "Whiche ys þy fayth, and þy lawe?" And he answerd
hym, "I trowe þat in heuen ys oon god, þat y worschippe,
and of him y holde [1]goodnesse and thankynges to my sawle,
and also to hem þat er of my lawe, of my fayth, and of my
byleue; and it ys lefuH to me to shede þe blood of him þat
acordys noght to my lawe, and take fro him his hauyng, and
aH þat fallys to him, wyf, ffader & Modre, and childryn. And

Have no trust in misbelievers.

Hear this tale of an Enchanter and a Jew.

The Magus was rich, the Jew poor.

They questioned each other of their law.

[1] Fol. 35 a.

The Jew said he was good to all Jews:

ouer þat, it ys holdyn to me a malysoñ if y holde hym fayth, *and kept faith with no other sort of man.*
or do him helpe, or any mercy, or if y spare him ought. Now
haue y shewyd þe my ley and my fey; make me now certeyn
4 of þy ley and þy fey." And he answerd hym, "My fey, My *The Magus said, "I do good to all men:*
byleue, and my ley, er þes; I wyll first good to myself, and
to þe sones of my lynage, and y wille non euyl to any godys
creature, no to hem þat folwyn my ley, no to hem þat dysa-
8 cordys with me, And y beleue, þat euenheed & mercy er to be
kepyd & holdeñ yñens vche man lenynge; no manere of wronge
lykes me; And me þynk if any euyl fall to any leuyng man, þat *If any living man is hurt, it is an evil to me.*
þat euele fallys to me, & troblys me, ffor y desire welfare, helth,
12 stryngth, and goodnesse, all holely to come to[1] vche mañ."
Þanne sayde þe Iew, "What if any man do to þe wronge, or
wreth þe?" þe Enchantere sayd, "I woot þat god ys yn heuene *If he hurts me, God will reward all men."*
rightfull, good, and wys, to whom no þinge ys hydde, ne no priue
16 þynge, ne no þing layned, þat rewardes þe good after hir goodnesse, & þe wyckyd and þe trespassours after her trespas." And
þe Iew sayde to him, "Why kepys þou noght þy ley and þy fey *The Jew said, "Give me your horse, since I am weary."*
yn þe werkes as þou confermes?" "In what manere?" sayde
20 þe enchantere. And þe Iew answerd & sayde, "y am a sone
of þy lynage, and þou seeȝ me goon on foote hungry and wery,
And þou art on horsse, hool and wel at ese." "Þat ys soth,"
sayde þe Enchantere, and lightyd doun of his Mule, & opynd
24 his male, and gaf him mete & drynke, and after he gart hym
styrt vp and ryde, and after [þe Iew] was byfore rydant, and
straak þe Mule with þe spores, and hastyd hym to forsake his *Then he rode off and left the Magus alone in the desert.*
felaw, and he cryed after him and sayde, "abide me, I am negh
28 shent of goynge." And þe Iewe sayde, "shewed I þe nogh my
ley, and þe manere þerof? I will now also fulfylle hit." And he
peyned him to hasty þe Mule, And þe oþer folwynge after cryde
and sayde, "O Iew, leue me noght yn þys desert, þat lyouns
32 deuoure me noght, ne þat I dye for hunger and [2]sorwfull threst, [2] Fol. 85 b.
But do mercy to me, as y haue don to þe." Þe Iew wolde noght
loke aȝeyn, no gyf entent to his sawes, But he cesyd noght, to
he was passyd his sight; And whenne þe Enchantere was yn
36 despayr of alle socours, he bythoghte hym of þe perfeccioun of *So the Magus called to God the rightful judge.*
his ley & of his fey, and of þat þat he sayde to þe Iew, þat in
heueñ was on god rightfull Iuge, to whom in creatures no þing
ys hidde, ne no pryue þing layned. He lyft vp his hondes to þe

[1] MS. *de*

"Confirm my heuen", and sayde, "God þat sauyst hem þat tristyn yn þy lawe,
praise of Thee
to this Jew." & shewys þe holy yn þy comandementȝ, conferme my louynge
in þe, ynens þis Iew"; after whenne he hadde sayd þys, he
Soon he wente noght ferre yn þe way; he fand þe Iew, cast of his Mule, 4
found the Jew
in evil case. & bette, and his thee brokyn, and his nekke cuyl hurt. And þe
Mule on þe oþer syde stood on farre; and whenne he saw his
meyster, by kynde techinge he com negh toward hym, and he
styrt vpon him, and he lefte þe Iew sorwand, and he departyd 8
fro hym. But þe Iew cryed after him, And sayde, "ffayr
broþer, for goddys sake, haue now mercy vpon me." And þe
The Magus Enchantere bygan þanne gretly to blame, & sayde him, þat he
reproved him,
leffyd him withouten mercy, and þat he hadde greuously synned 12
but the Jew vpon him; And þe Iew sayde to him, "repreue me noght of
said, "I have
done nothing þing passyd, ffor y shewyd þat þat was my lawe & my fayth, yn
but my religi-
ous duty." whom y am norshyd, & my kennysmen and ancestres yn þe
self lawe dwellyd, And here y dwelle all to-ffrushyd, & y haue 16
gret myster of pytee; haue mercy on me, for þe obseruance of
þy lawe, þat hauys geuyn to þe victorye vpon me." Þe En-
The Magus chanter hadde eft vpon him pytee, & bare hym byfore hym to
had mercy
on him, þe stede ordeyned, and bytoght hym to his ffolk; but he dyed 20
with-ynne a short while, And þe kyng of þat Citee whanne he
herde þe doynges of þat Enchanteour, he clepyd him afore him,
and was and for his pityuous doynges, and for þe goodnesse of his lawe,
brought to
great honour. he ordeyned him oon of his Conseillers. Louynge be to god, of 24
þis þing ys Ende.

Book V. Cap. 105. **To chese a Qweynte Scryueyn and Pryue.**

¹ Fol. 36 a. ¹It ys nedfull to þe, chese a sotell man, þat hauyn most stal-
Be careful in
the choice of worth tokenyng, and most rechand argument, to shewe þe quan- 28
your scribe.
tyte of þy hynes; ffor bytokenynge or enterpreteyson of wordes
ys so as þe esprit of word, and þe endytynge ys þe body, and þe
wrytynge ys þe clethynge of wordys and spekynge. And right
as þe nedys be, a man stryngtyd in substance, of fair beholdyng 32
and of ornementȝ, Al-so it fallys þat þou chese of wyse men &
He should be of Skreueyns, sweche þat hauyn perfeccion of enournede elo-
eloquent;
quence, & of sotyll record; And right as þe Skryueyn ys enterpretour of þy wyl, and ys ordeyned for þy consilles and 36
and faithful. priuyteeȝ, So it nedys þat he be of good ffayth, and of lele
knowynge of þy wyl, and in alle þy wirkynges, And þat he
besye hym to þy profyt and to þy worschipe, as it semys. And

Book VI. The Choice of Messengers. 107

it nedys þat he be qweynte and warre yn his werkys, and non   *He should be cautious.*
entre and byholde hys pryue wrytynges. And it fallys þat þou
mede his werkys, aftyr his seruyce þat he doos to þe, and þat he
4 laste curious yn þy gouernaiH, after þe terme sett of þy wyl. *Reward him well.*
Put hym þanne yn þe degree of þin auance3, ffor his properte
ys þin, and his corupcion þyn.

Book VI. Cap. 106. To teche a Messagere.

8   Wete ouer aH þinges þat þe Messager, whedyr þou sendys *Ambassadors are your eyes,*
hym, shewys þe wyt of þe, þat sendys hym, and he ys þyn eghen, *ear, and tongue in*
yn þat þat þou seest nogHt, and þyn ere, yn þat þat þou heryst *places where you are not.*
nogHt, and þy tonge, where þou art absent. Þanne þe nedys to
12 chese þe most worthy to sweche a seruyce, of hem þat er in þy
presence, wys and willynge, honourablyte, vnderstondynge, lele,
and eschewand ouer, fleand aH velanye and blame. And 3if þou *Choose among your*
fynde sweche oon, clepe hym to þe, and speke with hym of *best seruants.*
16 þinges þat he knowys nogHt of þy wyl, And þou shaH sone persayue, if it be yn him þat þou enquerys, ffor aH sone as þinges
ffonden he ys to be enhyed; And if he be nogHt in þis deter-
minynge, at þe leste be he to þe trewe secretary, no þinge addand,
20 no letiland, in þinges þat þou sendys hym, and þat he kepe wel
þy comandement, & þat he gyf good entent of þat þat he berys
of answers þat men makys hym. And if þou ¹fynde non ¹ *Fol. 30 b.*
swylke, be he nopeles a trew berere of þy lettres to hem þat þou *He must, at worst, be a*
24 sendyst hem, bryngand and telland þe answers a3eyn. And if *faithful messenger.*
þou persayue any of þy Messagers corious, and besy to gete
hauynge, and to geder hem yn þe places þat þou sendys hym,
Refuse hym vtterly. And also if þou see any Messager dronke- *Be not serued by drunk-*
28 lew, for þai er nogHt sent to þy profyt, ffor þe Persiens whenne *ards.*
any Messager come to hem, bare oon of hem to drynkyn mekyH
wyn; And if he dranke as surfete, þanne wyste þey wel þat his
lord was þe lesse wys. And kepe þe wel, þat þou sende nogHt *Do not send your great*
32 þy gretest conseiller in þy message, ne soffre him nogHt ferre froo *nobles on embassies.*
þe, ffor þat ys distruccion of a kyngdome. Now haue y shewyd
to þe qualyte3, and þe louynges and þe repreuynges of Messagers,
and þaire ordinance, & how þay er knowyn in vntreutH & in
36 good treutH; þanne, whenne a Messager ys nogHt swyche, and *Degrade couetous am-*
castys hym to giftes and rewardes, & tretys witH þe of þinges *bassadors.*
þat þou hauys enIoyned hym, yn þy gouernayH make him lesse.

Book VII. Cap. 107. **To gouerne þy self.**

Your subjects are the source of your wealth. I trowe þat þou hauys now vnderstandyd, þat þy subgitȝ er þe hauynge of þi hous and þi tresour, wherof þi kyngdom is confermed. Lekyn þanne þi subgitȝ to oon orche-ȝerd, þat *They are like an orchard,* hauys diuers trees berynge fruytȝ, and haue noght þare-ynne sedes bryngynge forth wedes and netles, and florysshe noght *and must be tended.* forth fruyt bryngand, ffor trees þat hauyn yn hem many braunches and rotes, and þe stoke vpsette, some of hem makys fruyt & seed couenable to multiplye þaire kynde, whenne þay er wel tylled and kepyd; þanne, after þe quantyte of þy tresour is þe lastyng and þe defens, of þy kyngdom and of þy myȝt. Now *Give good entent to their needs.* it nedys þanne þat þou gouerne hem wel, and þat þou gyf good entent to here nedys, so þat þou remowe fro hem aH þaire wronges. And be it neuer noyous to þe, to geue entent to here [1] Fol. 37 a. statys, no to enquere whare-[1]of þey haue myster, ffor þanne þay shaH haue oon purpos stabyld ynens þe, þat fallys noght to distruccion, but to conuersacion, þat þou ert wel ordeyned, of *If you do not, you encourage rebellion.* maners enfourmed, lastyng, wys, and sufferand; and if þou be noght swyche, þe hertys of þi subgitȝ saH be rebeH to þy gouernaiH, and saH bycome corumpyd by sweche thoghtes, þat byfore wer clene.

4

8

12

16

20

Cap. 108. **[Of expendours.]**

Do not have many stewards of your lands. And make noght many expendours of þin expensys to be maad, ffor þare-by may come to þe corupcion, ffor vche of hem wyH etyH to ouer-passe oþer in Corupcion of wyrkynges, & he shal peyne hym to shewe hym to be praysed and profytable to *They will oppress your subjects.* þe, in oppressioun of þy subgitȝ, And so shaH vche of þy conseillers doo, þat ouer-longe dwellys yn þe office. And many er swyche þat oon sayen, & oþer-wayes doon, and bryngeȝ many to here vndoynge, to may[n]gteyne hem & defende hem.

24

28

Book VIII. Cap. 109. **Off lederes off ostes and here ordinaunce.**

The utility of your Barons. Barouns er helpe and multiplicacion of þe kyngdome, by hem ys þe court honourd and gouerned, & ordeyned yn here degreeȝ. Goode ordinance is þanne yn degreeȝ necessarys, and be noght þe kyndrede vnknowyn to þe, whether þey be negh or farre, in þy ordinance yn þaire nombre. And þis ys þe ordre necessary afore-sette & seyd, nombre & brynge aȝeyn to a Nombre vndyr a Nombre; þanne say I, þat ffourfald ordynance

32

36

ys necessary, ffor vche a stede in erthe ys ffour parte yn his *Have them in fourfold ordinance:* dyfference, afore, byhynde, on þe Right syde and on þe left syde. And also þe kyndes of þe werld er ffoure, Est, West,
4 South, & North; þe ferthe part of þy kyngdome be yn gouernayll to vche a leedyr of þin oste, and if þou wyl moo, be þay tene, *or in tenfold.* ffor tene and foure er perfyt yn nombre, ffor yn ffourhede er *Ten is a perfect number.* oon, two, thre, and ffoure, and if þou geder hem to-gedre þey
8 make tene; þe nombre of ten ys þe perfeccion of hem þat enbracen ffourhede, & vmlappys it yn nombres; ffolwe þanne vche comandour tene[1] vicaires, & vche vicaire tene lederes, & *Let each have ten under him.* vche ledere tene denys, & vche deyn ten men, þanne er all þes
12 to-gedre a hundreth thousand feghtyng men. And whenne þou hauys myster of þe seruyce of tene thousand men, þou salt [2]comande to assemble oon oste, & þore þou sall putte oon *[2] Fol. 37 b.* comandour & tene vicaries, and tene lederes come with vche a *How to summon ten thousand men.*
16 vicayre, & with vche a ledere tene dyens, and with vche a dyen ten men; And þes makyn in somme tene thowsand ffyghtynge men. And yf þou haue myster of a thowsand, Comande oon of *How to summon one thousand:* þe vicaires and come with hym ten leddres, & with vche a
20 leddre ten dyens, & with vche dyen ten fyghtyng men, and alle makys a thowsand[3]; and if þe nede, comande to a dyen ten *or a hundred.* fighting men, and come with vche of hem ten fighting men, so shall þou spare þy vitayle, & þou shall allege þi folk, and þou *By this means your*
24 shalt come to þat þat þou desyres yn þi purpos. And þou shalt *work and expense will be lessened.* allege þy trauaill yn þy hegh men, ffor vche of hem shall gouerne tene vndyr hym yn his degree, and so shall þaire wyrkyng be allegyd in hem. And be þy comandour swyfte, &
28 qweynte, & ordinant; And it nedys to þe Barouns to haue a conyng man, wys, persayuand, lele, & preuyd in knyghthoode, to *The qualities of a war-leader.* take kepynge þat þay be noght corumpyd of gyftes, And þat he besily enquere þaire þinkynges; and whenne þou persayues any
32 swyche þinge in any, remewe hem, and assemble hem, and shew hem þat þou haues ordeyned þaire remouynge; and it nedys þat þou be tretable and curteys, And þat þou dyspise noght oon for oþer.
36 [Cap. 110. **Of the horn of battle.**]

And it nedys þat þou haue with þe þe, Instrument þat *Use the Instrument of Cenustinus.* Cenustinus made to þe vse of þe Hoste; and it ys a dispytous Instrument, þat outspredys it in many maners. Whenne þou

[1] "ffoure" in MS.   [3] "hundrith" in MS.

Book IX. Of the Conduct of Battle.

The great horn of battle.

nedys to vesyte þy Contree and þy kyngdome, and to assemble þy hegh men and þyne ffyghters in þe self day; or soner, or in oþer manere, as þe hoste shall haue myster; þe sounde of þe Instrument ys herd sextyl Mylee. 4

Book IX. Cap. 111. Off auenture off Batoylles.

[1] Fol. 38 a.
Do not risk yourself in battle.

[1] Wille þou noght haunte batailles, and putte þy lyf in auenture. Holwe oft-sithes þe conseill of þe most best manered men of þi court; And ocupye þe noght in þinges þat þei þat ere 8 ouercomen, or blamed, costomes to ocupye hem, vpon vaniteȝ of Batailles. Ne assaye noght, ne haunte noght bataille yn þy propre persone, And þe gretteste with-holde toward þe. Ne ocupy þe noght, no gyf entent to foltisch vndertakynges & 12

You might get killed.

hardynesse, ffor it ys a certeyn þinge þat kynge shal neuer assemble with kynge to-gedir, þat þe oon hauys hope to destruye þe oþer, And þat ys foundyn oft-sithes in kynde. Wete þanne þat enuy ys comynge & risyng, of þe body, and þe sawle, of twoo 16

No one fights without hope of victory.

opposisiouns contrarys, and þaire spryt ys hope & tryst of victory on þe oon syde & on þe oþer. And whenne mys-hope of victory fallys, þanne dyen and cesen batailles; And as longe durys bataill as lastynge to haue victory ys, on þe oon syde or 20

Keep up your men's spirits.

on þe oþer. Be all þy strynght and þyn entent, in lastyng and persoueraunce, and in stabelynge and sustenance of hem þat er of þy lyn; and espyse noght here persones, but speke faire to hem, and hete hem gyftes and worschippes, & ȝelde þy hetynges. 24

Be always armed.

Wende noght in host with oute haberion or quyrre, so þat if þyn enemy fynde þe sodeynly, all þi besynesse and purueyance be to kepe þi-self, of armes, of kepers, of spyes, and of necessary wacche, nyght & day & all tymes. And sette noght þy herbe- 28

Camp near water.

gage, but yn stedes negh & ioynant to hellys or to waters, and lede with þe many vitaylles moo þan þou mysters, and make

Try and frighten your enemies.

many rynnand, & oribles voyces, ffor sweche þinges makyn strynght and vertu to hem þat er with þe, and lastyng to her 32 purpos, and drede & shenshype to her enemys. & vse diuersyte of armes in þi Barouns, some in quarels and arwys, and ordeyne

[2] Fol. 38 b.
Use all kinds of arms.

þe oþer in wenges, & þe stoures all aboute; [2] and whenne þou ordeyns þy wynges to fighte, sende with hem a faire shape, and 36 toures of tree, In whom be armours of shotyng, sendand out brynnynge dartȝ; And if þou fynde hem yn hem, slakand or failland, comforte here hertes and enfourme hem, & ordeyne

Of Battles and Sieges of Walled Towns. 111

hem to perseuerance, as it ys afore sayd. Ordeyne þy wenges, on þe right syde of hem þat strykeɳ and assayllen, and of þe left syde hem þat shoteɳ; And in þe hert, or ellys in þe myddes of *Attack with the right wing.*
4 þi folk, hem þat sendys out brennand brandouɳs, & shotes hem out, & þat maken soundes of orible voyces, and makyn diuers sterynges. And þe stede þat þou fightys on with þy aduersers, be it semynge euer more seker, ffor þarfore shal þyn hoste peyne
8 hem mekyH more to fight, & stalworthly aȝcyn-stonde her enemys; eschewe tresouɳ, & namely whenne þou seeȝ þi aduer- saries forsake þe, & in þat partye dresse þy wenges to bataille, and þare-with putte to hem þy presence ofte-sythes, ffor þat ys *Look out for treason.*
12 a origenaH of victory. Whare fore men were costomed to say þat victory commes of noon, but if þay be ouercomeɳ of ffeyntise of herte. Ouer aH þinges, make many wacches, and assay þy spyes with howge soundes, ffor sweche er of þe nombre of hem *None are conquered till they fear.*
16 þat surmounteɳ and ouercomeɳ. And oon cautele ys þat bryngea to purpos, & oon of þe groundes of Batailles. And haue stedys determynd, appereld in some stede of þe hoste, to socoure & kepe wel þy meɳ with drynke and oþer necessaries; *Have plenty of food and drink:*
20 And haue many bestayle to bere warny stoor to castellys wher þou shalt fyghte, þis er ollyfaunȝ, espontous bestes; And right swyft, as dromyders, yn whom ys hope of flyght at nede, and er as castels. And if þou shaH assayH castels, vse Instrumenȝ *Elephants and dromedaries:*
24 castyng stones, as Mangoles or Perrerers, and make moo of hem after þou hauys mester, and oþer Instrumenȝ perceaunt & lanceaunt, and arwes and dartys enuemynd. And if þou mowe come to welle or stede where þi enemys focchyn water to *Artillery: and poisoned darts.*
28 drynke, caste yn hem venyms, and so þou salt make graues to hem. ¹Kepe in aH þinges stabilnesse, ffor þat ys a fuH louable þing, And so þou shaH fulfylle þy purpos. And folwe neuer moor hem þat fleyen, no be noght ouer-hasty yn þi werkys. *Poison their drinking water.* ¹ Fol. 39 a.
32 And if it mowe be, lat aH þi werkynges be tresoɳ and entrik- ynge to þi aduersers. Kepe þe wel yn þe first bigynnynge & þe endyng of þe batailH of þe folk, ffor þe folk of Iewes er properly traytours & entrykours, & þey haue no shame. þe Persiens & *It is better to cheat than to conquer foes: especially Indians.*
36 þe Turkeys, & þe perseis, er right coraious men, and of gret vndertakynge; þanne fight with vche men yn þe manere þat ys couenable; And make noght þe lesse greet, no sette noght byfore þat ys byhynde, But aH þy werkys be þai, in opyn & *Fight according to what your foes are.*
40 pryuee, yn þe manere afore sayd, And after þe qualyte or þe

112   Book X. Of Physiognomy.

Begin when Leo is in the ascendaut:

and the Moon in good aspect of Mars.

When you set out, start in the ascendaut of the city.

Let Mercury be in mid-heaveu.

¹ Fol. 39 b.

The moon must not be in quadrature with the Sun.

Let Mercury be in good aspect to complete the work.

ordinance of Astronomy, as y haue afore leryd þe. Whenne þou wilt attene to þe stabylnesse of þi purpos by þe ordinance of heuenly vertuȝ, Stable þou þe mountant, or þe vpspryngand, yn þe tokenynge of þe Lyon); And see þat þe mone and his ledere be in his good state, & in goode stede and vpstyand, And stable with þe mountant, or þe hous of þe mountant, yn þe house of Marȝ. And leue noȝht þe siȝht of Marcȝ with-outen triplycite, And byhold, þanne, all þe werkynge wherof þou wille haue þe nature of þe Planetys and here houses; And ordeyn þe self planetys, and þe tokenynges þat er of þe self nature, ffor þat ys þe chef; þanne whenne þou wilt wend, ordeyne mountant to þe way, or þe Cytee, or þe stede whedyr þou etyls, And þe wirk- ynges þat þou etyls, and ynens þat, þat ys þe moste lawnesse of þe erthe; And loko þat þe mone be noȝht wycked, no in eclyspe, no trouble, no vnder þe beem of þe sonne in þe sext or twelf degree, or aȝeyn-goyng, ffor þanne þe mountant shewys victory and prosperite; þe comyng shall be good, and namly whenne Mercurius shall be yn Middes of þe heuene, it shal shewe spedynge of þe werk & perfeccion). And whenne it shal be yn þe seuen) degree, myȝhtynesse of þe werke, and gladnesse, & prosperyte, and it shall shewe fulfillynge of þe purpos. And if it be abown) þe erthe, it shall bitakyn spedys of necessary þinges, & prosperyte of auenture. And loke þat þe mone ¹be noȝht in þe entree of þe way, in þe quarreure of þe sonne, or els yn his contrary. If þou fynde þanne þe vpspryngant or þe mountant in his contrary or quarreure, torne aȝeyn suyftly to þe greeȝ, and þe werk shal wel cheue; And if þou wille vnder- take bataill, ordeyne þe house of þe mone and þe myddes of þe heuen), & Mercury byholdant deuoutly & debonerly; And make Mercury yn þe fferthe degree, & reparaill þe mone, ffor in hold- yng of wayes it ys þe gretteste tokenyng vninersele.

4

8

12

16

20

24

28

Book X. Cap. 112. **Knowynge by diuers tokenynges.** 32

You should also know how to judge men by their outward tokens.

Among oþer þinges þat þe nedys to knowe þe konyng þat þe sawle folowys and knowys by noble tokenynges, whenne it ys drawyn fro dysirs and coueytis, And whenne it ys deliured of noysance, and þis diuision) ys knowyn by þoȝhts. ffor whenne [it] ys surmontant, and holdys lordschipe vpon þe body, þat greuys him, And a flawmyng vertu dwellys yn þe hert, & he holdys him to þe vertu of þe sawle þat ys yn þe harnes; þanne is þe

36

vnderstondyng helpyd, enhyed, and maad liȝtyd, after mesure.
Wharfore, if any aske þe encheson of þe clene vnderstondynge *These are influenced by the stars.*
of prophetes, wharof þai er approuyd and liȝtned, and of þaire
4 trew diuisiouns of natureles meruailles, wete þat it come to hem,
abown all oþer þinges, by þe accordance of þe sterres, þat er
clepyd þe constellacion of engendrure, folowynge þe vertu
generatyue, so as þe nedys to enquere þe tokenynges & þe *Learn the science of physiognomy.*
8 folwynge with þe ffayrhede of kynde, þat ys to wete þo science
of phisonomy, þat ys a ful greet science; And þe olde philosophers vsyd it by longe werldes, & þay made hem glorious in þe
enquerynge of fayrnesse of nature yn þis science; Of whom þe per-
12 feccioun of þe fore-sayd science ys ȝeuyn to a souerayn doctour of *Polemon was a great master of this science.*
þe olde philosophers, Philomen, Meistre of Phisonomy, þat atret-
ably folwyd of þe composision of man þe qualiteȝ and þe [1] natures *[1] Fol. 40 a.*
of his sawle; & he goth yn þe selue story, ffayre and straunge.
16 Vpon þis, wete þat þe discyples of wys ypocras peyntyd his *The disciples of Hippocrates tried to prove him.*
ffigure in perchemyn, and broȝt it to Philomen, and saide,
"byholde þys ffourme, and shewe vs þe qualiteȝ of his complexion;" and he byholdyng þe composicion and þe ordinance
20 of þe ffygure & of þe partyes, he lyknede þe partyes and saide:
"þis man ys lychcrous, deceyuant, and loufand lecherye." And *He judged evil of his character:*
þe disciples wolde haue slayn hym þerfore, and sayde, "O
foltisch man, þis ys þe ffygure of þe most worthy & best man of
24 þis werld." Philomen þanne apesyd hem, & chastisde, & sayde,
"þis ys þe ffygure of wys ypocras; whare-tyll haue ȝe askyd me
þerof? I haue shewyd ȝow aftyr my science, þat y fele by þe
ffygure." And after, whenne þay come to ypocras and sayde
28 him, what þat þey hadde done, and what Philomen sayde to hem,
and his Iugement, Ypocras answerd hem, "Certaynly, he sayde *and Hippocrates justified him:*
al soth to ȝow, & he passyd noȝht a lettre þerof. Noþelees,
sythen þat y saw and vnderstood þat þey were fowle þinges and
32 dampnable, I makyd my sawle kynge vpon it self, and y with- *and told how he conquered himself.*
drew me, & ouercome my self, for to withholde my couetyse." þis
is þe louynge & þe wyt of wys ypocras werkys, ffor Phisyke ys
non oþer þinge but abstinence & victory of couetable þinges.
36 Now y stable to þe reules of þis science of Phisonomy & con- *Now you shall learn the rulesof Physiognomy.*
stitucions suffyceantȝ abbreggyd, þat shal be greet profyt to
þe, and lerynge of nobleye of kynde, and in clennesse of þy
substance.

SECRETE. I

Cap. 113. [Off colour.]

Of men of light colour.

Wete þanne forsothe þat þe modere marriȝ ys riȝht swych to þe seede þat it conseyues, as þe pot þat ys resseyt of sethinge; þanne if it shewe it whit with ȝalowe colour & blew, It bytoknys þat it ys to lytell sothyn, þanne if sweche a diminucion) byfall yn a creature, his kynde also shall be lessenyd to hym. ¹þanne kepe þe fro a man þat kyndly is ȝalow and blew, ffor sweche er liȝhtly stirryd to vyces and licchery.

[margin: ¹ Fol. 40 b.]
Of yellow-tinted men.

4

8

Cap. 114. [Off byholdyng.]

Signs of a man who loves you.

If þou see a man oft-sithes byholdyng þe, & if þou byholde hym, and he be abayst and siȝhe, & teres shewe hem yn his eȝhen), Trowe of sweche oon þat he louys þe, and dredys þe; And if he doo contrary, holde hym enuyous and despytous.

12

Cap. 115. [Off þe mysauentrous.]

Beware of deformed men.

Also kepe þe fro vche mysauentrous man), þat ys lesnyd of any membre, and eschewe hym as enemy.

16

Cap. 116. [Off attemprance.]

The man who is evenly attempered.

Oon euenn) creature and attempre, þat acordys him to meen) stature, with blak eȝhen) & heer, & rounde chere; of whit colour mengyd with Reed & brown), þe body of riȝht and euen) stature, of a meene heued bytwen greet and lytill, latly spekyng but mystere be, and holdys him in a mene voys yn his spekynge: And ouer all, whenne nature bowys him to blaknes with ȝalownes; þanne ys þe attemprance good, and þis creacion) be lykyng to þe; hym haue þou with þe. And y make to þe oon enterpreteysoun by manere of departyng, And attempre þou it by riȝhtwysnesse of vnderstondynge.

20

24

Have him about you.

Cap. 117. [Of heer of men.]

28

Much hair and soft:

Many heres and softe bytoknys pesabilyte, and coldnesse of þe brayn. Greet multitude of heer vpon) bothe þe shuldres bytokyns ffoltynesse. Many heres in þe brest or in þe wombe bytokyns horibilyte & singularyte of kynde, & lessenyng of þe resceyt, and loue of wronges. Reed colour ys tokenynge of vnwyt, & of greet Ire, and of awaytes; And blake heer shewen) riȝhtwysnesse, and loue of riȝht. And þe menee colour bytwen) þes two colours, bytoknys loue of pees.

Red hair:
Black hair:

32

36

Cap. 118. [Of eghen.]

And he þat hauys greet eghen) ys enuyous & with-outen shame, slouthful, and vnobeyssant. He þat hauys lityll eghen), 4 lyk to heuenly colour, or blake, ys of sharpe vnderstondynge, curteys, and leel. He þat hauys steepe-owt eghen ys malicious & feloun. He þat haues eghen lyk to þe eghen [1] of a asse, ys vnwytty, and of hard kynde. He þat his eghen) steryn swyftly, 8 and haues a sharpe sighte, sweche oon is trechour, thef, & vntrewe. If eghen) be Reed, he þat hauys hem ys coraious, stalworth, and myghty. Þe werste eyen aren) þat hauyn spottys, whit, or blak, or reed, on all sydes, ffor sweche a man ys werst 12 of alle oþer, and most vicious.

marginalia: Great eyes: Little eyes: Red eyes: the worst of all.

[1] Fol. 41 a.

Cap. 119. [Of browes.]

Browes þat hauyn many heer bytoknys euyl manere of spek- ynge; And whenne þay reche to þe temples, he ys fowl þat 16 berys hem, And he þat hauys his browes departyd yn lengh and shortnesse, in mesure and er greet, sweche er of light vnderstondyng.

marginalia: Thick brows.

Cap. 120. [Of nees.]

20 A nose þat ys þynne bytoknys his lord ful Irous; and he þat hauys a long nose rechinge to þe mouth, ys prow and hardy. And he þat hauys a greet nose ys hastyf, And a nose þat hauys nosesterles oft greuant, & harde openynge, is Irous. And whenne 24 þe oon syde of þe nose yn þe myddes bowes toward þe heyghte, his berer ys a Ianglere, and a lyere. And he þat in nose ys most euyn, þat is yn meene long, of mene makynge yn þe ende, and hauys noght his nose-sterlys ouer greet.

marginalia: Long noses. The best nose.

Cap. 121. [Of face.] Of mouth.

28 A full fface, withouten) bolnyng, bytokyns a stryuer, a dyscordour, wrongys, and fowl. He þat hauys a mene fface, in chekys, and templys, bowynge to Lennesse, ys sothfast, louynge, 32 & vndyrstondyng, wys, and seruysable, wel ordeyned, & engynous. He þat hauys stalworth armes ys ffyghter & hardy; And he þat hauys greet lyppes ys ffoltysch, And þat is right full of flesch in þe vysage, ys vnwys, enuyous, and leghere; And he 36 þat hauys a lene vysage, ys wys yn his werkys, & of sotyll vndirstondynge. And he þat hauys a lityll fface, bowynge

marginalia: A full face. A good face. Great lips. A lean face.

toward ȝalownesse, ys wycked, and euyl-techyd, deceyuant,
and dronkelew. And he þat hauys right a longe vysage, ys
wrongwys.

A long visage.

Cap. 122. [Of þe temples.] 4

And he þat hauys bolnynge temples, and full chekys, ys ful Irous.

Full temples.

Cap. 123. [Of þe eres.]

He þat hauys right greet eres ys full ffoltysch, sauynge þat 8
he ys of good witholdynge, and of good mynde. And he þat
hauys right lytill eres ¹he shall be foltysch, thef, and leccherous.

Great ears.

¹ Fol. 41 b.

Cap. 124. [Of voyces.]

He þat hauys a greet voys, and wel sownand, shal be a 12
fyghter, and wel-spekand; And he þat hauys a meene voyce,
noþer ouer greet, ne ouer small, ys wys, purueyant, sothfast, and
rightwys. He þat ys hastyf yn wordys, namly if he haue a
small voys, ys dronkelew, enuyous, and lyer; and if his voys 16
be right greet, he ys Irous,² [hasty], and of euyl nature. He
þat hauys a swete voys, shall be enuyous, & suspect, ffor
fayrhede of voys shewys folye, and vnwyt, and greet wyll.

Loud voices.

Hasty speakers.

A sweet voice.

Cap. 125. [Of mouynge of body.] 20

He þat ofte-sithes is steryd, and with spekyng sterys his
hondes, he ys fowl, eloquent, and deceyuant; And he þat withholdys him to sterre his hondes, ys perfyt of vnderstondynge,
wel disposyd, and of hool conseill. 24

Much gesture.

Little gesture.

Cap. 126. [Of þe Throte.]

He þat hauys a longe necke, he shall be of good sound, but
foltisch ys he; And he þat hauys a short necke, ys queynte,
and deceyuant, engynous in euyl, & trechour; And he þat hauys 28
a greet necke, ys foltysch, and mekyll etynge.

Long neck.

Short neck.

Cap. 127. [Of þe wombe: of þe sholders.]

He þat hauys a greet wombe, ys vndiscreet, foltysch, proud,
and leccherous. Meenesse of wombe, with a streyt brest, by- 32
tokyns heyenesse of vnderstondyng, and of good conseill.
Broodnesse of brest, and greetnesse of sholdres and bak, bytokyns prowesse, and hardynesse, with witholdynge of wyt, and
vndyrstondynge; And a thynne bake and wayk, bytoknys a 36

The tokens of the belly:

and of the breast.

² A blank in MS.

Of Arms, Hands, Feet, and Knees.

man of discordant nature. Meenesse of brest and bak, & euen- *High shoulders.*
heed, ys good tokenyng, and preuyd. Vpraysyd shuldren)
bytoknys sharpe nature, and vntreuthe.

Cap. 128. [Of þe armes.]

Whenne þe armes rechyn so farre, þat þe hondes ateigne *Long arms.*
to þe knees, bytoknys hardynesse, and prowesse, with largesse ;
And whenne þay er short, it ys tokenynge of a man louynge
discord, & lytiH wys.

Cap. 129. [Of þe palmes of þe hondes.]

Whenne þe palmes of þe honde er longe, with [1]longe [1] *Fol. 42 a.*
ffyngers, it bytoknys his lord wel ordeynyd to many craftes, and *Long palms.*
wys yn wyrkynge, and it ys a tokenyng of good gouernance.
Greet ffyngers and shorte, bytoknys folye. *Short fingers.*

Cap. 130. [Of knees, Of þe soles of þe feet.]

Greet feet and fuH of fflesch, er tokenyng of ffoly, and *Little feet.*
louynge of wronges ; lytiH feet and ligĥt, bytoknys hardnesse ;
And smale thees bytoknys ignorance, and þaire gretnesse, hardynesse and strynthe. Brodnesse of thees and heles, bytoknys
stryngĥ of body ; And mekyH flescĥ yn þe knees, bytoknys *Great knees.*
febylnesse of vertuȝ, and heuynesse.

Cap. 131. [Of þe paas of men, & manere of goynge.]

He, þat yn goynge, hauys his paas large and latly, welfare *A long step ;*
shaH folwe him yn aH his werkys ; And he þat makys short
paas, ys hastyf, and suspecious, and nogĥt mygĥtfuH yn þe *A short one.*
wirkynges of his cuyH wiH.

Cap. 132. [Of þe tokenynges of good kynde.]

Þat man ys of good mynde, & wel dysposyd in kynde, þat *The tokens of a good body*
hauys nessĥ flescĥ, & moyst, and mene bytwen) sharpe and softe, *and mind.*
and ys nogĥt mekyH long, ne mekyH short, and ys whit, fallyng
toward reednesse, softe yn lokynge, his heer fuH, and his eigĥen)
of meene gretnesse, fallynge to roundnesse, and his heued of
euene mesure, and his nekke of euene gretnesse, wel dysposyd,
and his sholdren) bowen) a lytiH, witĥ-oute greet flesĥnes yn þe
knees, þat hauys a cleer voys, bytwen) greet and smaH attempred ; longe palmes, longe ffyngers, to sutillyte fallyng, of lytiH

laghynge, and of lityll bourdyng, & of noon fantome; whos
lokynge ys mellyd of gladnesse and auysement.

Cap. 133. [Of oon wytnesse in Iugement.]

Do not judge by one sign,

but compare one with another.

Noþeles, it nedys nogh þat þow be hastyf, by any oon of þe 4
tokenynges afore-sayd, in sentence or Iugement; But gedyr þe
wytnesse of alle to-gedyr, And whenne þou shal fynde dyuers
tokenynges & contrary, holde þe all-dayes to þe bettyr & more
preuable party. 8

**Heer endys þe Treetys of þe Secreet of Secreetȝ off Aristotyll.
Qui scripcit carmen sit benedictus.   Amen.**

THE GOUERNAUNCE OF PRYNCES

OR

PRYVETE OF PRYVETEIS.

[THE GOUERNAUNCE OF PRYNCES

TRANSLATED BY

JAMES YONGE

(1422).

Printed from MS. Rawl. B. 490.]

IN the Honoure of the Hey Trynyte, Fadyr, Sone, And Holy gooste, Almyghti god; oure lady Seynte mary, and al the holy hollowes of hewyn: To yow, nobyll and gracious lorde, 4 Iamys de Botillere, Erle of Ormonde, lieutena*un*t of oure lege lorde, kynge henry the fyfte in Irland, humbly reco*m*mendyth hym youre pou*er* Seruant, Iames yonge, to youre hey lordshipp: altymes desyrynge in cryste, yowre honoure and profite of body 8 and Sowle, and wyth al myn herte the trynyte afor-sayde beshechynge that he hit eu*er* Encrese. Amen. Amen.

IN oone techynge acordyth, *and* in oone verite Shewyth, the moste wyse clerkes *and* Maysteris of renoune that haue 12 beyn afor vs in al tymys, tretynge of prowes *and* worthynesse of Emp*er*ours, kynges, and al othyr gou*er*nors of chyualry; that Chyuary is not only kepete, Sauyd, *and* mayntenyd by dedys of armes, but by wysdome and helpe of lawes, and of witte, and 16 wysdome of vndyrstondynge. [1]For Streynth and Powe*r*e, w*ith*out witte and connynge, is but outrage and wodnys, And wysdome and connynge, wythout Streynth *and* Powe*r*e, Surly hym gidyth not. But whan w*ith* Streynth and Powe*r*e, hym 20 compaynyth witte *and* connynge, and witte dressith Powere, in goodnys may the Prynce Play, and w*ith* good men Surly walke. This apperyth by many olde stories, for the connynge and grete witte of Arystotle lytill hadd avaylid to kynge Alexandyr, 24 wythout the Streynth of the brut of his Powere. And the olde Pryncis of Rome conquerid more al the worlde by connynge

Marginalia: Fol. 28 b. — Dedication to James Butler, Earl of Ormonde. — All clerks agree that chivalry is maintained by wisdom, — and that wisdom needs power to sustain it.

---

[1] *nota, in margin.*

and Study of clergeable bokys than by assautes of battaiH, othyr Stroynth of Popill. And ther-for Tully the grette clerke Sayth, "than were wel gouernette Emperies and kyngdomes Whan kynges wer Phylosofors, and Philosofy regnyd." The whyche 4 thynge, nobil and gracious lorde afor-Sayde, haith Parcewid the Sotilte of youre witte, and the clernys of youre engyn, And[1] therfore I-chargid Some good boke of gouernaunce of Prynces out of latyn othyr Frenche in-to youre modyr Englyshe tonge to 8 translate. And for als moche as euer y hame bounde for youre gracious kyndly gentilnesse onto youre comaundement to obey, now y here translate to youre Soucrayne nobilnes the boke of arystotle, Prynce of Phylosofors, of the gouernaunce of Prynces, 12 the whyche boke is callid in Latyn **Secreta secretorum**: that is to Say, the Pryuete of Pryuetcis, The wych boke he makyd to his dysciple Alexandre the grete Emperoure, conqueroure of al the worlde. This Aristotle was Alexandyres derlynge *and* 16 welbelowid clerke, And therfor he made hym his maystyr and chyfe consailloure of his royalme. For arystotle was a man of grete consaiH, Of Profounde lettrure, And Percewynge vndyrstondynge, *and* wel kowth the lawes; he was of hey nourtoure, 20 wel prowed *and* I-lernyd of al Sciencis, Wyse, sotille, humbile, euer lowynge ryght *and* verite: And therfor many men helde hym approphete. And as y fynde writte, [2]hit is founde in olde bokis of the grecanys that god Sende His angill to Hym, 24 Saynge, "radyr I sholde cale the an angill than a man."

Arystotle Sende many Pystelis that men callyth nowe lettres of alexandre, of the Whyche this presente boke is oone, of the gouernaunce of kynges *and* Prynces. 28 The cause that Arystotle makyd this Pystill Was this; Whan alexandyr hadd conqueride perse, for-thy that Some of the Pepyl ther weryn agaynys hym and dysobeiaunt, he Sende to arystotle this lettyr in this forme. 32

"To a nobyl Maystyr of ryght gouernoure, and of verite, Arystotle, Sendyth gretynge his disciple Alexandre. To thy discresciou*n* I do to vndyrstonde, that y haue founde in the londe of Perse appeple ful of Reyson and of hey vndyrstondynge 36 and of Parcewynge engyn, the whych afor al otheres conveytyth dygnyte[3] of lordshup, and therfor we Purposyth to destru ham

---

[1] suttilte *crossed through here.*
[3] A Note ffor Ireland, *in margin, in a late hand.*

al. What the thynkyth vp this matyr do vs to witte by thy lettres." *Shall I destroy them?*

Wp whych matyr, Ary*stot*le answerid in this man*er*.

4 " Yf ye may chaunge the eyre and the wateris of that londe, *and* ou*er* that the ordynaunce of the Citteis, fulfill ye youre Purpos. And yf no, than gouerne ye hame wyth good Woil- launce and bonerte, for yf ye So do, ye may haue hoppe wyth *Govern them justly, and they will obey you.*
8 goddys helpe that al thay shal be to yow obeyaunt, *and* ye shall mow tham gouerne in good Pees."

Whan alexandyr hadd rescewid this lettyr, he did arystotles consaille, Wherfor thay of Perse were morre obieiaunt to alex- *So he did.*
12 andre than any othyr Pepill. And for als moche, nobil lorde, that I desyrynge more outre you*r* appryse, I writte to youre Excellence this boke, entremedelid wyth many good ensamplis *I have added to the book many stories.*
of olde stories, And wyth the foure cardynale vertues, and
16 dyuers othyr good matturis, and olde ensamplis and new.

Here begynnyth the Chapiter*es* and the tytles of this boke.

Fryst how *and* for whate cause this
    arystotle-is boke was makyd ... **Cap***itu***lum j**ᵐ.   Page 127.
20 Of the two thyngis Pryncipalle whych
    eu*ery* kynge be-howyth to haue ... **Cap***itu***lum. Secundum.**   Page 127.
Essamplis of olde stories, to p*r*oue the
    Same lesson trouthe ... ... **Cap***itu***lum. tercium.**   Page 128.
24 Of dyuersite of maners of kynges,
    whyche ben Preysyd and on-
    Preysid ... ... **Cap***itu***lum. quartum.**   Page 130.
Wherfor byth to Enchue folargesse *and*
28   scarsite, *and* what longyth to f*r*an-
    chise ... ... **Cap***itu***lum. quintum.**   Page 131.
Whath awaylyth Sotilte of vndyrstond-
    ynge *and* connynge, *and* how thay
32   byth y-know ... ... **Cap***itu***lum. Sextum.**   Page 134.
Of the two thyngis that makyth a kynge
    to haue good renoune ... ... **Cap***itu***lum. vij**ᵐ.   Page 135.
How a kynge sholde haue hym anente
36   his Pepille ... ... **Cap***itu***lum. octauum.**   Page 137.
How a kynge sholde hym haue anent
    hym-Selfe in vertues *and* clothynge **Cap***itu***lum ix**ᵐ.   Page 138.

	Of the custume of Iues, *and* how a kynge sholde his subiect*es and* namely his		
Page 139.	marchaundys mayntene	Capi*tu*lum. Dessimum.	
Page 140.	Of the Solace of a kynge	Capi*tu*lum. xj^m.	4
Page 141.	That a kyng is lykenyd to reyne, wynd*e*, vyntyr, a[n]d Somere	Capi*tu*lum. xij^m.	
Page 142. Fol. 29 *b*.	Of the Purveyaunce of a Kynge ...	Capi*tu*lu*m*. xiij^m.	
Page 142.	Of the mercy of a kynge	Capi*tu*lum. xiiij^m.	8
Page 143.	Of the thynges wher-of a kyng*e* shulde hym avyse, *and* feyth to kepe ...	Capi*tu*lum. xv^m.	
Page 144.	How a kynge shuld au*au*nce Prowid men of armys, *and* the study of clergi	Capi*tu*lum. xvj^m.	12
Page 145.	The prologe of the iiij^e. Cardynale vertues, declarynge the .iij^e. vertues of theologie, and foure man*er* of¹ goodis	Capi*tu*lum. xvij^m.	16
Page 146.	Of the foure cardynal vertues, whych ben y-callid pryncipal vertues ...	Cap*itu*lum xviij^m.	
Page 146.	Of the fryste cardynal vertu, whych is callit prudencia, *in* Englys, vysdome	Capi*tu*lum xix^m.	20
Page 147.	That a man shulde surmount al bestis in vertues, *and* Speciali in two ...	Capi*tu*lum. xx^m.	
Page 148.	Of Prudencia, and connynge to mayntene and haue	Cap*itu*lum xxj^m.	24
Page 149.	Of olde stories to Proue the Same techynge of Prudencia Sothe ...	Capi*tu*lum. xxij^m.	
Page 150.	Of the Parties of Prudencia	Capi*tu*lum. xxiij^m.	28
Page 154.	¹Of vndyrstondynge, whych is the Seconde Parte of this vertu Prude*n*cia	Capi*tu*lum. xxiiij^m.	
Page 155.	Of the thyrde Partie of Prudencia, that is y-callid Purueyaunce	Cap*itu*lum xxv^m.	·32
Page 156.	That Prudencia is moche to Preyse proueth dyuers reysonys	Cap*itu*lum xxvj^m.	
Page 159.	Of the Seconde vertu cardynal, that is y-callid in latyn, Iusticia	Capi*tu*lum. xxvij^m.	36
Page 161.	That a pr*i*nce sholde not truste to his enemy in no tyme	Capi*tu*lum. xxviij^m.	
Page 167.	Of the man*er* of correccion that a prince sholde haue agayn*es* his subiect*es*	Capi*tu*lum xxix^m.	40

¹ 3 *a* L.

Of the .iij⁶. vertu cardynal, that is
y-callid fortitudo, in Englysh,
streynthe ... ... Cap*itu*lum xxx^m. Page 170.
4 Of olde stories to Show the condycionys
 and propretcis of the hardy ... Cap*itu*lum. xxxj^m. Page 173.
Of the Pite and mercy that a kynge
sholde haue ... ... Cap*itu*lum. xxxij^m. Page 180.
8 Of the kynges tytles to the lande of
Irland aftyr the cronycles ... Cap*itu*lum xxxiij^m. Page 184.
Of the .iiij⁶. cardynale vertu, callit temporaunce ... ... Cap*itu*lum xxxiiij^m. Page 186.
12 Of olde stories of the comendacioun of
the vertu of temporaunce ... Cap*itu*lum. xxxv^m. Page 189.
Of the temporat loue that sholde be be-
twen a man and his wyfe ... Cap*itu*lum xxxvj^m. Page 191.
16 Of the comendacioun, and of the worke
of Matrymony ... ... Cap*itu*lum xxxvij^m.¹ Page 193.
Of the kepynge of body, aftyr the con-
sayl of lechis ... ... Cap*itu*lum xxxix^m. Page 195.
20 That astronomye is necessary to the kepynge of mannys body ... ... Cap*itu*lum xl^m. Page 195.
Of Stories and Ensamplis to proue that
Oryson is Soucrayne remedy in
24 euery trybulacion ... ... Cap*itu*lum. xlj^m. Page 197.
That god haue not in dyspyte the ory-
son of Pagans ... ... Cap*itu*lum xlij^m. Page 200.
Of dyuers ryght good *and* necessary
28 nobilteis of the vertu of orison ... Cap*itu*lum xliij^m. Page 203.
Of new Ensamplis that oryson is moch
vaylant agaynys the Malice of ²
ennemys ... ... Capitulum. xliiij^m. Page 205.
32 Of the vertu of Iustice ... ... Cap*itu*lum xlv^m. Page 207.
Of the gouernaunce of a man aftyr the
.v. wittes ... ... Cap*itu*lum xlvj^m. Page 208.
Of the man*er* of propyrteis of consail-
36 loures ... ... Cap*itu*lum. xlvij^m. Page 209.
³How a prynce shall assay his consail- ³ *Sb* L.
lores ... ... Cap*itu*lum xlviij^m. Page 210.

¹ 38 omitted [*in a late hand in margin*].
² of *repeated in MS*.

Page 211.	Of the propyrteis and condycionys that a good consailloure and a frende shulde haue	Cap*itul*um xlvix^m [*sic*]	
Fol. 30.	How a man Hath the condycionys of		4
Page 211.	al mane*r* of· Bestis	Cap*itul*um. L^m.	
Page 212.	Of Notaries, What condycionys thay sholde bene	Cap*itul*um. Lj^m.	
Page 212.	Of Messagers, and what condicionys thay sholde ben	Cap*itul*um. Lij^m.	8
Page 213.	How that the subiectis ben the tresoure of Pryn*ces*	Cap*itul*um. Liij^m.	
Page 214.	Of baronys, and whate of they Servith · in the roialme	Cap*itul*um. Liiij^m.	12
Page 215.	That a kynge sholde not entyr in battail in his owyn propyr Persone ...	Cap*itul*um. Lv^m.	
Page 216.	That Physnomie is a nessessary scyence to know the maneris of men ...	Cap*itul*um. Lvj^m.	16
Page 217.	Ensamplis to proue the same scyence sothe	Capitulum. Lvij^m.	
Page 218.	That the Sowle sowyth the condycionys of the body	Cap*itul*um. Lviij^m.	20
Page 219.	That the scyence of Physnomy, *and* of the iiij^e. mane*r*es of complexcions, *and* of al colours *and* lymmes of manys body, the tokenys of whate condycionys thay sholde bene, aftyr the same science	Cap*itul*um. Lix^m.	24
Page 232.	Of that Same science of Physnomye, in a shortyr mane*r*e	Cap*itul*um. Lx^m.	28
Page 236.	Of the gouernaunce of helth of manys body aftyr Physike	Cap*itul*um. Lxj^m.	
Page 236.	Of the .iiij^e. elementis whych bene in the Worlde	Cap*itul*um. Lxij^m.	32
Page 238.	Of two Pryncipale thynges whych helth kepyth	Cap*itul*um Lxiij^m.	
Page 239.	Of the gouernaunce of the body of a man aftyr slepe	Cap*itul*um. Lxiiij^m.	36
Page 240.	Of the ryghtful houres of ettynge and drynkynge	Cap*itul*um. Lxv^m.	
Page 242.	Of the gouernaunce of body aftyr mette	Cap*itul*um. Lxvj^m.	40

Why this Book was made. 127

	Of the .iiij. parties of the yere aftyr har kyndes / fryste of the veere	... Cap*itul*um. Lxvij^m.	Page 243.
	Of Somyr, *and* of his condycionys	... Cap*itul*um Lxviij^m.	Page 244.
4	Of herust, *and* his condycionys	... Cap*itul*um Lxix^m.	Page 245.
	Of Wyntyr, and his condycionys	... Cap*itul*um Lxx^m.	Page 245.
	Of thynges that makyth a manys body faate, moysty, *and* wel dyssposi*d*	Cap*itul*um	
8	Septuagessimum. primum	Lxxj^m.	Page 247.
	Of thynges that done the contrary	... Cap*itul*um Lxxij^m.	Page 248.

Expliciunt capitula Sequentis libri.

¹**Fryst, How and for Whate cause this arystotiles boke**   ¹ Fol. 30 *b*.
12   **Was maky*d*. Cap*itul*um pr*i*mu*m*.**   Cap*itul*um j^m.

f   Orto witte how this boke was makyd, ye shal vndyrstonde
that aftyr Alex*ander* had conquerit al the landis of Pers
and Mede, he Passyd wyth his retenue towarde the londe
16 of Inde to gete hit; and for that arystotille was than abydynge
in Grece at scoolis, And alex*ander* had grete nede wit*h* his wyse   Alexander had need of
Consaill*e*, and that he lowid hym so mych, He sende hym by   the counsel of Aristotle, and
lettyr to come to his Presence. And forwhy that ar*y*stoti*lle* ne   sent for him.
20 myght not in good maner, leue the scoolis, he wrote to Alexander in this forme, ² " O thou fulglorious³ Son*n*e, fulryghtful   ² 4 *b* L.
Emp*er*oure, god the conferme in hooly verite *and* wyth vertue,
and fro the wythdrawe al bestialle appetit*es*, and thyn engyne
24 allyght to the Service *and* honoure of god. Thyn Pistle I haue
receuyd wyth dowe reuerence *and* honoure, and fully vndyrstonde what desyre thow hast to my presence. But for als   Since he might not
moche as to the now I may not come, to the y sende now this   come, he sent him this
28 epystle, in the whych thow mayste thy Selfe consaill*e*, lyke as y   book.
wer wyth the. Forwhy the heynys of thyn Engyn lyghtly may
Parcew the depnys of Sotilte, and a lytil remembrance of connynge, in many weyes of verite may be thy gide."

32   **Of the two thyngis pryncipall*e* the wyche behowyth a**   Cap*itul*um
     kynge to haue. Cap*itul*um Secundu*m*.   ij^m.

W ho so wold lordshup pesebly mayntene, and a roialme to
  gouerne aryght, tow thyng*es* he moste haue. One is that   A king must judge righte-
36 he be wyse, suttyle, *and* remembrit that aftyr good lawes and   ously between folk.
ryghful wysely may and can to deme betwen al maner of folke,

³ Prynce *is crossed through here.*

A king must be able to maintain his right.

and afor althynge euynly betwene grete men and Smale, ryche and Power, wythout goynge assyd owt of lawe. That othyr is force of Powere, wher-throgh he may his reme kepe, mayntene, and defende. This may he do by the fryst lyghtly. For who- 4 So by witte and conynge doth ryght to euery man, wel as frende he owyth to be louyd of euery man, and as a ryghtful lorde to be dowtid and dredid. Onto Suche a prynce al men gladly obeyeth. This obeyaunce and force is not only by ryghtfulnes, 8

He must spend freely among his folk.

but also by fredome and larges, And therfor a prynce owyth frely despende amonge his folke, [1]and wysly eueryman rewarde aftyr his deserwynge. But whate myschefe folwyth of chynchry and folargesse, ye schal sene hit aftyr in this boke. 12

[1] 5 L.

Capitulum. iijm.

Here folwyth Ensamplis of olde stories to Prow the forsayde lasson Sothe.

I N olde tyme in kyngis ther was wondyrful reddure of ryght to kepe wel the lawys, wherof tellyth the wyse clerke 16

How Zaleucus made a law that adulterers should be blinded.

Valery, that kynge ʒalente stabelid many good lawis in his Cite of locre. Of the whych this was oone, "That who so euer were atteyntid of Spowse-brige, he sholde lesse both his eighyn." Aftyr hit be-felle his owyn Sone to be founde in the Same Syne, 20

[2] Fol. 31.

His son was guilty, and

and al the Cite atte the [2]Honour and reuerence of the fadyr, to the Sone relessid the Payne of the eighyn,[3] But the kynge ne wolde nat Suffyr by his will. They of the Cite so Entierly praid and bosoght the kynge, that he grauntid oone of his 24 Sones eghyne to be Sawid, But for-why he wolde not his law

he put ont one of his own eyes to save one of his son's.

broke, Fryst he makyd his owyn eigh to be out-rasit, and Sethyn oone of his Sonnes, And So he mayntenyd his lawe, and relessit the duresse of the laue. So that wondyrfull euenys 28 hym departid betwen the Pite of the fadyr, And the ryghfulnesse of the good Iuge. By this apperid wel, that by law he Iugid al otheres ryghtfully, that wold not spare his Sone. Of

Exemple of force.

force of Powere hit apperid also, and hit is to witte, Force of 32 Power is noght aftyr the nombre of pepill, but aftyr the myght of tham that in armes ben prouyd, and aftyr the good gouernance of the witti *and* wyse Prynce, wyth-out wyche nombre of

Another example of Xerxes.

pepil lytill is worth or noght. Of this We fyndyth i-write, that 36 Xerses, kynge of Inde, that wolde batailli wit*h* the Pepil of grece, strongly gederid huge hostis of whych [4]no man couth tell

[4] 55 L.

[3] eughyn, MS.

the nombyr. Wherfor some of his men sayde that the Grecans wolde not abyde to hyr tythynges of the battalle, but fle at the fryste hyrynge of hit. Otheris sayde that the grecanys (or
4 grekis, whych you semyth beste Englyshe) ne shold not be scomfite, forthy so few Pepill wolde not meld in battail, but a-noone thay wolde be al fallynge dovne, and take of the gastnys Of So grete an hoste. Otheris Sayde that hit was to drede that
8 thay sholde fynde the Cite of grece woyde, that the kynge sholde not fynde werre that he myght werre, othyr his Pouere Show. Otheris sayd that vnneth wolde Suffice to ar kynges hoste the largenesse of al Grece in lond, See ne hyre, for he had
12 So hugy a meney that the grece See was to streyte to hame, And that the Plente of his bachelerie was so grete that al the campany of the londe wolde not Suffice har tentes and Paueillons to Piche, And lasse to fyght, or any assaut to make, And that
16 the eyre myght not receue the Plente of har arowes an dartis.
 So hugely on Such maner thay losyngid the kynge of Wayneglory of the force of his hoste, that this losyngeris makyd hym ouer-sette the wysse consaille of Damazate, the Prowid wyse
20 clerke, That to hym sayde, "The flostrynge of the losengers that the Plesyn, thow sholdyst gretly drede, for soth hit is, that nothynge that is to mych may be aryght gouernyd, and that thynge that a man may not gouerne hit may noght endure.
24 Nothynge Erthely is noght so grete, that hit ne may Peryshe and faill." And aftyr hit befell that al that this good Clerke Damazates sayde betyde the kynge. For that grete hoste, for defaute of ryght Purveyaunce *and* wyse gouernaunce, was ouer-
28 come and scomfite of few Pepil, ordaynly gouernyd. ¹But victori in battail Pryncipal is in god. ²That Shewyth wel the deddis of the nobylle victorius Erle, Syr Iamys, yowre gravnde-Syre, whych in al his tyme lechury hatid : And ther-for god in
32 al his tyme granted hym mervellous victori vp his enemys wyth fewe Pepill, Namly vp the morthes, of whyche he slew huge Pepill in the red more of athy, a litil afore the Sone goynge downe, stondynge the Sone mervelosly still till the slaght was
36 done ; And no Pitte in that more lettynge hors ne man in al the slaght tyme. And sethyn, atte astoffy, As syr Edwarde Perrers the good knygh[t] can tell, how youre Same graunde Syre wyth few Pepill Arthure Macmurgho wyth myche pepill to scomfite
40 sette, *and* many hundretis of his men slew. That fredome

SECRETE. K

Side notes: His men said that the Greeks would not face him. Others were afraid to find the city void of folk. Others said the land was too small for his host. A wise man warned him against his flatterers, and it fell out as he warned him. ¹ Fol. 31 *b*. ² 6 L. Irelande It is God that giveth the victory, witness your grandfather, how he slew the Murphys, and the McMurroughs.

helpyth gouernaille, hit apperid in this ensampill. hit befell kynge Alexandre in a tyme that oone of his knyghtis for his Service askyd of hym a reward. And he that full was of fredome, and nedy men gladly wold hyre, and more gladly woldc auaunce, yaue hym a Cite ryche and grete. Than sayd the knyght, "lorde, So grete a yefte longyth not to my pouere estate." To whom answerid Alexander, "I behote not what longyth to the to rescewe, but what semyth me to yeue:" For the whych fredome and many othyres, al men gladly kynge Alexander servid.

Capitulum Of the dyuersyte of kynges of maneris wych ben Prasyde and vnPrayside. Capitulum. iiij^m.   12

IN fowre maners kynges ham demenyth. Some byth fre to ham-Selfe and to har subiectis, Otheris byth scars to ham-Selfe and to har sugettes. Of this two the ytaliance sayth, that in a kynge hit is noght reproue yf he be scarse to hym-Selfe. and large to his sugettes, But thay of Perse Sayth the contrary, that a kynge is noght worthe but yf he be large to hym-Selfe and to his sugettes. But amonge al othyrs, he is worste ¹and moste reprovabill, that is large and fre to hym-Selfe, And scars and harde to his sugettes, For his roialme may not endure. For the forsayd thyngis hit be-howyth to witte whate is Fraunchise. Fraunchise in Englyshe is callid frenys, or fredome. Nede hit is to witte how hit may be conquerid, I-had, and mayntenyd. Also nede hit is to witte whate harmes dothe folargesse and scarcite. Wherfor hit Is to wytte, that hard is to knowe in al poyntis to holde the meeñe, and lyght is hit to faille; As to hit the marke hit is harde, and to faylle hit is lyght. And there-for the more Maystri hit is, to know and conquere fraunchis, that holdyth the meen wey, than folargyse or auarice, that bene of two boundys. And therfor yf thow wolte largely lyue, and aftyr the vertu of Fraunches, thre thyngis thow moste beholde. The fryste, how moche thou mayste despende of thyn owyn propyr; The seconde take kepe in whate tyme hath yeftis most nede or defaute; the thyrde that ye can be viside,² and see the Services and meritis of thy Subiectes.

Thow shalte Vndyrstonde that thow mayste despende, that frely aftyr thy Power thow mayste yeue of thyne owyn. For yf

---

² Altered to aviside.

thow Spendyst or yeveste othyr men goodes, thow Passyste
Frauncesse, *and* out of Fredome thow walkyst. And who de- Nota p.
spendyth more than his Powere or his goodis strechyth, descende Do not spend
money you
4 he moste in Powerte; And that is ayeyño the vertu of larges. have not got.
And his rule oue*r*-Passyth. For-why who-so-eue*r* folyche hym
Mayntenyth in oue*r*-grete costis oue*r* his Poue*r*, *and* wyth-oute
nede, he is a wastoure of his goodes, and destrueth his roialme
8 whate he may: he is not wourthy to be a gouernoure. Suche is
callid a folle-large, or a wastoure, ¹that oue*r*-Passyth Wysdome ¹ 7 L.
and Purveyaunce. Of the Sede*n* thynge be wel avisid. For yf If you are
sparing, you
thow wysely the gouerneste, and Spendyst thy goodis aftyr thy can help the
poor in their
12 Poue*r*e, than namely shalt thow can thy largesse to showe to need.
thy good Pepill, whan thow seyste ham nedfull and poue*r*.
Than shalte thow be large to thy-Selfe *and* to thy Subiectis
both; Than shalte thow fynde Frendis wythout Fayle, obeiance
16 in al thynge; Than shall thy royalme endure and grow, in force
of Power and richesse. Suche a kynge men in olde tyme Then shall
you be
Preysid, Suche is callid wertuȝ, large, and a good prynce. Of praised of
men.
the thyrde thynge, bethynke the suttilly *and* vysely, that thow
20 the can Parcewe of the Seruyces of the good dedis of the
dyuersite of thy Pepill, whych to the bene profitabill, nedfull,
and trew; And to ham yeue thow lyke har deserte, and to tho Give to each
according to
that nedfull byth, wel rewarde. For who-so yewyth hyme that their need
and desert.
24 neddyth noght *and* hath noght deservid, that yefte is loste, For
hit Is not aftyr Fraunches and wertu. A ful thynge hit is to
a kynge *and* vnsemely, to be harde *and* scarse, For noone Suche
a man may loue, And wyth-out lowe a man may neue*r* duly and
28 trewely Serwe, And therfor yf any kynge hym fellyth othyr Choose servants who
scarse othyr folarge, yf he wolde do wel, he moste ordeyne some will spend
your money
trewe men that may duly, als hit longyth to a kynge, his goodis wisely.
to despende and ordeyn.

32 **Wher-for byth to Enchu folargesse** *and* **scarcite. And** Of fredome *and*
  whate longyth to Fraunchis. Cap*i****t***ulum* **V**ᵐ. Scarsite:

Alexandyr y do the to witte certeynly, that a kynge that The danger
of both
o   more yewyth than his roialme may sustene, he shal anoone foolish giving
and covet-
36   be destrued and broght to noght; And his royalme fail ousness.
moste, And whoso hard is, or noght yewyth, he may not
a roialme holde, And ther-for wite thow well that the honnoure
and glory of a kynges to enchu folargesse ²*and* scarsite, as two ² 7 b L.

N*ota*

[1] A little space in the MSS. after 'auere'.

Don't take your subjects' goods from them.

[2] Fol. 32 *b*.

Hermogenes gave the same advice.

Solomon.

The prophets.

Some princes take their people's goods to defend them.

Others only make a pretence of defending them.

Don't be vainglorious,

[3] 8 L.

or you will lose God's reward.

wickyd enemys to mayntene a roialme. Fraunchis and largesse auere,[1] makyth longe a royalme to Endure and wel y-kepid. And one thynge y shall say, that may the moche avayle; That thow take not gladly the goodis of thy subiectis nethyr har*e* aueres. And therfor Sayth the ful wyse Philosofoure [2]Hermogenes, That in a Kynge Hit is a Souerayne Bonyte, Sotylte and Vndyrstondynge, seurte of connynge, *and* of law, wyth Schewynge of Parfite vertue, Yf he Enchu to take *and* holde fro his subiectis har good*is* and har Possessions, For that destrueth remes; wher-for al tho that So do*n*ne, dure they may not longe. And therfor Sayth the prophete, "vnryghtful men shal not lyue halfe har dayes." And also, vnryghtuossnes disherityth kynges and Pryncis; And therfor sayth Salomon, "Kyngdomes bene translatid frame oone Pepill vnto anothyr for vnryghtuosnesse." And therfor the p*ro*phet forbedyth wrongis and Sayth, "Ne wole ye cowete raveynes or wrongfull takynges." The glose ther-vpon Sayth, "O yee dampnabill lucres *and* wynnynges, that getyth money *and* lesyth conscience." Many pryncis and lordis for nede takyn goodis of the com*m*yn pepill moche agayn*e* har willis, And ham therwyth fro myschefe defendyth. Suche a kynge is tollerabill, as many men thynkyn, for the mor*e* myschefe to Enchu. But Sum Pryncis ther ben*e*, that for thar owyn Synguler au*au*ntage, as they wenyth, by colour*e* of har Pryncehode *and* coloured defense of the com*m*yn Pepill, takyn atte har talent trew men goodis. Suche Prynces bene wors than Sathanas, lasse than thay amendis make. Now god of his endles goodnys eu*er* graunt yow grace, extorciou*n* and fals covetyse to enchu; and that ye eu*er* be wel war*e* that y naue no [3]vayne glory of yo*ur* good dedis, For than shall ye lesse the rewarde of god, For of euery good dede two goodis shal fall. One is godis rewarde to the doer*e* of the dede, That othyr is glory *and* wyrchippe of god. Than he that glorieth hym-Selfe or au*au*ntith of his good dedis, in that he berewyth the glories *and* the Vyrchipp*e* of god, and therfor he shal lesse the rewarde that he sholde of god resceewe, As clerkes sayth. Vaynglorye is oone the moste Pe*r*ueylosse synne that is, for hit comyth eu*er* of good dedis, and many a man that holili lyuen, hauyñ vaynglory of har good lyuen*e* *and* good dedis, Peryschyth. And ther-for entirly thynke *and* leue fully that al goodnes is, was, *and* eu*er* shal be in god, throgh god, and of god, and So hit lyeth in no

manes Power to do good, Saue oonly by the Specialle grace of godis Sufferaunce, as cryst in the gospell of goodnes spekynge, Sayth, **Sine me nichil potestis facere.** / "Wythout me ye may
4 nothynge do." In anothyr Place he Saythe, **Qui perseuerauerit vsque in finem, hic Saluus erit.** "Who-so contynuyth into the Ende, he shal be sawid." And therfor, gracious lorde, the good gracious gouernaunce that ye haue be-goone, do ye con-
8 tynow, as ye desyryth to Saue youre honeste *and* al trew lege Pepill So Specialy Shall pray for you yf ye So do, *and* sette in youre bannere godis blessynge and har, ayeynnes whyche youre ennemys shall haue no Pouer to wythstonde.

[marginalia: What the Scriptures say. Continue in; your good deeds.]

12 **Ensample to Prow this Sothe.** *[Irelande.]*

This wyrchipphul knyght Syr Stewyn Scrope, in kynge Richarde-is tyme and ¹Kynge Henry-is tyme the fourth Also, Hauynge the gouernaunce of Irlande, many extorcionys did,
16 Lyuerez takynge, lytill good Paynge, moche he traualit, lytille espolid in the Iryssh, enemys he had ²al the mene tyme. Atte the last the excellent lord, Thomas of lancastre, oure lege lorde is brodyr, that now is lyeutenant of Irland, makyd Stephyn his
20 depute, Irland to governe. Whan he was depute makyt, the nobyll lady his wyffe into the lond y-hadd he wolde, But she awow to cryste makid; lasse than he on a boke Swere wolde, al trew men for his exspensis Pay *and* noone extorciouns doun,
24 wold she neuer Into Irland in his company come. That othe he Sware. Into the londe he came, good Pament to al men he makyd, Grete grace to al gentil endaunger anent the kynge for lyfe and landis he grauntid. And therfor in his baner, trewe
28 men blessynge he bare. The vertue of thes armes was so myche that in one day, the grete prowte Artoure Macmurgh-is coun- trey, in yowre presence tendyr of age, he brente, many of his he Slow, the towne of Callan in Ossory y-wone, *and* yolde to
32 Waltere Bourke rebelle to the kynge, ³he restoride O'kerolle in the Same towne wyth huge nombyr of enemys there-In, and wyth-oute he Slowe the Same Waltere, wyth a grete kerne dyscomfitid, al in oone day in youre presence aforsayde: good
36 pees in leynstere that yere, and many othyr com*m*endable dedis of armes he did elsware. Al this grace hym befelle that yere as y vndyrstond, For-thy that he al that yere noone extorcioun did. **Now y leue of this matier. And wryte y will aftyr**

[marginalia: ¹ Fol. 38. Sir Stephen Scrope did evilly. ² 8 b L. ∴ Irlond. His wife said she would leave him if he did not swear to do better. Ireland. He did, and as a reward, he burnt McMur-rough's country, took Callan, and slew Walter Burke. ³ he he MS. This grace befell him because he was not extortionate that year.]

Aristotcles the boke, the whych as afore is write, Sayth; That extorcion takynge by a kynge of his subiectis goodys, destrueth the roialme. And shewyth that to be Sothe in this manere / Whan the Myses *and* the exspensis of folargesse ouer-Passyth the rentis re- 4 uenueth of the roialme *and* the reccitis, than moste the kynge of his Peple har goodis take. Than doythe he ¹harme in euery syde; harme to ham of whome he takyth, for he be-reuyth ham har lyvynge and hare Sustenaunce, And harme to hym that takyth 8 *and* ravyschyth; for he that is vndone by fals extorcioun takynge, he cryeth to god almyghty, fadyr of mercy and of Pite: And he hyryth hym well *and* blestly, And in dyuers wyse Suche an extorcionere kynge destrueth; harre roialmes ham 12 berewyth by werre or by defaute of heyrys, or by deth of Fadyr and Sonne, or by othyr ewill aduentures. To Fraunchyse in a kynge hit belongyth, that he be not enquerynge of the ryches of othyr men, nethyr of har pryuey Storis, Nethyr he sholde not 16 his yeftis remembyr; But whan a man yaue hym oghte he sholde wel theron thynke. To the largesse and bounte of vertue in a kynge hit longyth to hym reward tho men that bare ham
welle in the Service of hare auncestres, or in har owyn, thegh 20 thay olde men be, and helpe may noght armes to bere: ther-as thay hath longe afor wel deseruyd in battaille and dyuers Stowres stowtly demenet ham-Selfe in grete yonge-man-hode. And thegh they haue not myght and streynthe armes to bere in 24 har oldnysse, they hathe vertue and Streynth of consaill y-prowide. Oone may yeue a stronge stroke in estoure; anothyr yewyth a vyse ²consail and Sauyth al a roialme, And So may 28 noght do the Souleyñ streyth of one man. To a vertues kynge hit appendyth lyghtly to relesse the wronge that is to hym done, honoure tho that honorabill byth, helpe nedy men, Consall tho that vnvyse byth, Secoure and defende tho that gyltles byth, Answere gladly the Pepill, and benurly wyth ham speke, ³Speke 32 wysely and lytill, Fle fooly and euyl company: Thes maner thynges a man may not do wythout wysdome and vndyrstond-ynge *and* lyght of connynge.

What aualyth Sotilte of vndyrstondyng*e and* connynge and how thay byth y-know. Cap*itu*lum vj^m.

Cap*itu*lum v vj^m.

Ndyrstond alex*ander*, that connynge and vndyrstondynge byth hed *and* be-gynnynge of al gouernaunce, hele of

Sowle, and kepynge of vertues, vices to destrwe. For by witte and connynge of vndyrstondynge a man may well chese the goode and lewe the ewill, and hitte enchu. Vndyrstondynge is *Understanding is the beginning of all virtues.*
4 the begynnynge and will of al vertues, and rote of al goodnys. The desyre and willynge to good rennone is a signyfiance and a tokyne of connynge and vndyrstondynge, And who so weraly desyryth good rennoune he shall be renounet and Preysid; And *nota*
8 he that hit will not desyre, he shall atte the latyr ende be shente. Therfor good rennoune is Souerantly to be desyrid, For gouernaunce of a roelme is not doyne at will Saue by good renoune. *Good renown is to be desired.*
    Who-so covetyth a roialme or a lorchuppe to Purchase or
12 wel wyth-oute loue of good rennoune, than moste he begyn wyth Pryde wyche is begynnynge of al wickydnys. For Pryde Engendryth envye, Envye Engendryth falshede, falshede Engendryth lesynge, lesynge engendryth detractacion, detractacioun *The genlogi of Pryde.* *From Pride comes all evil.*
16 engendryth hatredyn, hatredyn) engendryth wronge and wrethe, Wronge and wreth engendryth vnreuerence, Vnreuerence engendryth enemyte, Enemyte engendryth dyscordis *and* werre, ¹And *¹ 10 L.* were destrueth lawes and the royalme, and that is agaynys
20 reysone *and* kynde. Therfor desyre thow good renoune, For So mayste thow conquere humylite that destrueth Pryde; Humylite Engendryth lowe that destrueth envy and hatredyn; Loue engendryth Verite, that destrueth fal[s]hede lesynge *and* *The genealogy of Humility.*
24 detractacion; Verite engendryth ryghtfulnes, That destrueth wronge *and* wrath and vnreuerence; Ryghtfulnesse engendryth frenshippe *and* destrueth enemyte; Frenshuppe engendryth consaille helpe *and* Pees. Aftyr this vertues was al the worlde *All good arises from this virtue.*
28 ordaynyd, The lawes y-stabelid in the Pepill, and acordyth to reysone and to kynde.

Of two thynges that makyth a kynge to haue good renoune. Als hit folwyth in this nexte Capytre. Capi*tulu*m vij^m.

32   Or-alsmoche as a kynge Soueranly in foryne gouernance
f   sholde desyre good renoune, and conquere hit in al that he may, two thynges he moste do and mayntene. Fryste is *How a king may have good renown.*
    that he be abow al thyngis subiecte and obeyaunte to the laue
36 of god and al his roielme, And aftyr that lawe hym gowerne and Sustene, For suche a Prynce worthy is to haue lordshupp. And he that godis lawe to his roialme makyth subiecte, ²ande *² Fol. 34.* ouermych ouerledyth Hit and emblemyshyth Whate He may,

If a king puts God's law below his own, he shall not be held in honour.
² 10 b L.

and Hys Fraunches *and* estatues¹ low makyth, In that he dothe to god ouer-grete veleny : he ouer-Passyth al maner law, ryght, verite, [and] god hatyth, indespite hym foryethyth wherfor ryght is, that al the ²Pepill of god hym haue lytill in honnoure. 4 The Philosofors sayth, that assemely thynge hit is into the magiste of a kynge that he be subiecte *and* obeyaunte to the stabylnes of good lawes, and abow all thynge to godis lawe, noght in fals Papelardry of word or of dede, but in Suche shew- 8 ynge and oppyne wyrchynge of good werkes, that al folke may oppynly Parcew that he doutyth gode, *and* that he is Subiecte to

His people shall dread him when he feareth God,

his myght. Than veraly hym shal drede his Pepill whan thay knoweth that he dreddyth gode and hym douly honouryth. 12 But whan a kynge Shewyth al only in worde that he god dredddyth, *and* in his werkes dothe the contrary, fro god he shall

in deeds as well as in words.

be forcloside ande his Pepill hym Shall dyspyse, For evyll workys may noght be y-hyde anente the Pepill : for the wyche 16 thynge lese he moste his lof, his roialme shall fall, the crovne of his honnoure and of his reuerence he moste faille. And aftyr there shall noone quylete of auere, ne no hepe of tresure that may make his roialme ayeyne come, ne his lordshuppe yf he 20

Inglande
Witness King Richard.

haue hit loste agayne to wynne. This was prowide to be Sothe in kynge Richard the Seconde, somtyme oure kynge, that y wel knewe. This kynge weddyd the wourthy Anne, of almayne

He married the emperor's daughter, and was happy.

the Emperour-is doghtyr. Noght longe ther-aftyr Pees he hadd 24 of al royalmys crystyn, In heyeste Prosperite of al kynges he stode. Whan anne was cryste be-take, he weddyt Elyzabeth of Fraunce, y-callid kynges doghtyr, of nynore age. Than regnyde

But after, he fell into evil,

avoutry and lechurie in hym and his howse-maynage, that al the 28 roialme thanne rumourt *and* lothit for that rousty Synne, For boldnys of this mariage, his hey allyaunce *and* his baronage. Thomas of Wodstoke, his owyn precious Vncle, at Calise he

² 11 L.
and slewjt many great lords.

makyd to be Mvrderide, And rycharde the ryche ruly Erle of 32 Arundelle ³atte londone, towre hille, his hede he makyd of- Smyte, and many othyr nobill lordis, in whom his wirchupp stode, full ille he be-ladde. Al this he didde for wrethe that this nobyll lordis hym roulide for the beste in his tendyr age. 36 Whyle he regnyd in this vnrule weneth thre yeere, Into the land of Irlande he arryuete, *and* lytill or noone esploit dit.

¹ al manere lawe, ryght, verite and good, *crossed through, with* vacat *written over.*

Than the mene-whyle, Duke henry of lancastre that he hadd *But Duke Henry came* exilid, by Eeste England arryuede. Than lordis and comynes of the lande atte Pomfrete into his helpe in euery Syde by many 4 thowsandis to hym gedderid. To weste Chestre he went; kynge Richarde out of Irlande into Walis arryuet, ther anoone spratlit al his ryche retenue, and at the Castelle of Flynt the Duke hym *and took King Richard* toke. To londyn he ladd hym, Parlement ther was sette, the *at Flint,* 8 Duke was coronyd kynge. But Richarde neuer aftyr that his kyngdome myght ¹reyose, Ande yette, hym to restore many a ¹ Fol. 34 b. thowsande men loste hare lywes. There-fore by this ensamplis *and thus he lost his land.* and many more a man may see, that lasse than a kynge or any 12 othyr gouernoure of a pepill dred god, and loue hym, and his lawe mayntene afor al thynge, he shall faade, and fall, and honoure forgo, in a shorte tyme. The seconde thynge is that makyth a kynge to haue good rennoune, that in spekynge he *A king should speak little* 16 gouerne his tonge wysely, that he be not of many wordys, but *and wisely,* that he be well avyside, reysonably to speke that he woll Schew, and Sethyn dyscretly and Sotily, and to effecte his Purpos to Say and Shewe. Ouer that hit behowyth that his dedis and his 20 werkys accorde to his wordis, that he be not variant and Vn-stabille. For Stablenys behowyth euery good prynce to haue *and be stable.* that a man may witte where he shall be yfounde. If this two thyngis aforsayde be in a kynge wel mayntenyt, Of god he shall 24 haue grace, And of his Pepill shal be wyrchippyd, ylowid, and *Then shall he be praised* ydreddyd. *and feared.*

²How a kynge shal haue hym̄ anent his Pepille. Capitulum viijᵐ.

² 11 b L.

28 t O a kynge hit appendyth to honoure tho that his lawes *A king should gladly speak* contreuyth, Haue in reuerence folke of Relygioun, Wyse *with wise men;* men auaunce and dyscrete; wyth thes men he sholde gladly speke, and aske of dyuers nedis and thyngis, that goode byth to 32 know and cun, Honystly and Swetly thyngis to Enquere, and vysilie ham to answere, The moste wyse and notabill of ham moste to honnoure, euery lyke his deserte. A kynge owyth to ensershe the defaute and the nede of Pouere men and myssayse, *and help all those that* 36 and he owyth hame helpe and Socoure, and har dyssayse hastely *are poor and needy.* releue. And hit be-longyth to the Pite that a kynge Sholde haue that he Purvey of men that can har langage, that goodly can wyth tham that neddy byth Speke, and that suche a

Spekere be ryghtfull and Pitteuous, that may in his stid, helpe, confort, Socoure, *and* dresse.

How a kynge hym Shall haue anente hym-selfe in vertues and in clothynge. Capi*tulum* ix[m]. 4

A king should foresee things that are to come,

monge al othyr thyngis and vertues a kynge sholde haue, He sholde be Purveyaunt *and* Pensyfe of thynges that may come aftyrwarde, and aftyr that ordayne his doynges, So that the adventures comynge aftyrward, he may the more lyghtly 8 Supporte. a kynge sholde be Pyteous, Enchu wreth, and the

and not easily show his wrath.

mowrnynges of his corage to hyde *and* hele, that he be not y-holde hastly by lyght Shewynge of his wrethe, othyr vnwyse.

Nota

If hit happe a kynge to do any thynge vnawyssely, he owyth 12 hit repel vmbethoght avysely, and wyth reyson know his de-

[1] 12 L.

faute. Full grete vertu *and* Souerayne vysdome of connynge is

He should not be hasty or overslow.

hit in a kynge that he can gouerne hym [1] selfe aryght, And that he hym Selfe well demene. And whan a kynge shall do any 16 thynge opynly, he shall not be ouer hastely ne ouer Slowe, that he be not holde hasty ne Slow. O alexa*n*der, desyre thow not the thynge that may not endure *and* anoone Passyth, *and* that

And desire things durable above all.

thow most quykly forsake and leue, apparaill the to-geddyr 20 richesse and tresure that may not rootte, the Perdurabill lyfe, the roialme wyth-out ende *and* yoy wythout doloure. Guy al

[2] Fol. 35.

thy thoghtis al tyme to do [2] well, And Shewe thy Selfe glorious

He should flee the manners of beasts,

and hardi; Fle the manere*s* of wylde bestis *and* wode that can 24 not haue mercy, and the fiersnes of the lyoone, and abow al thynge the filthede of the Stynkynge fleshly lust of a Swyn. This is sayde in lyckenys. Thow shalt not be crwel as a beste wit*h*-out reyson that Pite can not haue, But be merciable anent 28 ham of whom thou haste the maystri or lordshuppe. Vmbethynke the of that, that may befall, Forwhy whate shal of aduenture to-morrow betyde thow knoweste noght. **But gracious lorde how ye shall haue yow anent enemys rebelle**, *and* 32 **thewis, aftyr in this boke ye shal fynde y-writte.** Now yewe

nor should he imitate the lusts of swine.

the not aftyr thy desyris, in mete, in drynke, in company of women, ne in ou*er*-longe Slepynges, as doth a Swyn. **In vyue thyngis ye shal kepe yow fro lechurye, whych ben prowid** 36 **by this two versis:—**

speche	syght	touchynge	kyssynge	laghynge
Colloquium,	**Visus,**	**contactus,**	**basia,**	**risus,**

Of his Clothing and Speech. 139

Sunt fomites veneris, hec fuge, saluus er*is*.

This byth the norchynges of lechurie; enchu ham, and thow shalte be sawid. What glory or what valure the may be-tyde, 4 yf thow the accustumyst to the workys of bestis wythout reyson, Trow thow me wythout dute, that the foly company of women destructh the body, sortlyth ¹the lyuedayes, ondyth al vertues, ouerpassyth the lawys of god, And doghty men and 8 hardy hit makyth lyke women, neshe and feynte, dedis of armys to done. Moche hit appendyth a kynge to be rychely and honestly y-clothyd ouer al otheris, that the heynesse of his dignyte may appere in his vesture, that men sette not the lasse 12 by hym, but do hym du reuerence, and that his Pusaunce be not emblemyshit. a kynge sholde be good of Speche and Softe in worde, enchu moche speche, and Speke but lytill, but yf he nede haue. For bettyr is that men desyre hym to hyre, than of 16 his Speche men fulfillit be. For whan a man is trowbelit *and* nvit of many word*es*, he hyryth wyth the lasse wille.

He should flee the sources of lechery.
¹ 12 *b* L.
which shortens life, and causes many evils.
A king should be nobly dressed,
and soft of speech.

Of the costome of Iwes, ànd how a kynge shold his Subiectis ańd namely his marchaundis mayntene. Capi*tu***lum x**ᵐ**.

20   O a kynge hit appendyth noght that he hym company
t   ouer-mych wyth men that lytill bethe sette of, or dyshoneste Personys, For company mayntenyth anent ham
that lytill byth of value, as folis and dyshonest lyueris, makyth
24 the honnoure of lordshupp rebutte in dyspite. Therfor ther was
a fayre custome amonge the Iues, for onys a yere the kynge
sholde haue of his Pepill *and* his hoste a monstrison, and in
ryche apparaille richely enarmet, sittynge on his stede, shuld
28 shew hym to his Peple; the Pepill beneth hym, his Erlis, his
nobill folke and his baronys hym aboute. Than Esploite he the
grete nedis, Than wer Shewyd *and*² tolde the dyuers aduentures
that were the roialme betyde, the grete contencions *and* Enuyes
32 and cures of the neddis of the roialme. Atte that day of
custume he yaue grete yieftis, giltles men out of Pryson de-
lyueret, relessit greuous dettis, and ³many othyr grete workys of
Pite didde. Whan this were don than sholde the kynge go
36 Sitte afore his Pepill, and than anone scholde stonde afor al the
folke one of his consaillours that wer y-callide ⁴amonge ham
costeers, that is to say sitter*es* bysydde, for thy sholde sitte in

His company should be well chosen.

In old times he was seen only once a year:

on that day he gave great gifts, and did works of pity.
³ 13 L.
⁴ Fol. 35 *b*.

² *and and*, MS.

How a King should encourage Merchants.

Then a wise man rose up and praised him;

euery syde of hym. Than the moste Vyseman of ham and beste of facunde, to wyrshippe of the kynge sholde yelde lowynges *and* thankynges to god, that wel thare kynge gouernyde *and* the roialme of Iude *and* that god the reame so enourned 4 *and* endowet of so vyse a kynge *and* wytty, that the pepill of Iude into that tyme was to preyse in obeissaunce, accorde,

and bade him govern well.

stablit, *and* confermyd. Than aftyr that he had god commendid and preysid, and the kynge, he sholde Prise the Pepill tellynge 8 hare good vertues *and* maneres, to conquere and haue har good will. Than he sholde ham amoneste by good ensamplis *and* reysonys to obey *and* honoure *and* humblie Serwe hare kynge,

So all the people rejoiced in their king.

and trewely lowe; Therfor criet the pepill, har kynge and his 12 good werkes with hey woyce commendid and Preisit, and preyet god that har kynges lyfe holde and kepe. Atte the Departynge they went by Cittcis *and* lynagis, and Praysid har kynge and his workis. Thes Pepill taght har chyldryn to loue, honoure, 16 obey, drede, *and* doute har kynge, and So encresid har renoun. Atte that tyme the kynge was wonyd to deme the mysdoers wythoute mercy, to haue that thay shold no more do amysse,

At that time the king would lighten the dues of the merchants.

that otheres were therof chastisied. Atte that tyme the kynge 20 wolde allcege truages, *and* relese to marchandis of har rentis, and ham in trouth defende and kepe. And therfor is Iude full of Pepill. For thedyr comyth Merchandis of al landis, and ther byth wel rescewid *and* moche good wynnyth. Ther may 24 wynne ryche and pouere Citeseyns and foreyns. And there

[1] 136 L.

encressyd the truages [1] of the land and rentys. Wel Sholde men enchu to ennue or wronge do to Marchandis, For they Passyth fro londe to londe, and expaundyth the rennons of kynges and 28 roialmes lyke as thay fyndyth. And ouer that there nys no

So that there is a great resort of merchants to that land.

roialme that nathe nede of some thyngis that byth in othyr landis, And tho thyngis byth cariet fro lande into lande by Marchandys, And therfor who so ille demyth Marchandys in 32 his lordshupp, the goode and the Prowe of the pepill he dystrowbyth and gretly amenusyth. And therfor he nys noght worthy, a roialme or a lordshuppe to haue or mayntene.

Of the Solace of a kynge. Capitulum Vndescimum. 36

A king should glad him with music.

t   O the magiste of a kynge hit is auenaunt that he haue Some Pryue trew Pepill amonge whom he may glad hym, and aftyr nves and dyssesis haue dyuers Instrumentes of

myrthe afor hym to oppyn his herte *and* conforte. For the Sowle of a man hath delyte in instrumentys of myrth, kyndely the wittes enorchyth, contencio*u*n *and* dyssayse and heuynes of
4 cure away-Puttyth, and al the body therof streynth takyth. And yf in such man*er* thow wilte the sporte Pley and Solace, hit Suffysyth thre or foure dayes aftyr thy Plesynge; That shal be p*r*iuely don *and* stilli. Whan thow shalt be in Suche Solace,
8 drynke but lytill, make al otheris drynke att har talente, Feyne the to be dronke, And than ¹maystow many secrete thyngis to Parcew and Hyre. This owyth noght to be don, but twyes or threes by yere. Ou*er* that thow owyst to haue of thy maynye
12 wyth the, that the may tell what that men sayth or doyth in thy Roialme. Ou*er* the tyme of Solace, hit appendyth to ͏a kynge that he be of demure berrynge *and* fayre, And that he be not ou*er*-moche laghynge, *and* of lyght contena*u*nce hym kepe,
16 For ofte laghynge Puttyth away the reuerence of a prynce. ²This prouyth Sothe by this wers. **Per multu*m* risum, potes cognoscere Stultum.** A*ngl*ice. "By ofte laghynge thow mayste know a fole."

side notes: For body and mind are rejoiced. In mirth, too, a king may learn many things from his company. ¹ Fol. 36. But still he should be of grave countenance. ² 14 L.

20 **That a kynge is lykenyd to reyne, wynde, wyntyr,** *and* **Somyr. Cap***itulu***m xij**ᵐ.

a lykenys is betw͏een a kynge and the rey*n*ne, wynde, wyntyr, *and* Som*er*. Fryste betwen a kynge *and* the reyne: For of
24 reyne comyth ile *and* good; good for hit moystieth the herbis, trene, and gardynes, And aftyr hit makyth herbis to ryse, cornys, treis and rootes sprynge, blowe, *and* kerne, and lewis, flowris, *and* frutis to bere: And of this comyth moche othyr goodis. Of
28 the Reyne also comyth many otheris mesaduentures and many harmes, As thondyr, laitynge, the ryuers *and* water*e* makyth ou*er*-Passe har boundys, bestis and Pepill peryschyth, wherof comyth moche harme. And thegh therof comyth so many
32 harmys, yette men lewyth not therfore god to thanke that sendyth the reyne, of the wyche comyth full mych good to the land' and to the Pepill. The seconde lyckenys is be-twen a kynge and the wynde. Of the wynde comyth good' and ille:
36 Good, for hit makyth cornes grow, and makyth frutes to ripe, hit makyth the reyne to fall, and makyth ham wey that Passyth the See, and many othyr goodis makyth the Wynd*es*. But ther-ayeyn*e*s dyuers Perillis and illis *and* destourbaunce fallyth,

side notes: A king is like rain—it is cause of good and evil. Yet men thank God for rain. He is like the wind.

throgh the wynde a-land and in the See. The Pepill in tempestes lesyth har good*es and* har lyues, of the wynde comyth
the corrupcion of the eire, Venymes ther-of be noryschyd, and
othyr illis. And albe thes illis fallyth throgh wyndis, hit wer 4
noght profitable to the pepill to be wythout the wynde. The
thyrde lyckenes be-twene a kynge, wyntyr an*d* Somyr : For the
coldis and the hetis of the Som*er* and the wyntyr helpyth to
the Spryngynge and the bourgynge of naturall thyngis. Albe 8
that of ham ¹comyth many Perillis and illis. So is hit of a
kynge as of the thre thynges. For by the good kyngis, is wel
gouer*n*et the roialme *and* duly mayntene, and many othyr
goodis he dothe to the Pepill, And al he dothe many thyngis 12
aftyr lawe *and* ryght wherof Some byth damagid, Some byth
myslade, And albe that he do wherof somen byth myspayed,
And he² doth ham dysplesynge, men owyth not therfor to leue
to do har Preyer to god, that he mayntene and Sustene har 16
kyn*g*e to the profite of the realme, and to the good of the
comyne; and god ther owyth to thanke, that So good a kynge
to ham hath yowe.

Of the Purweyawnce of a kynge. Capitulum. xiij^m. 20

³Alexandre, bethynke the that thow be well y-storid of
whete and of corne, *and* of euery maner of greyne that
good is for lyuynge, throgh al thy realme, that yf derth
fall thow mayste Socoure thy Pepill by thy Purveyaunce in har 24
dyssayse sufferynge. In Suche a tyme thow shalt thy g*r*aunges
and thy gerners opyn, thy Sillers disclose, that al thyn may
felde the Fraunches of thy bounte, and Prayse the worthynes
and dyscrecioun of thy wysdome. This grete witte and Pur- 28
veyaunce confortyth the realme, Sawyth the Pepill, kepyth the
Citteis,°*and* makyth the kynge of his subiectis to be dreddid.

Of the mercy of a kynge. Cap*itulum* xiiij^m.

lexandyr, ofte-tymes y haue sayde the and consaillid, And 32
a ytte agayne y say and the amoneste, that the blode of a
man gladly ne do noght Shede, for that longyth to god
that knoweth the thoghtes *and* pri*u*eteis of hertis, wherof Sayth
the vyse clerke Hermogynes; Whan a man sleyth anothyr the 36
Vertues of hewyn Shal crye to god and Say, " Lorde, lorde, thy
⁴Servant wel be lyke the," And yf the slaght be vnryghtfull, god

A King should always keep Faith.   143

shal answere, "Who-So sleyth, he shal be slayne: the venge- *God re-*
aunce longyth to me, and y shal therof vengeaunce take." For *vengeth man-slaughter.*
the dethe of a man that giltles is Slawe Shal cry the vertues of
4 hewyn, Into the tyme that vengeaunce therof be take.

**Of thre thyngis wherof a kynge or a prynce shulde hym
a-vyse. And pryncipally of the thyrde, that a man
sholde kepe fayth in his othes makynge for any thynge,**
8 **&c. Capi*tu*lum xv^m.**

Lexandre, remembyr the of the dedis *and* werkis of thyne *Remember*
a auncestres and to haue a papyr of al har actes *and* har *old times.*
lyues, for so shalte thow many good thynges Parcewe by
12 the Ensamplis of har actis. Of the Seconde thynge be avysid,
that thow haue not in dyspite men that fro riches byth falle *Do not de-*
into pouerte, For he that is now lowe by Pouerte, may by *spise the un-fortunate.*
fortune be heyet and ryche y-makyd and relewid, And than he
16 may nve and damage. The thyrde thynge for-yete not in no
maner; Neuyr breke thy feyth that thow haste yowe, ne ally- *Never break*
aunce confermyd: For that appartenyth to vntrew men. And *faith.*
ouer that hit is to witte, that an evil ende followyth vntrowthe.
20 And thegh hit happe that throgh a feyth y-broke any good
befall atte that tyme, more harme therof shal fall in anothyr
tyme, than that goode afor amounted by falsnes gotte. Ouer
that he that feyth brekyth, Of falsnes and vntrowth he shal be
24 Proclamyd *and* knowe.

Wytte thow, alexandyr, that by lewte and trowthe and *The praise of*
feyth the Pepill byth vnyette, Citteis fulfillid, *and* mayntenyd *good faith.*
lordshuppis. And yf feyth or lewte be forsake, than shall hit
28 of the Pepill be and of lordshuppis ¹As of wylde bestis, amonge   ¹ 15*b* L.
woche euery olt hym abow hym to whome he is prere. For the
whyche thynges, ful trewe Emperoure, kepe thy feyth, thyn
vndyrtakynges, and thy Serementz In al Poyntes thegh thay
32 nvous be, the whych thow haste take an hande. Witte thow,
alexandre, that as Hermogenes seyth, that there byth two *Two spirits*
Spiritis abowte the; that oone is atte thy ryght hande that the *attend man—*
kepyth, And that othyr in thy lyfte ²hande that the beholdyth.   ² Fol. 37.
36 This Spyritte that al thy workys Seyth ande Parcewyth, yf *one to keep*
thay be not good, he writyth ham *and* showyth ham to god that *him, the other to mark his*
the makyd. This thynge ounly Sholde wythdrawe the, *and* *deeds.*
make alle men enchu il workys. Ther-for forswere thou noght

Do not swear readily, thy-Selfe in no vyse, ne thy feyth breke. Therfor thow moste enchue to Swere gladdly, For a kynge sholde not swere, but yf hit were for a grete encheson, ffor a kynge that gladly wolde swere, dothe dyshonoure to his roialme. ffor that appendyth to 4 subiectes and to Serwauntes, and noght to gentiles ne to nobles. And know thow that the encheson of the destruccioun of the roialme of ambage and of the Cite. was be-cause that hare *and never break your oath.* kynges weryn to moche costumabli to Swere flasly for whan 8 hit be-felle ham any serement othyr feyth to make, that one Parti begilid that othyr and brake har Serementes *and* hare cownauntes. And thay brake the lewted that Stablid was to Profite of mann *and* hole. For the whyche thynge ham ne 12 myght not longyr suffyr the fulle ryghtwysnesse of almyghty god.

Capi*tulu*m xv*iij*. **How a kynge shulde auaunce prowyd men in armys, and the Study of clergi to hawe wyth hym'. Cap***itu*lu*m. xvj*m*. 16

Make your young men warriors, lexandyr, make thy bachyllers and thy yonglynges to be
¹ 16 L.   a   prowid in armes to yousty, and Serche and thay in al maner
               ¹of assautes be enfourmyd for al maner of battaillis *and* of
estowris. And many tymes do commande throgh thy roialme 20
and your children scholars. that al pepill hare chyldyr putte to scole, and make ham be taghte and study in hey scyencis *and* nobles that byth callid libral Sciencis, that is to Say fre scyencis, as gramer, arte, fisike, astronomye, and otheris: And thy Purveyaunce ham owyth to 24
Help them that study. fynde har lywynge. To tho that wel Studyeth ye shall some auauncement yefe, So that otheres therof haue the bettyr wille to lernen. Hyre ham gladly in hare nedys, and auaunce ham that byth to rewarde. That shall make the of clerkis to be 28 praysid *and* commendit: That shall make ham thy good workys, thy Fraunchis, *and* thy bounteez to writte; So that thy good
The praise of clergy. rennone thy shall make euer to Endure. The estudy of clergi well mayntenyth, is the wyrchipp of the Empire, the beauute of 32 the realme, the lyght of the lorshuppe, the remenbraunce of all goodys. For by wrytynge of bokis, the whyche makyth clerkys to be Studiers, thyngis that Passyd byth men may cun ayeyñe,
What clergy does for a land. and in bokis a man may See ham oppynly. Throgh the whyche 36 thynge was Enhawsid the realme of Grece, that makyth har renoun throw all the worlde to be know and So longe Endure. Certeynly that was throw the Clergy and Study that ther was so

The Prologue of the 4 Cardinal Virtues. 145

grete, and by the full wyse Philosofours that ther dwellid in har
study. So myche was the Study in Grece mayntenyd, that the *The learning of Greek maidens.*
yonge damselis in har Fadyr howses cowthe the courses of the
4 Sterres, and of the yers, the Encheyson and the dyuersite of
Shorte daies and longe, of Shorte nyghtes *and* longe, the courses
of planetes, the mesuris of the Serclis, the signyfiaunce of the
Sterres anent thyngis that were to cum, and many othyr thyngis
8 appertenynge *and* Shewynge of Sterris.[1]   [1] 16 b L.

[2]The Prologe of the foure Cardinall Vertues, declaryng the Cap*itu*l*u*m
[3]vertues of theologi, and fowre manere of goodis. xvij^m.
Cap*itu*l*u*m xvij^m.   [3] Fol. 37 b.

12   Obyll and gracious lorde, atte the begynnynge of this *This is not in Aristotle's book.*
  n   presente to boke I Sayde that y wolde writte to youre
     excellence Of the iiij^e. cardynall Vertues, Vndyrstondynge
     that thegh be not writte in arystotle is boke aforsayde, thy byth
16 writte in othyr good bokis of latyne, And thay byth no lasse
     profitable than the beste thynge in A*ris*tot*l*is boke. But fryste
     vndyrstonde ye, as hooly writte Sayth, that ther byth thre *The three theological virtues,*
     Vertues prynciopalle of theologi or dyuynyte, y-callid in latyne
20 **Fides, Spes, Caritas**, In Englysch, Feyth, Hoppe, *and* Charite. *Nota bene*
     Feyth is a belewynge of thyngis that oure bodeley eygh may not *Faith,*
     see, As the xij^e. articlis of oure comyn " credo in Deu*m* P*at*rem."
     Hoppe is a ryghtfull tryste for a ryghtfull Werke, i-put be-twen *Hope,*
24 wanhoppe and dysspayre, or presompsion of goodis to come aftyr
     to be hadde, And of illis to come afftyr to be Enchued. Charite *Charity.*
     as the Maystyr of Sentence saythe, is " a loue, wyth the whyche
     god is lowid for hym-Selfe, And oure neghbore for god or in
28 god." Also as Seynte Austyne seyth, " Charite is the fulfillynge [Au]gus-
     of law, And of al dyvyne Scripture or hooly writte," That is to tinus.
     say the p*er*fite loue of oure god, and of oure neghbore. Than
     Sethyn that Charite is the fulfillynge of lawe and al dyvyn *The praise of Charity.*
32 Scrypture, thegh a man haue al othyr vertues, with-out charite
     he may not be Sawid, and therfor, nobill lorde, Punysħ ye neuer
     mysdoere, newer noone enemy for noone hattrede ne for no *Never punish for hatred of the offender.*
     covetyse of har goodis, Sauc for lowe of Iustyce, and ryght duly
36 ham Punysshe, lovynge by wey of charite hare Sowlis, And hat-
     ynge hare evill dedis, *and* so ye shall youre Charite kepe. And

  [2] At top of fol. 37 b. :—Of the Prologe. Of the fowre Cardynalle
Vertues.

yf ye done the contrary, ye Passyth the boundis of good governance. The grete clerke Seneca Scyth, "If þou wilt submyt or vndreset al thyngis to the, submyt thy-selfe to reysone." Sothly, nobill lorde, many Pepill shall ye well gouerne, whyle that reyson gouernyth yow. And yf ye, as my hey tryste *and* prayer to god is, youre-Selfe gowerne aftyr this boke, *and* aftyr the iiij^e cardynale vertues that here lyke as y fynde writte in dyuers bokis ¹declarid shal be, than shall ye doutles youre-Silfe gouerne by reysone, to godis wyrchupp *and* youris, and profite to al youres, to your wel-willynge ouer al.

Marginalia: Seneca's saying.
¹ 17 L.

Of the foure Cardynal vertues. Cap*itul*um xviij^m.

Ardynal vertues byth callid Pryncipale vertues: the fryst is callid in latyne Prudencia; the Secu*nd*e, Iusticia; the thyrde, Fortitudo; the fourthe is Temporancia. Thes byth callid in Frence, Visonge, or Purveyau*n*ce, Dreiture, Coerance, *and* Temporaunce. Thes byth callid in Englyshe, Wysdome, Ryghtfulnes, Streynthe, and tempure. And for-alsmoche as lateyn is the moste stydfaste langage, Als ofte as in this presente wrytynge of translacion shall speche of the names of this foure vertues, I putte lateyn in the stydde of Englyshe: For a man may sette dyuers Englyshe for euery of ham.

Marginalia: Prudence, Justice, Fortitude, Temperance.

Cap*itul*um xix^m. Of the fryst vertue cardynal, that callit is, Prudencia. Cap*itul*um xix^m.

tte the begynnynge of the declaracion of this vertu, Pru- ²a dencia, vndyrstonde ye that there is foure mane*r* of goodys, that is to witte, good of kynde, good of fortune, goode of science of clergi, and good of grace. Good of kynde is streynthe of body, fayrnesse, helthe, delyuernesse, and many othere*s*. Thes goodes byth comyn als good to willde bestis as to men. Goode of fortune is riches of golde, sylue*r*, yowelis, and othyr worthely possessionys *and* richesis, and byth comyn als well to ewill men as to good, like as thay were to the blessid Iope and to the cursid Emperoure Nero, *and* many othere*s* Sethyn *and* in oure dayes. And therfor men sholde sette lytillie at this goodis of Fortune or of kynde, for thay be not werry goodys, for now thay byth, *and* now thay byth agone. And so hit is to Vndyr- stonde, that goodes of kynde, *and* of fortune byth all goodis that appartenyth to Sustentacioñ, or anowrnement, othyr protec-

Marginalia: ² Fol. 38. There are four manners of good. Good of kind, which comes to beasts as to men: Good of fortune, which comes to evil men as to good:

cion and defence of body. Goodis of Science of clergi, byth *Good of Science:*
bettyr than goodis of kynde or of Fortune, for ¹they byth goodis *¹ 175 L.*
of the Sowle, natheles thay makyth not the Sowle good of
4 necessite, for good of Science is comyñ to good men *and* to
bade. The beste good of all is good of vertues *and* grace: *Good of Grace, which*
vertue is not oonly a good, but it is also well a goodnesse, *is best of all.*
makynge good necessarly his possessoure: And therfor no man
8 dute that vertues makyth the Sowle altherbeste.

That a man sholde surmonte al bestis in vertues *and* namely in two. Cap*it*ulum xx^m.

*Cap*it*ulum .xx^m.*

Itte is to witte, that lyke as a man of al bestis that eue*r* *A man has reason and*
12 h god makyd surmountyth in nobelesse of kynde, So he *will.*
sholde ham surmounte in vertues, *and* namely in two, that
byth two begynnyngis *and* hedis of al mane*r* mankynde workis,
that is to wyttynge, vndyrstondynge or reysone, *and* wille. And
16 therfor euery vertu that is done by good vndyrstondynge or *Prudence comes from*
reyson is y-callid Prudencia; And euery vertu by the wyche a *reason:*
man doith any worke Duly *and* ryghtfully. hit is y-callid Iusticia, *Justice comes from will.*
and appendyth to wille, for the Ryghtfulnes of workis or of
20 dedis comyth and rysyth of Ryghtfulnesse of wille. But of this
two goodis hit is to say of the goodnesse of reyson, *and* of the
goodnesse of wille, and of har profiteis, a man is destourbet in
two maners: In oone mane*r*e by the wickydnesse of Fleshly *Fleshly appetite is restrained by Temperance:*
24 appetites, that is to witte by glotony *and* Lechurie, and for thes
wyckydnes to refrayne, hit be-howyth haue the vertu of temperance; In an-othyr mane*r* thay byth destroubid by the wickydnesse of corage, the whyche comyth of foreyne thynges, as drede
28 that a man hath of Perelis, othyr of trauals, for the whyche is
nedfull thynge to a man that he be Stabelid and confermyd by *Fortitude gives him*
the Streyth of the vertue that gothe not out of the wey, ne *strength to abide in the*
ouerpassyth that that reysone yewyth; this vertue is callid *right way.*
32 Streynthe of corage or of herte, In latyn as aforsayde hit is
callid Fortitudo. And as y-aforsayde thes bene the foure cardynall vertues, that is to witte Pryncipall vertues or Soue*r*ayns,
For to ham byth remewid al that othyr vertues as to har cheffs.
36 And thegh vertu appendyth to al men, namly hit appendyth
to a kynge *and* to a prynce, ²and to al others that ³owyth any *² 18 L. ³ Fol. 38 b.*
Pepile to goue*r*ne ande redresse. Amonge thes vertues that we *A king should have these*
haue namyd aftyr ryght ordyr, Hit be-howyth to begyn) wyth *virtues.*

Of these virtues Prudence comes first.

Prudencia, for by vndyrstondynge will is gouernet, for wille nothynge may not desyre, but yf by vndyrstondynge to hit by shewid. And therfor holldyth vndyrstondynge and reysone the forwarde. And for-als-moche as Prudencia is the Parfynesse of good, and the vertu of reyson as afor is sayde amonge the vertues afor towchyde of Prudence, hit is by ryght ordyr to begynne. 4

Ca*pitu*lum xxj^m.

Of Prudencia and cunnynge to mayntene and haue. Ca*pitu*lum xxj^m.

8

*These virtues are profitable to king and subjects. no*ta

Plato.
Solomon.

Valerius.
Boethius.

Policraticus.

Policraticus.

¹ 186 L.
Solomon.

Solomon.

Rudencia and Cvnnynge behowit*h* a Prynce namly to haue, p for thay byth profitabill to hym and to his Subiectis both. And therfor Plato the grete Philosofoure sayth That "than was the worlde y-blessyd whan wyse men regnyd and wyse kynges were." Salamon sayth **Multitudo sapientu**m **sanitas est orbys terrarum.** That is to say, "The multytude of wys men, Is the helthe of al the worlde." Valery in his vij^e. boke, and boyce in his fryst boke, Sayth, that the nobill Clerke Senec called the worlde the gyldyn worlde, whan roialmes weryn gouernyd by wys men. Of this sayth Policrat in his vj. boke, that " iij^e. thynges makyd the romanys to conquere londe and ouer-come Pepill, that Is to say, cunnynge, and wysdome y-prowyd of armes, and hey feyth and trouthe mayntenyd." The Same clerke also saythe in his iiij^e boke, " I ne may not mynde me that the Emperours of Rome ne the dukes wer vnlettride while that hare lordshupp was well gouernyd in his streynth." But y ne wote how, Sethyn that in prynces was extentid the lyght of letterure, is enfebelid the streynth of all chyualrye, of Prynechode, and rialtee, as the rote y-kyde. But hit is no wondyr that ryaltee wythout wysdome and cvnnynge ne may not endure. For god that is Hym-Selfe connynge, Sayth ¹in the Persone of cvnnynge, in the boke of Proverbis, " By me, þat Is to say, cvnnynge, kynges regnyd." Salamon in his boke of wysdome' Sayth, "A wyse kynges is the Stabelynge of the Pepill." And ther he Sayth agayñ, " ye kynges of the Pepill, If ye delytyth in ryall Citees and in Septris, loue ye wysdome. that ye may regnyne longe tyme, Loue ye the lygh of cvnnynge for al the Pepill ye haue to gouerne. A wyse Iuge his Pepill shall Iuge, and har Prynce shall be Stabill: An on̄ne-wyse kynge shall lese his pepill, and the Citteis enhabited shall be by the witte of an on̄ne-wyse kynge Destrued." Ouer al thynge the

12

16

20

24

28

32

36

wysdome of a kynge sholde his law gouerne aftyr the law of
god, and the law of god haue *and* cvnnynge. Therof wrotte the
Holy Prophete Moyses in the boke of Deutronomye; Aftyr that <small>Moses.</small>
4 a kynge is sette in his heynesse of his roialme he sholde make
the lawe of god be writte, and the Ensampill of the Prestis take;
the whyche lawe he sholde al tymes wyth hym haue and rede,
that he myst can dred god and doute, and the comandmentis and
8 estatues of his lawe mayntene and kepe. For manys lawes byth
good alwey, Whan thay dyscordyth not from the laue of god.
By that hit [1]apperyth that a kynge sholde be wyse that he be   <small>[1] Fol. 39.</small>
not y-callid an ape. As Seynt bernard Seyth " An ape Envy- <small>S. Bernard.</small>
12 ronyth the fole kynge, that sittyth in See, And therfor yf a
prynce be vnletterid, he sholde aftyr the consaill of letterid
men wyrche, and hym and his realme gouerne." And therfor
hit is writte in the boke of Deutronomye, That "a kynge sholde <small>Moses.</small>
16 take ensampill of the law of Prestis," that is to sey, of letterid
men, as helemaund sayth.

**Now here begynnyth olde stories to prowe the forsayde
thechynge of Prudencia trowthe. Capi*tu*lum xx[ij]**[m].

20 f   FOr cunnynge and Prudencia to haue *and* conquere, olde
kynges [2]weryn full couetouse, Pensifs, *and* desyrynge, and   <small>[2] 19 L.</small>
that apperyth well by this stories. In the thyrde boke of <small>How Solo-
mon prized</small>
kynges we fyndyth y-writ, that oure lord apperid on a certayn <small>wisdom above
long life,</small>
24 nyght to kynge Salamon in slepynge and to hym sayde, " Aske <small>riches or
glory:</small>
thow that thow wylte, And I the hit yeue," and Salamon sayde,
" Thow hast makyd thy grete mysericord anent thy seruant
Dauy my fadyr, But y ham but a lytill chylde that can not ly,
28 and my issue y know not, and thy servant is Putte to gouerne
thes full grete Pepill that thow hast chose. Graunt thow than
to thy Seruante an abill herte to witte, and wysdome that I may
Iuge thy Pepill, and depart the good from the evill, for who
32 myght Iuge or gouerne this thy Pepill that is so grete." And hit
Plesid god tha[t] Salamon Suche a thynge askyd. Than sayde
god to Salamon, " For-why that thow haste Suche a thynge
askyd, and thow ne hast not askyd longe lyfe, ne ricesse, ne the
36 conqueste of thyn enemys, but thow hast askyd wysdome for to
Iuge and deme ryghtfully, I make the aftyr thy Demaunde; and
I graunt the a wyse herte and vndyrstondynge, in-so-mych that
none afore the hath be y-lyke the, ne aftyre the shall come.

150   *Of the Parts of Prudence.*

God's reward to Solomon. Ouer that y shall the yewe that thow haste not askyd, that is to say, rychesse, nobelesse, and honnoure, ouer al the kynges that afore has bene, and yf thow my comandmentes kepyste, I shall yeue the longe lyfe." Werby hit apperyth that Prudencia in 4 a Prynce, vnto whyche Prudencia longyth witte and cvnnynge, as is aforsayde, hit Plesid myche god, Whan Salamon his desire
Great princes had their masters. to haue cunnynge was so myche. And therfor had this olde Pryncis wyth ham hare maistris, as Alexander, arystotle; Nero, 8
Polleraticus tells of Philip and Aristotle. Seneca; and Troiane, Plutark. Of this sayth Policrate in his vjᵒ boke, that when Alexander was borne, kynge Philippe that was his fadyr Sende to Arystotle a lettre in this forme, "Kynge
¹ 19 b L. ¹Philippe Sendyth gretynge to arystotle. Witte thou that a 12 Sone is to me borne, but for-thy that he is borne in thy tyme, ffor I hoppe that he by thy techynge and enformacion he shall be to vs couenable and worthy to the gouernance of a realme." Of this tellyth Policrat, that the Emperoure of Rome consaillid 16
The King of France and Fulk of Anjou. the Kynge of Fraunce, and hym amonestit, that he sholde make his chyldryn to lerne fre Sciencis of Clergi. For he sayth, that a kynge vnletterid, is lyke an hornyd asse.

Capitulum xxiijᵐ.   **Of the Parties of Prudencia. Capitulum vicessimum 20
                                           tercium.**

Vlly Sayth, and shewyth in the Secunde boke of retoryke,
² Fol. 39 b. ²t that Prudencia hath thre Parties, that is to witte, mynd,
The parts of prudence. Memory: understanding; forethought. vndyrstonddynge, and Purveyaunce. Mynde by the whyche 24 a man recordyth hym of thynges that byth Passid; By vndyrstondynge a man avysyth hym of thynges that now byth; By Purveyaunce a man aymeth aftyr reyson thynges that byth to com. And aftyr the dyuersitee of aduentures a man hym storyth 28
Memory teaches that all shall pass, as all hath passed. and Purveyeth. By mynde, a man sholde hym recorde of thynges that afore hath bene, ffor as this bene, wer thay in har tyme, and lyke as tho thynges that than weryn bene passid, So shall Passe that now byth. Therfor Sholde a mañ lytill cowete othyr 32 desyre the heynesse, the honnoure, the yoy, or the gladnysse of this worlde. Anothyr lyfe behowyth vs Purchase, For ,this vs be-howyth forsake and lewe. Than vmbethynke vs of the moste noble lordis as to worthely lorshuppe that afor this tymes weryn). 36
    Whan the grete kynge alexander by conquest had gettyn the Emperie Of the worlde than he dyet, and he that all Pepill leuynge Demenyt, of othyr men dede into Erthe he was ladde.

Than Sayde a clerke, "Moche is to dyspice the heynysse of the worlde, the rcalte of the Emperie and þe honoure of richesse, [1] for his Frendshupp is but wrathe of doloure, his gladnys rynnyth al-way into worse, all nys but as a floure in the felde." O Alexandyr the myghty Emperoure, make we vs a merroure, For hym myght not Suffice the brede of the worlde, the nauy of the See, of all to be lorde, al the landys he conquerid fro grece into the este, Darry the grete kynge he slayne, al his pepill he did ouercome; but whan the dethe hym caste doun, hym Suffysid a lytill graue of v^e foote. for his Pallis, for his halle, and for his roob; euery man of this take Ensampill. Whan alexandyr was dede, hym was made a graue of golde. To his enterment came many Philosofors, of the whych oone sayde, "tresure in his lyfe makyd alexandyre of golde, but now wythout any duris,[2] makyth golde of hym tresure."

Anothyr sayde, " yestyrday hym suffisid not al the worlde full of Precious stonys, ne no Palis of golde; to day hym Suffice a lytill bounde of two ellis othyr thre."

The iij^e Philosofoure sayde, "yestyrday he hadd of all men the lordshuppe, to-day hauyn al men of hym the maystri."

The fourth Sayde, "yestyrday he ladd his hostis vpon the Erthe, to day thay ledyth hym into the erthe."

The v^e sayde, "yestyrday he hadd erthe vndyr his fete, to-day he is of erthe oppressid."

The vj^e sayde, "yestyrday he hadd frendys Speciall, but to-day he haue ham all y-lyke."

Therfore hym sholde no man of heynys, of lordshuppe, of richesse, or of Powere to haue Pryde, for thay may not longe Endure. And ouer al that, god ne holde noght moche of Erthely heynysse, and So hit semyth well. For lordshupp and heynysse god yewyth to coursid men as well as to good men. [3] But of the roialte and riches of goode men comyth goodnys, Ande of the lordshupp of Cursid men comyth many lostis *and* myschefis. That apperid well in Nero [4] to whom god grauntid of al the worlde the lorshuppe *and* the Empire of Rome. Of whoos magiste, felonye, and cruelte men fyndyth y-writte. Nero hadde the wyse Clerke Seneca to his mayster; This wourthy Clerke Seneca longe abode and hadde hoppe of grete reward for his trauaille and his good Service. To whom sayd Nero, " chese in whate tree thow wilte be on-hangid, for that

<small>The reason why Nero slew Seneca.</small> is the rewarde of thy trauaille." And Seneca askyd hym in whate maner he hadd the deth I-deseruyd and Suche rewarde. Than makyd Nero a Sharpe Swerde to florysh ouer Seneca is hede. And Seneca that the deth dowtid, wriet the hede atte the tretyngis of the Swerde. Than sayde Nero, "Maystyr, why wryest thy hede for the Swerde?" Seneca answerid, "I ham a man and the drede of deth me nuyth:" to whome sayd Nero, "I dowte the nowe als moche as a chylde and lyke as y a chylde, werre-ffor y may not lyue in ese, Whyle that thow lyueste." Than sayde to hym Seneca, "Sethyn that y moste dy, graunt me that y may chese a maner of dethe." Nero to hym sayde, "chese hastely the dethe, and tary thow not." Than he makyd hym a bathe to be ordeynyd, and of bothe his armes in the bath to lette blode. So myche he bledd that in <small>Boethius.</small> the bath he diet. Boyce in the boke of consolacioun seyth, that this Nero makyd his brodyr to be slayn, and his modyr he made be slayñ and oppenyd, for that he wolde witte and See, how he was in the maris y-bore and fedde. And for-als-moche as the Feciciens and lechis hym reprouyd of the deth of his modyr, for hit was agaynes reyson and kynde, that the sone sholde do slee his modyr that grette doloure for hym sufferid <small>Nero would be with child.</small> and with grete trauaill hym norishid, Than sayde Nero, "make ye me with chylde, and ber a chylde that I may knowe how grete doloure and Payne hadd my modyr wyth me," and the <small>¹ 21 L.</small> Ficiciens sayde, ¹"That may not be, for hit is agaynys kynde." Than sayde ham Nero, "If ye make me not wyth chylde, wyth cruel dethe I shall make you al dye." Sethyn thay hym yaue <small>How his physicians gave him a toad in his drink.</small> pryuely a lytill toode in a drynke, and by crafte thay makyd hit grow in his bely, and his bely sawlte hit wax grete, that hit suffyre he ne myght, a thynge agaynes kynde; Wherfor he demyd that he was wyth chylde. And the lechis makyd hym Suche metis to het whyche makyd the litill toode grow accordyngo to hys kynde, and to hym sayde, "Sethyn thow wilte concewyn and chylde bere, women mettis wyth chylde thow moste ette." Hitte be-fell that throw the growynge of the <small>How Nero could not abide the child bearing.</small> toode, So grette was his doloure that longyr he myght not suffyre, and ther-for he sayde to his lechis, "Haste ye the tyme of my chylde berrynge, for the doloure is to me so stronge, that wyth nede y may my breth wyth-drawe." Than thay yaue <small>² Fol. 40 b.</small> hym a drynke to caste owte, ²and he keste owte a toode strongly

The Crimes and Death of Nero. 153

fowle *and* hydows. Nero be-helde his chylde, and grysnesse *How Nero marvelled* therof hadd, and hym merwelid of Suche an shape; And the *at his child.* lechis hym sayde, "The shappe is suche, for-why thow woldyst
4 not abyde the tyme of chylde-berrynge." Sethyn he commaundid to kepe his chylde *and* welle to norryshe, and that hit were Enclosid in a vaut of stone. This Nero slowe seynte Petyr and Paule : ther-aftyr he hym be-thoght *and* merveillid of the
8 brandynge of Troy. And forwhy that he wolde witte how grete *He set Rome on fire to* was the fyre-blaste therof, he makyd the Cite of Rome afyre to *realise the burning of* sette, and Sewyn dayes and Sewyn nyghtes to brente. On *Troy.* Passynge faire towre huge of heyght in the Cite afyre was.
12 Nero of the fayrnys of the fire-blaas stifly hym reioiet. He was wonyd to fysshe wyth gildyn nettis. Whan thay of Rome ^{1} 21 b L. Sawe this wodnys, *and* longyr thay myght not hit Suffyre, ^{1} thay *Then the Romans pur-* assaylid the Tirande *and* hym oute of the Cite chasid and Pur- *sued him till he died.*
16 suet, and whan he apercewid that scappe he ne myght, he raane to a stake *and* hym Stickyd throw the body, *and* so he dyet. Than he that the Emperoure of al the worlde hadd *and* lordshupp in his lyue, he nad noght aftyr his dethe so moche
20 honoure, that any man wolde hym byrry, but he was lefte wit*h* wilde bestis *and* fleynge fowlis to be deuourid. Nero in ill tyme hym myght not Suffice the lordshupp of Solerne ther' as the day *The lordship of Solerne* dawyth, nethyr of galerne the baillie, ther as the nyght nyghtyth. *and the Baillie of*
24 Aftyr all this glorie, hy*m* befell the fowle dethe ; al men hit *Galerne.* haue in mynde, Of that there is noone resorte. Therfor hit apperyth well that god grauntyth the heynysse of honour herthely als wel to ewill men as to good men, And therfor sholde no *All earthly greatness*
28 mane hym Pryde of heynysse, or of richesse, of Empire, of *shall pass away.* roialte, of lordshupp, ne of erthely honoure, for abyde thay may not endure, but Sone shall Passe, *and* as flouris shall fade. And therfor sayth seynte Austyñe in the boke of verray Innocence, *Augustin.*
32 "Ife of riches that floryshith of the genterie of thyn auncestris the aua*u*ntest, of beauute of body, of streynth, or of honouris that the Pepill the dothe, be-holde thy-Selfe, that thow arte Erthe and into Erthe thow shalte wende. Remembyr the of
36 tho men, that to-fore the haue bene in beaute of glorie, wher *Where are all the great of* bene thay, that emyronnet were wyth grete Powere of Citeseyns, *past times ?* where bene the wyse legistres, that by witte ne myght not be surmountid? Wher ben thay that helde the grete festes *and*
40 grete mangries makid? Where ben thay that noryssheth the

Remember that Death levels all Men.

The power and might of death.

grete horsyn of pryce? Where ben tho that ladd the grete hostes? Where ben the Weldy Werriours, the Dukes and the tyrauntes? Al thay byth into Powdyr *and* to askis turne, and in voyde ¹wordis onely is hare memory makyd. Be-holde hare graues! deme yf thou cannyst, who was serwaunt, who was lorde, who was riches and who was Pouer. Discerne yf thou canyste the Persone of the kynge fro the Person of the knawe, the stronge fro the febill, the fayre fro the fowle. Therfor remembyr the of thy kynde that thou Pryde the not; therof haue mynde, yf thow kepe thy Selfe."

¹ 22 L.

Capitulum xxiiij^m.

²**Now of vndyrstondynge, that is the Seconde Parte of this vertu Prudencia. Capitulum Vicessimum quartum.** 12

³ Fol. 41.

³He Secunde Parte of Prudencia is vndyrstondynge, as y t afore Sayde. By this vertu a-vysyth a man hym of thynges that nowe bene. Amonge al thynges that byth to vndyrstonde, oone Soueraynly nedyth, that a man know hym-Selfe. For in vayne othyr thynges hym Paynyth to know, that hym-Selfe wolde for-yete.

With all thy knowing know thyself.

Ieronimus

Therfor, as seynte Ierome vs tellyth, in olde tymes whan the Pryncis of Rome retorned fro bataillis there as thay had victorie, the romanes makid thre maneres of honoures. The fryste was that al the pepill yede agaynes the Prynce with grete gladnys; The ij^e was that the Prysoneris and hostagis that were takyn in the battaille sholde follow the Pryncis chare on har fete, thare handis bounde be-hynde har backys; The iij^e was that the Prynce sholde be clothid in Iubiter thare godis cote, sittynge in a chare that iiij^e whyte horsyn drewe. But for-als-moche as the romanys wolde that the Prynce for his honoure hym-Sylfe sholde not foryete, thre dyshonoures in the same day he moste Suffyre. The fryste was that ther as the Prynce sate in his chare a bond-man and of fowle condycion to signifie that euery man of the Pepill sholde haue hope to come to glorie of a Prynce or of an empyre, by prosse and vasselage. The ij^e Dishonoure was that the bonde-man that wyth the Prynce Sate ⁴buffetis and Strokis hym yaue Saynge in gru, **Notisclotos,** that is to Say, haue knowynge of thy-Selfe, and be not Prute of so hey vyrchipp; mynde thow how thow arte dedly. The thyrde

Three honours in a Roman triumph,

and three dishonours.

⁴ 22 b L.

16

20

24

28

32

36

² Of vndyrstondynge, the whych is the Seconde Parte of Prudencia (in margin, at top of page).

dyshonoure was, that euery man myght wyth-oute Payne or
reproue *and* myssayne the Prynce for that Iorney.

In this wyse Iulyus Cesar the forte werryor, whan he came *In this way*
Julius Cæsar
4 agayñ to Rome aftyr the conqueste of his enemys, many reprowis *triumphed.*
and Indyngnacionys of the Pepill recewid, of the whyche he
neuer vengeaunce toke. Dauid the Profete sayth of men that *Dauid*
in honoure byth *and* knowyth not ham-Selfe, **Homo, cum in**
8 **honore esset, non intellexit,** *etc*, That is to say, "Whan a man
was in honoure, he ne vndyrstode not, he is lykenyd to wylde
bestis wit*h*out reysone, as he is makyd alyke to ham." Also
Dauy Sayth, **Nolite fieri sicut equus et mulus, in quibu***s* **non**
12 **est intellectus,** *etc*, that is to say, "Ne be not as an horse *and*
a mule, in whome is noone vndyrstondynge."

Of the thyrde Partie of Prudencia that is callid Purvey- *Capitulum*
aunce. Capitulu*m* **Vicessimu***m* **qui***n***tum.** *xxv*^{m}.

16 the thyrde Partie of Prudencia is Purveyaunce, by the *Every man*
has need of
wyche a man hym avysyth of thyngis that byth to come. *forethought.*
Thegh a man haue neuer so good fortune, hym nedyth of
Purveyance; And the more ryche mañ be *and* manau*n*t, the
20 more hym be-howyth that he be vmbethoght. Therof Tullyus *Tulliu*s
the wyse clerke tellyth in the boke of questions Of oone Denys
the cruel tyraunt, kynge of the realme of Cezile, That oone of
his frendis that callid was Damocles hym Sayde, "Moche hath *The story of*
Damocles and
24 god the endowet wyth grace, Rriche thow arte *and* manau*n*t *Dionysius of*
Syracuse.
grete lord-shippes, Castelis, toures, Powere of Pepill, fayre
horsyn, clothis of Sylke, *and* ryche kynne, no man is the y-
lyke." And the kynge hym answerid, "Wylte thow my
28 fortvñe proue?" "ye," sayde that othyr gladly. Than the
kynge ¹ ordaynyd that Damocles ² Where sette in a fayre bedde ¹ 23 L.
² Fol. 41 b.
of golde, and made Sette afore hym a fayre tabille full of precious mettes, *and* makyd sette afore hym̄ fayre yonge women
32 stonde hym̄ afore hym to Serwe. And whan he was in al this
delitis, the kynge co*m*maunded that men sholde hange ouer his *The sword of*
Damocles.
hede *and* his neke a Swerde of stelle Sarpe, So that nothynge
the Swerde helde, Saue oone hors-here. Than he that in the
36 delytis satte behelde the Perill in whyche he was sette: for drede
of dethe he foryate the delytes, so that no kepe he toke of the
bede of golde, ne of the delycious mettis, ne of the fayre yonge
women that hym Serwid. Than Sayde the kynge, "Suche is al

my lyfe that thow So myche preysyste." "I pray the," sayd
Damocles, "lette me Passe hens." Al the day of oure lyfe in
grete Perill we byth, for thre enemys ws werryth, dayes and
nyghtes in vs hare assautes makynge; The worlde that vs 4
drawyth to cowetyse; the fleshe vs chasyth to lecheri; the
Deuyl vs assaylyth by Pryde and envy. Moche is he a fole
and vncu*n*nynge that in so cruel a battaill noght dreddyth ne
helpe sechyth. There-for Sayth Iope, that chyualrie is manys 8
lyfe in erthe. While that we lywyth in manere of knyghtes we
fyghtyth, For whan this lyfe an ende takyth, neue*r* aftyr
chyualry shall be. And whos[o] altyme of hes dethe thynkyth,
he shall of this enemys victorie haue; therfor Sayth Salamon, 12
"Fayre Chylde, haue mynde that thow shalt dye, and neue*r*
more thow shalt Syne." the best worde that eue*r* was founde
is, that thow shalt dye.

That Prudencia is moche to Prayse, Prowyth well this 16 reyson*es* folwynge. Capitulum vicessimum Sextum.

Vlly Spekynge of Prudencia in fayre mane*r* he Sayth, "If
t that thow desyre Prudencia to haue, by reysou*n*e thy lyfe
thow shalt lede": and al thynge aftyr har kynde, and not 20
aftyr men Saynge thow shalte deme, for many thynges semyth
good *and* byth not, And other*es* semyth not good *and* byth good.
Hit is not al golde that [1] Shynyth as golde, Thou shalt not mych
holde ne Preyse the goodys that some moste Passe. The good 24
that god haue youyñ the, thow sholdyst not hit kepe as anothyr
manes good, but as thyn owyn despende *and* vse hit. Ife thow
p*r*udencia haue embraset, thou shalt neuer be vnstabill; but
aftyr that the tyme *and* the thyngis wolde aske thow howeste 28
the dresse and a-wyse. So that atte euery node that thou shalte
do, thow mayste be abill, and acordynge. ffor that is not the
honde y-meuet ne chaunged, that nowe in leynthe othyre in
Palme hym streythyth, agayñ into a wyste hym closyth. Hit 32
is propyr to Prudencia, and to hit appendyth, to examyne and
to Proue his consaille, *and* not by lyght credence to fall in
erroure or falsnesse. Of thynge that is in dowtaunce, thou shalt
not defyne, but into the tyme that thou there-of fully asserted 36
be, thow shalte abyde. Ne yeue thow not lyghtly thy sentence,
for hit is not al tymes sothe that Sothe semyth; Ofte tymes

The Advice of Prudence. 157

verite hath a vysage of lesynge, And ofte tymes a lesynge hath a *Oft-times lies look like*
coloure of verite, As he that is a frende oftymes he Shewyth *truth.*
drowpynge chere, And the losyngere *and* a dysceyuoure lagh-
4 ynge *and* a fayre [1]chere. If thow desyryste to be wyse *and* by   [1] Fol. 42.
Prudencia worche, vmbethynke the fro ferre of all that may be-
falle, that nothynge befall Sodaynly. Whoso is wyse he Seyth
not, " I wende noght that this me sholde haue betyde," but *A wise man is ready for*
8 " wel wiste y that this myght me haue betyde, And therfor *ill haps.*
agaynys that y was Purveyed." al thynge that thou shalte do,
loke that hit be good to begynne*n*, And Sethyn what ende hit
shall haue, thow moste bethynke, For wyth-out a good ende,
12 lytill is worth a good begynnynge. Whoso wyse is *and* vmbe-
thoght, he wille not begyle, ne begilid he nel not be. Swift *He will not act on sudden*
thoghtes that lyke byth to Swevnes, ne rescewe thow not, for yf *thoughts.*
thou the in Suche thoghtes delyteste, Whan thou haste all y-
16 thoght, mowrnynge *and* wrothi thow [2]shalte reme. lette thy   [2] 24 L.
thoght be stabill, certayne, and trewe, thy worde be not in
vayne, but be hit of Solace othyr of Prowe. thow shalte Preyse
and co*m*mende scarsly *and* seldewannes, but thou shalte blame
20 more scarsly, more a-vysely, and more selde. He is to reprowe *He will not praise or*
that ouer-myche Preysyth and to ofte, as he that myspreysyth *blame out of measure.*
and blamyth ouer-meswre. Ouer-myche to Preyse is suspecte of
losengry; and ouer-myche mespryce, of felony. Thou mayste hit
24 vitnesse to verite, and not to Frendshupe: a frende is to lowe,
and verite moche more. And therfore he is an onwyse man that *So don't give to Rhymers,*
audyence or Yeftis yewyth to Rymoris othyr any Suche losyn-
geris, for thay Praysith hare yeueris be thay neuer So vicious.
28 Who-so ham any good yewyth brekyth the statutis of kylkeny, *or you break the Statutes*
and he is acursid by a xj bisschopis, as the same Statutes *of Kilkenny.*
makyth mencion. Sodaynly no thynge be-hete, for whan thou
haste be-hote, more shalte thou yeue. If thou wyse be of corage
32 thou moste thynke of thre tymes, that is to witte, thyngis that *Think of three times, present,*
now byth to ordeyne, thyngis to cume to Purvey, And tho that *future, and*
ben Passyd to remembyre. Who-so nothynge thynkyth of *past.*
thyngis y-passet, a sote *and* a fole he shall be callid. And who-
36 so nothynge rekyth of that, that may falle, In sodayne myschefe
he moste falle. And who-so rekyth not whate he dothe, Sone
he shall come to evyll esplete. Remembyr the of thynges good *Both good and evil may*
and ewill that myght falle, that thou mayste adversite the *happen.*
40 bettyr Sustene, and prosperite the bettyr mayntene. Ne be not

al tymys in traualle *and* in thoghtis, but in tymes in Ioy and
Solace wythout Syn*n*e. And whan thou arte in reste, kepe the
fro ydilnesse : For holy write sayth **Ociositas inimica est anime,
et radyx viciorum**, That is to say, "Idylnysse is the enemy of 4
the Sowle, and rote of vicis." The wyse and the welgouer*n*ed
man*n*e, whan of grete [1]cures he wille hym wythdarwe, Of ydyl-
nesse ne of folye he hath not to do. To hym longyth nedes to
Esplete, domes to meswre, Dures to relesse, wronges to redresse, 8
Stryffes to allege ; al that he owyth to do Sone he Parcewyth,
he dreddyth to done amyse. His good dedis *and* workys wythout chydynge, Awantynge, or grete noyse-makynge, he fulfillyth :
Suche byth the vyse manys gyse *and* his maneris. Lette not the 12
autorie of the Seyere meve the ; take no cure of the Seyere what
Pe*r*sone he is, but take kepe what menyth that he sayth "Many
a pore man shewyth [2]wysdome and reysone, And many a Prynce
grete foly wythout reysone." Ne haue no cure to Please al men, 16
but good men, ne to be praysid of folis and Shrewis, but of good
men and wyse. To dysplese il men and Shrewis, hit is grete
honoure and Praysynge ; and to be of ham Praysid, hit is blame
and reprowe. Suche thynges thou owyste to Desyre that good 20
men Desyrith and praysyth. Desyre not the thynge to the, wyche
thou mayste not come to. Whan thou arte in p*r*osperite, thynke
vppon aduersite, and of were in tyme of Pees, for hit is to late
whan thou art y-take. The wyse man may not be mystake, for 24
he will afor-hande be remembrid. To the Offyce of Prudencia
appendyth the dedis of all othyr vertues redresse, To hit appendyth to show whate, whan, and how hit is to done ; To hit
appendyth to Purvey that oure workys to god be acceptabill, 28
profitable to vs, and not wrongefull to oure neghbors, that god
be glorifiede in oure workis, *and* rewarde to vs be gette, and
goode essampill to oure neghbors be yeue. Also to the office of
Prudencia appendyth aftyr trowthe Suppos, and not aftyr the 32
oppynyon of dyuers Pepill. Also to the Office of Prudencia
appendyth to be stabill, and not variable. Salamoñ Sayth,
"An holy man in wysdome abidyth as the Son*n*e, And a foole
chaungyth [3]as the moone." Also Prudencia dyshoneste in pryuyte 36
also well as in oppyn placis enchueth. Also in prosperite, rathyr
than in adue*r*site wysly dothe. And hit is to witte that he that
Synnyth dedly, Doth hym Selfe vij grete folies. Fryste he
b[l]yndyth hym Selfe, for the boke of wysdome Sayth "The 40

Marginalia:
Don't be idle.
A wise man will find plenty to do. [1] 24 *b* L.
He will weigh advice, not the person who gives it.
[2] Fol. 12 *b*.
He does not fear the blame of evil men.
Prudence is the director of all other virtues.
Solomon. [3] 25 L.
Secu*n*dum parisiensis.

Justice: The Second Cardinal Virtue. 159

malice of Synneris ham-Selfe blyndyth." The ij⁰ is, that he byndyth hym-Selfe to the Deuyl, As Iob Sayth, **Misit in rethe Pedem Suum,** "He hath Putte his foote in the nette," but as
4 gregory Sayth, "he shall not, whan he will, drawe hit oute."
The iij⁰ Is, that as a woode man hym-Selfe he Puttyth his haundis, yeuynge hym-Selfe a wounde vncurabill; For that Salamon Sayth, "By malice he hath his Sowle Slayne," for
8 Synne is the dethe of the Sowle, for hit departyth god from hym, the whych is his lyfe. The iiij⁰ is, that he castyth his goodys a-way, For who-so doth a dedly Synne, al the goode dedys that euer he did he hath loste, Into the tyme that he into
12 good lyfe turne. And also the good dedys that he doth in that synne, thay byth not veray good, for thay byth not to hym merytorye. The fyfte that he goth avay fro the makere of al thynge, For Osee, the holy prophete, Sayth, **Ve eis quoniam**
16 **recesserunt a me,** "Wo to them, for-why thay haue lefte me." The vj⁰ is that he to al-myghty good presumyth were to make, the whyche were sone were endyth, yfe the mercy of god hit wolde suffre. The vij⁰ foly ys that he the yatis of Paradyse to
20 hym-Selfe he S[t]oppyth, and the kyngedome of hewyñ Sillyth for a lytill price, lyke as esaau didd, that for a lytill Potage solde the ryght of his herytaunce.

The 7 follies of deadly sin. Job.

Gregory.

Solomon.

Who sins, loses all his good works.

Hosea.

¹**Of the Seconde vertu cardynall that is y-callid in latyn**
24 **Iusticia. In englysshe ryghtfulnesse othyre ryght. Cap**_itu_**l**_u_**m vicessimum Septimum.**
²t He lawe of Emyle³ exponyth this vertu Iusticia, in this maner in latyne: **Iusticia est constans et perfecta voluntas,**
28 **Ius suum vnicuique tribuens,** That is to Say, "Ryght is a stydfaste and a perfite wille, yewynge to euery man that to hym is ryghtful." Saynte Austyne Sayth, that there byth two Parties of Iusticia, that is to witte, "leue harme, and do good." Of
32 this Sayth the Prophete, **Declina a malo, et fac bonum,** And cryst Sayth in the gospell, **Primum querite regnum dei et iusticiam eius,** that is to Say, "Fryste haske ye the kyngdome of god and his ryghtfulnesse"; And in anothyr Place he Sayth,
36 **Beati qui esuriunt et siciunt iusticiam,** that is to say, "I-blyssyd be thay that hungeryth and thurstyth ryght." Some clerke dyuydyth the vertu of Iusticia into v⁰ Parties, Fryste into obedience, for the Suffrayne; In correccioñ for the Subiecte;

¹ 25 b L.

² Fol. 43.
³ civille Lain.

Capitulum xxvijᵐ.
Of Justicia

Agustinus.

The five parts of Justice.

In equyte for Pere and pere; *and* in verite and feyth, whych appertenyth to al men. Seneca dyscrewynge Iusticia sayth, **Iusticia diuina lex est, et vinculum societatis humane**, that is to say, " Ryght is the lawe of god, and a bonde of manys fello- 4 chippe." For the lawe of god chargyth the forto do to thy neghbore, lyke as thow woldyst he sholde do to the. Ife thou the vertu of Iusticia desiriste, loue god, do profite to al men, *and* Dyssesse no man; *and* il men that nve wolde thou shalt 8 lette, that thay shall not mow trew men to dyscsse, chaste dystorube; and Punyshe mysdoeris, the whych appartenyth to the vertu Iusticia: he consentyth to wickyd men, that wickydnesse will not destru. In the boke of kynges the scripture vs 12 tellyth, that helye the Prest was a full good man *and* an holy, But for-als-moche that he his Sonnes tha wickyd men were *and* lecherus, slackely reprowid* *and* not chastid, by reddoure of the lawe, god ther-of toke grewos vengeaunce. For thar Syne they 16 where slayune in battaille, and xxx^{ti} Mt. wyth hame of godis Pepill, by assaute of mysbelewyne men; And the arke of god, of the whyche the Iues makyd so myche ¹drucrie,² was rauyshid a-way. And ther-for, when helye herde the newe thythynges, 20 he felle out of the cheyre ther as he Sate; His neke was broke, and there he dyet. The good kynge Dauy the worthy hardy, the loset of force and of vertue, of witte and of bounte, of whom god Saythe, " I haue y-founde a man aftyr myn herte," ffor-als- 24 moche as he was ouer-tendyre of his chyldryne *and* ham chastyd not in har yonge age, he founde ham aftyr when they were full woxeñ Prowte, onreuli, fiers, *and* presumpteous; so that thay wolde haue regnyd lyvynge hare fadyr, And oone of ham that 28 was callid absoloñ Pute hym out of the realme, and ouer-lay his fadyr Concubynes; And werre longe tyme Durid betwene the fadyr and the Sone, til god abbatid the wickyd presumpcion of the tyraunt, ffor he was slayne in battaill, and his men Discom- 32 fitd. That god punyshid hame that chastenet not hare subiectis, ³me-thynketh hit apperyth oft-tymes by dyuers Englyshe captaynys of Irland* that haue bene *and* now byth, whos neclygence in noñ-Punyshynge of hare nacionys and Subiectes haue destrued 36 ham-Selfe, har naciones, *and* har landis. The names of thes captaynys hit awaylyth nat, ne hit nedyth, *and* also hit were henyouse *and* Perelos to reherse. And so fore thay thre causis, I leue of that matiere, *and* also leste y sholde be shente in this 40

parti, the Sothe forto telle, ffor Salamon in his proverbis Sayth, Solomon.
"Verite getyth hatredyñ, and good Service gettyth Frendis."
And there-for Sayth the apostill in his Pistill that he wrote to Paul.
4 the Galathis, iiij^{to} "I ham," he sayde, "makyd an enemy vnto
you, tellynge to you the verite." verite in this dayes is myssayd,
Verite in this dayes is wyth-holde, bonde, *and* prisone*r*, ¹for ¹ 26 b L.
vnneth, as Parisience sayth, is founde the man that hit wolde Parisiensis.
8 say. And therfor Sayth Senecka, a notabil worde fore Prynces Seneca.
and ryche men forto know, he sayth thus, "I shall show the what
is hit that thynge that lackyth vnto ham that haue al richesis in
Possession. I Sey that ham lackyth men that Sholde Say to
12 haṁ the Verite, or the trouthe." Verite in this dayes in eue*ry*
Syde impugned, So that hit hath ofte-tymys necessite for to fall
aftyr the worde of ysay, Saynge, **Veritas cecidit in platea**, that Isaiah.
is to say, "Verite is fall in the Pament." Verite caste doune,
16 whan any vnryghtly thynge is preferrid to trouthe, But verite Truth is little
that so now is despied and lytill Settyn of, in tyme comynge set by now.
hit shall delyue*r* his louers, and condempne his enemys aftyr the
worde of oure Sauyoure, Saynge, "ye shall knowe verite, *and*
20 verite shall delyue*r* you." Perisience Sayth, "As the false Peny Parisiensis.
hathe hyṁ-Selfe vnto the trewe, So hath hym-Selfe the false
man, vnto the trewe man." Also he Sayth, "we Sholde do
trouthe vnto al men." And there-for Sayth seynte Austy*n*ne, Augustin.
24 "Eue*ry* man that lyeth doth ille *and* wickydly, for no man
lyenge, in that that he lyeth, kepyth trouthe or feyth."
Salamon Sayth, "a lyynge man is hatfull vnto god," ffor whan Solomon.
al tresure is tried, trouthe is the beste. Now leue I of this
28 mane*r* matire, *and* Speke ferthyre of chastesynge of ill men *and*
tresspasoures. I Say that Goue*r*nours of the Pepill sholdyn
correcte ille men, whyle thay may not longe abyde, for a Poete
Sayth, **Qui non wlt dum quid, Postea forte nequibit**, that is to
32 say, "who so will not whan he may, he shal not when he
wille"; The grete Poet Ouydie Sayth, **Pryncipijs obsta**, "Wyt- Ovid.
stonde the begynnynge," ffor lyghtyre is a fressh wounde to
hele, than a festrid. And whyle an hooke is a ²yonge Spyre, ² 27 L.
36 hit may be wonde into a wyth, but when hit is a wixen tree, an
hundrid oxyn vnneth hit may bowe. Salamon sayth, **Qui parsit** Solomon.
virge odit filium, "who Sparith the yarde he hatyth the
chylde"; And whoso sparith the thefe, he sleyth the trew man.
40 That a prynce Sholde execute the dynte of Swerde in his enemy,

Specialy in fals Pepill, not ouersettynge the houre of fortune,
Shewyth this stories Suynge. The fryste boke of kynges tellyth
that ¹oure Lord god cnoyntyd Saule Kynge vppon Israell, and
Putte Hym in the way and Sayde, "go thou and Sle the Synners
of Amaleth, And thow shalt agaynys ham fyght, tylle thay be
dede." Saule forthe wente, Agage the kynge of amalech into his
prysoner he toke, the Pepill he slow, Saule his Pepill of the
beste oxyn and Shepe Pray thay makedyñ. Than came the
hooly Prophete Samuel to kynge Saule and Sayde, "Why ne
hardyst thou the voyce of oure lorde, but thou hast y-do ille in
the syght of god; And for-als-moche as thou haste y-Putte of
the worde of god, god hath caste the avay that thou shalt not be
kynge of Israell": and So was he onkynge makyd̃, and the holy
Dauy anoyntyd kynge of Israell, lyuynge Saule: and merouer,
for-als-moche as Saule fulfillid not the execucion of dynte of
Swerde in amalich as he was chargid̃, he was ytraualid with the
Deuyl. And the hondis of this holy prophet slowe the cursid
kynge Agage. Also Dares a clerke that was att the Segee of the
nobill Cite of Troy, and therof the stori-makere, tellyth and
affermyth for sothe that atte the Seconde battaill betwen the
Troians and the grecans, that aftyr Monestus the Duke of
Athene hadd wondyd hectore, the kynges Sone of troy, Priames,
in the Same day ²this nobill knyght hector Slow of the grecans
more than a thowsande knyghtes. Where-for the hoste of
grecans he broght into so grete febilnes that none of ham had
herte to defende, ne Agomenon har kynge powyr hym in battaill
to Sette. Therfor the troians vertuosly the grecans into hare
tentis fleynge suyt, and as men that victorie hadde hare Shippes
brente, hare golde, Syluyr, armure, and Iowell with ham thay
tursid. This was the day that an ende was makyd of the
battalle, the troians victors for ay myght haue be. But, O, how
lyght cause blynde the troians eyeñ, and namely hector that the
vndoynge of hym-Selfe and al hissyn myght haue enchued, for
that day the troians so myghty were, that al the grecans that
there agayns ham was, yslayñe thay moght. Discression in none
wys man is to Preyse the whyche whan he is in hey nede or
in morteH perill yssette, And a good fortune hym befallyth, that
of Suche nede or Peril he may Sudaynly delyuerid be, the grace
that fortune hym yewyth nel rescewe. But as anone gracious
man forsakyth the grace in oone houre, that neuer aftyr he shal

and destroyed for lack of Prudence and Justice.

mow comyn to, So hit befell of the onsely hector in that day, in whyche of his enemys wyth grete wyrchippe he myght haue y-hadd the victory. whan al his enemys faste fro hym flowyn, *(4)* than Aiax, the Sone of Thelamon the kynge, an hardy knyght, strongly in hector assaute makyd. But as thay in battaille atte that tyme to-giddyr spake, hector hym well knew and that he his neye cosynne was; gladd he was that he his cosynne Aiaxe *(8)* Sawe, his armes away he Putte, grete chere to hym ¹he makyd, his Cosyn to Plese more entyerly. honestly hym he Prayed the fayre Cite of Troy wythin to See, and wyth his grete Perentele awhyle hym dysporte. Than Aiax Hector louely Prayed, that *(12)* yfe he so myche hym lowid as he Sayde, that he ²wolde make and Procure that the Troians for that day agayn the Grecans of battalle wolde cesse, and no more the chasce followe, but home to the Cite wende. Hector therto grantid, the trues weryn *(16)* trumped vp for that day, The troians wyth grete doloure the battaill lefte, and home thay wente. This was so lyght a cause, that the troians that day of the entente of har victorie cessid: Vnto the whyche neuer aftyr thay ne myght not come, but in *(20)* Sorte tyme aftyr, this hardy knyght Hector was Slayne, the Pepill al slayn *and.* flemyd, and the excellent Cite of troy for aye Subuertid and destrued was. This Cite, as dares Sayth, was th[r]e dayes iornay in leythe, and also myche in brede; the wallis *(24)* of hit weryn of marbill, in heght CC cubites, wyth many toures in grete heghte the wallis abow. Heuery hous of the Cite was marbill, LX cubitis in heghte; the Sigee of Troy durid ten yere. The fryst cause of al the werre, now shortely to telle, was this:— *(28)* Pelleus, kynge of thesaly in grece, Sende an hardy and a bolde knyght, Iason, his brodyr sonne, *with* a fresshe felloshippe, into the Ile of Calcos to wyn the wethyr fleis of golde of Oetes the kynge. This Iason Saylynge thedreward landyd at Troy, hym and *(32)* his men to refresshe, wittynge came to Lamedanton, the kynge of troy, of the fresshe array of Iason³ and his men. This kynge therof hawynge envy, sende Iason by message that he sholde his londe lewe wyth-out delay. Iason so did, and Sayde, "Gentrie *(36)* ⁴wolde that the kynge to estraungeris none harme doynge bettyr chere sholde make. And Peraduenture, are this yere passe, y shall here lande, whedyr that he will or no": and So he dide, the kynge he Slowe, Troy he brente, and the kynges doghtyr

but he stayed the fight

Ector.

to make cheer to his cousin Ajax,
¹ 28 L.

² Fol. 44 b.

and granted three days' truce.

So the victory ceased, and at the last Troy was taken.

De longitudine et latitudine troie etc.

The first cause of the war.

Troia.

Jason and Laomedon.

⁴ 28 b L.

How Jason burnt Troy.

³ by message, *marked for erasure here.*

rauyshid. But Priames, son to lamedanton, and fadyr to Ector,
restorid troy So excellently as I afor-Sayde, that hit sholde
neuer haue be take, ne hadd traysone beyne¹ begonne. And hit
is to witte that Rome, Venys, Italy, Lumbardy, Fraunce, England, and many othyr Prowyncis weryn, *and* yette byth, inhabite for the moste Partie of the Pepill that Scapid out of this
nobill Cite, the Newe Troy, whan hit was won.

> **Nobyll and gracious lorde**, thes two stories afore-writtyn
> considerit, Sethyn god and oure kynge haue grauntid you
> Powere, do ye therof Execucion in opyn fals enemys, traytouris,
> and rebelle, trew men quelleris, whan thay fallyth Into youre
> handys, by the thow Sharpe eggis of youre Swerde, that is to
> witte by rygoure of lawe and dyntes delynge, hauynge in mynde
> that I Sayde afore of the Poet, "wi*th*stonde the begynnynge."
> For as a Sparke of fyre risyth an huge fyre able a realme to
> brente, So rysyth of the roote of an fals enemy, appert traytoure,
> othyr rebellis, many wickid wedis sone growynge, that al trewe
> men in londe Sore greuyth. Therfor, whan thay fallyth into
> youre handis, Raase ham a⸺ out of rote, as the good gardyner
> dothe the nettylle. I know welle the roote of the nettille, One
> dough O'dynicis, fadyr of hym that now is, Of whom spronge
> the wedis that als myche in mi tyme haue destruede of the
> comyte of Kyldare as al Irysh men of Irland aftyr. this nettle
> in Poynte was to haue be rasid out of roote, ²whan ye, gracious
> Lorde, the castell of Ley out of the fals nettle-is Handys
> wyrchiply wan. In the yere of oure lorde Ihe*s*u cryste, M⸠.
> CCCC xx^{ti}. And ye the same castell, to the lorde therof, the
> Erle of kyldare aforsayd, delyuerid. In the Same yere the
> Same fals nettles lyghtly agayn hit gotte.

Capitulum xxviij^m. **That a prynce sholde not truste to his enemy. Capitulum Vicessimum octauum.**

S. Bernard.   b   Ernard Sayth, **Debilitas inimici non est Pax, Sed ad tempus treuga,** that is to Say, "The febilnes of the enemy nys not a pees, but a truse for the tyme," And yf thou trystis that thyn̄ enemy thynkyth not the Same sotilte that thou thynkyste, thou Puttyste thy-Selfe in drede, and therfor Salamon Sayth,

Solomon.   **Non confidas inimico tuo in eternum,** that is to say, " Tryste thou neue*r* to thyn enemy." And touchynge this matiere y

The Story of the Jew and the Philosopher.

fynde write in this maner. Two men haue ben companyed in one way, that oone was an Philosofoure and feythfull man, that othyr was a man the whych was an Iewe. The Philosofre rode *The Philosopher and the Jew.*
4 vpon a mule that he hadd fosterid atte his owyñ plesynge, and bare with hym al necessaries for a man that ride sholde; the Ieue went on his fete, and noothynge he had to ette ne noone othyre necessari. they talkid togiddyr, and the Philosofre to
8 the Iwe Sayde, "What is thy law *and* whate is thy feythe?" the Iue answerid, " I belewe that in hewyn is oone god whyche y honoure, and y will good to al men that accordyth with me in my feyth, *and* in my law, *and* my belewe, and good wolde to *They tell each other their law; first the Jew,*
12 me. And who-so dyscordyth fro my lawe, hit is laweful to me hym to Sle, his mony take of hym, his wyfe and his chyldryn also, and abowe al tynge I ham acursid in my lawe, yf y kepe feyth and trouthe to hym, othyr hym helpe, or mercy do, or any
16 [1]thynge hym Spare." Aftyr thys Sayde the Iue to the Philosofre, " I haue now shewid the my law and my feyth, now shew thou thyne to me." The Philosofre Sayde, " this is my feyth *and* my lawe. Fryst y desyre good to my-Selfe and to [1] 29 b L.

then the Philosopher.
20 my chyldryne *and* to my cosynys, and y will none harme to noo creature of god Of my lawe ne of noone othyr. And y belewe that mercy and ryght is to be doñe to euery man lyvynge, and no wronge me Plesyth, and as me semyth yf harme is befall to
24 any man, that hit me touchyth *and* nuyth. I desyre Prospe*r*ite, helth, Solase, felicite, and goodnesse to al men in Comune." Than sayde the Iue, " And whate yf a man haue y-do the wronge or offence?" The Philosofre sayde, " I wonte that in
28 hevyn is oon god, good, ryghtful, and wyse, and nothynge fro hym may be hydd, that rewardyth good men and il aftyr hare deserte." The Iue answerid, "why kepist thou not thy lawe, And why confermyst thou not thy feyth in ded doynge?" and
32 he answerid, " how shal y hit do?" the Iue hym answerid, " See me here, a man a-foote, hungry, thursti, *and* for trauaille recreiet, and thou rydest thy-Selfe atte aise." " Soth sayst thou," quod the Philosofre, and anoone lyght doune of the *The Jew asks for a ride,*
36 mule, he opynyd his male, and yaue hym mette and drynke; And aftyr he sette hym on his Mule. Anoone aftyr the Iue Saw that he was wel ydressid, and that the mule was swyfte, he smote the mule wyth the sporis, the Philosofre behynde fere *and runs away from his companion.*
40 he lefte. And therefor he cried " alas, I ham [2]confused." The [2] Fol. 45 b.

Iue a lytill the mule¹ restyd, and Sayde, "I Sewyd the my lawe and his condicion, and y wille hit conferme." Than hastly the mule forth he drowe; this Philosofre sayde, "Leue me not in this deserte to ben Slayne of lyons, othyr of othyr wylde bestis, or of ¹hungre, myssayse, thurste, or Some othyr myschefe dey; but haue mercy of me as y hadde of the." The Iue endeynyd not bakeward to be-holde hym, he wolde not hyre, he stynte not, tille he out of his syght y-Passyd was. And whan the Philosofre was so in dyspayre wythout Socoure, he remembrid hym of his Perfeccion *and* his feyth, and of that that he hadd sayd to the Iue, that in hevyn was oone god ryghtfull Iuge, vnto whome nothynge may be conseylid ne hid: than he lyfte vpe his hede to god, and Sayd, "lord god, thou woste that y belew in the, *and* in thy lawe, and in thy comma*n*dme*n*tes, I preyse the a*n*d magnifie the, And therfor conferme thyn honoure anent this Iue." whan he hadd thus Sayde, he wente not fere thennes, ther-as he founde the Iue falle doune of the mule, that brake his thegh and his neke hurtdet, and the mule on his belly stondynge; and when the mule Sawe his lorde that hym nurchyd, he knew hym and agaynys hym wente. the Philosofre lepid vp the mule *and* departid fro the Iue, that ther In Peril of deth abode. The Iue cried, "a, fayre brodyr, haue mercy of me, for I dey. kepe thy lawe, for god hath graunte the victory." Than he began more besilli the Philosofre to blame, "Thow synnest vickydly yf thou me leuyste wit*h*out mercy." Than Sayde the Philosofre, "thou synneste cursly whan thou leftyste me wyth-out mercy." the Iue answerid, "reproue me not of trespasis y-Paste, for y Sayde to the that Suche was my law, *and* my feyth in² whych y was norshid in, *and* in whych y founde all myne auncestres ynorshid *and* myne eldryñ therin contynue." **Therfor, nobill and gracious lorde, consydyr ye that youre yrysshe enemys ne hare auncestres wyth-nede any of them was trewe to you or to youre fadyr, than ye ³were strongyr than thay, wytnysse on youre-Selfe, that arthure M^cmirgñ was no longyr trewe ne pees helde, than youre fadyr lyuet, for al the grete othis that he Sware.** This Phylosofre aforsayde had mercy of the Iue, *and* makid hym ride behynde hym into the Place there-as he desyrid to be amonge his owyn Peple. Not longe aftyr the

¹ nule, MS.   ² in in, MS.

How a Prince should use his Power. 167

Iue died, And whan the kynge Of the Cite herde of this matiere, he sende for the Philosofre, and makyd hym his prywey consailloure, for that Piteouse worke and for the bounte of his 4 lawe. *The Philosopher has mercy on him, and is rewarded.*

Of the manere correccion that a prynce sholde haue anent his Subiectis. Capitulum vicessimum nonum. *Capitulum xxix^m.*

h Itte Is to witte that correccion sholde come of lowe, acord-
8 ynge to holy writte, **Ego quos amo arguo, et castigo.** "I blame and chaste tho men that y loue." But Sume prynces and Iuges wolde correcte tho men namely to whome thay haue Envy, whos correccion nys not but an enemyly persecucione.
12 Isay the holy prophet Sayth, **Egredietur virga de radice Iesse,** that is to say, "A yarde shall out-Passe out of the roote of Jesse." Iesse is noone more to say, but a brandynge, for of the brandynge of lowe the yarde of correccion shuld oute-Passe.
16 There-[1]for ye shall not correcte youre Subiectes as an enemy, but as[2] a brothyr. For correccion with-out mercy is a blyne wodnys, And lyke a blynd archere, whyche wenyth to smyte a dere, and hittyth a man, as lameth did, that Purposyd to shote
20 a wilde beste and smote Cayme and hym killid. The lowe of Iusticia and ryghtfulnesse of Dome regnnyd in Prynces, that Paganes where in olde tyme, moche more than hit dothe now in oure crystyn Prynces. For as valery Saythe, A kynge that
24 Cambises was callid founde that oone of his Iuges, that he [3]hadde y-sette to Iuge his Pepill, yaue a fals Sentence, wherfor this kynge comandid that he were y-hillid, and did couere whyth his Skyñne the Seete therin as he was woned to sitte
28 whan that he was Iuge. And commandid that his Sonne, that Iuge was aftyr hym in the Same Cete, shulde Sitte and deme, that he mynde haue sholde of the Payne of his fadyr, wpon whos skynne he Sate. In this maner a newe Payne he founde,
32 by the whyche fals Iuges queyntly he chastid. Arystotle preysyth the vertu of Iusticia, and Sayth, that hit is the moste faryste vertu of all vertues, more bryghtyr Shynynge than the day-sterre. And therfor wyth-out this vertu may no Prynce
36 ryghtfully regne. For the Powere of a prynce that is not ryghtfull demenyt, ys lykenyd to a sharpe Swerde in a wodemanys honde. Al othyr vertues bene vayllaunt to tho men

Isaiah.

[1] Fol. 46.

Correct your subjects as brothers, not enemies.

Valerius.

[3] 31 L.

The judgment of Cambyses.

Aristotle on justice.

[2] as as, MS.

The justice of a king profitable to his subjects.	that ham hath, but the ryghtfulnesse of a prynce strechyth hym to al tho that Subiectes to hym byth. And therfor Sayde the Pepill of Iude, that the ryghtfulnesse of a prynce ys more profitabill to his subiectis, than Plente of mettes and drynkes. 4
Helinaund.	Helinaund, that stories of Romanys wrote, tellyth in his boke that Traiane the Emperoure of Rome leped vp to hors and redy
A widow prayed Trajan for justice.	was to go to battaill. there came forthe a widdowe and hym helde by the fote, and delfully hyr Playnyd, and with wepynges 8 hym Prayed, that he wolde do hyr ryght, Of tho men that hyr Sone had Slayne, whych was not but an Innocent, And Sayde, "Syre, thou arte Emperoure, and I haue Sufferid the cruell
He promised it on his return.	wronge." the Emperoure answerid, "whan y come agayne, I 12 shall do thyn asseth." She sayde, "and whate yf hit happe that thou neuer agayne come?" "My successoure shall do the
1 31 b L.	ryght." She answerid, "whate ¹shall hit availle the, the good that anothyre man thy Successoure shall do? Thou arte my 16 Doctoure, and aftyr thy deservynge thow shalte mede rescewe: hit is wronge and dysceyte, noght pay the dette that is owynge.
She sued for it on the spot.	Thy successoure, to ham that wronge Sufferyth, for hym-Silfe he shall be bounde; Anothyr manys ryghtfulnes may not Saw the. 20 Hit shall be honoure to thy Successoure, and well hit shall hym befall, yfe he may Sawe his owyne." To this wordis the Emperoures herte, tendyr of Pite that he toke of hyre wordis,
And he lighted from his horse and did justice.	Anone he lyght doune of his hors, and Saate in Iugement, and 24 anone he did to the widdowe fully ryght. And therfor the Romanes makyd to hym an ymage in myde the Strete, to Show how to the widdow he didde ryght, ar that he yede in werre vp fellons and enemys of the Empire. Anothyr tyme hit happid, 28 that Traiane his Sonne rode an hors vndauntdid, that ouer-trade a weddowes Sone in the strete into the tyme that he died.
² Fol. 46 b.	²She makyd Pleynte to the Emperoure, and there-of ryght
Moreover, he gave up his son, who had killed a widow's child.	askyd. He toke his owyn Soñne, and hym to the widdow 32 yaue for his sone, that dede was, to do hyre wille wyth hym. Therefor hit was cried in the Sene of the Senatoures of Rome in audience of all the Pepill, "No man is more bessid than Cesar Augustus, ne noo man bettyr than Traiane." Moche 36
Christian Princes, take shame of this Pagan.	sholde oure crystyn Prynces reede and be ashamyd, whan thay doth no ryght to the Pepill, or slackely and Slowely hare wrongis amendyth, whan Iusticia, as well to Pouer as to ryche sholde be done frely, Delayeth for fawoure or for hate, or hit 40

for Penyes sylle and Sauyth gilti men, and dampnyth gylteles
men. Tho men ben lykenyd to the Iues, the cruel [1]fellons, the [1 32 L.]
whyche Sauyd baraban the thefe and a man murderere, and
crucifieddyn Ihesu, the verray Sauyoure. More deppyr in the *Ill Princes shall lie*
turmentis of helle shall bene the ille Prynces, than the ill *deeper in hell*
subiectes; And more the crystyn Prynces than the Pagan *than Pagan ones.*
Pryncis, yf they do not ryght to al men. And yfe thay done
welle thay shall haue more rewarde. Wherof hit is writtyn in
the boke of wysdome, " to Smale Pepill mercy shall be grauntid,
but the myghty men *and* stronge, more strongyr' turmenty shall
suffre." Ther was an heremyte Sumtyme, that al tyme Prayed *The hermit and Pope*
god that he wolde shewe hym of whate merite he was and in *Gregory.*
whate degre, Atte the laste a voyce frome hevyn hym answerid,
" Of the Same merite thou art, tofor god, as gregory the Pope."
than Sayde the heremyte, " Alas, In ille tyme came I into this *The hermit complains.*
deserte, In ille tyme Saw y this hermytage, in myssaisse and
defaute, in full grete Sufferaunce haue I be so many Ieris, and
now ham I but y-like gregori the Pope, that hath So grette
honoure *and* reuerence *and* riches. he hath so hey glorie and
Pouer, that all the worlde to hym Enclynyth *and* Subiecte is."
whan this heremyte so hym demenet he fell neygh in dyspayre;
the voyce of the augill hym Sayde, " Thow arte a fole dotdrat *The angel answers.*
and ouer-trowes. how darryst thow make comparisone betwene
gregory and thy-Selfe? thou lowist more the catte that thou
haste, than gregory al the worlde." Bi this hit apperyth full
well, that riches and heynesse of the worlde ne takyth away *Riches do not take away all*
good vertues: But more byth to Prayse the grete lordis, that *virtue,*
by witte *and* vertues ledyth and gouernyth the Pepill har *they make it more difficult.*
Subiectes, than Power men that nothynge haue to gouer[n]e
ne to mayntene [2]but ham-Selfe. This gregory as the stoory [2 32 b L.]
tellyth, For-why that he hadd harde of Traian the Emperoure,
that he was full of ryght, he was delfull that on so ryghtfull a
prynce was Per[s]hid. And Prayed god bysely wyth entyere *Gregory prayed to God*
herte that yf hit hym Plesid, he sholde take this Emperoure *for Trajan*
out of hell, and hym to Sawe. An angill to gregori Sayde, *the Emperor:*
" atte this tyme god hath herde thy Prayere, Traian is sawid, *and his*
But fro hens-forward bid thou no more Suche Prayeris." A, *prayer was heard.*
lord god, moche louyst thou the vertu of Iusticia, whan for hit
thow haddyst mercy of a pagane, And the blysse that neuer
ende shall hawe in hewyn, for Iusticia to hym thou grauntyste.

To the whyche blysse vs brynge Ihesu cryst, [1]Hevyn Kynge, Amen. Here endyth the boke of Iusticia and begynnyth the thyrde vertu that is y-callid in latyn fortitudo. In Englysshe Streynth of herte, othyr boldenys, othyr manhode, othyr hardynesse. Cap*itu*l*u*m tricessimum.

Capitulum xxx[m]. *Augustin.* He thyrde cardynalle vertu ys y-callid fortitudo. Saynte t Austyn Sayth in libro de morali*bus* ecclesie, **ffortitudo vero est amor facile om*n*ia tollerans propter id quod amatu*r*.** that is to Say. "Fortitudo is a loue al thynge lyghtely

The Gloss. Sufferynge, for that thynge that is y-lowid." The [glose] vpon the gospell of Matheu Sayth, **ffortitudo est firmitas animi contra molestias seculi,** that is to say, "Fortitudo is a stid-

[2] *gouernance, MS.* fastnes of the Soule, agaynes the grieuance[2] or heuynesse of the worlde." Tullyus in Secu*n*da rethorica, Sayth, **Fortitudo**

Cicero. **est considerata pe*r*iculor*um* suscepcio *et* labor*um* pe*r*pessio,** that is to Say, "Fortitudo is a considerid v*n*dyrstondynge of Peri*ll*, and a sufferaunce of trauai*ll*." Also Tulli Say3 that,

Cicero. **Fortitudo e*st* magnar*um* reru*m* appeticio et humilium con-

[3] 33 L. **tempcio et cu*m* racione humili[3]tatis labor*um* perpessio,** that is to Say, "Fortitudo is a desyre of grete thynges, and a despysynge of lowly thynges, and a sufferance of trauaill*e*, wyth

Fortitude bears both good and evil. the Pro*fi*te of reyson*n*e." By thys vertue Fortitudo, a man may Susten*e* w*ith*out feyntyse of herte, trybulacions and adversitees and harde chaunces, And well berre his good fortunes wythout any Pryde. By this vertu Is the herte of a man I-Stabelid, in so myche that for no chaunce hit is not y-nued, but hym

It makes him steadfast and unchanging. holdyth Stydfastly and Strongly in al adventures, good and ill, not chaungynge the herte. This vertue had heyly al this holy martires and wourthy men of armes that afor vs were.

Cicero. Tully Say3 that who-so hathe the vertu of Fortitudo, he shall lyue w*ith* grete treste, frel*y* and wythout drede. Moche is hit grete to manes corage noght to fless*h*, but stabilli Stonde, and the Ende of lyfe to yelde wythout drede. If thou haue this

What a strong man says of his enemy. vertue Fortitude, thou shalte neu*er* say, that wronge ys done to the, but of thyne enemy thow shalt Say, he grewid me not, but he hadde wille to grewe. He that is wyse and hardy, he haue the vertue of Fortitudo p*r*oprely, and Su*m* men hym callyth a corageous man, or a manful man. Suche a corageous man, of

He speaks no evil; noo man he shall Say i*ll* in p*r*esent ne in absente; Opynly he will take battaill, for deceit and trechuri appendyth to hym that

is feynte of herte. Than shall he be holde hardy and corageous, *he is neither foolhardy nor cowardly.*
that desyryth not gret pereiH, as doth the fole-hardy ; ne ouer-
myche doutyth, as doyth the feynte coward. Arystotle, in the *Aristotle.*
4 iiij⁰ boke of Ethic, descreuyth the hardy in thys mane*r*, " The
hardy puttyth not hym-Selfe in pe*ri*H by Smale thynges that
lytill avalyth, For so done thes foolis, that So myche thay
Preysyth thynges ¹that lytill wourthe bene, that thay Puttyth ¹ 33 *b* L.
8 ham-Selfe in pe*rei*H of lyfe for ham. And that appartenyth to
a feynte herte to lowe myche a thynge of lytill waluc. But the
hardy for a grete thynge and of grete Pryce gladdly hym *The bold man puts him in*
Puttyth in pe*ri*H of lyfe, As for com*m*une Profite of the Cite, *peril for things of*
12 Contrey, othyr a roialme, to sawe holy churche, to enhanse the *great price,*
vyrchippe of god ; In Suche case Puttyth the hardy boldely his
lyfe in pe*ri*H, And leue*r* hym Is to lyue*n* in honoure, than to
lyue wit*h*out ²vertue in dyshonoure." So did the good Kynges, ² Fol. 47 *b.*
16 Pryncys, Erlys, Baronys, *and* Knyghtes that afor vs were ; as
did kynge Dauy, Sampson, Iudas Machabeus *and* his bretherin, *as all the worthies did.*
Arthur, Charles of Fraunce, the good Prynce Edward, James
youre g*r*aunt-sire, Maurice fitz Geraud, Robert Steuenes son,
20 Reymond le grose, Ihoñ de curcy, *and* many othe*r*es of the
quenqueste of Irland. The hardy more gladly yeuyth than
rescewyth, largely he rewardyth, Amonges hey men and lordes
he contynueth hym heyly, Amo*n*ges mene Pepill menly, So
24 that he may acorde to ham all. The hardy of few thynges hee *He takes few things in*
hym entremyttyth, and takyth few nedys in hande, *and* they *hand, and those of great*
shall ben of grete nobelesse, and of grete renoune. For-why to *price.*
entremytte of al thynges, appendyth to hym that hath a lowe
28 herte, and lytill vertu. The hardy or the manfull in hidlynges
he nendeynyth not any-thynge to do, For he wille do nothynge
where-for he sholde be reprowid. He will haue opyn frendis *He has open friends and*
and opyn enemys, So that al men may know whyche ben both *open enemies.*
32 oone and othyr. why, forto lowe pryuely or forto hate, appertenyth to Poue*r* men that dare noght to take an hand opynly. ³ 34 L.
The hardy ³wille not leue that he takyth in hand for speche of *He cares not for the*
the Pepill, For he hath more cure of verite, than of the *opinion of the people :*
36 oppynyou or ortrow of the Pepill, And ther-for he is trew in
dede *and* worde, And haue no will to ly, but yf hit be for
myrthe and Play : he will haue no company but wyth his
Frende*s*, why, forto Please al men, hit were oue*r*-moche thral- *nor will he please all*
40 dome, but the hardy ne may hit endure. But thay that byth *men.*

He is not easily astonished. of lowe herte ben lowely to al men, and mervelyth of Smale thynges that thay hyryth. But the hardy wyse man mervelyth hym not but of thynge of grete value. The hardy, of dysayses *He remembers not past ills.* that he hath Sufferyth he wile haue no remembrance, for-why, 4 he ne holdyth hym not y-lowet ne vndyrfote of the dyssayses whyche he hathe escapid. And for-why that he toke not to hevynesse the damagis that hym befell, but by vertue of stronge corage ham rescewyth lyghtly, he may not of ham haue remem- 8 braunce, for a man lyghtly for-yewyth *and* Some thay thynges that he lytill telle of. Anothyr maner hathe the manfull or the hardy that he Spekyth lytill, and thynkyth that beryth *He has no will to speak of himself.* borthom, And also he haue no will to Speke of hym-Selfe, ne 12 of none othyr moche: he haue no cure that he be y-praysid ne that otheris be blamyd, And ther-for nethyr hym-Selfe ne otheres he praysyth, ne wil not say harme of his frendis ne *He does his deed without bobaunce.* of his enemys, but al that hym owyth to do, he hit doth 16 wit*h*out bobaunce wisely, and wyth-out feyntyse actifly. Anothyr condicion hath the manfull othyr the hardy, that neuer he Playnyth hym of defautes that he hath hadd, nethyr of mette, drynke, ne of othyr thynges necessaries, but Plente and 20 *He changes not for plenty or default of necessaries.* defaute of al thynges he rescewyth evynly, so that no man may Percewe nethyr by worde ne by semblaunt, that he hath the herte y-changed fro ayse to mysayse, ne for scarcite, ne for Plente. And yf hit befall that he haue defaute of any thynge, 24 he ne Prayeth gladly anothyr manes helpe, but yf the grete ¹ 31*b* L. nede therto hym drywe, ffor hym ¹rechyth not moch, but of com*m*yn Pees of the Pepill, Iustice, and ryghte, and the honoure *He desires Justice, right, and the honour of God.* of god aboue al thynge. More desyryth the hardy, honest 28 thynges wythout wynnynges, than dyshoneste thyng*es* wyth gret wynnynges, And therfor he desyrith more grete lordshupp*e*, ² Fol. 48. ²othyr lytill rente, than a townshup of londe othyr a grete Some of catele to charlys appertenynge. To charlis appertenyth 32 *He is not like the churls.* to Prayse moche, *and* to loue grete hepis of money of golde and Siluer, For-why, they haw lowe hertis *and* lytill, But to nobill Pepill of hey Parage and of grete vertue, longyth to loue chyualry, lordshup; to desyre Streynth, Doghtynesse, *and* ryght- 36 *He is slow in moving, for he finds little worth hastening for.* fulnesse wythout queyntise. By kynde the hardy shal be of Slow mewynge, for he fyndyth but Seldome a thynge for the whyche he hym endeynyth to haste, And he sholde haue a stronge voyce *and* grete, *and* treely Speke, ffor that betokenyth 40

Old Stories of the Hardy and Manful.

a stronge herte and a stabill. And therfor women, that by kynde bene more febelier than men, haue Smale voyces. And tho men, that by rancoure of herte chydyth hastely, thay haue not har Spyritis in thare Powere, But whoso hath the vertue of Fortitude, he ne deynyth not to chyde, And in Spekynge he haue not mestere to hafe [haste], for his Spirite is not by rancoure y-trowbelid.

He has a strong voice and great, and he de-signeth not to chide.

8 Here begy*n*nyth old stories to Shewe the condicionys and the propirteis of the hardy or the manfull. Capitulum Trycessimum Prymum.

Oche desyre thes olde Pryncis to Putte hare lyues in balaunce for come*n* Prowe of the Pepill, and they were so hardy, that in Suche a Poynte thay douted not the deth; for as Valery Sayth, and Seynte austyn*n*e hit rehersyth in the boke of the Cite of god, Codre, Su*m*tyme kynge of the Cite of 16 Athenys, whan he had vndyrstonde by the Answere of his godys, are that he to a certayñ battaille agaynes his enemys wente, that thay the victori sholde haue in battaill whos kynge or duke sholde be slayne in battaill, He onlasit his riche armes *and* roial array,[1] 20 and hym clothed in Pouer [2] array, *and* wythout any drede he went al dysharmyd ayeynnes the hostis of his enemys, and by contencion ham taried, wherfore they hym Slewe anone. For leuer hym was deth to suffyr, that his men had the maystri, than lyue *and* 24 See his me*n* to bene ouercome. The Prynces in olde tyme ne were not covetous of golde ne Siluer, And therfor more gladly they yawyn than resceuet. Vegesce tellyth, that a nobil con- sailloure of Rome that Fabrice was callid, a wyse and a worthy 28 man *þ*at lowid not yftis to rescewe, Answarid to an Ambassa- toure of a fere Estraunge contre, that hym proferid a grete Some of golde, "Go," Sayde he, "to thy contrey wyth thy golde, I haue no cure to resceue; Leuer is hit to me to comaunde tho 32 that the golde haue, than thare good to haue." Sypion, the nobill duke of Rome, whan he Saue well that haniball the kynge of Cartage, that is Souerayne Cite of affryke, had besiegid the Cite of Rome longe tyme, and So hugely slayne of 36 the romanys that in oone day he dide fill thre bushelis of golde ryngis, that weryn of the Pryncis *and* of the wourthy men of

*Capi*tul*um xxxj*m*.*
Valerius. Augustin.
The death of Codrus, king of Athens.
[2] *35 L.*
Vegetius.
Fabricius and the ambassadors.
Scipio.
When Hannibal besieged Rome,

---

[1] x *partially altered to* y.

174   Stories of Scipio, Alexander, and Cyprus.

<small>Scipio carried the war into Africa,</small>

<small>and caused Hannibal to return.</small>

<small>[1] Fol. 48 b.</small>

<small>At the last Hannibal died of poison.</small>

<small>[2] 35 b L.</small>

<small>Valerius.</small>

<small>Alexander and the cold knight.</small>

<small>Orosius.</small>

<small>Cyrus was besieging Babylon.</small>

<small>The river slew one of his knights,</small>

the Same Scypion, than, this Scipion, wyth his Chiualrie Passid the See, and Came to Cartage and hit assiegid, wyth grete manhode he makyd stronge assautes and harde; The Pepill by Swerde and hungyr he Slow; thythyngis therof to Rome wente. 4 Haniball the Sige forsoke, hastely to Cartage he wente, wyth Streynth he entried, by grete vertue the Cite restorid, he makyd engynes, he gederid grete hostis, the Cite defendid, He ordaynyd his shildrymes, steryn battaill he yaue, but atte the latyste 8 Scipion hym ouercome. Than flow haniball throght al affrike into A Castelle, [1]and Into Streynthis. Scipion hym chased as a grefhound dothe the Fox. Atte the latyr ende by wenym, that [2]he dranke of his owyn will, he died, that he wolde not to 12 be takyn or Slayne of the Romans. Than Scipion toke al affrike, and So hit makid Subiecte to Romanys, and Payedyn grete truage of golde and Siluer; he came agayn to Rome, hole and mery, and Sayde to the Romanes, " Fayre Sirres, affrike to 16 yow haue y conquerid, And nothynge of the conqueste haue y rescewid Saue the Name." As the tyme and the nedes askyd, the Princis in olde tyme they contynued ham, Some tyme as a lorde, anothyr tyme as a fellow, this wittnessyth Valery, that 20 tellyth that kynge alexandyr lad in a tyme a grete hoste in full colde weddyr. atte evyn when he restid, he satte in oon hey sette by a fyre; he rewardid aboute, and Sawe an olde knyght quakynge for colde. Anoone he descendid fro the Seete, And 24 toke the knyght in his armys, and Seete hym in the Sette by the fyre, there as he hym-Selfe Sate. And therfor hit was no merveill that men wolde so gladly Serwe Suche a lord, that bettyr lowid his knyght than his owyn dignite. Grete and hey 28 dedys toke on ham Prynces in olde tyme, And Smale thynges thay lettyn to Smale men. Ensampill of this vs tellyth Orosie, that well couthe the Stories. Cyrus, the kynge of Pers, hym besied to conquere babilon, the grete stronge Cite; but he was 32 moche y-lettyd by an hugy ryuer rennynge by the Cite wallis. In a day whan thay wolde assaute make, a knyght fryst by foole-hardynys hym-Selfe to the ryuer Sette. The course of the ryuer So stronge and So styfe rane, that the knyght and his 36 hors rauyshith, doune hym bare, and dreynte. Cyrus, the hardy and manfull kynge, in grete wrathe Sayde, " So crowel wengeaunce of this ryuer shal y take, that a woman wyth chylde hit Shall mow Passe without Perill." Than he did assembill worke- 40

men by thowsandis, and trenchyd and dalwe the growne, and
departid the ryuer in CCC *and* lx Parties, wherthrogh that al — and he took vengeance on
men Smale and grete hit myght Passe wyth-out ¹any damage. it.

⁴ than he toke the Cite, hit destrued, and the wallis therof he did — ¹ 36 L.
down-caste into the fundemente. Hit was not y-holde proesse ne
chyualry to assayle a man vnwarnyd, but olde men helde hit for
cowardy. And therfore was alexandyr, the kynge Piames Sone — The treason of Paris
⁸ of Troy, moche to blame, that in the tempill of apollyn by — blamed.
dysceyte and treyson slow achilles the worthy and doghty
knyght. Holy writte reprowyth Ioab, Prynce of kynge Dauyes — Joab reproved.
hoste, for that he had Slayn by trayson two prynces bettyr
¹² that he was, Abner *and* amasam. And therfore Salamon, kynge
Dauyes Son, therof Vengeance toke, *and* makyd hym be Slayne,
as the boke of kynges vs tellyth. Trouthe and verite, more than
oppynyon or falsnesse, lowid olde Pryncis. Ensampill of that
¹⁶ vs tellyth Valery, and Sayth that in olde tyme wher two — Valerius.
frendys, that oone was callid Hamound, that othyr Phicia. On — The story of Damon and Pythias.
of this was take by Denys, the cruel Tyraunte, kynge of Cezillie,
he wolde haue Slayn hym, he askyd of his dethe respite in-to
²⁰ the tyme that he had y-makyd his testament and dysposid his
godys. The tyraunt hit grauntid vp that covnantte that he a
plege for hym wolde Putte into a certayn day. He Putte In his — One friend becomes surety for
frende for hym *and* went forthe. Many dayes Passyd, the
²⁴ terme neyghed, and he came not. Euery man helde hym a fole — the other's return.
that faste was, *and* sayde, "²folych Haste thow done, to Putte — ² Fol. 49.
thy-Selfe in Hostage for thy frende. He will not agayne cvm,
dey thow moste." he answerid, "I kno well my frende, that he
²⁸ atte no tyme couaunt wold broke: well know I, and Sertayne I
haue of reuenine." Whan the terme came, his frende repairet — His friend returns,
and hym presentid, And to the tyraunt Seyd, "see me here, lete
my frende Passe, for y haue hym acquited." Denys remembrid — ³ 36 b L.
³² hym of So grete ³trouthe, frendshupe, and lewte, *and* for-yaue his — and Dionysius pardons
male talent, And prayet ham bothe to rescewe hym to ben thare — him.
fellowe. By losyngrie to Plese grete or Smale, hyt is contrary to
the vertue, Fortitudo, and therfor the Phylosofers that were full
³⁶ of vertues, Leuer was to ham to Suffyr grete myssayse, than by
losyngerie grete auere to gette. Als Valery tellyth, Dyogen the — Diogenes
Philosofre. in a certayn day gederid wourtes to his mete, And
therfor a losynger Aristipus to hym Sayde, that was with denys — Aristippus reproves
⁴⁰ the tyraunt, "Diogen, thow sholdyst haue no mestere to ette — Diogenes.

wortes, and thow woldist losenge kynge denys." Dyogen answarid, "and thow woldiste ette Suche mette, thou Sholdyste
neuer nede to losynge kynge denys." None hardy or manfull is
not lyght of thoght, nethyr haue no mervelle that many pouer 4
men mervelyth of. Of thes vs tellythe Valery, that in a certayn
battaill descendyd an halte man, and therfore Some of the
Same battail hym Scornyd. the halte man answerid, "I ne
ham not maymet in handis ne in armes, thegh y be halte-footed : 8
moche more bettyr I shall fyght, for y ne haue noo hope to fle."
Of anothyr he tellyth vs, to whom his fellowe sayde, "So grete
Plente thay of Pers haue of Arowes that the Sonne Vixith all
durke, whan they begynnyth to sote ; bettyr is to fle than so 12
many Pepille to assaile." That othyr as an hardy man answarid,
"the Plente of arowes that thow spekyste of sholde vs Plese
moche, ffor the weddyr is ful hote, And there-for moche the
bettyr we shall fyght vndyr the shedow of the arowes." Ouer- 16
mych to thynke dissayse and aduersiteis that ben Passid, appertenyth not to hym that hardy is, for that shal make hym feynte.
For yf kynge Alexander had moch thoght of tribulacionys and
peynys that he Sufferid in Perse, he nade neuer be hardy to 20
entyr in Inde. And yf Scipyon had ouermych chargid the
damages of Rome, he had neuer ben hardy to entyr in affrike.
Of the comendacion of Scipion we [1]fyndyth y-writte, that als
longe as he hadd to done, hym thoght that nothynge was done. 24
Iulyus Cesar gladly for-yaue the wronges that to hym was done,
and by So mych the lordshupe of al men he gette. The hardy
hath grete Sufferaunce, bonerte, Stabilnes, and verite, and therfor he chargyth not of preysynge ne of myspreysynge, for hit is 28
a grete noun certayne of good renoune, that a man Putte hym of
anothyr manys mouthe to be Praysid. For by Speche of the
Pepille, a coward may be as Prowos as Ector of troi. Natheles,
as is afore in this boke declarid, in foreyne gouernaunce a prynce 32
sholde desyre and gete good renoune, by obeysaunce to god, and
in Vyse gouernance of his speche to godis wirchippe and profite
of the Pepille, and for no bobaunce as dyuers men dothe, whych
yewyth yeftys to Rymoris whyche Praysythe [2]Hym Beste that 36
moste Ham yewyth. Eeuery Wyse man, as a poet Sayth, ofte-
tymes sholde Enquere whate that the Pepill of hym spekyth,
Sepius inquiras quid de te fama loquatur, that is to Say,
"Enquere thow ofte-tymes what thynge is hit that fame Spekyth 40

of the." Kynge Alex*ander* was callid of many a man that hym *A flatterer called*
losengit, 'Iupit*er*, the grete god'; but he wyste weH that thay *Alexander Jupiter,*
lied. And therof happid in a tyme that he assieget a Cite, his
4 hoste makid therto assaute, The Cytteseynes ham defendid,
Alexandyr was woundid in the thegh, but he wolde not departe
fro the hoste, tille the assaute was fulfillid. aftyr, he lyght fro
his hors and in Softe laghynge Sayde, "This wounde shewyth *but his wound told*
8 wel that I is not god, but a dedly man, for hit grewyth me sore." *him another tale.*
Abow al thynge lowed Prynces in olde tyme the com*m*yn prowe
and the auctoricement of the Pepill, and therfor thay soght not
riches ne tresures to har owyn prow, but for the com*m*yn prowe, [1] *37 b L.*
12 ne delycate [1] mettes ne drynkes thay soght not, but als lytill as *Princes in war seek not*
thay myght; And more for othyr men than for ham-Selfe. And *delicate meat.*
therfor as me-thynkyth the grete abstynence that oure Irysh *Neither do our Irish*
enemys Supportyth in mettes and drynkes, is moche the cause *enemies, and so they often*
16 that thay in were often-tymes haue thare Purpos. For of a *win.*
gouernoure of Rome tellyth Valery, that Marcus Curius was *Valerius.*
callid a man of grete witte, hardy and Chiualerous, and wel
gouernede the Empire. to hym came messangers of a grete
20 Cite, and hym̄ founde Sittynge by a fyre vpon a lytill chaire,
ettynge of a tren dysshe, and hym Prait, yf hit were his Plesynge endeynet to rescewe a grete Some of golde, that thay had
broght hym for har lordis. This worthy lorde began to smothe *The Roman Lord who*
24 lagh, and answarid, "Say ye to youre lordys that hedyr you *would rather command*
sende, that Marcus Curius hath leuer to comaunde riche men *rich men than be rich.*
than be ryche; witte ye that y shall not be corruptid by frend-
shup, enemyte, nethyr by golde, ne by Siluer." For as Valery
28 Sayth, "euery good Emperoure loueth bettyr to be Powere in a *Valerius.*
ryche Empire, than be riche in a pouer Empire." And Seynte
Austyne Sayth, "that more is to playne that the Pouerte of *Augustin.*
the Empire of Rome is Perishit, than the riches: For whyle
32 that the Pryncos were Pouer the Pepill was riche, and when the
Prynces were riche the Pepill was Pouer." And therfor as vs
tellyth Eutropias, in the Stories of Romanes, That constance the *Eutropius.*
Emperoure in al his tyme desirid to make his Pepill riche, and
36 more-ouer, the same clerke vs tellyth, that bettyr is that riches *Riches should be in many*
be in the handys of many men, than they in oone Place be *men's hands, and not in one*
enclosyd; for the richere that the Pepill be, In So myche thay *place.*
may ham-Selfe the bettyr defende, and therto thay haue the
40 bettyr talent. And who-so lytyll hath, the lasse talente hath;

And therfor yf the [1]Prynce Empoueryth the Pepill, he may haue the lasse truste that the Pepill will helpe hym wyth good will. All the entente of good Prynces that euer were, was to mayntene the prowe of the commyn pepill, for in that dede thay trysted the bettyr to be lyke oure lord [2]god, Kyng of al Kynges, that al creaturis gouernyth aftyr Hare degre. Therfore by gret study the lawes weryn stabelid and mayn-tenyd, Marchaundises vsed, Dyuers moneis contreuet, and al that myght bene y-sayde that good was, al was Purveyet to the comyn Profite of the Pepill, and not to make riche the Prynces; that wittnessyth al bokis that tretyth of Empires or realmes. Tully askyth, "yf the Sone shall Spare the fadyr yf [3]he do any thynge agaynes the commyn Profite of the Contre." Therto he hym-selfe answarith, "That fryst the Sone shall pray the fadyr, that he wythdrawe hym, and yf he will not he shall trete hym, and aftyr yf nede be, he shal acuse hym, and more shall will that his fadyr be slayne, than the comyn Prowe of the contre and the Peese be distourbet." Of grete abstynence were this olde Prynces, ffor at noone tyme he may be chyualryous, he that Is a glotoune. Of this we redyth in gestis of Romanys, that Cesar auguste, lorde of al the worlde was of grete abstyn-ence; he nad noo cure of delicate mettis, but helde hym appayed of commyn brede, and grete fleshis, and chese of the bugle, for he wolde not yeue ensampill of delytes to chyualrie. Glorie, honoure, and noblesse, more desyryth prynces in olde tyme, than hepis of golde, Siluer, or precious stonys. Ensamples of thes ben grete plente, but Sortely to passe ouer, hit suffichyth that in the stories of Romanes we fyndyth y-writte, that oone forcible kynge of grete Pouer, assiget the Cite of Rome. Cruel assautes therto makyd; [4]Grete nombyr of Pepill he had Slayne, wherfor out of mesure he was dreddid and dowted. the Sinatouris of the Cite that hadd the Pepill to kepe aforsid har consaille, moche thay peynyd ham to contreue how thay myght ouercome the tyraunt, and the Sige a-way Putte that longe tyme dured. Atte that tyme in a Pasture wythout the Cite was a kepere of Mulis, that Romanes callid a mulion. this Mulion euery day be-helde the hostis, he rewardid har battaille, he deuysed har armes, hare contenaunces, and hare out-Passynges, herly and late, and Saw the kynge ofte-tymes goynge out of his tentis priueli to go to

[3] De patrie per amorem, MS.

The Muleteer who saved Rome. 179

sege ; he knew hym well by Sertayn tokenys. The Mulion hym *and came on their king*
Sawe in a day by-cause of goynge to pryuely fer fro his men, *as he was far from his men.*
thedyr besili he hastid ; thes carle was stronge in armes, the
4 kynge wyth grete streynth he caght, and hym trused hym before
on his Mule. he hastid fast in his way, and neuer cessid tille
he came to the Capitolle ; ther as the Senatours weryn atte *He led him to the Capitol,*
consaille, he smote atte the dore and askyd entre. The Po[r]terys *and asked entry.*
8 haddyn of hym grete endeyne, there hym lefte, Vp thay went,
his message thay did. the Senatours were grewid to be destowr-
bete for a carle. Atte the laste sayd on Senatoure, "we sholde *At the last a Senator*
not haue despite of the Carle, we know not whate thythynges he *granted it.*
12 hath broght. For but he hadd sume grete message, he ne were
not bolde to come hedyr." And so by commyn assente the carle
hadde entre. a fayre Presente he shewid, the kynge of barbrie
he hame [1] presentid, to done thar will Wyth Hym. The barbrions *[1] Fol. 50 b.*
16 Had Har Kynge loste, hit was no wondyr thegh thay espaunted *Then he brought them*
were ; the Romanes ham armyd faste. The barbrions were *the king of the bar-*
encumberid, thay Soght har kynge, he myght [2] not be founde, *barians. [2] 30 L.*
they turned har backys, but lytill ham a-vayillid ; the Romanes *The Romans fell on them*
20 ham Suet, they smote, they hewyn and Slowen, and home *without a king, and de-*
repairet wyth grete victorie ; golde, siluer, precious stones, riche *feated them.*
clothis, and grete nobeldi wyth ham bare into the cite ; thay
Slow the kynge, and So they makyd a good ende of the were.
24 Aftyr this the Senatours bethoght whate rewarde sholde thay
yewyn the Mulion ; thay callid hym forth, Golde, Siluer, and *Then they offered a re-*
othyr auauncement hym proferid, and hym askyd wherof he *ward to the muleteer,*
hym wolde be content for his good Service. He answarid as
28 manfull and hardy man, that more lowid honoure than riches
that Sone Passyth : "Of golde ne syluer I ne haue no cure,
Graunt me oone thynge and that me Suffisyth. Do ye," sayde *and he asked for an image*
he, "make an ymage of brasse of my lickenesse, and a coronet *of brass in his likeness, with*
32 kynge ouercome by me." thay did So, and Sette the ymage *a crowned king before*
amyd the strete, that al pepill that ther went myght haue *him.*
remembraunce of that victorie. Therfor aristotle Sayth, that *Aristotle.*
"honoure is the moste hey thynge that a man may haue in this
36 worlde." To the hardy hit appartenyth to be slow of mewynge,
but whan he shal battail in honde take, he is so ferce that he
dreddyth no man. In the stories of Romanes we redyth, that
Tyberius the Emperoure of Rome in al his dedis was taryynge, *Tiberius.*
40 and wythout ripe consaille nothynge he didd that bare burthyn,

The Story of the Sick Man and the Flies.

<small>Tiberius charged not his officers.</small> For ouermyche hastynes nys not proesse. [1]Thys Emperoure any officere that he had makyd with nethe he chaungyd' but yf hit were for opyñ falsnys.[1] This emperoure askyd in a day on of his pryuc men, why he so did : he answarid and Sayde, that he So did for Prowe of the Pepill, and that he shewyth by this
<small>A man was lying wounded.</small> Ensampli.[2] A man Somtyme was, that hadd many wondis, and lay nakyd in a wodd ; the flyes thyke lay on hym̄ that his blode soke. anothyr man Passyd by the way and Pite hadd on hym, and
<small>One drove off the flies.</small> away the flies drowe. "Alas," sayde the wondid man, "moche
<small>3 39 b L.</small> harme haste thow done to mee and greuet, ffor the flies that
<small>He blamed him sore.</small> now haste away chassid thay [3]ben full and haue ettyn y-nowe, and thes newely come me shale moche more Smertre assayle." So is hit in the same manere of new officers, that like ben to newe hungri flies, and "therfor," sayde he, " y wille not lyghtly chaunge ne remewe officers, ffor al tymes the latyste byth moste greuous, for they ben moste nedy, and leste Sparyth the Pepill."
<small>These are the tokens of the hardy.</small> To Speke wyth good Spirite and breth appartenyth to the hardy, for that tokenyth hardynesse of herte, grete takynge on, and Stowtesse. Spekynge of a lytill Spirite Signyfieth and Schewyth a feynte herte wyth-out boldenys. Now haue y Sewyd yowe the tokenes and propirteis of the hardy, the whyche arystotle vs techyth.

4

8

12

16

20

Of the Pite and mercy that a Prynce sholde haue.
Capitulum xxxij^m.

24

<small>Capitulum xxxij^m.</small> Itte is to witte that thegh mekenys is necessary to al men, namely hit is in Prynces. Therof hit is to witte that god'
<small>4 Fol. 51.</small> [4]ordeynet the fryste Prynce of His Pepill, Moysen the
<small>Meekness especially necessary to Princes.</small> whyche was Hardy, a ful meke man abow al men that in Erthe wonned. In Matheu is gospel written, **Ecce rex tuus venit tibi mansuetus, et lex eius vocabitur lex clemencie**, that Is to Say, "See thy kynge comyth to the meke, and his law is callid the lawe
<small>Proverbs.</small> of mekenesse." The lattyst boke of prouerbis Sayth, that in tokyñ of mekenes, crystyne kynges and prelatis of holy churche
<small>Seneca.</small> byth ennoyntid. Seneca sayth, **Nullum ex omnibus clemencia magis quam regem aut Pryncipem decet**, that is to say, "No man of the Pepill mekenesse makyth faire othyr Semely, more than a kyńge or a Prynce." For mekenesse is the Soue*r*ance and

28

32

36

[1–1] This insertion is written in the margin of the MS.
[2] An ʙ *is erased*.

the difference betwene a kynge and a tyraunt. And hit is to
witte that the vertue of mekenesse kepyth the mene betwene
Sparynge and vengeaunce, ffor Seneca Sayth, **Tam omnibus** *Seneca.*
4 **ignoscere crudelitas est, quam nulli, Medium tenere debe-
mus**, that is to Say, " Hit Is cruwelte als welle to foryewen al
men, as no man, therfor we sholde holde the mene wey." He
that is a gouernoure in tymes he shall Spare, and in tymes *Sometimes forgive,*
8 vengeaunse take. The vertue of Temporaunce, namely in a *sometimes punish.*
Prynce appartenyth to mekenesse, in vengeaunce-takynge of the
wrongis that byth y-do to hym-Selfe. For lyke as hit be-fallyth
not to a manful man to be liberall of anothyr manes goode, but
12 forto be lyberall of his owyn, So Is the Prynce y-callid [1] meke, [1] 40 l..
noght in his Pepill lost-is for-yewynge, but in his owyn noght
goynge owte of the vertue of Temporaunce. And therfor grete
honoure, glorie, and Perpetuel virchippe, is to the Prynce, *Princes should re-*
16 namely in redressynge by force of Pouer and lawe, the wronges *dress wrongs from ene-*
that ben done to the comyn Pepill and his subiectes, by enemys, *mies, thieves, and extor-*
thewis, And othyr extorcioners. That a prynce sholde be *tioners.*
Paciente and meke, Seneca Puttyth oone ensampill and tellyth, *Seneca.*
20 that the bee is a Passynge wrathfull beste *and* full of fyght,
and for vengeaunce they lewyth thar Styngill in the wonde, but
the kynge of bees Is wythout a styngill. this is a kyndely
nobelesse of the vnreysonabill creature, yewynge essampill to al
24 pryncez *and* gouernores of the Pepill. Anothyr ensampill I
fynde writte of the lyon, that thegh a man haue hym Sore *The lion does not hurt*
hurte, and than he that hym hurte falle doun to the Erthe, as *a wounded man.*
he wolde cry hym mercy, he wil hym not dyssayse in nothynge.
28 Therfor Iulyus Cesar for-yawe lyghtely nothynge Saue the *Cæsar for-gave all his*
wronges that men did hym, and yf any man hym myssayde, he *personal enemies.*
hym answerid neuer, nethyr Vengeanse therof toke. We redyth
of thys Emperoure that a man by ewill will hym callid,
32 "Tyraunt"; and he answerid, "yf y were a tyraunte, thow
sholdyst Say no more so;" and Sothe hit was, for he myght haue
hym Slayne. The emperoure Teodosie makyd a statute and *Theodo-*
Sayde, "If any man myssay oure names, we wil not that therfor *sius*
36 he be Punysshid; ffor yf that come of lyghtnesse, hit is to dyspise; and yf hit come of wodnesse, a man sholde therof Pite
haue; And yf hit cvme of malice, hit is to be foryeue." Seneca *Seneca.*
the good clerke tellyth, that the Citeseynes [2] of athene Sende [2] Fol. 51 b.
40 messagers to Philippe Kynge of Macedone. Whan thay hadd

Timoehares and Philip of Macedon.	done har message the kynge to ham Sayde bemurely, "Telle me ye whate thynge is, that y may done Plesynge the lordys that yow to me sende"? They to hym sayde, and speciali oone of them that was callid Tymokares, "If ye wolde make your-Selfe
¹ 101 L.	an-honged bene, hit wolde gretly ham plese." whan ¹the kynges knyghtes hardyn that, anoone thay wolde hym haue hewyn in Smale Peces, ne hadd the kynge hym defendid. "lete of," he sayde, "no man be So hardy to do hym any harme." Than Sayde he to the messagere, "go thow to thy lordes that hedyr the Sende, and Sai tham in my be-halfe, that thay bene more Prowte, and lasse ben to Prayse, tho that Suche message Sende, than thay that the message herde and no vengeaunce toke."
Cato.	The Vise Poete Caton Sayth, **Vtilius regno, meritis adquirere amicos**, that is to say, "More Profitable thynge is than a kyngedome, by good deseruynge frendis to gette." But So did
De Dermicio Memurgh. Irelande.	not Dermot M^cmurgh, Prynce of leynystere, whych is the v^e parte of Irlande, For a gret Clerke, Richard Cambrensis that makyd the Story of the conqueste by kynge Henry the Seconde in Irland, tellyth that this Dermot in the begynnynge of his regnacioune, he was an oppressoure and an extorcionere of vertues men, and a crowel Tyraunt ontollerabill, vpon the grete lordis of his londe. Anothyr myschefe hym befell, O'rooryckes wyfe,
O'Rourke's wife ravished away.	kynge of Mythe, by hyr owyn assente, in abscence of hyr lorde, he rauysshed. And for-why that, for the more Partie al myschefe, witnessynge olde stories many, and newe also, the wiche by women began. This kynge O'rorike, mor for shame than for the hurte heyly grewid, wox al venomowsly wrothe. And therfor he gaderid many strangeris, that is to say, Rourike of Connaght, that tyme kynge of Irlande, whyth his Pepill and his owyn, A-vengid to bene. Than the grete lordis of laynyster,
Dermot is besieged on all sides, and forced to flee.	Seynge har Prynce i-Putte to myschefe, and in euery Partie vmbesegid wyth enemys, olde wronges that he hadd done ham thay rehersid; thay rose al atte onys wyth his enemys, And So fortvne and his Pepill hym lefte atte ones. Than this Prynce Dermot, Seynge hym-Selfe on euery Side besieget, wythout helpe and fououre, and hugely ouersette with enemys, aftyr many Sore battaillis, to the laste remedy, he flow ouer the See
He gets help from Henry.	into Normandy in the parties of Fraunce, to kynge henry the Seconde aforsayde, and hym besely besoght of Socoure. He
² 41 L.	was ²wirchiphully rescewid of the kynge, and hym his gouern-

4

8

12

16

20

24

28

32

36

40

aunce tolde. Whan the kynge hadd herde the cause of his
comynge, he rescewid of hym the bonde of Subieccioun, and *and receives letters of*
fewtee, and hym toke his letteris of bienvoillaunce wher-by he *commendation.*
4 broght Pouer of Englyssh-men, Normanes, and Walschemen into
laynystere, the whyche wyth that othyr fowre Parties of the
londe by the Same kynge henry was for the more Partie I-con-
querid. Thus did this Prynce Dermot hym-Selfe and al othyr *Thus evil princes bring*
8 Prynces of his Nacioñ in lond for euer encombre by oppressyoñ. *their land to subjection.*
¹And therfor Hit Is more Sure to euery Prynce to comaunde *¹ Fol. 52.*
His Pepill well willynge to hym, than ewill willynge. this felit
Nero and Damaciane, Emperoures of Rome; And so filit kynge
12 Richard the Seconde and many mo afor and Sethyñ. This *Cambrensis.*
Clerke Cambrens tellyth in the Same story, **Expedit subiectis** *begyn [in margin]*
Principi cuilibet pocius amari quam timeri, that Is to Say,
"Hit Is Spedful to euery Prynce radyr to be ylowid, than to be
16 dreddid," of his subiectes, And hit is Spedphull to be y-dreddyd,
So that of loue radyr than of correccioñ that drede confortyth.
For whate-euer man is y-lowid, hit semyth that he is dreddid.
But euery Extorcioner Is hatid of the commyn Pepill, and he that
20 hatid Is of the commyn Pepill, he shal be vnsocowrid whan he
moste nede hath, lyke as Dermot the Prince was. I fynde In a *Nota.*
Sermonde writte, that an extorcionere is wors than the deuyll. *An extortioner is*
For the deuyll takyth in prei and turmentyth but corsyd men, *worse than the devil.*
24 And the extorcioner rubbyth and Preyeth good men and trew;
And therfor the Deuil may Iustifye hym in rewarde of extor-
cioner, For the Deuyl may Say to god, "I haue turmentid oonly *The devil can justify him-*
tho men that the haue hatid, but this extorcionere hath tur- *self to God.*
28 mentid tho men that the lowid." And So we may vndyrstonde
that an extorcioner Is the deuyll-is angill, for thay ben sende
Into this worlde to do ther that thynge the wyche the deuyll
doth in helle, that Is to Say, to do turmentrie.
32   But for-alsmoche, gracious lorde, as I haue now her towchid *Now shall we rehearse the*
of the conquest of Irland, I shall now declare yow in Partie as *title of the English to*
y fynde in croncles written, many titles of oure ²lege lorde the *Ireland.*
kynge of Englandes ryght to this land of Irland, agaynes t[h]e *² 41 b L.*
36 errourse and haynouse Iryshmenes oppynyones, saynge that thay
haue bettyr ryght.

Of the Kynges titles to the land of Irland, aftyr the Cronyclis. Capitulum xxxiij.

Capitulum xxxiij^m.

Ingllandis title to Irelande.
Ryste atte the begynnynge, afor the comynge of Iryshemeñ into the londe, they weryñ dwellynge in a syde of spayne 4

First, because Irishmen came from Bayonne, which belonged to the King of England.
whyche is callid basco. Of the whyche Basco, Bayon Is the chefe Cite, and basco a membyr of hit. And atte yryshmen comynge Into Irland, kynge Gurgonynce, Soñ to the nobill kynge Belynge, and kynge of Britane the more, whyche now Is 8 callid England, was lorde of Bayon as oure kynge now Is. And therfor thay sholde be his men, and Irland his land. The Seconde tytle is this; Atte the Same tyme that Iryshmen came out of basco in Sixti Shippes exilit, thay mete wyth kynge 12

Second, because our king granted them Ireland.
Gurgnynce vp the See at the Ile of Orcades, atte his comynge fro Denemarke with grete victorie. Than har Captaynes hyberus and herymon wenten to this kynge, and hym tolde the cause of har comynge, and hym Prayed with grete In- 16 staunce, that he wolde graunt ham that thay myght enhabite Some lande in the weste. Atte the laste the kynge, by avyce of his consaille, graunted ham Irland to enhabite, and assygned

[1] *Fol. 52 b.*
ham gides for the See thedyrwarde. And [1]therfor they Sholde 20 ben our Kynges men. The thyrde title Is, As I haue afor

Third, Dermot became liege man of King Henry.
declarid, that Dermot, Sumtyme Prynce of leynestere, in Normandy became lege man to kynge henry the Seconde, conqueroure of Irland. Wherthrogh he broght Pouer of Pepill 24 aforsaydyñ into the land, and mariet his eldyst doghtyr Eue at Watyrford to Syr Richard fiz Gilbert, Erle of Sragnylle in Walis, and hym graunted the reuersione of laynestere wyth Eue his doghtyr. Aftyr that the Erle graunted to his kynge henry, 28 Deuelyñ wyth two candredes nexte to Deuelyñ, and al the havyñ tounes of laynestre, to haue that othyr Parte in Pees,

[2] *42 L.*
and [2]the kynges good lordshup. And therfor M^cmurgh hath leste ryght to haue lordshup of al othyr Irysh Captaynes; And 32 oure kynge in especial haue good ryght to laynystre. Hitte Is

What is a candrede, a hundred, or a weapontaille.
to witte, that a Candrede in frensh and in Irysh, Is a Porcioñ of grovnde that may contene an hundrid villachis. In England Suche A Candrede is y-callit an hundret othyr a wepyn-tale. A 36 wepyntaille Is as myche to Say as a takynge of wepen, ffor In olde tyme in England atte the fryst comynge of a newe lorde in-to an hundret, the tenantes of the Same hundrede Sholde delyuer to har lorde har wepyn as for har homage. The iiij^e 40

title of ryght that oure kynge hath to Irland Is, that Sethyn in
the yere of Oure lorde M⁺. C. and lx^ti, ij, the forsayd kynge
henry landyd atte watyrforde, and there Came to hym Dermot, Fourthly, all the Irish kings yielded them freely to King Henry in 1162.
4 kynge of Corke, and of his owyn propyr wille became liege
trybutarie for hym and for his kyngedome, *and* on this he makyd
his Serement and yawe his hostagis to the kynge. Than the
kynge rode to Casshell, and ther came to hym Doneuald, kynge
8 of lymerike, and be-came lyege man as did the kynge of Corke.
Than came to hym Duneualde, kynge of Ossori, and M^csaghlyn,
kynge of Ofaly, and al the Prynces of the Southe of Irland, and
be-came lege men as Is aforsayd. Than wente kynge henry to
12 Dyuelyne, and ther came O'kernel, kynge of Vriel, O'rorike
kynge of Mythe, and Rothorike, kynge of al Iryshmen of the
londe, and of Connaght, with al the Princes and men of value
of the lande, wythout-take the Pepill of Vllystere, and by-came
16 lyeges *and* Subiectes tributarijs by grete othis for ham and hare
kyngedomes *and* lordshuppes, to the forsayd kynge henry, and
that by hare owyn good wille as hit semyth wel, for the cronycles
makyth no mencion of no chyualry ne werre done by the kynge 1 426 b.
20 al the tyme that he in Irland was. The V^e title Is this, the Fifthly, all his lands belong to the Pope, and he granted the lordship to King Henry.
Pope Adriane, for-as-moche as Irland ¹Is an Ile, and hit and al
othyr Iles cristiens to the ryght of Seynte Petyr and the churche
o Rome appartenyth, he grantid the lordshupe of Irland to the
24 forsayde kynge henry, to encresse therin crystyn feyth *and*
holynesse, And to sette the Pepill of the londe in gouernaunce
of good lawes *and* vertues, vices to enchu, This yfte and graunt
of Pope Adriane, Pope Alexandyr his Successoure confermyd.
28 this titles of ryght oppynly apperyth by the ²Same Popis Bullys, ² Fol. 53.
the copyes of Whych Bene ryued ynow. Sethyn came³ Vyuyen,
a legate fro the Pope, into Irland and assemblid atte deuelyne al The Council of Dublin.
the Clergi of the land atte a consaill, atte the whyche Consaill
32 this legate declarid and affermyd to the clergy the kynges ryght
to be good to Irlande, *and* comandid *and* also denunced al the
Pepill of Irland on the Payne of cursynge, that no man sholde
presume folyche to departe fro the liegeaunce and the fayth of
36 the kynge of England. The Syxte title Is, that assemblid atte Sixthly, the Council of Armagh decreed that the land belonged to England.
Ardmagh, the Clergi of al the land atte the tyme of the con-
queste vp the comynge of Englyssh-men, by the Same Consaill
hit was decrewite and demet, that throght the Synne of the

³ came came MS.

Pepill of the londe by the Sentence of god, the myschefis of the
conquest ham befelle. The vij^e title Is, For atte the fryste
comynge and beynge of kynge Richard the Seconde in Irland
atte the Cite of Deuelyne, and othyr Places of the londe, there 4
come to hym wyth hare owyn good-wille, O'nelle, Captayne of
Iryshemen of Vluestere, O'bren of Thomon, O'conghoure of Connaght, Arthure M^{c}murgh, Captayne of Iryshmen in laynystere,
And al othyr grete Capitaynes of Iryshmen of Irland, and be- 8
came liege man to the Same kynge Richard, And to hym did
homage liege, And for more [1]grettyr Surte thay bounde ham in
grete Somes by dyvers Instrumentes to Pay to the Popys Chamer,
to trewely kepe and holde hare legeaunce in the fourme afor-.12
sayde. There-for, fro the begynnynge to the End, good is oure
kynges ryght to the lordshupe of Irland. And therfor hold thei
ham still for shame, that therof the contrary Sayne.

Nowe here y an end makyth of the thyrde Cardynal vertue 16
that ycallid in lateyn, Fortitudo, in Englysh Streynthe,
And trete of the iiij^e cardynal vertue, that Is in latyn
callid Temporancia, Is myn entente god helpynge. Amen.

Capitulum Tricessimum quartum. 20

He fourthe vertue Cardynal, Clerkes callyth Temperance,
t   by the wiche a man kepyth and holdyth mesure in ettynge
and drynkynge, and surfetyth not, as in women, and from
al Surfetys hym kepyth in al his dedis and Syggynges. And 24
therfor Tully Sayth, "If thou desyriste Temperance Put away
euery Surfete, and restrayne thy desyres; Reward thow how
myche kynde askyth, and not how mych couetyse desyryth."
Ife thou haste the vertue of Temperance, therto shalte thou 28
comme, yf thou be Payet of thy-Selfe without couetyse of more
to haue. For y-now he hath, that Is ap-Payet of that, that he
i-richet Is, ffor more he will not desyre. And he that more
couetyth, than he hath, he knowlechyth that he y-now haue 32
not, And therfor to thy couetyse Sette thou the bridill, in
ettynge and drynkynge be thou y-temperit, And aftyr that
kynde askyth, put mesure. Bettyr Is lytill than to mych, but
the mene alboth Surmountyth in bountee. Whan thou art in 36
company, that thynge whych thou haste blamet, thou shalt not
ette ne drynke. To the Delytes whych now byth present, ouermoche thou shalt not the yeue, ne tho [2]that ben absente, thou

shalt not gretely desyre. See that thou can lyue ¹Of Lytill [1 Fol. 53 b.]
mette and Drynke. Drynke not for Delite, as doth the glotone, *Temperance in eating and drinking.*
But for nede that thou haste; lette hungyre yeue the talent,
4 and not Sause ne Saueure. If thou be attempret by the vertu
aforsayd, thou shalt enchu foule thynges ar that thay falle, ffor
no man Sudaynly taken, may not well kepe hym-Selfe. And
whoso will not enchu evil company, Sudaynly he shall fall in
8 fowle thynges. Be-holde wel al the meuementis of the body *Be watchful of your body.*
and of Corage, that ther be not in ham no filthehede. Be neuer
the more hardy to done amyse, be-cause that thou arte alone by
thy-Selfe, and no man Seth the; ffor a man may for euyl dedys
12 be shent, thegh othyr men See ham not done. Thow shalt not
drede no man more than thy-Selfe, ffor Sumtyme euery man Is *Fear no man more than thyself.*
absent to the, but thou art al tymes presente to thy-Selfe, And
al that thou doste Pryueli, god Seth hit opynli. Foule and
16 vnclene wordys thou shalt enchu, ffor hit is not fere fro the
herte, that the mouthe Spekyth, and that that Is in the mouthe,
Sone to the dede approcedyth. Thyñ accusementes thou shalt
medill euenly *and* menely wythout empeirement of dignyte,
20 Play not to myche, ne lagh not moche, ffor Salomon Sayth, *Solomon.*
"laghynge Is alway in the mouthe of the fole," and the fole
enhawsyth his voyse whan he laghyth. The wys man wenethe
he Softe laghyth. Ther is tyme of laghynge, tyme of wepynge,
24 tyme of Speche, and tyme of beynge stille. In two causes *Two causes at which a wise man will not laugh.*
sholde no wys man lagh, that Is to witte, in despite of anothyr
man, ne for that myschefe anothyr Is betyde. Who-so laghyth
when he sholde not, he Is holde ²dyshoneste; And who-so [2 " L.]
28 neuer laghes, he Is ouer estrange in company. Shewe thy *Show thy wit, and grieve no man.*
witte, and greue no man; whan thou shalt Play, Of veleyny
the nedyth to kepe. Thou Shalte lagh wythout grynnynge,
Speke wyth-out cry or noyse-makynge, Goo wythout Slouthe,
32 Reste the wythout dyshoneste. Ouer al thynge thou shalte *Hate flatterers.*
enchu and hate Parfitely losengerie in thy-Selfe *and* otheris, ffor
losengerie destrueth euery vertu; the losengeoure shal Sayne to
the, " god thankid, thou doste welle, and thou arte ful of *This is what they say.*
36 vertues and of witte, riche, estable, stronge, worthy, hardy,
Semely, *and* fayre of body, large of herte, wel despendynge, a
nobill man and of grete Parage, well prowid in dedys of armes;
so god me helpe, In al this land nys none thy Pere." Who-so
40 suche losengeris belewyth othyr trowyth, they shal falle in Pride

and ouertrouth, wherthrogh thay shal Suche thynges take in
hande, that neuer they shall mow well brynge to a good ende.
Solomon. Salamon Sayth, "the losengeoure whyth his mouthe begilyth
Cato. his frende"; And therfor Catoñ Sayth, **Plus alijs de te, quam** 4
tu tibi credere noli, that Is to say, "Belew thou not anothyr
man of the, more than thy-Selfe." Thou shalt wythstonde a
Withstand losengeoure vtreli, that he be rebuked, and So Shalte thou done
flatterers. thyn owyn profite and his also, for So thou shalt not be dys- 8
cewid, and he shal not entremyt hym to discewe. Warnynge and
amonestynge recewe thou gladly, and reprowynge wythout wrath
or gurchynge. Ife a man reproueth the ryghtfully, thou houyste
¹ Fol. 51. to evne hym thanke, And yf he doth ¹Hit Wrongfully, ²hyt 12
may be þat he wende that he did ryghtfully.² And yf Hit be
that he the reprowe Wrongfully, the trouth tell hym benurly, ffor
Solomon. ther nys no man but he Sumtyme mystake. Salamon Sayth,
"A blessyd answere abbatyth wrethe, and an harde and a 16
thawrtouer worde raysyth³ Stryfe and wodnesse. Reproue thou
a vyse man, and he shall loue the; reproue a fole and he shal
Cato. the hate." Catoñ Sayth,

Virtutem prim**am Puta compescere linguam.** 20
Proximus **est ille deo qui scit racione tacere,**

that Is to say, "Trow thou the Pryncipal vertue to refrayne
thy tonge, For he Is negh to god that can be still by reyson."
Nature has And therfor hath kynde enuyronet a manes tonge wyth tethe 24
surrounded
the tongue and lippes as wyth two wallis, to Sygnyfie that no word Sholde
with two
walls. out-Passe, but yf hit were triet wyth reyson. Kynde vs hath
grauntid two eighen and two eeris, Saue but one tonge, vs to
Show that more we sholde see and hyre, than Speke. Salamon 28
Solomon. Sayth, "Al that the fole thynkyth he Spekyth, but the vyse
man abydyth the houre couenyable to Speke." In Spekynge a
poete consailyth vj Poyntes to be-holde and kepe by this versis.
Six points to **Si Sapiens fore vis, Sex ser**u**a que tibi mando:** 32
be regarded
in speaking. **Quid loqueris, et vbi, de quo, cui,⁴ quomodo, quando.**

that is to Say, "Ife thou wylt be wyse, Sixe thynges kepe
whych y comande the: That Is to witte, what Is that, that thou
Spekyste, whare, and of whome, to whome, whate manere, and 36
in whate tyme." Vices and ewil taichis thou shalt enchue and
hate in thy-Selfe, but anothyr manes vices thou shalt not to

---

²⁻² in margin.   ³ Mysyth *in MS.*   ⁴ cur *in MS.*

besy encherch, nethyr aspy, For Suche a man by reysone is to hate; whan the ¹behowyth an² ill doer to reproue, thou shalt hit not done ouersharpely, but in fayre manere. Reprowe was
4 founde for amendement of hym that Is reprowid, But whan a man Is ouer-harde reprouet, he hatyth his reprowere, and So· therof he is empeyrid and not amendyd. Therfor Sayt[h] Salamon, whoso ouer-harde Snythyth the noos, he draueth blode,
8 and therfor wyth benurtee and fayre chere thou Sholdyst reproue, and the trespace lyghtely foryewyn. whan a man Spekyth the wyth, fayrly hym hyre, And whath that his answere shall ben, gladely hit hym Sayne. And yf he thyn
12 answere in dispite haue, neuer for that be thow ymeuet, ne chydynge make, ne thyn endyngnacion to hym Sayne. For hit is grete honoure to a man hym to wythdrawe fro chydynge. By this forsayde vertue of Temporance, of al Pepil thow shalte ben
16 ylowid, yf thay that ben lowyr than thow, thow haue not in dispite. And to thyne Souerayns doste honnoure and reuerence, And to thy felowis due company. To Souerayns reuerence and honoure, to Subiectes helpe and Socoure, to fellowis company
20 and douceoure, to al men be benure, to no man flatterynge; haue thou fewe Pryue men, be ryghtfull to al men, Slow to be wroth, Redy to mercy, In aduersite Stydfaste, In prosperite wel avysete and humble.

24 **Thus myche haue y Sayde of this vertue Temporance for this tyme: Now here y write olde stories in comendacion of the Same vertue. Capitulum xxxᵐ q**uintum.
a Rystotle, Prynce of Philosofers, Sayth, that to the Vertu
28 of temporance two thynges appertenyth, That Is to witte, Abstynence of mette ³and drynke, and chastite of Body : ⁴And therfor olde Vertues men thes two thynges thay kepedyn. this apperyth by this Story : Alexander the conqueroure So mych
32 he myght endure abstynence, that oftetimes whan he was in trauaille, he askyd none othyr mette but brede only. A grete Clerke Vegece vs tellyth in his boke of Chyualrie, that hit appartenyth not to a good knyght to lowe ayse ne delytes of
36 body. Alsmoch is abstynence auenaunt to a knyght and mesure, as to a monke. Valeri tellyth that women of Rome in olde tyme, Dranke no Wynne. For throgh glotony and dronke-

² and in MS.

Side notes: How ill-doers should be reproved. ¹ 45 L. Solomon. Speak fairly to him who reproves you. Do honour to your Soverayn, and due company to your fellows. Capitulum xxxvᵐ. Aristotle. ³ Fol. 54 b. ⁴ 45 b L. The abstinence of Alexander. Vegetius. Valerius.

nesse men fallyth ofte-tymes in lechurie, wyche Is contrary to
chastitee and to chyualrie. And therfor as Valery tellyth, that
Cornelyus Scipion whan he was sende by the Romanys in-to
Spayne to make hit Subiecte to Rome, anone he comandid that 4
no bordelle were founde in hare company, and ther-for thow[1]
thousand women wereñ dryueñ away from the hoste. Well
wyste the wyse Prynce that loue of women *and* brandynge
fylthed of lechurie nesshyth a manes herte and hym makyth 8
lyke a womoñ, So that he lesyth his Streynth, *and* hardynesse,
and manhode, *and* chyualrie. More accordyth to a lechurere a
Styfe-stafe than a Swerde, and an hechil than an chelde or
a boklere. And therfor Sayth Poetes in fable, that the welle of 12
Salynace makyth men that therin ham bathyth chaunge in-to
women, In sygnyfiaunce and tokyñ, that tho men whych ham
bathyth in the welle of lechurie lesyth Vertu and Valure, and
becomyth feynte and cowardys, *and* febill as Women ben. The 16
Same Clerke Valery vs tellyth of a nobil yonge man that was
callid Spurina, that was so fayre of face, of body *and* fetares,
[2]that al Women Wer meuet and tempted of his grete beaute.
This yonge man that well Parcewit, but he had not talent of 20
foly, And therfore als-moche as he wolde not be suspecte of foly
ne yeue occasion ne encheysoñ of ille and Syne, he wondid al
his face, and many wondys ther-In maked ; Wherfor the beaute
a-way wente and the Synne cesyd. The loset clerke Vegesce 24
of kynge alex*ander* tellyth, that aftyr a grete battaill y-don and
grete Pray taken, A nobill damysell of grete beaute was presentid to the kynge. But he that al was yewyñ to chiualry he
nad no cure of lechurie, And therfor he endeynet not ons hyr to 28
rewarde, but sende hyr to the Same Prynce that She afor was
Spowsyd to. Whan this Prynce and his men Sawe this, they
Preysyth moche the vertue and the grete leaute of alex*ander*,
And ther thay hym rescewid as kynge and lorde. Suche 32
anothyr tale vs tellyth Valerye and Sayth, that atte that tyme
whan Scipion had won *and* conquerid Cartage, as is in this boke
afor-written, amonge al othyr hostagis a fayre mayde of grete
Parage to hym was presentid. And whan this conqueroure had 36
vndyrstonde that a gentill-man of the contrey had hyr trouthid,
he[3] makyd brynge afor hym hyr fadyr *and* hyr modyr *and* the
gentill-man that hyr trouthyd, *and* to ham Saydyñ, "This golde

[1] thowo, MS. [3] ha, MS.

Of the Temperate Love between Man and Wife.

that ye haue broght to me for this damycelle raunsone, I hit yeue and graunt in free mariage to hyr *and* this gentil-mañ,[1] that hir has trouthid." Of this grette Ientrie alle men mervelith, *By Temperance a man*
4 And this nobille lord mor gladly for ay servid. By this Vertu *governs himself, by Justice others.* Temporancia a man gou*er*nyth hym-self, and wi*th* the Vertu of Iustice othir men. But rathir and more ²Providabille ys to a ² Fol. 46 *b* L. man to gouern hymself than othir mene.

8 **Now her is to wit of the temporat loue that shold be betwen A man and his wif, And how he shold know and us hir temporaly. Cap**i**tulum. xxxvi.**

T he loue and the dred of almyghty god, maker and fourmer *Twelve reasons why a*
12 of al thing, frust aboue al thing preferid, xij⁰ cau*s*es en- *man should love his wife* duceth a man to loue his wif reissonnabli and tempora[t]li. The *reasonably.* furste caus is for that holy writ so bidith: " **Viri diligite vxores vestras Sicut et** *Christus* **dilexit ecclesiam et Semet**
16 **ip***su***m tradidit pro ea**": That is to sey: " O ye men, loue yo*ur* wywis as crist lowith holy church, And hymself yaw for hit." Therfor a man shold loue the helth of his wif bodely and gostely; for why: criste diet for the helth of man*n*es Soull and
20 remissioun of his Sin, And therfor a man shold *mer*ciably fforyew his wif repentaunt v*er*aily hir trespace. Vppon this matier Seint Austeyn saith " **Cur en***i***m ad huc reputam***us* **adulte***r***os** *Augustin.* **quos credim***us* **penitencia esse sanatos.**" That is to sey—
24 " Why shold whe now hold men adulteours which whe trowith wi*th* repenta*u*nce I-maked hole." The Seco*u*nd caus that shold *The second cause.* enduce a man to loue his wif is, for hir body is the body of hir spous, And therfor he shold loue hir body as his owyn bodi, for
28 the wif hath no pou*er* of hir owyn body. The iij⁰ caus ys that *The third.* non of tham ys Sufficiant to bring forth fruyt alon of Ieneracioun. The iiij⁰ caus is that woman of manys Ribe was fourmyt; *The fourth.* God wold not fourm woman of the Slyme as he dud man, but
32 of manys fleshe and bon, that he shold loue hir as him Self; ffor holi writ saith, " whoso lowith his wif he lowith himself." The v⁰ caus is that a ³Man be-hettith woman loue when he Set ³ Fol. 47 L. the Ring on hir fynge*r*, and at mas in p*r*esence of cristes body *The fifth.*
36 he doth kis hir. The Sixt caus is that they ar cossinis both *The sixth.* of man and woman, for the vedlak louene eue*r*y ethir, And therfor hit is wondir sethyn So many for ham lowen othir that

---
[1] From here to p. 196, l. 5, supplied from MS. Lambeth 633, fol. 46, l. 21.

How a Man should love his Wife.

thay hamself shold discord; ffor ofte tymys two realmes for on matremony is broght to on accord. The vij⁰ caus is that a wif leuith fadir and modir and all hir kyn, and anheyrryth to hir spous, And therfor he doth ontreueli but yef he hir loue. The 4 viij⁰ caus is that but yef they loue both othir thay shall be in gret myssais, for lik as a man ne restith not well vndir a dropping hous, namely in cold tym, So a man restith not with his wif yf contencion be tham betwen. The Philosofre saith, 8 "**Vxor est aut perpetuale refugium aut perhenne tormentum**": That is to sey, "A wif is a perpetuall refuyt, Othir an euerlesting tormenty." the ix⁰ caus is that hit is hugeli pleassant to god, and man loue wedlak; for Salamon Saith, "In 12 thre thingis my spirit is pleassit, that ben aprowid afor god and man; that is to sey the accord in brethereth, loue of negheboris, And man and his wif well togeddir assentyng." The x⁰ caus is that a wif is a solas to a man of godis yefte, And therfor 16 Salamon saith, "**Ve Soli**"; That is to sey, "Woo to hym that is allon." But he is not allon that livith in chastite, as oneste maidenys and widowis vnto the worshup of god. But a fornicatour is hold allon which is acursid of god, that whan he seth 20 and covettith a woman fleshely, his dissolacion Radir þan ¹his consolacioun he seth; he seth the swerd with the which the dewill hym kittith and fro god hym departith. The xi⁰ caus that a wif is lik an ornement of an houshold; ffor Salamon 24 saith, "**Sicut sol oriens in mundo in altissimo dei, Sic mulieris bone species in ornamentis domus eius, et mulier diligens corona² est viro suo**"; that ys to sey, "As the son ryssing in the world in the heghest placis of god, So is the 28 fairnys of the woman gode in the ornamentis of hir hous; And a lowing woman ys a croun to hir spous." And Salamon, speking of fairnys, saith, "**Sapiens non corporis sed anime respisit decorem.**" That is to sey, "A wise man beholdith 32 not the fairnys of the body but of the soull." And a fole in flesly thyngis is ouer-taken. The xij⁰ caus is that the sacrament of matremony is a dingnite ordeyned of god and in paradis afor that euer enny syn was wroght. And therfor crist in the 36 gospell saith, "**Quod deus coniunxit homo non separet**"; That is to sey, "That thing which god has bound, no man depart." Of the loue that a vif shold haue to hir spous, A doctor tellith, ffurst euery woman shold loue and dred hir 40

The Commendation of Matrimony.

housbond so heyly that she shold troue no man fayrir, wisser,
ne stronger than hir housbon; And thegh anny' othir man
fairer, wiesser, othir stronger wher than he, she shold not troue
4 that.

Of the comendacioun and of the werk of matrimony.
Capitulum xxxvij^m.

H   It ys to wit that matremony ys to be commendid for many   Five reasons
8 caussis, and in exspeciall at this tym for v^e; fruste for the auc- why marriage is commended.
torite of almyghty god, ordyner of matremony; ¹And for honor   ¹ Fol. 48 L.
of the place that hit was maked In; ffor thereas Seint benet   s. Benedict.
ordeyned the monken rull, and Seinte Austeyn chanoun Rull in   s. Augustin.
12 erth, allmy3ty god that may not erre maked the Sacrement of
matremony in paradis. Therfor yef he trespassith that breketh
the rull of Seint benet, moche more hugely he tresspassith that
matremony whiche god makyd breketh. The ij^e caus is that   The second cause.
16 matremony ys to be comend is the oldennysse of hit, ffor this
ordir ys not nyowely maket, but of oldennys hit passith all
manner of orderis in erth, ffor hit was maked afor that euer
man synnyt: the therd caus is ffor that god at Noes flod, whan   The third.
20 all the world was dront, only he sawid the ordir of matremoney.
In Noes ship he and his wif, har thre sonys and har wiffis
sawid were, but all the lechurreris and concubynes were drond.
The iiij^e caus is for criste Ihesus and his modir Seint Mari and   The fourth.
24 his dessiplis by thare bodies presence—as Seint Iohn In his
gospell telith—wirsshuppeden at the feste of wedlok, and there
ettyn and dranken; but lechurris & concubyns may not sayn
that euer criste or Seint mary his modir etten and dranken in
28 enny of thar houssys, But rather the deuyll, of whom thay
maked Sacrefiz of thare bodies. The v^e caus is for that our   The fifth.
lord Ihesus wold be born of oure lady Seint Mari in matremony.
Morouer hit is to wit that the work of matremony may be ussit
32 and don, as sarteyn tretis of wertius tellith, without anny ²Syn   ² Fol. 48 b L.
and meritori in thre cassis; ffrust whan hit is don ffor caus of   When the work of matrimony may be used.
cheldryn to ben concewid, and to the wirship of god to be
bro3t fforth, with othir due sircumstanceis accordyng to Reysoun.
36 This is the principall caus and office of the werk of matrimony.
The ij^e caus is whan that the work is don for remedy, that is to
wit to enchu fornicasion. The iij^e caus is whan det is payed to
the asker; vppon the which matier Seint Austeyn saith thus:

SECRETE.   O

Of the Work of Matrimony.

Augustin. "**Redde debitum coniugale nullus est criminis. In hoc causu mouet Iusticia.**" That is to sey, "To pay wedlak dette hit is of no syn, rightfulnis meuyth in this caus the." The *The fourth cause for demaunding the debt.* iiij[e 1] case Is whan a man asketh that worke to mak his wif, that she fal not in sin; as whan a man knowing his wif shamfaste and neuer to ask that dette, and he dredith of hir fallyng in Syn, he asketh that dette. In this casse pite meuyth. But sothely yef a man use that work to fulfill his concupiscens *When it is venial or mortal sin.* ther is sin, othir while venyall syn and othir whill dedely syn; hit is veniall sine whan concupiscence is so ferforth subiecte to Reissoun, that he wold not know hir but yef she wer his wif; hit is dedly syn whan that concupiscens Is so vnmessurable that he wold knov hir thegh she wer not his wif. *John de Burgh.* Also hit is to wit that a worthy clerk, Iohn of Burghe, in a bok which he maked, that is calit in latteyn "**pupilla occuli Sacerdotum**," tellith that a man is note bound to pay his wif the dette of wedlak in an holy place, ffor so as sum men saith [2 Fol. 49 L.] the place myght be [2]Polut. But yef a man and his vif were *When the debt may be paid in a holy place.* long tym in that place vyolenly enclossid, hit wer laffull to tham to do that ded. Also in hey festis & solempne dayys, in tymys of fasting and processiones a man and his wif shold not neghe togedir, for in such solempne tymys specyaly honnoure is to be don to god, And therfor hit Is to abstene fro leuefull thingys, that thyng which is asked may be getten the mor *When asked for it must be paid.* lyghtelier. Natheles, who so is askede, he owith hit to pay, but yef he may defer hit viesly and without pereill, but he shall not aske hit in the forsaiden tymmys. Therfor whoso asketh that ded in tho tymmys he syneth not, but whoso asketh I-styrryd with con[cu]piscens, but nozt for contempe of the tym othir holi churche consaill, Senneth venialy. And also in tym that a *When the woman is with child.* woman is with child, zef without pereill of the chill hit shall mowe be don, that ded I-asked owith to be payed, And also hit may be asked without dedly Syn; natheles yef hit shold torn to pereill of the child, nethir shold hit ben asked ne yewen. In which cas beste is that a man haue his wif lik his Suster, And do nat that charnell worke.

    O ffe the foure cardinall wertues, by the which a man gidith hym rightfully in the wey of gode maners, ware that

[1] MS. iij[e].

How the Body is to be governed.

many pepill gon out of the wey into this tym I hau
tretid; Now will I retourn to that place theras I left
of the bok of gouernance of kingys and princys in this
4 . sam maner suante.

Off the keping of the body after the consaill of Lechis.
Capitulum xxxviij^m.

 a lexander, in exspeciall kep the fro venym and pusouns: <small>Beware of poison:</small>
8 well ¹Whe wot that many kingys and princys that myght not <small>¹ Fol. 49 b L.</small>
be ouercome with armys by wenym loste thar lywis, And othir
whillis by þe hand of that man in whom moste thay trustid,
And namely by whemen, for loue of whemen blindith the <small>and especially of women.</small>
12 vndirstanding of men, and ham makith ouer moch to truste of
Wemen. Therfor thou shalt not trust in wemen ar that thou
han ham approvid, ffor alsson that thou trust the in a woman
thy lif is in hir handis. Alexander, well sholdiste thou re-
16 menber the þat Sum tym the Quen of Inde the send fair yeftis <small>Remember the Queen</small>
and gret, Among which she send the a ful fair damsell, Of whos <small>of India,</small>
beaute thu wer anon I-caghte. But I, that present ther with
the was, besili beheld that damsell, and hir contenaunce, & hir
20 lokinge; And I apparcevid that she had frekelit eyen, and
without sham fichit hir sight in men vesagis, by the which I <small>and the poison-maiden,</small>
vndirstod well that euery man that hir tuchid Anon shold be <small>from whom I saved you.</small>
enfectid with wenyn without hop of lif, for she was of a child
24 I-norshit with venym, And therfor she was all venym; And
yef I had not varnyte the therof at the furste tuching she had
shent the. Therfor thou sholdiste haue with the in al tymmys
gode lechis and fi[si]ciens; And thou shalt not truste the in on <small>Don't trust in one</small>
28 lech, for he myȝt the priuely don the harm, The lighter that he <small>physician.</small>
is alon. But manny lechis togedir wold not consent so lighteli
to mys-don, ffor euery of tham shall dout othir; therfor of
[lechis in] Sciens and wiesdom beste I-provid and of the be beste
32 fam, by thar consaill tak thou medesyne ²What the nedith. <small>² Fol. 50 L.</small>

That Astronomy is necessari to the keping of mannys body.
Capitulum tricessimum Nonum.

 a S galian the full wies leche Saith, and Isoder the gode <small>Galen and Isidore teach</small>
36 clerk, hit witnessith that a man may not perfitely can the sciens <small>that a leech must be an</small>
and crafts of medessin but yef he be an astronomoure. And <small>astronomer.</small>
therfor thou shalt nothing don, and namly of that which

appertenyth to the kepping of thy body wit*h*out consaill of
astronomoure. Beleue not folis that sain that no man may cu*m*
to the Sciens of steris and planet*is*, ffor thay ben so fer fro vs,
the which by ofte beholding, gret waking, and studi, the old
philosofors [1] that crafte Haue contreuct and Sertayñ Rulys
makyd of the mevynges of the Sterres. Morouer hit is not to
beleue to folys that Sayñe that god hath prouydet *and* ordeynet
al that is to-comynge, And therfore hit nys noñ profyte to can
aforhand that Is to cvm, and by this reyson, hit is no3t wourth
the Science *and* Iugementes of the Sterrys. But I the Say,
alexandyr, that the gloryous god hath so y-stabelid, that the
elementes bene gouernyt by the S[t]erris *and* by the Planetes
that We opynly Sene. The See mevyth *and* hym wyth-drawyth
aftyr the mewynge *and* growynge and drecresynge of the mone,
that hath maystri and lordshupe vpon the watyr and vpon al
thynge that hath kynde of watyr. And therfor oystres and
crabbes, the brayne and marrowe of al bestis wixen and de-
crescen aftyr the mone. And neuer the latyr hit is good to
witte aforhande thynge that is to cvm by kynde of Sterres, for
a man may the bettyr Purvey hym agaynes that is to cvm, yf
he hit knowe afore, and be not Sodaynly ouertaken, as yf a man
wyste that a ful colde wynde *and* wyntere were to cvme, yf he
were wyse he wolde Purvey hym of hote clothis, wodde, and
colle, and of [2] othyr thynges necessari, by the wych he myght
escape wythout empeyrement the grevaunce of the wyntyr. In
Somer a man Purveyeth hym of colde mettys, and drynkes
attemperid, *and* of colde houses. And yf a man wyste derthe
to cvm and grete hungyr, the bettyr he wolde Purvey hym of
corne and othyr vitaille. And therfor hit Semyth well that tho
men bene grete folis that Sayne that the Science and Iugementes
of Serris is not profitable to cañe, Setheñ that therby a man
may dyuers aduenturis the bettyr to vndyrstond aforhand, and
enchu harmys by witte and Purveyaunce. But for-als-moche
that the witte of a man ne Suffysyth wit*h*out the helpe of god,
the Sufferayne remedy agaynes al harmes Hit is, to Pray god
almyghty that he for his grete mercy wolde turne harme Into
good, for his Powere ys not makyd lasse, defuylet, ne destourbet,
by the vertues of the Sterres. Therfor his mercy is to Pray by
deuocion, orison, fastynge, Sacryfice, *and* by almes-dedys, that
he haue mercy of oure Synnes. And yf we So. done, we may

Prayer is a Remedy in every Tribulation.

haue hoppe that of the harmes that we haue deserwid well, he will vs delyuere.

Herre begynnyth stories and ensamplis to proue that oryson
4 **is Souerayn remedy in euery trybulacion. Capitulum quadragessimum.** *Capitulum xl.*

Ho-so will enserche the olde stories Sethyn the worlde began, opynly he shall fynde that nothynge that man may
8 done is of so grete vertu as is orisoun. Abraham the nobil *Abraham prayed for* Patriarke, as the boke of genesi sayth, Prayet god for Sarra his *Sarah, and had children.* wyfe for she was barayne and Passyd the age of chyld-berynge, ¹And She concewyd ysaac. this Same ysaac had a wyfe barayne ¹ 51 L.
12 ycallid Rebecca, he Prayed god that he wolde yeue hym genera- *So did Isaac.* cion, And She concewid Iacob, the holy and nobyl Patriarke: of this thre descendet Marie the ful blessid virgyne modyr of oure lorde Ihesu cryste. In the tyme of Moyses, the ledere and *The story of Moses and*
16 gouernoure of the Pepill of Israelle, we redyth, that a pepill *Amalek.* y-callid amalech faghten agaynes Israell. Moyses ne wolde not entre into the battaill, but rerid his handys toward hevyn, and Prayet god wyth fyne herte that he wolde ham helpe. And hit
20 be-felle that ²Whyle that He hadd His Handis vprerid Israel ² Fol. 55 b. ouercome Hare aduersaries, But whan he avelid his handis, Amalech ouercome Israel; and therfor two men Sustenyd the handis of Moyses, into the tyme that amalech was ouercome and
24 Slayne: where-for we vndyrstondyth that oryson bettyr de- *Prayer better defendeth in* fendyth a man in bataill than a sshelde othyr a targe, and bestyr *battle than a shield.* is in estoure than a sharpe Swerde of Stele. Iosue the Wourthy and wyse weryor, in his grete destresse by Oryson ouercame his
28 enemys as we redyn in the bibill. whan this Iosue, Successoure *Joshua conquered five* of Moysen, had entrid the lande of behoste, and y-take the Cite *kings by prayer.* of Gabaon, and grete goodis and riches goten, fywe kynges of the lande ham dressid agaynes Iosue; that is to Say, the kynge
32 of Iachis, the kynge of Ierusalem, the kynge of Ebrone, the kynge of Iermoth, the kynge of Eglon, wyth hare hostis. Iosue went agaynes ham, wyth his chyualry, and prayet god to be his helpe; God hym answarid, "Neuer doute thou ham, I shal the
36 helpe, No man shal the wythstonde." Iosue hardely ham assay-lid, and god ³ham espaunted so hugely that thay ne durste tham ³ 51 b L. defende, Anoone thay turned har backis; the childryn of Israel ham chaset wyth grete spede, hewedyn ham, and Slowen, and

als many as scapedyn the Swerde of [Iosue] god keste ham
dovne wyth grete Stonys of hawle that than felle throgh godis
biddynge, to whom al thyng Servynne, as Sayth the holy Prophete Dauy. And moche Pepill more were dede by the haule, 4
than by Swerde. Iosue doutid moche that the day hym faillid,
that he myght ben fully avengid : by the grete treste that he had
in god, comanded the Sone and the mone that thay Sholde not
mewe tham fro that place ther as thay weryñ atte that houre, 8
into the tyme that he were avengitte of his enemys. God that
hym granntid, and the Sonne stode amyddis the firmament the
space of one hole day, So that afor ne aftyr ther was noght had
So longe a day, that vnethe any escapid of fywe hostis, And the 12
v kynges weryn taken and hongid. Ezechie the good kynge of
Ierusalem bettyr hym defendyd by Prayer than by Swerde, ffor
as the boke of kynges vs tellyth, Senacherib kynge of assyriens
destrued the Citteis of Iude and aftyr assieget Ierusalem, And 16
fore-alsmoche as ther was had so gret Pouer that he vndyrstode
not that any man myght hit wythstonde, he sende by thre messagers to kynge Ezechie that he were a fole yf he thoght hym to
defende agaynes hym, for non kynge of othyr landys myght not 20
hym wythstonde, and that neuer he shold hym treste of the
helpe of his god, for noone god of al that weryn ther al-aboute
in al regions ne myght ¹not defende thar land agaynes the
assiriens. This kynge Ezechie hym trested in god, and hym 24
clothid in a sake, he Put hym-Selfe to Penaunce, and Prayet,
he Sende to ysay the holy Prophet that he sholde Pray for
hym and his roialme. Alboth Prayet to god that makyd hevyn
and erthe, in whos Powere al thynge was, that he wolde opynly 28
Showe to al naciones that he aloone was god almyghty, And
maystri yewyth to them that he will. Thar Prayer was not in
wayñe, for in oone nyght the angil of god came to the hoste of
assiriens, and Slow of ham an hundrid and Sixti and xx⁺¹ and 32
vᵉ M̃ ²Whan that Saw Senacheribe, hit was no wondyr thegh
He had no wille Longir to abide, and therfor he hastid hym
faste till he came to the grete Cite of Nenuve, but he myght not
so mych hym hast that myschanse nas atte his bake, for his both 36
Sones hym Slow whan he honouret his god atte his tempill.
Hit be-fell ther-aftyr That ezechie wax Seke to the dethe, And
ysayo the Prophete came to hym, and to hym sayde, " Oure
lorde sayth, that thou Shalt dey, and noght lyue." The kynge 40

was sorowfull, *and* hym turned toward the walle, *and* tenderly weppet, and hym praiet of longyr lyfe. Ysaye his way wente, but hit was not longe aftyr that god to hym sayde, "Turne
4 agayñe to Ezechie the ledere of my Pepyll, and Say to hym in my behalfe; I haue hardyn thy Prayer, and Seyn thy terris, *and* I haue helit the *and* Sauet. The thyrde day thou shalte gonne to the tempill, and y graunte the xv yere more to lyue
8 than thou sholdyst." And therfor hit is to vndyrstonde that euery manes lyfe is y-markyd by kynde, how longe he [1] shal mow doure, and that terme may no man Passe: but by foly and evile kepynge, he may hit abregge. But god that Is abow al kynd,
12 may alboth fulfill aftyr his owyn wille. And therfor Ezechie lyued more longyr by the grace of god, than kynde hym grauntet. Manasses the Sone of Ezechie was a ful cruwel tyraunt, he Slow ysaye the Prophete, that helid his fadyr and Sauet the realme,
16 *and* the Pepille; he maked fals oratories to fals goddis and ham honouret; he fulfillit Ierusalem wyth Innocent blode, and beleuyd swenys and sorsrie, *and* hym yaue to euery ewil crafte. And Sortely to Sayne, he Surmountet in Shrewednnesse not
20 only the kynges of Iuda and Israel that weryñ afore hym *and* aftyr, but wyth that he passet in shrewetnesse *and* malice al the Paganesse *and* mysbelewynge men, *and* mysturnet al the tempill *and* hit makid like as hym-Selfe was. And therfor' god that
24 may not suffre vickidnesse aldaies endure, sende a tyraunt that othyr to chastyce, for the Prynces of assirieus came wyth full grete Powere, and conquerid the Cite of Ierusalem, and token Manasses the kynge and hym lad in cheynes to the Cite of
28 babilon, *and* hym in preson sette. Than he hym bethoght of the grete noble that he demenyd in Ierusalem, ther as he was kynge y-cronet, and he became mournynge *and* Sorefull *and* hugely hym peyset that he had god so mych y-grewid, *and*
32 mercy hym criet of his Synnes. And hym entierly Prayet that he wolde hym delyuer, *and* amendynge promysid yf he ayeyn myght to his realme covme. In this wyse he knew god ayeyne in angwysche *and* in [2] myssayse, whych he had foryetene whan
36 he was in his goodnes, ouerwel atte ayse; God whych is [3] ful of mercy *and* no man refusyth, haue he neue*r* so myche hy*m* wrethyd, yf he will hym repente of his mysdedis *and* of Parfite herte mercy hym cry, he foryaue manasses his orribill Synnes,
40 *and* hym agayn broʒt into Ierusalem, *and* the regalite hym yaue,

Hezekiah fell ill, and prayed for health.

Then fifteen years were added to his life.
[1] 52 b L.

Manasseh, his son, was a tyrant.

God punished him by the Assyrians.

He repented and prayed to God,

[2] 53 L.
[3] in, MS.

and God heard and forgave him,

and restored *And* he cownant kepte: he be-came a good man, *and* destruct
him to his
kingdom. the auteris *and* oratories that he had edified to do his sacrifice to
fals godes, *and* servid god in al his lyue wel and trewely, and
diet aftyr he had regnyd lv yere. 4

¹ Fol. 56 *b*. ¹**That god nath not in dispite the orisones of Paganes.**
Capitulum **Capi*tul*um xlj^m.**
xlj^m.
² Pleyer MS. f the grete Vertue of Preyer,² that god Shewyth to tho
 whych the law of god kepedyn, *and* the ryght belewe 8
couthe, thegh Some of tham wickid were into this tyme, I
haue Sortely tolde you; but now wil y now Say more grettyr
God hears mervelis, and I Shall Show *you* that god nath not in despite the
the prayers
of Pagans. orisones of Pagans, yf thay hym w*ith* good herte Pray. God 12
Sente the prophete Ionas to the grete Cite of Nynyvee, wyche
Jonah was was a thre-dayen Iornay. "goo," sayde he, "to the Cite of
sent to
Nineveh. Nynyvee, *and* Say to hit, that afore this xl. dayes Passyd beñe,
the Cite shal be destruct." Ionas entrid the Cite one-dayes 16
Iornay, *and* prechit to tham of the Cite that Paganes weryñ, al
They repent- that god had Sayde to hym. They belewid anone the worde of
ed on his
preaching god, and weryn Sorefull *and* repentant of thar*e* Synnes, and thay
fastid *and* tham clothid in Sackis, Smale *and* grete. of this 20
Came tythynges to the kynge of the Cite, and he anoone arose
³ 53 *b* L. fro his roial Siege, *and* Put of hym ³his clothis *and* hym clothyd
In dust and in Sake, *and* hym Sette in the powdyr, *and* makid cri throgh
ashes,
al the Cite that men and bestis sholde faste *and* clothid in 24
Sakkes, and that euery man sholde turne from his Ille lyfe, and
and God his wickidnesse. Whan god Saw that, he chaungid his Sentence
changed His
sentence. *and* for-yaue tham thar Synnes, for that they w*ith* Pure hertes
hym mercy criden, thegh that thay Paganys weryn. Anothyr 28
mervelous ensampill to p*r*oue the Same I Shall you telle. Whan
Alexander alexandyr had conquerid Egipte, Perce, *and* Mede, he Passid
found the lost
ten tribes in toward the mountanes of Caspies; be-twene whych mountes
the Caspian
mountains. dwellit the tene lynagis of the Pepill of Israel fro the tyme of 32
Salmanasar the grete kynge of assyriens, whych destruct al the
lande of Samarie, *and* token the childryn of Israel, *and* tham
translatid into his lande, as vs tellyth the boke of kynges. And
hit was providet and ordaynet by the assiriens that the childryñ 36
of Israel were not hardy to passe the mountayns aforsayd wyth-
They asked out lewe. And therfor whan kynge alexandyr came to the
his leave to
go out. mountayns, thes chyldryñ of Israel askedyñ lewe to gone out,

yf hit Plesit the kynge, for he was kynge at that tyme of that
lande. Than the kynge enquerid wherfor the were y-ladd out of har land, and he vndyrstode by tham wych the verite knewen
4 that for that thay weryn into that traldome, that thay no helde
not the lawe of god of hevyn wyche thay had rescewid by
Moyses, and wyrsepedyñ fals goddis whych maket weryn by
mannes handis; And therfore the prophetis of god prophiseden
8 of hare thraldome, and Sayden that thay sholde not ¹come agayn
of that exil. Whan alexandyr had that vndrestonde he answarid
tham, that he wolde not yeuen tham noone lewe to goone out,
but mor fastyr he wold tham enclos. Than he began to stope
12 the issues betwene the mountayns; but aftyr he apperceiwid
that the worke of man ne myght not to that suffice, he Prayet
god that he wolde fulfill that worke. And anone this mountayns
tham Ioynet to-gedyr so stydfaste that none of tham myght out-
16 gone by none engyne ne none othy[r] man to tham entre by no
crafte. And therfor hit Is not mervell yf god ²moch done for
the oryson and Prayer of a crystyn good man of good Lyfe,
whan he did So myche for Pagans and Synnyers. **Now gracious**
20 **lord, to youre excellence here I write dyuers rygh good and**
necessary notabilitees of the vertu of Prayere, fryst in
latyn and **Sethyñ in Englysh, aftyr dyuers moste autentike**
auctoritees of holy wryte. Capitulum Quadragessimum
24 **Secundum.**

f Ryste hit is to witte, that Prayer othyrwhyle is sadyn a
good worke, on wych matyer Seynt Paule Sayth, **Sine inter-**
missione orate, that is to Say, "pray ye wythout any Stynt-
28 ynge." vp this matiere the glose Sayth, **Semper orrat qui**
bene agit, that Is to Say, "He prayeth al tymes that al tymes
doth well." Also the ryghtfull man neuer styntyth to Pray, but
that he Stynte a ryghtfull man to be. Whoso will fryste pray
32 he moste consydyr his owyn fautes, tham amende, and than
Pray; for Salamon Sayth in the thyrde boke of kynges, **Templo**
edificato Si quis cognouerit Plagam cordis Sui, et extendit
manus suas in domo hac, tu exaudies illum in celo, That is
36 to Say, "The tempill y-bylid, who³so will know the wonde of his
herte, And Pute vp his handis in this howse, thow thalt hyre
hym̄ in hevyñ." Also the glose Sayth, **Oracio est cultus deo**
debitus, que comprehendit fidem, Spem, et caritatem, that is
40 to Say, "Preyer is a wyrshupe owyn to god, the whych compre-

Marginal notes: Alexander asked why they were left captive. They told him. ¹ 51 L. He would not let them go. He prayed that the mountains might close up, and so they did. ² Fol. 57. Capitulum xliiⁿᵐ. Prayer is a good work. First learn your faults, then pray. Salamoñ ³ 54 b L. The gloss on prayer.

hendyth feyth, hope, *and* charite." And therfor Seynte Austyne *Augustinus* sayth, **In fide, Spe,** *et* **charitate continuato desiderio Sempe**r **Orem***us*, that is to say, "In feyth, hope, *and* charite, wyth *con*- *Matthew.* tynuel desyre Pray we altymes." Seynt Matheu Sayth, **Et nunc** 4 **clamem***us* **in celu***m*, "Now cry we to hevyñ." Seynt Luke *Luke.* Sayth, **Petite et dabitur wobis, querite et invenietis, Pulsate et appe***r***ietur Vobis,** " Aske ye, And hit shal be yevyñ to you; Seche ye, and ye shall fynde; knoke ye, and hit shal be oppenyd 8 *Augustin.* to you." Vp this texte Saynte Austyn Say[th] thus, **Non tantu***m* **hortaretur deus vt peterem***us***, nisi dare vellet, erubescat hu***m***ana pigricia, Plus wlt ille dare, quam nos accipe***r***e; Plus wlt ille misereri, quam nos a miseria liberari.** " God ne 12 volde not so mych amoneste, that we sholde aske, but yf he wolde yeue. Manys Sleuth vix hic assamyd, for he will yew more than we will taken, he wil more haue mercy than we desyre *James.* be delyuerid of myssayse." Seynt Iames Sayth, **Si quis indiget** 16 **Sapiencia Postulet eam a deo,** *et* **dabitur ei,** " Whoso nedyth wysdome, aske hit of god *and* hit shall ben yeue to hym." Isodyr *Isidore.* Sayth, **Qui vult oracionem suam volare ad do***m***i***n***um, faciat illi duas alas, Ieiuniu***m* **et elemosina***m*, " Who-so will his 20 Prayer flee to god, make to hit two wynges, fastynge and almes-[de]de. And hit Is to witte, that Prayer helyth Sekenys of *Solomon.* [1]body, as Salamon Sayth, **Fili in tua paupertate ne despicias te** [1] 55 L. **ip***s***um, Set ora do***m***in***u***m et ip***s***e curabit te,** " O thou Sonne in 24 thyn Sekenesse ne dispise not thy-Selfe, but Pray oure lorde, *James.* *and* he shal cure the." Seynte Iames Sayth, **Oracio fidei Sanabit infyrmu***m*, " the Prayer of feyth shall hele the sekeman." Also Prayer longyth a mannys lyue, like as is afor-sayde of 28 kynge Ezechie. Also Prayer delyuerith a man fro Shame and Perill of deth, As hit did the good holy wyfe Susanna. Also [2] Fol. 57 b. Prayere delyueryth a mañ fro [2]the Power of Wickyd Prynce*s*, Prayer delivers from many evils. as hit did Baruc and many othere*s*: Also fro Prison as hit did 32 Seynt Petyr; And fro wickyd worme*s*, as hit did Seynt Margaret, Saynt George and the kynges doghter*e*; And also Irland by Seynt Patrike-is Prayer is for ay delyuerit *and* clensit from al venemouse bestis: also the holy p*r*ophet Ionas by Prayer 36 *Jerome.* was delyuerid out of the whalis bely. Saynt Ierome Sayth, **Ieiunio Sanantur Pestes corporis, oracione Pestes mentis**, " Wyth fastynge is sawid the Sekenys of body, and wyth Prayere the Sekenesse of Sowle." Also **Prayer in bodely** 40

battaille ouercomyth and hath victori. This proueth the boke
of exody, siggynge, **Cum leuaret manus Moyses, Vincebat** Exodus.
Israel, "Whan that Moyses vprerid his handis, Israel ouer-
4 come." Of this Spekyth the boke of Iudyth, **Memores estote** Judith.
Moysi Serui Dei, qui amalech non ferro pugnando Sed pre-
cibus sanctis deiecit, " Be ye myndful of Moyses the Servaunt
of god, whych amalech noght fyghtynge with Iren, but wyth
8 holy Prayer keste doune." Vp this texte Sayth the glose, **Plus** The Gloss.
[1] **vnus sanctus** proficit orando, quam innumeri **Peccatores** [1] 55b L.
**Preliando. Oracio Sancti celum Penetrat quomodo in terris
hostes non vincat. Plus vetula vna adquirit de celo vna
12 hora orando quam mille milites armati adquirant de terra
longo tempore preliando.** "More oone holy man profityth in One prayer more use in
Praynge, than out of Nombre of synnyers battaillynge. The battle than many war-
prayer of the holy man thurlyth heuyñ : why sholde not hit than riors.
16 enemys ouercome. More one olde woman gettyth of hevyñ in
oone houre Praynge, than a thowsand k[n]yghtes enarmet gettyth
of londe in longe tyme battaillynge." To Prow that Prayere
hugely a-walyth agaynes the malice of enemys, dyuers good olde New examples.
20 ensamplis abow in this boke y han writte; But for-als-moche as
good newe ensamples sholde not ben vnremembrid for lerynge
of tho that arne to come, Oone of tham now her y write.

Of dyuers ryght good and **necessary nobilteis of the vertu
24   of orison. Cap**itu**lum. xliij**m. Capitulum xliij m.
ftyr the Incarnacioñ of oure lorde Ihesu cryste, Mt. cccc In 1422 at Dublin the
a   xxij[tl2] yere, al the Clergi of deuelyn considerynge the grete clergy were grieved by
myschefe of Iryshh enemys and rebell were in the land the Irish enemy.
28 Surdynge in acte, that is to witte the brenys of Thomon, the Irelande
bourkenys of Connaght and monstre, The morthes of leys, the
Mcmahens vp the contrey of vriel, hit more depyr than euer
afore brandynge, And O'neyle-boy, Grayfergowse and Vlucstre
32 atte his owyn wille brandynge and wastynge, This clergy twyes They went in procession
in euery wike in oppyn processyon god Prayeden for the good twice a week
esplaite of the forsayden oure kynge henry, than beynge in praying.
Fraunce, and for the forsayd Erle his lyeutenaunt of Irland,
36 anent the malice of the forsayden enemys. Thys erle [3] throgh the [3] 50 L.
grace of god and dewout Prayere aforsayd, beynge wyth hyṁ the
hoste of deuelyñ, alle [4] the moste Inly streynthes, p[l]aases, and

[2] ij are run together. L. 1421.   [4] atte MS.

tonnes of leys, wyth moche of hare stode and har cornes, than
aftre eke he braunt and destruyet. And anoone aftyr he
rebukid the forsayden breenys and bourkeyns wyth dyuers otheris,
¹and Ham to Pees reformed. Aftyr that beynge in His company
the Same Hoste of Deuelyn and many mo, this erle by Doun-
dalke roode and by M{{c}}genons countre, and throgh o'haghuraghtes
countree, into the moste Inli Streynthes of M{{c}}mahons contre,
thre nyghtes therin I-logid he was. his stronge newe castell, his
townes, his fayre toures, and his stronge P[l]aases into the
grownde brake, brande, and destrued, and many of his Pepill
this Erle Slowe, and al the remenaunt were scomfited. The
fourth day wyth his Pepill throw the mydstreynthes of Manus
M{{c}}mahons countrey Sauely wythout any fyght or Shote of any
enemy to the toune of Arthyrde hit repayred. The nexte wyke
aftyr that, al the moste stronge Pases of the Same Manus countre,
wyth his cornes, this Erle did kutte, brant, and destruet; noone
henemy ther Seyñ forto wythstonde, ther as euer afore were
wonnet to fyght with englysh men. Aftyr this wythout delay
this Erle into O'neel-boyes contrey wyth his retenue roode,
gracious esploit ther god hym sende; fro trayson hym Sauyd;
And this o'neel boy wyth al the grestis enemys of vlnestere vnto
Pees refourmyd. Than to the towne of Drodath this Erle with
all his retene Sauely repayrid, And there this M{{c}}mahons with
dyuers othyr enemys, fynes with hym makid, Pees forto haue.
Al this forsaydyn hostynges, viages, and trauaiH doñe and fulfillid weryn in lytill more space than thre Monthes by the grace
of god, in whome Is al, and deuoute Prayer, without that that
the kynge anny liege man loste. Also this Erle a litill afore
the forsayd hostynge rode Thomoñ xl. dayes, the wyche is the
moste Inly Streynth of Iryssh of al the land, and hit brante, and
many men therin Slayne, And damagelees forto accompte fro
thens repayrid, And dyuers othyr processes did, in they yere that
he lyeutenant was. For the whyche processes this nobill erle
shold nat vaynglory haue for foure causes: the fryste cause Is
that the fryste Parte of the Profite of euery good worke, as
Parisiens Sayth, is glorie appertenynge to oure lorde god, And
ther-for the apostil sayth, "Honoure and glorie bene they vnto
you, oonly god." The ij{{e}} cause Is, that the Seconde Parte of
the Profite of euery good werke Is good ensampill, appertenynge
vnto oure neghbore; And therfor cryste in the gospel of Matheu

Sayth, "Youre lyght so lyght afore men that thay mowen See youre good workys." The iijᵉ cause is that the thyrde Parte of the Profite of a good worke Is a mede or rewarde appartenynge 4 vnto hym̄ that dooth good workys. And therfor he that Sechyth his owyn glori of good workes that he doth, he defraudyth god of his Parte of the profite, And ther-for barnar vp this vers, **Scuto circumdabit te veritas eius,** *etc*, Sayth, that vayn glorie 8 Is an arow of the deuyll that Is to drede, fleynge lyghtly in thy lyfe-day, but hit makyth a full heuy *and* a full Soore wounde. The iiijᵉ cause why that this nobill erle sholde not haue vayne glory of this forsayde processes is, the lytill thanke that he had 12 of ¹ham that hym shuldyn beste haue rewardid *and* commendid. And ther-for this nobill erle may Sey that, that the appostill Sayde vnto thymothe, "know thou," he Seyth, "that in the latyste dayes ther shullyn be Perillous tymes, And men Shullyn 16 be lowynge ham-Selfe, couetous, Prowte, heygh, claundrynge, inobedyente, *and* vnkynde wyth-all." Of vnkyndnes spekyth Seneca, *and* Sayth, "He is an onkynde man that denyeth hym to haue recevid a good dede : He Is vn-kynde that feynyth : he 20 is vnkynde that rewardyth not ne commendyth benefactis, but reportyth ille dedes : ²And He is moste vnkynde of all that foryetyth Benefactes." But yet, wer Hit So that no mañ wolde rewarde ne thanke anothyr for benefactes, neuer-the-lasse shulde 24 a man in any tyme cesse forto do al the good that he may. For the prophet biddyth, "Declyñe thou fro harme and do good." And also oure lorde god Sufferyth nooñ ille dede forto be vn-punyshyd, ne nooñ good ded vnrewardid. **I declarid as here-** 28 **afore Is writtyñ, how that Prayere moche availlyth agaynes bodely enemys: Now hit is to witte that Prayere moche a-waillyth agaynes gostely enemys.** The grete Clerke Isodyr Sayth, **Hoc est remedium eius qui viciorum temtamentis** 32 **exestuat, vt quociens quolibet tangitur vicio, tociens se ad oracionem subdat, quia frequens oracio viciorum inpugnacionem extinguit,** that is to Say, "This Is the remedi of hym whyche brandyth with temptacioñ of vices, that als often he 36 is touchid wyth any wyce, so often-tymes Put hym-Selfe to Prayer ; fore ofte Prayer quynchyth the Pryckynges of vices." Also Prayer Puttyth a-way deuyll, as mathou in the gospell Sayth, **Hoc genus demoniorum non eicitur, nisi per oracionem** 40 **et Ieiunium.** ³"This kynde of Deuelis his not Put out, but by

margin notes: But there are four reasons · why he should not be vainglorious. · Bernard. · He got little thank for his services from those who should have rewarded him. ¹ 57 L. · Timothy. · Seneca. · ² Fol. 58 b. · Still we must do right if we are not rewarded. · Isidore. · Matthew. · ³ 57 b L.

Prayer *and* fastynge." Also Prayer turmentyth the deuyll:
Also hit lightyth a man to the lowe of god: Also hit Puttyth
away Syn̄: also hit confortyth a man in trybulacion̄: Also
Prayer is good for tranquyllite *and* pees: of this y shal fynde
many auctoriteis in holy writte. Sayn̄te Gregory sayth, **Magna
virtus oracionis que, effusa in terra, in celo ope*r*atur. Ang-
lice,** "Moche is the vertue of Prayer, wych out-sayd in erthe,
worchyth in hevyn̄." The glose Sayth, **Oracio velut quoddam
Scutu***m* **ab ira dei protegit,** that is to say, " Prayer defendyth
the wrath of god as a shelde." But who-so will that his
Prayer be herde wyth god, kepe his comaundmentes; for
Isodyr Sayth, **Qui a p*r*eceptis dei aue*r*titur man***us***, quod
in or*acio*ne Postulat non meretur, nec impetrat ab illo
d*omi*no bonu***m* quod Poscitur, cuius legi non obedit: et Si
id quod deus precepit facim***us***, id quod petim***us*** sine dubio
optinemus,** That Is to Say, "He that is turned fro the com-
maundmentes of god, He deservyth not thynge whych he
askyth in praier: nethyr he gettyth of that londe the good
whych he askyth, to whos law he noght obeyeth: And yf we
donne that god comaundyth, that thynge whych we askyth
wythout doute we shall gettyn̄." Ther-for Seynt Austyne
Sayth, **Citius exaudytur vna obediens oracio quam decem
Milia contemptor***um*, that Is to Say, "Soner Is graciously
hardyn oone Prayere of the obedient, than ten thowsante of oon
rebelloure othyr an evill lyuere." In tyme of Prayer a man
sholde onely thynke in god, therfor Isodyr Sayth, **Pura est or*acio*
quam in suo tempore secu*l*i no*n* interueniunt cure: Longe
autem a deo est a*n*im***us*, qui orac*i*onibu***s* cogitacionibu***s* seculi
fuerit occupatus,** that Is to Say, "clene Is that Prayer whych
in his tyme the curis of ¹the worlde ne entremedelyth nat;
ffer fro god is the Sowle, wych in Prayeres occupacions of the
worlde Is occupied." Ther-fore oure Prayer sholde benne sayde,
havynge hooly oure hertes in god, for an holy abbote Achon
Sayth, **Diabolus eni***m* **nullum opus tantu***m* **conatur interum-
pere, quantu***m* **orac*i*onem deuotam,** that Is to say, "the devill
no worke is so besy to lette or destrube, as deuoute Prayer."
Also we sholde Pray god hauynge hope wythout any doute.
For Seynt Bernard sayth, **Indign***us* **celesti benedictione esse
conuincitur, qui deu***m* **querit dubio affe*c*tu,** that is to say,
"He ys co*n*uictid to be onworthy the blessynge of god, that

How Aristotle commendeth Justice.

askyth god with dowtfull wille." Also hit is to witte that we
sholde Pray in euery Place, ffor in euery Place perilles, [1] And
in euery Place we nedyth the Helpe of god; But Isodyr Sayth,
4 **Specialiter Locus ydoneus orandi est secretus,** that Is to say,
"A Specialy behouabill Place of Prayynge is a pryue Place."
Also hit is to witte that in prayer is to be askyd in especial
and atte the begynnynge, the blisse and the kyngdome of
8 hewyn and the ryghtfulnes of the kyngdome, O this Seynt
Matheu Sayth, **Primum querite regnum dei, et iusticiam eius,
et hec omnia adicientur vobis,** that is to say, "Fryste aske ye
the kyngdome of heuyn and the ryghtfulnes of hit, and al thes
12 shal ben to you yeuen." But god byddyth vs not that we
sholde aske fryste temporal thynges; ffor temporal thynges
bene owyt to this men, whych haue the ryghtfulnes of hewynly
kyngdome.

Marginalia: We should pray everywhere. [1] Fol. 59. Isidore. Matthew. What we should ask for first.

16 ### Of the vertue of Iusticie othyr ryghtfulnesse.
Capitulum xliiij^m.

Capitulum xliiij.

F the vertu of Iustice afor in this boke Is largely Saydyn,
o but for-als-moche as Aristotle-is boke makyth [2] mencion of
20 Iustice, the best wordys that therin benne I shall here-to
youre nobellese writte. Iustice Is a vertue that mych is to
Preyse for hit is appropyrte of the glorious god. And therfor
tho Pryncys and lordys whych har Subiectis by Iustice gouern-
24 yth, and thar nedys auauncceth, thare bodyes and Possessions
defendyth, they ben lyke to god the Souerayne gouernoure.
God gouernyth al the worlde by witte and Iustice; And to tho
two vertues ben contrary foly and wronge. And therfor Iustice
28 of a kynge, othyr of a gouernoure, Is more profitable to subiectis,
than Plente of riches; And a ryghtful lorde bettyr than seyson-
able rayne. And hit is to witte, that hit was foundyn y-writte in
oon stone, in langgage of galde that a kynge and vndyrstandynge
32 bene two bretheryn, of wyche ethre hath nede to othyr; That
oon ne suffice nat wythout that othyr. Iustice wyth ryghtfullnes
is departid in two maners; that oone maner is whan the Iuge
doth ryght to al men, smale and grete, aftyr the lawe, That othyr
36 maner Is whan the Iuge hym holte ryghtfull as anent god; that
he kepe hym fro synnes wych ben agayn the law of god; alboth
this thynges owyth euery good Iuge to haue. By Iustice Is al
the worlde y-gouernet, the worlde Is lyke a gardeyn of god, the

Marginalia: Aristotle praiseth Justice. [2] 58 b L. Princes who govern justly are like God. Justice is more profitable to subjects than riches. Two manners of justice, to others and to God.

wallis whych hit emyroneth bene ryghtfulnes: And the ryghtful Iuges is as a lord emyronet wyth lawe, and the lawe is a
yarde by the wych a kynge goue*r*neth the roialme; And the
kynge is an herde, whych is defendet by his barones; the
baronys ben as soudyorus sustenyd by mony; money is fortune
y-gaderid of Subiectis; Subiect*is* bene as Servant*is* by Iustice
y-gouernyd; [1] And Iustice Is the helth of Subiect*is*.

Of the goue*r*naunce of man aftyr the v wittes.
Capitulum Quadragessimum quintum.

Od fourmyd man *and* hym makyd abow al bestis, and hym
yaue hys comandmentis, and hym promysid rewarde aftyr
his deseruynge, and yaue a body as a Cite to gouerne, and
put therin vndyrstondynge as a kynge, and hit sette in the
moste heyest Place of man, that Is, the hede, and to hym
estabelit v messagers to fette and presente al that to hym Is
necessarie, tho bene the v wittys; of the wych euery of ham
hath his Propyr dome, *and* bene in Sartayn Place*s* I-sette, in
eighen, in the nose-thurlis, in tonge, in handys, and in eeris.
By the eyghen know we ix. thynges, that Is to witte; lyght,
derknesse, coloure, body, shape, thynges neygh *and* ferre, meuynge, *and* restynge. By the eeris we haue knowlech of Sovne,
wych is in two maner*es*; Soune [2] Wych is callid voyce of man
othyr of Beste, as speche of man, neynge of hors, syngynge
of birdis: Anothyr Spice of vitte is callid Sowne of thynges
that bene not quycke, as the Sowne of watyr, *and* brekynge of
trees, thundyr, Harpynge, and othyr Instrumente*s*. By the noos-
thurles we haue knowlech of odeurs *and* stynches. By the tonge
we felen the dyuersite of Sauores, Swetnes and bittyrnesse, Saltnesse and egyrnesse, and othyr Saucoure. The taste is a com*m*yn
witte, Spraden throgh the body, but hit Shewyth hym most by
the handys than any othyr lym of the body; by that witte we
knowen hote, colde, dry, moyste, and othyr Suche thynges.
Thes v wittes al that thay [3] rescewyth of thynges that ben wythout, thay presentyth to the ymaginacioñ, and othyr more, they
ben presentid to the vndyrstonddynge, that hath to deme al
thynges.

The Properties of Councillors.

Of the manere of the propirtees of consaillours.
Capitulum quadragessimum sextum.

Capitulum xlvj^m.

ike as the v wittes bene as v messagers, wyche Serwyth
to the vndyrstondynge, so oweste thow, Alexander, to haue
v messagers and v consaillours, and euery of tham shall
be seuerall, for so shall they bene to the moste profitable. kepe
with thy-Selfe thyn secreete, and tell hit not tham, that thou
haste atte herte, And take kepe that thay Parcewe not that
thou haste mestere of thar consaill, for than they wolde despice
the. And therfore thou sholdyste fryste assaye thar wille and
thar witte, And so thou mayste bettyr avise the, well sayne and
done. And there-for Sayth hermogynes, the Philosofre, that
the Iugement of that man of whom consail is asskyd of, is more
to Preyse than the Iugement of that man that consaill askyth,
thegh he say bettyr and wisere, for he that hyryth the reysones
of many men may lightyr well sayne, than he that erste Spake.
And whan thou haste assemblid thy consaillours any consail to
yewen, thou shalte no3t medle estraunge consaill to yewyn, that
they be not destourbet; Sethyn shall thou hyre what they shall
sayne, And yf they answere anone and accorde, thou shalt than
agayñs sigge and by Sum reysoun, Show the contrarye of that
whyche thay haue sayde, to make tham thynke and bene avysid
more deppyr. Sethyn whan they haue all consaillet and thare
reysones is i-shewet, thou shalt not show to whate ¹thynge thy
will moste enclineth, into the tyme that hit cum to the dede and
to the proue, and thow shalt sutely and besely auise the, whych
of ham beste consaill yewyth to the, and moste appartenynge to
the moste Profitable Prosperite of thy gouernaunce. And Putte
notte that oone more heyere than that othyr, nethyr in wordis ne
in yeftis ne degrees of dygnyte, for as for that ofte-tymes comyth
destruccion in roialmes. Noone grete thynge shalt thou done
wythout consaill, for the Philosofre sayth, that consaill is the
hegheste of thynges wych bene to come, and that the cunnynge ²
and wysdome of the wyse kynge is encrescid by consaill of good
consailloures, like as the See is encressit by receit of freshe watyr
and ryuers. And myche thou mayste conquere by wysdome of
good consaill, moore than thou shalte Purchas by myght of men
of armes. Noone harme may cvm of consaill, for yf a man
yeuyth good consaill, thou mayste hit ³Su; And yf Hit Be vn-

A king should haue five messengers and five councillors.

He should keep his own wish secret from them.

Hermogenes.

Seem to uphold the contrary of what they advise.

¹ 60 L.

Do not tell them what you decide on.

Do not exalt one above another.

² cummynge MS.

No harm can come of taking counsel.

³ Fol. 60.

SECRETE P

profitable, thou mayste Hit enchou. I yeue the full good
consaill that thou make not kepere of thy reame only oone man,
whan thou goste in anothyr Place; for throgħ his wickid consaill, myght the baronage be corrupted agaynes the. Oone othyr 4
consaill I yeue the, that neuer thou spare thyn enemy dedly, but
euery tyme that thou mayste, Show thy Victori ouer hym̄; And
kepe the, that in no tyme he haue Powere on the, for in no
manere thou shalt on hym tryste. 8

Sidenotes: Do not make one man keeper of thy realm. Never spare your deadly enemy.

Capitulum **How thow shalte assay thy consaillours.** Capi*tu*lum xlvij^m.
xlvij^m.

Ne thynge by whych thou mayste assay thy consaillours
is, that thou shalt make ham vndyrstonde that thou haste
nede to money; and yf thay Sayne to the that good is, that 12
thou take of thy tresure, witte thou that thay maken of the
lytill Price. And yf thay Sayne the, that thou take largely of
the money of thy Subiectes, witte thou that thay hatyn the Out
of mesure: for that is but corrupcioñ of thy realme. And yf 16
thay Sayñe to the, "Al that we haue, we haue hit Purchasid in
youre lordshupe by youre grace," thes arne to Prayse *and* worthy
to co*m*mende, as thay whyche desyryth the honoure of thar lorde
as hare owyñ. In anothyr maner thou mayste assay thy con- 20
saillours. For in case that thay gladly rescewe yeftes *and*
besyeth ham to gadyr tresure, neuer tryste thou to suche; ffor
thay Servin the to Purchas golde, and har cowetyse neuer shall
take ende; ffor the moore that mony growyth, the more couetyse 24
encrescyth. And euer suche may be lyghtely corrupted, and by
auenture y-broght to that they wolde thy deth, by the entyce-
ment of tho wyche woldyn the harme, and hym yeuyth largely
of harme. Therfor good hit Is that thay be not fere frome thy 28
presence, and comande tham that thay haue not acquentaunce ne
famulyarite to noone othyr kynge ne Prince, and that thay sende
not letteris to tham ne yeftes of tham rescewe. And yf thou
mayste suche thynge Percewe, redresse hit in haste, ffor men 32
corages ben ful changeabill *and* lyghtely enclyneth to behostes.
And he is moste Profitable of thy consaillours and moste worthy
to be lowid, wyche lowyth thy lyfe and to the dethe obedience;
And he that moste demeneth thy Subiectes to thy ²lowe, And 36
he that abbaundeneth hym-Selfe and his goodis atte thy wille,
And he that hath the vertues and the maners that y shall tell
here-aftyr.

Of the tokenesse and condycions that a good Consailloure and a frende sholde haue. Capitulum xlvi[i]j^m.

nota Capitulum xlviij^m.

T the begynnynge, thy consailloure and thy frende [sholde
4 a haue] Perfitnesse of lymes, well to fulfill al thynges for
wych he is chosyn. Sethyn he sholde haue good vndyrstondynge, and good will to vndyrstond that a man hym̄ Sayth.
Hit be-howyth that he be of good mynde to remembyr that
8 wyche he hath vndyrstonde, so that he foryet not. And that
he be Parcewynge of that thynge wych berryth charge, and
wyche noon̄, and that he bene corteyse, wel Spekynge, and
eloquente wythout Ianlynge: he sholde be cvnnynge in dyuers
12 sciences, he sholde bene Sothefaste in worde and dedd, and lowe
throuth abowe al thynge, and hate lesynge. And he sholde
beñe Softe, bonere, and tretabill. Glotony, dronknesse and
euery Surfete of ettynge and ¹drynkynge, Lechurie, fule plaies,
16 and foule delytes He shollde enchu. Aboue al t[h]ynges he
sholde bene hardy, stabill of Purpos, and loue honoure and
heynesse; golde, Siluer, and othyr erthely thynges, he sholde
haue in dyspite: And nothynge he sholde holde moch of, Saue
20 dignyte, honours, and lordshuppes. he sholde loue and haue in
charite good men and ryghtfull, hate wronges, yeue euche man
hesyn̄, helpe tho that nede haue, and whan he shall Iustificacion̄
done, he sholde noone dyuersite of Persones make; for-why, god
24 made al men̄ y-lyke. he sholde beñe of grete Perseueraunce in
purpos ²and in dede that he shall do, that he Pursu ham and
fulfill ham wythout drede and couwardy. He sholde know the
yssues of the exspensis of the realme, he sholde not be of lyght
28 Semblant that he cvm not in despyte to the Pepill, neuer-the-
lasse courteisly he sholde answere the Pepill, his courte sholde
be opyn̄ to al tho that thedyr comyth, and he sholde besely
enquere and aspi al maner of tythynges: he sholde conforte the
32 subiectes, amende har dedis, and ham Solace in aduersitees; In
tymes suffyr har vncunnynge and thar Symplenesse.

These are the tokens of a good Councillor: good understanding and memory; courteous, wise and truthful; temperate and kind; ¹ Fol. 60 b. bold and loving honour; helping good men, and persevering; ² 61 b L. cautious, and of noble bearing, yet long-suffering.

How a man hath al condycions of bestis, Hit is to Witte. Capitulum xlix^m.

Capitulum xlix^m.

36 Itte thow Alexandyr, that god the gloryous ne maket noght
w noone creature bodely more visyr than man. And a man
may not fynde in no beste, custume ne thegh, wyche is
noght in a man. For a man his hardy as a lyon̄, Feynte as an

Man has all the qualities of beasts.

The pro-
perties of
animals
found in
man.

hare, couetous as a dogge, hardy *and* fierse as an harte, Piteous as a turture, Malicious as a lyonesse, Pryue and tame as a culuere, Deccyuaunt and¹ trechurus as a fox, Sympill and blesfull as a lambe, Swyfte and delyuer as a kyd, Tyraunt *and* Slow as a bore, precious and dere as an oliphaunt, lytill worth and dull as an asse, Prophitable as a bee, wancraunt *and* dyssolute as a goote, Ondauntit as a bulle, reysonabill as an angill, Lecherus as a swyñe, malicious as a toode, Profitable as an hors, nuous as a mows. And Sortely to Say ther nys noone creature in the worlde, of wych a man nath Sum propirte: And therfor a man is callit the lytill worlde. 4

8

Man is the
microcosm.

Cap*itu*lum L^m.

Of Notaries. Cap*itu*lum L^m. 12

Notaries
should be
wise and
eloquent.
² G² L.

A Lexandyr, to chese the be-houeth, to writte thy Pryuyteis *and* priuey workys, wyse men of Parfite eloquence, and of good mynde. For that ²is a tokyn of a grete lorde, and a stronge argument to Shewe the heynesse of thy myght, and the Sotilte of thy knowleche. For the tokyñ and vndyrstondynge of worde is as his Spirite, And the wordes ³yspokyñ ben as a body, but the wrytynge ys as a couertoure of the worde³; and afor al thynges that he be of good feyth hit nedyth. And that he know thy wille in al thynges, and that he wyllyth thy profite *and* honoure afor al thynges; he sholde be curteyse *and* Parceuynge in his dedis, And that no man entyr in sygh of thy Preveyteis of wrytynges. And yf thou mayste fynde hym Suche, Pay hym well for his Service, so that he hym holde apayed to do the bettyr.

16

Writing is
a coverture
for the word.

20

24

Pay your
secretary
well.

Capitulu*m*
lj^m.

Of messagers, and wych thay shold bene. Cap*itu*lum quynquagessimum Primu*m*. 28

An ambassa-
dor showeth
the wit of the
lord who
sends him.
⁴ Fol. 61.

Choose the
most worthy
you can find.

Itte thou, Alexandyr, that the messager shewyth the witte W of that man that hym sendyth. And he is his eigh in that whych he seth not, And his eeris in that wych he heyryth not, And his ⁴tonge in his absence. And therfore the nedyth to chese the moost worthy that arne in thy presence, wyse, wyrchipphull, *and* commendabill, that hat[et]h euery manere of filthet *and* vyleny. And yf he may noght al haue thes condycionys, for hard hit is to fynde Suche, atte the leste he sholde be Pryue and trew, and nothynge he sholde amenuse, make lasse, ne

32

36

¹ as, MS.   ³—³ This insertion is in the margin.

aneche, of the messagis or nedis whych he Is sende for. And yf *Let him be such as can heed all he heareth.*
that he kepe thy commaundment, And that he be takynge hede
to the answare that he hyryth, so that he tham can say agayñ
4 whan he comyth. And yf Suche ne may noȝt be founde, atte *If not let him be a bearer*
leste he sholde be a trew berrere of letteres that bene sende, and *of letters.*
agayñ to be broght. Of¹ thes thre messagers the fryste is mooste
Profite, And the Seconde mooste Sertayñ, And the thyrde lest
8 Perelouse. And yf thou mayste Parcewe that any of tho mes- *Do not choose one who can be bought.*
sagers be y-temptid to geddyr mony ¹ or Purchas of the placis
wyche he is sende to, refuse hym atte al poyntes, for he goth not   ¹ 62 b L.
for thy prou. Ne sende not a dronkelewe messangere, ffor the *Nor a drunkard.*
12 Pepill of Pers bene y-wonet to afforce messangers to drynke good
wyn, and yf the messager wix dronke, by that they knoweth
that hare lordis ne byth not wyse. The grettyste of thy Pryue *Nor the greatest of your lords.*
Consaillours thou shalt not make thy messager, nethyr he shal
16 not be fere from thy presence, ffor that sholde bene empeyr²e-
ment of thy roialme. Al thy messangers thou sholdyst ofte-tymes *Prove them oft, reward the good.*
Prowe, of what witte thay bene, and of what gouernaunce and
of what maner. Thay that good bene and trewe, thou shalt ham
20 wel rewarde, And yf any of ham bene founde that is fulli sette,
yeftes to resceue, and to couetyse, and to dyscouere thy priuetyes,
he sholde be Punyshid aftyr his deserte; but the mesure of the *Punish the ill.*
Punyscement I nel noght telle the.

24 **How that the Subiectes bene the tresure of Prynces, and lyke a gardyñ of dyuers trees growyn there-In. Capitulum Lij^m.**

Elle woste thou that thy Subiectis bene thy tresure, by *Your subjects are your chief treasure.*
28 w   whych thy roialme is confermyd. Thow shalt lewe well
that thy subiectis bene lyke a gardyñ, in wych bene dyuers
maneres of trees, and thou shalt noght holde ham as londe
berrynge thornes wythout frute. Whyle that thy Subiectis *While they are well all is well.*
32 duryth in estate, shall dure the defense of thy realme and of thy
Powere, And therfor the be-houyth hame to gouerne wel, and fro
wronges ham defende, and that thou ham helpe in al hare nedys.
And therfor the nedyth to haue a Constabil that shal not bene a *Have a Constable who shall guard them.*
36 destruere of thy trees, but a kepere and a Sauere. He sholde be
full of good maneres and vertues, wyse and Sufferynge; And of
³oone man make Suche a Suffreyñ, ffor yf they were many, that   ³ 63 L.

² n alterd to r.

oone Sholde haue enuy to that othyr, that he sholde not ouer-
passe hym, And therof myght many harmes cvme. Sum manere
of baillifes bene that Shewyth ham trewe and profitabill to the
kynge, And neuer-the-lasse they destrueth the Pepill, And euery
of ham thynkyth in dyuers veyes by wych he may longe abyde
in his office. And Such ther bene had, that oone thynge sayne,
and anothyr thynkes done, and mayntenys and defendyth Sum
evill dedis by hare yeftes: Of Suche hit is nedfull the to kepe.

Marginalia: Some bailiffs are true to their lord and evil to his subjects, and some are false speaking. Beware of these.

Of barons, and wherof thay Serwyth in the roialme.
Capitulum Liij[m].

[1] He barons anecheth and multiplyeth the roialme; By ham
Is the contre I-wyrshupped, the Empyre I-ordeynet in his
degrees. And therfor thou sholdyste Put ham in certayñ
dignytees and Powere. Ful wel thou mayste ham ordeyne in
forwe yf thou wylt, for foure differences bene chose that is to
witte; afoor, behynde, on the ryght syde, and one the lyfte
syde. And foure parties bene in the worlde; eeste, weste,
north, and South. And therfore thou mayste ordeyne that in
euery fourthe Partie of thy realme bene oone gouernoure. And yf
thou seyste that they bene manyer; do thou that they bene ten,
fore tene is a perfite nombyr, and hit contenyth[2] in hym-Sylfe
foure nombres, that is to witte, one and two, and thre and
foure; the whyche yf they bene assemblet, makyth tene. Therfor me sholde ordeyne that euery gouernoure had tene Vicaries
in his hoste, and euery vicarie ten lederis in his whele, and
euery ledere ten doiens, and euery doiens ten men: al thes
assembled makid an hundrid thowsand fyghten men. And
whan thou haste mestere to the Service of ten thousand men,
thou cal a gouernoure, and hym shal Serve ten vicaries, [3] and
wyth euery vicarie shall cvm ten leders, and wyth euery ledere
shal cvm ten doiens, and wyth euery doiens ten men, and that
shal make the nombyr of ten thousande fyghtyn men. And so
thou mayste vndyrstonde of manyer, othyr fewere. By this
ordynaunce and this accompte, thou maiste be y-lyghted of
costagis, and thou shalt haue thy Purpos, and thou shalte lyght
the trauaillis of thy baronage; and take hede that al thy captaynes bene chose men. Ful necessary hit is to barons that
thay haue wyse notaries and discrete, trewe and welle Prowid in
chiualrie, that can discrewe tho whyche ben worthy armes to

Marginalia: [1] Fol. 61 b. The use of barons to the kingdom. Have four of them if you will. [2] couetyth MS. If you want more have ten, for that note is a perfect number. Let each have ten subordinates, and each of these again have ten. [3] 63 b L. Thus you can raise your army quickly. Take heed that your captains are picked men, and that they have wise heralds.

berre. Al knyghtes thou shalt wyrchippe, noone havynge in
dyspite, Pouer ne ryche. And the behowyth to haue wyth the, *The horn of Themistlus.*
the Instrumentes wych demesteus maket, for hit shal the awaill
4 moche to assembill many Pepill Sodanly, in oone day or lasse
fore grete nede. This Instrument may be herde Sixe myle fere.

That a kynge sholde not entyr in battail in his owyñ Propyr Persone. Capiitulum Liiij^m.

8   how shalt noght vse bataill in thyn Propyr Persoñ, ther-as *Don't fight yourself if*
t   þou mayste hit enchu. holde al tymes wyth thy Selfe the *you can help it.*
beste and the grettyste of thy Powere. Be-hete thou to
knyghtes honours and rewardis, and kepe thy Promesis. Whan
12 thy-Selfe moste go in hostes, go thou neuer disarmyd, for Sodeyn *Never go disarmed.*
chaunchis ; Haue good kepers, and good Spies, and good kep-
ynge, namely be nyght. whan thou shalt make thyn hoste
arreste and thy tentis Piche, Purvey the yf thou mayste, that *See your camp pitched*
16 thou be negh Sum montayñe or watyr, and be well y-vitaillid ; *near water, and well*
and Purvey more than thou vndyrstondyste that nede the shal. *victualled.*
thou shalte haue many rynnynge engyns to make horribill
Sownes to gasten thyn enemys. Thou sholdyst haue in battaill *Have all sorts of arms*
20 al manere of armes ; Sum of the hoste shall stabill bene in oone *in your host.*
Place, and otheris shal ¹ gone al aboute. Thoures of trees remeable   ¹ 64 L.
thou shalt I-have ² ouer al, *and* Knyghtes there-in wel armyd,   ² Fol. 62.
archeris, abblastres, *and* Lanceouris of Dartes brandynge ; and
24 yf thou Seiste ham adrede othyr doutfull, conforte thou hare
hertys by good confurtabill techynge. and thou shalt ordayne
thy knyghtes in this manere, In the ryght hande of thyne *Swords on the left wing,*
enemys, the Swerde mene ; In the lyfte hande, the Iusters wyth *lances on the right,*
28 Speris ; amyddys, tho that shall caste brondys of fyre brand- *archers in the middle.*
ynge, the Archeris and Criours wyth horribil voices,³ And al
tymes yf thou mayste be, thou in the heiere Place of thyñ enemys, *Secure rising*
and yf thou Seyst any bataill faille, socoure thou hit anoone. *ground.*
32 And whate Parte of thyñ enemys that thou Seiste faille, anone
haste thou the to that Parte. And ouer al thynge to haue
victorie, moche worth is stablenys *and* abydynge. Of this
matiere men Sayñe comynly, and Soth hit Is, that oone man
36 may not ouercome his enemys, but yf he haue radyr ouercome
covardy. And thou Sholdyst haue many aspies, and busshe- *Have spies and am-*
montes with oribles sownes, ffor that is the moste Pryncipall *bushes, with horrible noises.*

        ³ vioces, MS.

queyntyse of bataile, victorie to haue. And thou shalt haue
certayne Places I-ordeynyd by the hoste for drynkes and othyr
necessaries. Olyfantes thou shalt haue, to bere castellis of trees,
and knyghtes enarmed wyth-In, for they benne horribill hugely, 4
and berryth grete hydoure. Dromydaries and Othyr Swyfte
bestis shall ben in the hoste, ham to helpe that nede haue. And
yf thou shalt fyght in a castelle thou shalt haue dartes *and*
arowe envenymet, and yf thou mayste cvm to the watyr of 8
whych thyn enemys drynkyth, envenyme thou hit. Ne be not
to hasty in thy workes, fyght wyth eue*ry* Pepill in thar manere.
In al thy workys take thou consaill of astronomyours, ffor by
the Sterres bene gouernyd al erthely thynges, And the Sterrys 12
makyth many mewyngys in the coragis of mene, and of that
comyth discencion, [1] bataillis, victories, and dyscomfites.

Margin notes: Have elephants / and dromedaries. / Poison your arrows and your enemy's water. / Take counsel of your Astrologers. / [1] 64 b L.

That Phisnomye Is a necessarie scyence to knowe the Maners of men. Capitulum Lv^m. 16

Capitulu[m] Lv^m.

Fte we haue afor sayde, that dyuers maneris of Pepill of
o   consaillours, knyghtes, constables, Marchalis, Notaries, Messagers and otheris that shall kynges and Empe*r*ouris Serwe,
shuldyne haue certayne condicions whych bene aforsayde. But 20
for-als-moche as stronge is to fynde and know condycones and
good vertues and maneris of Pepil wythout longe Prewe, hit is a
ful couenabille and profitabill thynge to euery Prynce, that he
cane the scyence of Physnomy, by wyche he may know by 24
syght euery man of wych maneris and thewis he sholde be by
kynde. And there-for hit is to witte as we haue aforsayde, al
bodely thyngis be gouernyd and ordaynyd by the Planet*es* and
Sterris. And therfor euery man, of the begynnynge of his berth, 28
by the vertu of the Sterris wych than haue rewarde to hym, Is
disposid dyuersly to vertues and to vices. But Soth hit is, that
euery wyse man haue vertu and will; by whych he may kepe
hym anent kynde, *and* vertues of [steris [2]] as Sayth Bug[usa]rus 32
the Phil[osofre], in the begyn[nyng] of the centiloge of tholo-
mewe. This tellyth vs that boke, by Ensampill; Su*m*tyme two
Philosofers astrono[3]myours weryn Herhrowid in a weveris House.
In that nyght was Borne to the wevere a Sone, And the astro- 36
nomyours beheldyne the constellacions of hys bryth by thare
castle, *and* foundyn that he sholde bene wyse and curteyse,

Margin notes: By their physiognomy you can judge the fitness of men for their service. / All men are ruled by the stars which have regard to them at birth. / [3] Fol. 62 b. / An example of a weaver's son.

[2] Some letters cut off the margin; inserted from L.

Examples to prove the Truth of this Science. 217

good of consaill *and* wel belowid of kynges, and that thynge
thay hyddyn fro the fadyr. The chylde wox, *and* his fadyr
and modyr wende that thay myght wel teche hym thar*e* craft*e*, <small>The child would not</small>
4 but for no-thynge he hit myght lerne; for betynge, thretynge, <small>learn the craft of</small>
ne fayrnesse, And ther-for they lettyn hym y-wourthe. Sethyn <small>weaving,</small>
this yonglynge Sette hym-Selfe to Scolis,¹ *and* be-came a good <small>but became a great wise</small>
clerke, and couth the courses of Sterris, and lawe *and* gou*er*n- <small>man.</small>
8 aunce of realmes, and aftyr be-came a grete Sire in the realme.
Anothyr tyme befell the contrary, of the kynges Sone of Inde.
For the kynge wolde that he sholde can Philosophye and al
Sciences, And therfore he sende throgh Inde and in othyr con- <small>The king's son of Ind</small>
12 treis, for Maistres his Sone to teche clergi, lyke as hit appendet <small>would not learn clergy,</small>
to So grete a kynge. But that ne mygh not availle, for that he
ne myght noght turne his corage to scien*c*is of clergi, but to <small>but only a handicraft.</small>
honde-craft*es*. For the whyche thynge the kynge was ful sore-
16 full *and* trowbelid, and he callid to hym al the wyse men of his
roialme, *and* ham askid how that myght be. And al accordid,
that kynde lad the chylde that to done, And oft-tymes hath <small>Nature so ordered it.</small>
Suche cases befallen.

20   **Ensamples to Prow the forsayde thynge. Cap*itu*lum
    quinqu[a]gessimum Sextu*m*.**   <small>Capitulum Lvj^m.</small>

    He dysciplis of yPocras the wyse, depeyntid an ymage in
t   Parcemyn̄ allyke to Ipocras, and hit bare to Philomon, <small>The image of Hippocrates</small>
24   wyche was a maystyr of Phisnomye; *and* hym Saydyn, <small>brought to Philemon.</small>
"Rewarde this figure and telle vs the qualyteis, the mancrys,
and the compleccion̄, of Suche a man as this figure Presentyth."
He behelde besely the figure, and al the makynge of the body,
28 and Sayde, "Suche a man is lechelorus *and* disceyuous." Whan <small>His judgment.</small>
that herde ²the disciplis, they wolde haue hym Slayn̄e, *and* to <small>² 65 b L.</small>
hym Saydyn̄, "O thou foole, that is the fygure *and* the ymagy- <small>They reprove him.</small>
nacione of the beste man of the worlde." Phylomon ham
32 Peiset, *and* sayde, "who-so Is this ymage, that ye haue Shewid
me?" They sayden̄, "this ys the Semblau*n*t of the wyse
ypocras." "Wherfor," Seyde he, "wolde ye aske me? I haue
answarid you like as y felde by my Science." Thay retourned
36 agayn̄ to har maystyr Ipocras, and hym tolde that whych <small>They tell Hippocrates.</small>
Philomen saide of his dome. Ypocras ham Sayde, "Sothely Is
hit al that Philomon̄ Sayth Noght for than, sethyn I-vndyr-

¹ Sclolis, MS.

He says that Philemon judged truly. stondenge that, y toke kepe to thynges wych y was enclinet to, that they were fowle *and* reprouabill; I stabelid myn vndyr-stondynge as a kynge ouer al my body, and y haue wyth-drawe me fro al folies, *and* haue had victorie *and* maistrie agayns al 4 foole delytes." This is the comendacion of ypocras the Philosofre; Philosophie is no more but loue of witte *and* cvnnynge, and abstynence of foly, and Victorie of foole wille.

Here is I-prowid that the Sowle Sueth the condycionys of the bodyes. Capi*tul*um quinquagessimu*m* Septimu*m*.

Capi*tul*um Lvij^m.

Ertayne thynge hit is that the Sowle whyche Is the fourme of the body, sueth the kynde and the complexcion *and* the propyrteys of the body, for ofte-tymes we sene opynly that the coragis of men ham chaungyth aftyr the Pascionys of the bodyes, and that apperyth in ¹Dronknesse, In amours, In frenesy, in Dreddys, in Soroufulnesse, in desires, and in delites. For in al this Passions of the body, the Sowle and the corage ham chaungyth. And kynde is so grete a fellowe betwen body and Sowle, that the Passyons of body chaungyth the sowle; and the Passions of Sowle, chaungyth ²the body. And that apperyth in the Passione of Dronknesse, whyche is bodely. For dronk-nesse makyth for-yetynge in the Sowle, by reyson that the grete smokkes gone vp to the brayn, and troubelyth the ymagynacion, whych Scruyth to the vndyrstondynge, and hym presentyth the lykkenesse of bodely thynges, and so puttyth away al the remembrance of thynges wych weryn afor-honde vndyrstonde, and destroubyth the knowlech of thynges that bene to vndyrstond. More-ouer the Sow[l]e is the begynnynge *and* cause of al the natural mevynges of the body, and neuer the latyr this vertue fro hym is takyn away by dronknesse, whyche is a passion of the body. For a dronken man whan he sholde gone in his ryght hande, he goyth in his lyfte hande. In the Same manere may we Showe the contrary, that is to witte, that the Passions of the Sowle makyth the body chaunge, and his meuynges to dyuers. And that may a man See opynly in wrath, in dred, in lowe. For thes Passion makyth grete chaungynge to the body, as knowyth euery man that ham hath Prowid. And in mevynge hit apperyth also. As yf a man goo vpon a narrowe tree lyggynge in an hey Place, only by ymagynacion and thoght of fallynge, ofte-tymes he fallyth. And

The soul follows the condition of the body,
¹ Fol. 63.
² 66 L. as appears in the passion of Drunkenness.

The soul is the cause of the movement of the body.

Passions of the soul change the body.

yf the Same tree were vpon erthe, here as drede ne perill were noght, he wolde neuer falle. More-ouer we sene that euery beest hath his propyr Sowle, and his Propyr body. Of thes 4 Speces neuer faillyth, ne neuer was founde that any beeste had a body of oone spice, and a sowle of anothyr Spice. As hit may not be that oone beste haue the body of ¹an harte, and a soule of a lyoñ. More-ouer we seeñ that knyghtis knowyth the 8 goodnys of horsyñ, and the hunteres the goodnesse of hundis, by hare Shappes *and* faucundes. Of al thes thynges aforsayde, we may reysonably conclude that the company and the accorde be-tweeñ the Sowle and the body is so grete and so myche 12 confermyd and stabelid by kynde, that [in] the Passions of that oone, that other² is Parcenere, or Partifelewe. And euery body hath a propyr sowle, And euery beste hath a propyr amanere *and* condicioñ in dyuers Spyces, as amonge horsyñ that oone is 16 lasse than that othyre, or in goynge or in coloure, and of othyr bestis in the same manere, as we haue aforsayde and shewid wythout doute, in manys Spice. O man is of oone maneres *and* condicioñ, and anothyr is of anothyr manere *and* condicioñ, in 20 fygure and in face; and by othyr thynges that apperyth in the body, a man may deme the condicions *and* maneris whych he hath, othyr sholde haue by kynde. This Prouyth Aristotle at the begynnynge of his Phisnomye, y-translatid out of grue Into 24 latyñ.

Beasts do not change their souls.

Lions have not the souls of harts.
¹ 66 b L.

Knights judge their horses by their shape.

² *ouer* MS.

Thus by the figure and shape one may judge the soul.

Of the Science of Physnomye. Capitulum Lviijᵐ.

P Hysnomye is a science to deme the condycions or vertues *and* maneres of Pepill, aftyr the toknesse or syngnesse that 28 apperyth in facione or makynge of body, and namely of visage *and* of the voyce *and* of the coloure. One lyght manere *and* general of Phisnomye is to deme vertues *and* maneris of man aftyr the conpleccioñ. Compleccions bene iiijᵉ for a man is 32 sangyne, or flevmatike, or colerike, or malyncoly. And ryth vp thes foure ³complexcions of foure Humours ⁴of the body, whyche answaryth to the foure Elementes, And to the foure tymes of the yeere. The bloode Is hotte and moysti to the lyckenesse of the 36 heiere; ffleme is colde and moysti aftyr the kynde of the watyr; Colre hoote and drye aftyr kynde of fyre; Malancoly colde and dry aftyr kynde of erthe. The sangyne by kynde sholde lowe Ioye and laghynge, *and* company of women, *and*

What is Physiognomy

of judgment by complexion.

³ Fol. 63 b.
⁴ 67 L.

The four humours answer to the four complexions.

moche Slepe *and* syngyn*g*e : he shal be hardy y-nowe, of good
will and wythout malice : he shalbe flesshy, his complexcioñ
shalbe lyght to hurte *and* to empeyre for his tendyrnesse, he
shall haue a goode stomake, good dygescioñ, and good delyueraunce : and yf he be wovndid he shalbe sone be holde, he shall
be fre and lyberall, of fayre semblaunt, *and* dylyue*r* ynowe of
body. The fleumatyke by kynde he sholde be slowe, sadde,
ful stille, and Slowe of answere: febill of body, lyghtly falle
in palsey ; he shalbe grete and fatte, he shalle haue a febill
stomake, febil dygestioñ, and good delyueraunce. And as
touchynge manere*s* he shal be pitenouse, chaste, and lytill
desyre company of women. The colerike by kynde he sholde
be lene of body, his body is hote *and* drye, and he shalbe
Su*m*what rogh ; *and* lyght to wrethe and lyght to Peyse ; of
sharpe witte, wyse and of good memorie, a grette entremyttere,
fulle-large *and* foolehardy, delyue*r* of body, hasty of worde and
of answere; he louyth hasty wengeaunce ; Desyrous of company
of women moore than hym nedyth. he sholde haue a stomake
good y-nowe, namely in colde tyme. The Malencoly man
sholde be lene of body and dry, he sholde haue [1]good appetyde
of mette, and co*m*onely he Is a glotouñ and good delyueraunce
hathe of his belly. And as touchynge maneris, he sholde beñe
pensyfe *and* Slowe, and of stille wille, still and dredfull, and a
smalle entremyttere. More latre Is he wourthe than a colerike
man, but he holdyth longyr wreth ; he is of[t] sotille ymagynacion
as of hand-werkys, And well arne wonyd the malencolik men to
be Suttill werkmen. The sangyñ men shulde bene ruddy of
coloure, The flevmatike whyte and Pale, The colerike sholde
haue yalowe coloure Sumwhate medelit wit*h* rede, The malencolike sholde be Su*m*whate blake and pale.

Of whyte coloure.

Hite coloure Svmwhate medelite wyth rede in a man,
tokenyth that he is hote of kynde, and of sangyne com-
pleccioñ ; but rede coloure tokenyth complexcioñ wel tempe*r*it,
yf Suche colour*e* be in al the body noght roghe. This sayth
aristotle here sortely, but here-aftyr he will hit say mor opynly.

Of Physnomye aftyr the here.

n esshe heere tokenyth a dredfulle, and harde here tokenyth Soft hair;
hardy and stronge, and that apperyth in dyuers bestys.
4 For an hare *and* a sheppe bene ful gastefull, and haue full
nesshe here. And the lyone *and* a boore bene full stronge, and
haue stronge here. Also in fowles, by kynde tho whyche haue strong hair.
harde federe*s* bene stronge and corageous, as a cooke, And tho
8 that haue nesshe pennes bene dredfull, as turtures beñe *and*
curlyours. So Is of dyuers Pepille aftyr the Place whyche thay
dwellyth In. For thay that dwellyth towarde the northe, bene Northern men.
stronge and coragious, and haue harde here. And tho [1] whyche [1] 68 L.
12 dwellyth towarde the Sowthe, bene gastefull and haue nesshe
here, as thay of Ethiopy. Plente of here aboute[2] the wombe Hair on the womb.
tokenyth a Iangloure and full of wordys, and thay bene lykenyd
to birdys whyche haue Plente of federis in the wombe.

16 Of complexcioun of Flessh, ut sequitur.

Arde flesshe throgh al the Body tokenyth a man of Lytill Lviij^m.[3]
h Vndyrstondynge, Suche beñe the grete karlis massies, [3] Fol. 64.
whyche bene of harde vndyrstondynge, but thay bene good Hard and soft flesh.
20 to work*es*. Flesshe in tempure neshe, noght slake, tokenyth
good vndyrstondynge; but if hit be ful nesshe *and* slake as
women bene, tokenyth a chaungeabill man *and* variaunt: but
yf suche flesshe be founde in a stronge man of body, hauynge
24 stronge extremytee3, ne tokenyth not that wych y aforsayde.

Of complexcione aftyr the mevynge.

s lowe mewynge tokenyth a dulle and slowe vndyrstondynge, Galt.
and quyke mevynge and delyuer*e*, tokenyth good vndyr-
28 stondynge and hasty witte.

Of the complexcione o voyce als hit folwyth her nexste.

a grete voyce and wel y-harde, like a trompe, tokenyth an Strong and feeble voices.
hardy man *and* bolde: a smale voyce and febille like a
32 womanes voyce tokenyth a feynte man. And therfor the
stronge beestis *and* hardy haue stronge voyc*es* and hey, As
lyones, bullis, *and* houndes; and kokkes whyche bene strongyr
than othyr *and* more corageous, syngyth heyghere *and* more
36 strongyr. Of the hare we seene the contrary.

[2] abouute *in MS.*
[3] *At top of page*, Capitulum Quinquagessimum octauum.

Of the coloure of the visage hit Is here to witte.

The colour of the visage.
¹ 68 b L.

Whan a man hath a visage y-like and of coloure as lye of fyre, he Is wrathfull, and by kynde ¹he sholde be lyght to wrethe. The forsayde tokenes of figures and of mevynges *and* likenesse of vissage byth moste certayñ amonges al othyr toke-

Do not judge by one sole sign.

nesse. And hit Is to witte to deme a man aftyr oone tokyñ hit Is grete foly, but thou shalt rewarde al the tokenys, and yf many or al accordyth than mayste thou than moore Surely deme; and whate Parte the moste of syungnes *and* tokenys ham holdyth, holte the to that Parte.

The tokenesse of stronge Corage.

The eleven tokens of a great-hearted man.

A levyn tokenys bene whych tokenyth Streynth and corage-ous. The fryste is harde heere; the seco*n*de Is evyñ stature of body; the iijᵉ grete stature of bonys and of rybbes, *and* of handys *and* of fette; the iiijᵉ Is a large belly *and* to hym retreted; The v grete braons and massy; the vjᵉ a Synnevey neke and grete, and noght myche fatte; the vijᵉ Is a grete breste and brode, vpreri*d* *and* Su*m*whate fatte; the viijᵉ large haunges of good proporcion; the ixᵉ eghyñ grey or broune, y-lyke a camail here, that bene noght oue*r*moche opyñ ne cloos; The xᵉ broune coloure in al the body; The xjᵉ a sharpe straght farred, noght gretly lene ne al full, nethyr al frouncet.

The tokenesse of a dredful or a feynte man bene x; fryste, als follwyth:

Ten tokens of a coward or weakling.

Nesshe heere; the ijᵉ a man stowpynge. and noght vp-ryght; the iijᵉ whan the entraillis of the wombe gone vp abowe the nawle; the iiijᵉ Is yolow coloure in the face meddelite wi*th* palnesse; the v Is febill lokynge of the egħ *and* closynge; The vjᵉ lytill extremytes; The vijᵉ Is longe hond*es and* smale;

² 69 L.

²The viijᵉ smale reynes *and* febille; The ixᵉ a man lyghtely agastnet; The xᵉ is oue*r*lyghtely mevynge of coloure and sem-blante, and haue semblant to be Pensyfe, and full of thoghtes.

The tokenesse of good complexcio*u*n.

The tokens of good complexion.

The fryste tokyñ of good complexcioñ Is temperid flesshe betweñe nesshe and harde, and namely be-twen lene and fatte. The ijᵉ tokyñ Is that a man be leene in the neke and in

al the braones of the body. The iij⁶ Is that the visage be opyñ and wel departid̃. The iiij⁶ Is ¹that the Vysage Be opyñ and well depertyd̃. The fourthe Is that the rybbis Bene wel
4 departid or Seueret and wel taillet. The vᵉ Is that a man haue quyke coloure. The vjᵉ Is that he haue a softe and a tendyr skynne. The vijᵉ Is that the bake ne be not flesshe. The viijᵉ Is that the heere ne be not ouer harde, ouer-charce, ne
8 ouer blake. The ixᵉ Is that he haue blake eighyñ othyr broune, Sumwhate moiste.

[marginal note: The tokens of good complexion. ¹ Fol. 64 b.]

The tokenys of ille complexcioun.

he fryste Is a man ouerchargid wyth flesshe aboute the
12 ᵗ neke and the leggis fro the kneys evile y-seueret. The ijᵉ a grete farret rounde as the draght of a cumpas. and fleshy. The iijᵉ yelow eighyñ. The iiijᵉ grete chekes and fleshy: the vᵉ fleshy reyns: the vjᵉ longe legges: the vijᵉ a fatte neke,
16 and the visage fleshy and straght.

[marginal note: The tokens of an evil complexion.]

The tokenys to know shamels men.

f Ryst opyñ eighyñ and glysinynge, and the eighliddes full of blode and grete, and shorte; Hey vprerid shuldris; the
20 body Sumwhate Stowpynge.

[marginal note: The tokens of a shameless man.]

The tokenys of honest meñ.

ᵗ he honeste and the shamefast man Is circumspecte and wyse in al his dedys, ruddy of colure as sanguyne, the
24 visage is rounde, the breste Sumwhate vprerid̃, tarynge of¹ speche, the voyce ²ful and stronge, the eighyñ stydfaste and Sumwhate broune, and not glysinynge ne ouer-oppyñ ne ouer-close, and that his eighen ne cloose not to ofte-tymes. Tho
28 thynges bene tokenyd by the eighen, othyr that a man Is dredful or vicyous.

[marginal note: The tokens of an honest man. ² 69 b L.]

The tokenys of the Corageous.

he tokenys of the coragious beñe a grete forhede and flesshy
32 ᵗ and full, and he lokyth not ouer sharpe as doth woode men, ne ouer dedly as dothe the cowarde; Fayre of visage and wel disposid̃, laat of mevynge, and Slow to take nedys but yf thay bene grete.

[marginal note: The tokens of a courageous man.]

¹ *At top of page:*—Capitulum Quinquagessimum Octauum. Lviijᵐ.

The tokenys of the cowarde.

The tokens of a coward.

Lytill vysage and leene, and frouncet, lytill eighyn dede lokynge, lytille of stature and lowe, and of febill mevynge; thes bene the tokenys of cowardy. 4

Of the tokenys of thralle.

The tokens of a thrall.

Nsemely eighen and frouncet, the hede bowynge towarde the ryght syde, knelynge to euery man for noght, the mewynges of his haundys bene vnsemely, dishordeynyt, and his goynge also bene tokenys of the thralle. 8

The bittyr man.

The tokens of a bitter man.

The tokenys of the bittyr man; he hath the hede bowynge and Stowpynge as a man pensyfe and fulle of thoght, he is blake of coloure, a lene visage and frounset, noght rogh, and blake here and smothe. 12

The angry man.

The tokens of an irascible man.

The angry man Is wonyt to be of straght body and corageous, that Is to witte, full of hotte Spyrit, and therfor he Is fulhardy, Sumwhate ruddy of coloure, Grete shuldres and large, 16

[1] entremytez, MS.

grete extremytez[1] and stronge, and noght moche rogh the breste, a semely chyne and accordynge to the visage, and liggyne here. Who-so no hym wrethyth whan he sholde, and theras he sholde, and agaynys tham ther as he sholde, he nys noght a man of 20

[2] 70 L.

[2]ryght witte : thus fynde y writtyn, but me-thynkyth that suche wrathe sholde cum of charite, wronges to restrayne. 24

The benure man.

The tokens of a kind man.

The condycions of the benure man Is shewid Pryncipaly by his lokynge, and comynly he Is flesshy and hath moiste flesh, and he Is of meene stature and wel mesurid, and he hath Sumwhate lowe here and Sumwhate scarse. 28

Of the smale herte.

The tokens of a little heart.

The tokenys of a lowe herte bene lytill visage, lytill eighen, and lytill all othyr lymes of the body, and lene y-flesshide. 32

The chyderis.

The chyderis bene wonyd to haue the oue*r*-lippe grete and lollynge oue*r* the emyste ¹Lyppe, of coloure Su*m*dell rede Hare
4 Visage.

The tokens of a chider.
¹ Fol. 65.

The tokenesse of the Pyteous and merciabil man.

P yteous and merciabill man tokenyth whitte coloure and cleene, the eighen redy to wepe, gladly they lowyn pyteous
8 stories and newe, and ham Puttyth in mynde, and whan thay hyryn Pyteous stories lyghtely thay wepyth, And namely aftyr wyne. they bene Parcewynge wythout malice, thy lowyñ women, and ofte they gettyth doghteris. In proue*r*bis hit Is
12 sayde, that the Piteous man hath iije vertues, that Is to witte, wysdome, drede, and honeste, and the tyraunt or the cruell man, the contrary.

The tokens of a pitiful man.

The Lechurere.

16 The lechure ofte-tymes Is whyte of coloure, the heere rogh, grete, and blake; rogh temples, fatte heyghen, and rollynge Swyftly in syght like a wode man; of suche lokynge bene bestis in ruthe.

The tokens of a lecher.

20 ### The slepere.

The slepere oft-tymes haue grete hedis, grette nekkis, and thay arne Sum-whate fatte of body and fleshy, and rogh al aboute the wombe.

The tokens of a sluggard.

24 ### The myndefulle man.

Of good mynde bene thay comynly, that haue the lymmes mor large *and* moore corssife and moore flesshe fro the Ioyntures ²vpwarde, than fro the yontures downwarde; they haue rounde
28 hedis wel amesurid to the body.

The tokens of a mindful man.
² 70 b L.

Condicions of women.

He moste opyñ dyue*r*site in bestis Is that oone Is male and
t that othyr female, and aftyr thay dyue*r*syteis we vndyr-
32 stondyth that the maners and vertues of eue*r*y othyr chaungid. For amonge al bestis that bene nuryshid or dauntid by witte of man, the femalis bene moste mekyste and lyghtiste to teche and leste worthy. And noght for that they bene moste
36 febill of body and leste of Pouer ham to defende, and the same Is hit of wilde bestis. But women beene more meuabill and

The diversity of male and female.

SECRETE. Q

Women are feebler of body and less endowed with reason. dyuers, namely fro male than men bene. For like as thay bene more febill of body and of complexcioñ, so in the same mane*r* they bene endowid lasse of reysoñ. And therfore lyghtly they[1] wixeñ wrothe, and askyth hastely wengeance; And full yll they mowen wythstonde temptacioñ, and namely temptacioñ Of fleshly delyte. 4

The tokenys of the feete.

The tokens of the feet; Who-so hath the fete well shappyñ, grete toes and synnowy, sholde bene stronge and hardy, for he hath the condicioñ of the male. 8

little feet; he that hath lytill fete and streyte, shorte toes and noght synewy, and more delycious to se than stronge fette, thay bene *crooked toes.* febill and feynte, and like to women. And he that hath crokid toes, comynly is shameles, and like in manere to byrdis, that wythout shame taken har Prayes. 12

The tokenys of the Ancles.

The ankles. Thay men whych haue synowy ancles and opyn sholde ben corageous, and the haue the condycion of the male, and tho whych haue fleshly ancles and not opyñ, bene nesse of corage an lyke to women. 16

[2] *71 L.* ²**Thokenys of the legge.** 20
The leg. Tho men whyche haue wel-makyd and synowy *and* stronge legges, shold be corageous, and haue the condycioñ of male; and tho men whyche haue smale legges and synnowy bene luchrus;
Small knees. and tho men wyche haue oue*r* lytill kneis they bene stronge of corage like as women bene, and that apperyth by thare facioñ. 24

Tokenys of the theghes.

[3] *Fol. 65 b.* ³Tho men Whych haue bonny theghes and Synnowy, bene *The thighs.* stronge aftyr the Propirte of male, And tho men whyche haue fleshly theghes and not bony, they bene nesshe aftyr the Propyrte of women. 28

Tokenys of the breste.

The breast. Tho men whyche haue bony brestis and sharpe, thay sholde bene stronge; And tho men whych haue flesshly and fatte brestis bene nesshe men. And tho that haue the flesshe of the brestis lytill and dry bene ille-ymancrite and bene lykenyd to apys. 32

36

¹ we *in MS.*
² At top of page:—"Capitulum Quinquagessimum octauum. Lviij^m."

Of the bely.

Tho men whyche haue belyes menly fatte and not grete, <small>The belly;</small>
bene stronge and of good complexcioñ, and haue the Propirteis
4 of male, And thay whych haue leen belies and hungri, beene <small>lean beilies.</small>
nesse.

Of the chynne.

Tho men whyche haue grete chynnes bene stronge and hardy, <small>The chin.</small>
8 and haue propyrteis of male, And tho that haue the chynne
smale *and* febille bene nesshe and lyke to women.

Of the Ribbys.

Tho men whych haue goode ribbys bene stronge and hardy <small>The ribs.</small>
12 aftyr the Propirte of the male, And tho whych haue febill Ribbis
bene aftyr the Propyrte of women; tho that haue ribbis boech-
ynge owtwardes like as they weryñ y-swolle, bene yanglours, and
folis in wordys, and bene like frusshes and toodes.

16 ### Of the shuldres.

Tho men whych haue shuldres heygh vp-rerid, the synnowes <small>The shoul-
ders.</small>
and braones apperynge, they bene stronge and hardy aftyr [1]the <small>1 716 L.</small>
propyrteis of the male; And tho that haue the contrary bene
20 aftyr the Propyrteys of women. And thay that haue the
shuldres hangynge downe-ward and welle taillet, bene fre and
lyberall; And they whyche haue the contrary, bene harde and
hungry.

24 ### Of the Neke.

Tho men whych haue the neke wel dystyncted by his yontes, <small>The neck.</small>
and wel delyuerit, they bene of good witte and good vndyrstondynge, for that tokenyth good vndyrstondynge and delyuernesse
28 of witte, and that thay Parcewyth lyghtely the mevynges of
witte. And thay that hath the neke of contrary makynge and
dysposycioñ, bene of Slow witte. A grete Neke noght fatte <small>Big necks
are to be</small>
tokenyth streynthe and hardynes aftyr the Propyrte of man, <small>preferred.</small>
32 And a smale neke the contrarie. A grete fleshy shorte neke
tokenyth wrothynesse like as a bull Is; A longe neke and not
ouer grete tokenyth corageous like a lyoñ; An ouer shorte neke
tokenyth a gyloure and a deceyuoure like the wolfe.

Of the Lippes.

The lips; thin lips.

Who-so hath mene lippes betwixe thyknesse and thynne, and the homyste lippe comyth dovne and closyth to the Emyste lippe, he Is corageous and hardy, y-lykenyd to the lyoñ, and that a man may see in grete houndes and stronge. And tho that haue thyne lippes and harde aboute the teth, and the tethe vp-rerid outward apperynge, byth chorll and fowle, y-lykenyd to swyne; tho that haue grete lippes and that oone hangynge and descend-ynge ouer that othyr, they bene folis y-lykenyd to assis; tho that haue the ouer-lippe vp-rerid, and the gomes gretly vprerid bene endeynous and cuyl-sayeris, lykenyd to baynge houndys.

Of the noose.

The nose;
[1] 72 L.

Tho that haue grete Noosys [1]lyghtely bene talentid to couetise, and bene desposyd to concupiscence, and bene lykenyd to oxeñ. And thay that haue the butte of the noose grete and rounde, bene rude of witte and lykenyd to Swyne. And thay that haue the butte of the Noose sharpe, bene strongly angry and lykenyd to houndys. And thay that haue rounde noosis and not sharpe, bene hardy and bolde and bene lykenyd to lyonys. A stovpynge noose [2]and brode Betwene the Brewis, tokenyth a coragious man y-lykenyd to the egyll. Tho that haue the noose crokyd and the forhede roune, pershaunt vpward, bene lechurous *and* angri and likenyd to Apys. Opyn noose-thurll tokenyth angry; For whan a man angryth, his noose-thurlys oppenyth.

round noses;

[2] Fol. 66.
crooked noses.

The vysage.

The visage.

Tho that haue grete visachys and fleschy bene dysposyd to concupyscence of fleschy lust*es*. A leeñ visage tokenyth study and besynes. A fate visage dredfulnesse; And a lytill visage, a lytill herte. A grete vysage and broode tokenyth slewthe in manere, as Oxeeñ *and* Assis. A streyte lytill visage of Pou*er* semblant, tokenyth an harde herte *and* hungri. An opyn vysage and fayre semblaunt, tokenyth a lyberal herte; a lytill smale forhede, tokenyth lytill witte, il to teche, *and* ill condycions.

The forehead.

The forhede al rounde, harde witte; a longe forhede ou*er* mesur*e*, a slow witte: a quarre forhede of meeñ gretnys tokenyth feyrnysse and corage; A playne straght forhede tokenyth a losenger*e*; the forhede sumwhate trowblit in semblant, tokenyth fiernysse and hardynesse.

Of the eyyñe.

Tho that haue reede ey-liddys lowyth comynly wel wyñ, and bene gret drynker*es*; heuy ey-liddys tokenyth good slepere; [The eyes and eyelids. 1 73 b L.]
4 ¹lytill eyyñ tokenyth a lytill herte and a slowe; gret eyeñ tokenyth a bowsty witte; Men*e* eyen, nethyr grete ne smale, tokenyth good complexioñ wyth-out vice. Depe eyeñ, malyce; Ou*er*-oppyñ eyeñ, lyke as they were y-thryste owte, comynly tokenyth a foole: [Deep-set eyes.]
8 Somwhate depe eyeñ tokyneth hardynesse, but eyen nethyr to depe ne to fer out but menly bene beste.

Of the eeris.

Lytill eeris tokenyth good vndyrstondynge; grete eeris dul
12 vndyrstondynge; And mesurabill eeris bene beste. [nota. The ears.]

Of the colure.

Tho men that bene ou*er* blake bene dredfull, and lykenyd to the Egipcians *and* ethyopiens; And tho whyche bene ou*er* whyte [Black hair; white hair;]
16 bene dredfull, like to women: Tho that bene of men coloure betwen*e* blake and white, Is a tokyn that thay bene stronge and hardy: Tho that bene yelow of colure, bene coragious i-lyke to the lyons. Tho that bene rede men, bene Parceuynge and [yellow, red,]
20 trechurus, and full of queyntise, i-likenyd to Foxis. Tho that bene Pale and trowbely y-coluridꝗ, bene dredfull, for thay berryn the colur*e* of drede in thare farret*es*. Tho that bene rede coloure, bene hasty and egre, for whan a man Is I-chafet by rynnynge [pale, red,]
24 or othyr mevynge, he wexet reede. Tho that haue a brandynge colur*e* like the lye of fyre, lightly wexeñ woode; and tho that haue Suche colure abowte the brestis bene eu*er* wrothy; and that apperyth, for whan a man Is hugely wrothe, he felyth the [flame colour.]
28 breste al brandynge. And tho men whych haue the neke abowte and the temples, grete ruddy weynes, bene wrothy *and* hugely angry; and that apperyth, for a man that Is wrothe hath the same Passione. Tho that haue the face sumwhate ruddy bene [Veins on temples.]
32 schamefaste, *and* tokyñ of honeste shew*ith* in har visage; ²tho that have the chekys al reede as thay were dronken, Is a tokyñ that thay lowyth ryght wel good wyne. [² 73 L. Red cheeks.]

Of the colure of the eyeñ.

36   Ho that haue fulli blake eyen tokenyth that thay bene
t   feynte, for blake colur*e* aprochyth neygh to derknesse, and in derknesse a man lyghtly is a-drede more than in lyght. [Colour of the eyes;]

And tho that haue eyen not wel blake, but declynynge to yelow, bene of good corage. Spleket eyen *and* whyte eyen tokenyth dredfulnesse, for whyte colure tokenyth drede. Tho that haue eyeñ of ¹the colure of a camel Heere, bene coragious, y-likenet to the Lyoñe and the egle. And tho that haue eyen y-colorid like rede wyne, ben dysposyd to woodnesse, y-likenyd to bestes whych may not be daunted. And tho that haue eyen like ly of fyre brandynge and sprakelynge, bene angry and shameles, y-lykenid to houndes. tho that haue eyen discolourid and trowbelid tokenyth drede, for he that Is a-drede wexit pale, and thay that haue eyen schynynge bene lecheours y-lykenyd to rookys and cokkes.

Of the sygnyficacioun of dyuers lymmes.

ho that haue rogh leggis bene lechureris, and thay that haue the breste and the wombe mochedell rogh, bene full vnstabill *and* varyant : tho that haue the neke be-hynde rogh bene liberal, i-likenyd to lyonys. Tho that [haue] sharpe chynnes bene of good corage, i-likenet to houndes ; tho that haue the browes negh to-gyddyr bene heuy and Sorrofull of chere, for thay berryth the sygyñ therof. Who-so hath the browes stikkynge vp anent the noose into the templis in euery syde, bene foolis *and* likenet to Swyne : tho that haue the lokkes vp-stondynge bene dredefull ; that apperyth, for tho wyche bene a-dred haue hare lokkis stickynge vp : tho that ²haue hare lockys or heere as cryspe tokenyth dredfulnesse, but lokkis cryspe towarde the ende tokenyth good corage : tho that haue the forhedes vprerid afoore, bene lyberall and likenyd to lyones : tho that haue a longe heede, and the ceris to-growynge to the forhede negh to the noose, bene slowe of witte. And the heede rounde, as we haue aforsayd, Is more tokyn of witte.

Thokenys of goynge.

Ho that have the braons of the shuldres ryght strayghtly whan thay mewyth ham, tokenyth that thay bene stronge and hardy and lykenyd to horsyn. And tho that haue lytill fette and febill legges, bene febill and feynte alyke women. And tho that haue eyeñ moche mevynge, bene sharpe and raueners y-like to the gosehauke. And tho that oft-tymes closyth hare eyeñ, bene dredfull. Tho that in lokynge or in rewardynge ficchyth hare syght and hit holdyth stabill, they bene studyous

and of good vndyrstondynge. And that apperyth, for whan a
man studieth deply, he holdyth his syght stabely. *firm eyes.*

Of the voyce.

4 Ho that haue a grete voice and orible and not ful hey, done *Great voice;*
t gladly wronges, and bene likenyd to assis. Tho that haue
the voice atte the begynnynge of the worde grete and lowe,
and aftyr that endyth hit al smale and hey, as kynde of oxen
8 bene wrothy. And tho that haue the voyce hei, smale and swete *high, small voice;*
and plesaunt, bene neshe, and haue lytill of manhode, and
i-likenyd to women. And a grete hey *and* stronge voice tokenyth a stronge and an hardy man, likenyd to a lyon, *and* to a
12 stronge hounde. A nesh brekynge *and* Plesaunte voice tokenyth
a bennure and wel y-manerit man. A smale hey stronge voice *small, high, strong voice.*
tokenyth a man lyghtely to be wrethyd.

Of the body tokenys.

16 Ho that haue a lytill body, bene sharpe of body and of *Little body;*
tt witte, for-why, har hertes bene ney the [1]extremytee3. And [1] 74 L.
ther-for in schorte tyme they hame mewyth and the vertue
of herte spredith throgh-out al the body, and comyth to the
20 brayne ther as the vndyrstondynge is fulfillid. Tho that bene [2] Fol. 67.
full grete of body, bene slow and taryenge of body [2]and vndyrstondynge, for-why, hare Hartis Bene fere fro the extremytee3 of *full great body;*
Hare bodyes and the brayne. Tho that haue dry flessh and hote *dry flesh;*
24 and bene lytill of body, bene variant and vnstabill, and afor
that, that thay may not fulfillen that thynge whyche thay haueñ
begonne, thay Puttyth ham in othyr thynges. And tho that
bene moche and haue moisti flesh and lytill hette, bene slow and *moist flesh.*
28 of slow vndyrstondynge. Tho that bene grete of body and haue
dry flessh and coloure accordynge to the hette, bene of hey vndyrstondynge and ful myghty to fulfille that they thynkyñ, for thegh
thay bene moche thay haue the body and the complexcioñ wel
32 mesurid. But amonge al othere*s* tho bene of beste complexcioñ *Mean complexion is best.*
that byth not oue*r* grete ne oue*r* smale. And thay whyche bene
ill mesurid of body, bene dysposyd to trechury and othyr ill
tecchis. And thay wyche bene wel mesurit of body ben Iuste
36 and ryghtfull men. By that whyche we haue afor-sayde, hit
apperyth that al Phisnomye to iiij^e thynges takyth hede, that *Take heed of four things.*
oone Is the Propirte3 of male and female; The ij^e Is the Dis-

posicioñ aforsaydyñ of the body of man; The iij⁹ Is the liknesse of man and the facioñ or makynge, and the maner of othyr bestys; The iiij⁹ Is the semblant or liknesse of the Passion by whych a man Is knowen by tokyñ. And thegh they haue many 4 tokenys or syngnes by wych a man may deme the Physnomye, Neue*r*-the-latyr, su*m* bene more certayne than otheris and more apperyth, And thay tokenesse whych bene in the hede moste Pryncipal, the tokenys whyche bene about the eyen *and* the 8 hede and the vysage, holdyñ the fryste and the soucrayne degre of Iugement; And the tokenys wyche bene aboute the breste and schuldris, holdyth the Seconde¹ degre; The iij⁹ degree holdyth the tokenys wych bene aboute the leggis and the fette; 12 The tokenys whych bene aboute the wombe holdyñ the fourthe degre and bene leste certayne: and the maner of tokenys accorden, the more certayne is the Iugement.

Now gracious lorde, wylle I translate the scyence of Phys- 16
nomye to you in a shortyr manere, for Su*m* bokys of arystotiles makynge haue that scyence shortyr than othyr: And so may ye chese wych ye beste Plesyth.
Capitulum Lix^m. 20

h it Is to witte that the seede wythyn the marice is defiet, like a messe w*ith*in a potte to sethe, And therfor Pale coloure and saad is a tokyn that the decoccion Is not Parfite, and therfor yf thou fyndyst in a man suche coloure, and he be a lytill man, 24 hit is a tokyn that the Perfeccioñ of his kynde Is makyd lasse and amenuset. Suche a man thou shalt enchu, for he is disposyd to ille tecchis. And whan thou seyste a man that ofte-tymes rewardyth the, and whan thou rewardys hym̄ he dredyth *and* 28 wixeth ruddy, and namely yf he syche, in his visage, *and* wepynge hym takyth atte the ey, that man lowyth the and dreddyth: and yf he haue condycions contrary, he Is envyous, and tellyth not by the; and like as he is to enchue, that hath defaute of 32 kynde; of quyke coloure; So is he to enchue, *and* more, that fautyth any lyme atte his byrth, or hath in othyr manere the lymes dyfformyd out of kynde: Suche bene to enchue as enemys, for to wickidnesse thay bene enclynet. 36

E that complexcion in tempure hath, wych Is of meen
² 75 L. h ²stature, he hath the eyen gray, the lockys browne, the

¹ seedne, MS.

chyer laghynge; broune coloure or yelow mellit wyth reede, *The tokens of a good man.*
the body al hollo and wel y-mesurid, ryght estature, the hede of
mene quantyte, and lytill of speche but yf hit nede be, þe voice
4 ne ouer grete ne ouer smale but meene, and wel harde, suche
men sholdyst þou haue in thy company.

heere.

¹Lente of Lockys softe, tokenyth Bonerte and colde brayñe. ¹ Fol. 67 b.
8 P Plente of Heere on euery ethre shuldris tokenyth foly and *The meaning of much hair;*
vncunynge. Plente of here in wombe and in breste, tokenyt
oribilite and syngulerte of kynde and smalnys of vndyrstondynge and loue of body. Reede coloure tokenyth a man angri *red hair,*
12 and vicious. Broune lockys and a-broune tokenyth loue of *brown and auburn.*
ryght and Iustice.

Eyeñ.

ho-so hath ful grete eyen, he is enuyous and not shamefaste, *Large eyes;*
16 W slow and Inobedyente, and namely yf he haue Pale eyen:
he that haue the eyen of meen gretnysse, blake or grey, he is of *mean eyes;*
Parceuynge vndyrstondynge, courteyse and trewe; who-so hath
longe eyen and straght, and the visage moch straght, Suche is *long eyes;*
20 malicious and felonous; who so hath eyen y-like an asse his eyen,
he Is a sotte and of harde vndyrstondynge; who so hath eyen
meuynge and fleynge and sharpe lokynge, he is a dysceioure, a *shifty eyes;*
thefe, and a giloure: he that hath rede sparkelynge eyen, his
24 fierse and corageous: Eyen that bene whit y-freklet, or I-sprotid, *speckled eyes.*
or blake, or reede y-spratelid throgh the eyen, bene moste to
blame amonge al otheris, and moste reprouabill; and suche a
man is worst amonge al otheris.

28 ### Browes.

ho-so hath the browes ful rogh, he fautyth eloquence: he *Eyebrows,*
W that hath gret browes strechynge to the templis, Such is
foule and lechurous: he that hath browes noȝt ouer thyke, of
32 ²heere of meene Leynth, and grete y-now, he is of good vndyr- *the best.*
stondynge and lyghtly Vndyrstondyth. ² 75 b L.

Noose.

h E that hath a sharpe noose and smale, he is wrethfull: *The nose;*
36 And he that hath a longe noose and Sum-whate stowpynge
and strachynge toward the mouthe, he is worthy and hardy: he

that hath a crokyd noose, he is hasty, malicious, *and* angry:
nostrils; who-so hath the noose-thurlis moche opyn, he is strongly angry:
who-so hath a lei and Plate noose amyd, stoupynge to-warde the
butte, he is a iogoloure and a lyer. And that noose is beste 4
the best nose. to Prayse that is meenly longe and menly brode, and the butte
not oue*r* coppyt ne oue*r* Platte ne stowpynge, and the noose-
thurlis menly grete.

Vysage. 8

Of the face: Who-so hath a playne visage and nothynge fleshy, he is a
chydere, a barratoure, il-taght, wrongfull, and foule: who-
an honest face; so hath the face meen in chekys *and* templis, and Sum*w*hate
fatte, he is sothefaste, louynge, vndyrstondynge, *and* wyse, com- 12
paygnable, honeste, and of good engyñc. Who so hath a grete
large mouth; mouth, he is chyualerous and hardy: And who-so hath grete
large lips; lippes, swollen, he is a fole. And who-so hath the face oue*r*
fleshy *and* oue*r* grete, he is vnvyse, enuyous, a lyer: who-so 16
a straight face; hath the face straght *and* wel y-mesurid, he is wyse and redy
in his dedys, and of sutille vndyrstondynge. And who-so hath
the visage litill and streyte, yelowe and discolourid, he is ful
malicious, ful of vices, dysceyuoure, and dronklewe. Who-so 20
hath the vysage longe and straght, he is angry. Who-so hath
swollen temples; the temples swollen and the chekis also, he is ful angri. whoso
great ears; hath the eeris full grete, he is a fole, saue in that wyche he
hath lernyd. That wych he hath lernyt and vndyrstonde, he 24
holdyth hit well, and wel hit remembrith. And whoso hath
little ears. litill Eeris he is a sot, a thefe, and a lechurere.

[1] 76 L.

[1]Voyce.

A great and pleasant voice; Who-so hath the Voyce grete and Plesaunt and wel hardyñ, 28
he is chyualerous, Plesaunt, and eloquente. Who-so hath
the voice meene betwen grete and smale, he is wise, Purueyaunt,
hasty speech; veritable, and ryghtfull. Whoso hath the worde hasty, yf he
haue a smale voyce, he is angri, fole, Enuyous, *and* a liere: And 32
yf his voice be grete, he is angri and hasty. And whoso hath
the voyce ful-swete, he is enuyous and suspicious. Ful grete
sweetness of voice. swetnesse of voice tokenyth foly and vnevnnynge; Whoso in
[2] Fol. 68. spekynge meveth [2]oftymes His Handys, and makyth many con- 36
tynauncys, He is enuyous. A Softe spekere is a dysceyuoure,
And he that spekyth wythout meuynge of[1] handys, and wythout

The Tokens of Neck, Shoulders, and Feet. 235

chippes and contenaunces, He is of perfite vndyrstondynge, wel
dysposid, and of¹ hole consaille.

Neeke.

4 ho-so hath a smale neke, he sholde haue a swete voyce and *A small neck;*
w   wel y-harde, but he is vnvyse. Whoso hath the neke ful
    shorte he is voucheous, deceyuant, and trechure. And *a short neck.*
    Whoso hath the neke ful grete, he is a fole and a gloton. And
8 who-so hath the belly grette, he is a Sotte, wythout dyscrecioñ,
    Proute and lecherous. But a meen belly and a meene breste *The tokens of the breast.*
    tokenyth heynesse of vndyrstondyng and of consaill. A broode
    breste hey vp-rerid and gret nynesse of shuldres and of the
12 chynne, tokenyth Proesse, hardynesse,¹ wythholdynge of vndyr-
    stondynge and of cunynge: the bake and the chynne whan
    thay bene ouer-smale tokenyth febilnesse and dyscordaunt kynde:
    Meenesse of breste *and* of ch[i]nne is a good tokyñ, *and* is to
16 Preyse.

Of the Shuldres.

w han the shuldres bene moche vprerid, thei tokenyth orribill *The shoulders;*
   kynde *and* vntrouthe; whan the armys bene longe and *long arms;*
20 rechynge to the kneis whan thay ben straght, tokenyth hardy-
    nesse, Proesse, and fraunchise; and whan the armes bene ful *short arms.*
    shorte thay tokenyth lowe of dyscorde, and ²vncunynge. Longe   ² 76 *b* L.
    Palmes and longe bake tokenyth good dispocicioñ to many
24 craftes, and namely to hand-werkys, and tokyn of good gouern-
    aunce. A shorte grete bake tokenyth fooly and vncvnnynge.

Of the feete.

       t He fette gerte and fleshy, tokenyth fooly and lowe of *Great feet;*
28   wrongis; the feete litille and febill tokenyth febilnesse of
    kynde. Ful smale leggis tokenyth vnconyngnesse; grettnesse
    of leggis tokenyth streynth and hardynesse; grete brednysse of
    heelis and of leggis tokenyth febilnesse of naturall vertue, And
32 tho that ham haue, bene neshe in maner of women. Whoso
    hath the Paas large and slow, he is wyse and wel spedynge in *slow step;*
    al his dedys, and who-so hath the Paas litill and Swyfte, he is
    suspeccious, of euyl will, on-myghty to werkys.
36 h   E is wel dysposid aftyr kynde that hath tendyr flesh, the *tender flesh.*
      body nethyr ouer roghe ne ouer Playne, of meene estature,

¹ 164 in ink figures, in margin, about 1850 ?

<small>The tokens of a perfect man.</small> of quyke coloure, wyth reede Sum-whate medelit, benure lokynge, Plente of lockys Playne Wythout moche cryspynge : The eyen sumwhate reede, opyñ and grete y-nogh, the heede rounde *and* of meene quantyte, the neke euyñ and wel dysposyd, the hede well y-mesurid, the shuldris sum-whate hangynge, the leggis and the knees synnowy and noght fleshy; the Voice clere and temperit betwen grete and smale, The Palmes longe and brode, the bake nethyr ou*er* grete ne smale, of lytill laghynge, fayre of semblaunt,

<small>Judge by all tokens, not by one alone.</small> sumwhat Ioyous. Many tokenys y haue tolde yow, but ye shall noght anoone yeue a Iugement ne a sentence for oone of the tokenysse, but ye shall gadyr wyttnesse of al the tokenys, and yf thay ben contrary, ye shall Iuge ther as moste of the tokenysse, *and* wych moste bene verray, ham accordyth.

Capitulum lx^m. [1] 77 L. **Here endyth the tretyse of Physnomye, and begynnynge the tretyce of gou*er*nance of helthe, of the body [1]of man, aftyr Phisike. Capitulum Sexagessimum.**

<small>Health is the thing to be most desired.</small> monge al thynges he[l]th is moste desyrid. For a man haue nothynge, that soore seke is, that he nolde hit yeue helth forto haue *and* mayntene; What were wourth al the worlde to haue, *and* languyre by sekenysse? Sertis lytill, or noght; ffor sekenys enfebelyth not only the body, but also [2]al

[2] Fol. 68 b. Wyse resou*n* and mynde. And therfor Hit nedyth euery man, and namely Pryncis *and* grete lordys, helth to haue, and bodely <small>Every man should be able to keep himself in health.</small> streynth for comyn Prowe of the Pepill; And that he cane kepe hym-selfe in helth of body, that he ne be not euer in kepynge of Phisiciens, like a chylde in warde of his tutoure. And therfor, sethyn gracious lord, that I, Iames aforsayde youre servaunt, haue y-translatid to youre excellence by this boke afor, the techynges, by dyuers autoriteis and ensamplis, how that ye shal kepe youre sowle fro vices and ill maners, and vertuosly to lywe:

Now here y translate yow, out of latyn into englysh, the techynges Whyche ye shall mowen kepe helth of body *and* **of corage, that ye may the moore Worthely by bounte and delyu*er*nesse, gouerne al that in youre** Capitulum Lxj^m. **iurysdiccio*un* Is. Capitulum lxj^m.**

<small>There are four elements in the world.</small> L the wyse Philosofers in oone accorde sayne that iiij^e elementes bene in the worlde, Wherof euery corruptabill thynge is makyd; that Is to witte, Erthe, Watyr, Ecyre,

and fyre : And euery of thes hath two ProPyrteis ; The Erthe is colde and dry ; The watyr is colde and moiste ; The eeire hote and moyste ; The fyre hote and dry. In the body of euery man
4 ben iiij^e humorus, answarynge to the iiij^e element*es* : and like propyrteis therof they haue. Malencoly, colde and dry ; Fleme, colde and moysty ; Saugyne, hote and moyste ; Colerike, hote and dry ; And for-als-moche as thes Propyrteis bene contraryus,
8 ne may not the body alway endure, but hit moste turne and repayre into the iiij^e ¹Element*es* of wych hit was makyd. And thegh the body may not alway endure, hit may endure longe tyme, yf the kynde of man be Well y-noryschid and in due
12 mane*re*, by ettynge and drynkynge like as we sene the mecche of a candill whych is y-lyghtid, Is y-nurshit by the oile Wych is about hit, and yf the oy[le ne]² were, the mecche shulde bene anoone brent and destruet. In the Same mane*re* yf [th]e
16 kyndely hette ne were y-nurshit by mette and drynke, in shorte tyme hit wolde destru the body. Ouer that hit most haue mesure and proporcioñ, for yf the mecche be ouer depe y-sette in the oyle, hit shall anoone be y-queynte ; And yf a man do
20 surfete of mette and drynke, the kyndely hette shal be enfebelit ; and anoone by that may a man fall Into Sekenys and aftyr that dey. for Salamon Sayth, "Many Pepill bene Perishid by glotony." Mesure in al thynge helth kepyth, and therfor haue
24 mesure in mete and drynke, in slepynge in wakynge, in trauaill in reste, in blode-lettynge and in all othyr thyngis. And whoso doth not so, he shal fale into dyuers sekenys Sudaynly. And who-so may not atte the ryght mesure, radyr hym holde to the
28 lytill than to the moche ; More lyghtyr may the defaute be restorid, than the super-fluyte be y-Put away. Of ypocras the vyse leche hit is writte, that grete abstynence he dide, and therfor in a certayne tyme he wox febill of body, and oone of his
32 disciplis to hym sayde, " Fayre Maystyr, yf ye wolde ette welle, ye sholde not be so febill." Ypocras answarid, " Fayre sone, I wolde ette forto lyfe, and not lyfe to ette." Wel hit Is knowen that tho men whych kepyth reysonabill diette *and* lywen tem-
36 prely, bene more hole of body, of bettyr vndyrstondynge, more delyuerir, more strongyr, more lyueloker, more sufferynge and durynge trauailles and dyssayses, and bene of more longyr lyfe.

Each of these has two properties.

The four humours answer to them ; and since their properties are contrary, they cannot endure for ever.
¹ 77 *b* L.

Man's body requires food as a lamp needs oil.

But the food must be in measure.

Solomon.

Measure in all keeps health.

Hippocrates' saying,

I eat to live, not live to eat.

² Blotted here.

Of two Pryncipall thyngis [1]**that helth kepyth. Capitulum Lxij**^m.

[1] 78 L.

[2] Fol. 69.

Custom is second nature.

²O Kepe Helth of Body two thynges Bene Pryncipaly necessary, The Fryste Is that a man vse mettis and drynkis couenables and acordynge to his nature or kynde *and* to his complexcioun, as in tyme and in houre *and* in seyson and as atte his costome. For as ypocras Sayth, "costome is the seco*n*de nature or kynde." The seco*n*de thynge is, that a man hym

Due purging of corrupt humours.

Purge in due tyme of supe*r*fluytez and humours corruptes, and ther-for he is to wyt that aftyr the iiij^e humore*s*, the ³ complexcion dyue*r*syn and varien; for Sum men bene sanguynes, other*is* Fleumatike*s*, the thyrde colerike, the fourth Malencolike. In the maner dyue*r*syth nature of mettes aftyr hote and colde, moisty and dry, and therfor while that complexcioun holdyth hym in estate, and gothe not away out of euynnesse *and* ryght mesure, a man is hoole of body; and therfor a man sholde vse mettis accordynge to his complexcioun, but whan the complex-

The complexions must be brought to evenness.

cio*u*n Passyth mesure, ther hit be-howyth to vse mettis *co*ntraries to remeue or brynge the complexcion to euenesse *and* mesure: And most be done cisili, by litill and by litill, that the kynde ne be not y-greuyd, for the kynde hatyth Sudayn eschaunge. Ensampyl y shal you telle that ye may the bettyr Hit vndyrstonde. The colerike is hote and dry, the fleumatike is moisti and colde, and therfor eue*r*ye ethre couenable may vse mettis of oo mane*r* of kynde, while that noone humoure ne synnyth in ham by excesse. But whan the humours Passyth ryght mesure by diet

By the use of suitable diet,

discordeynet, or by kynde of tyme or of⁴ regioune, they sholde vse contrary dyetis to redresse the excesse and the sorfete. The colerike sholde vse colde diet and moisti, and the Fleumatik

which should be varied with age, season, and place;

hote diet *and* dry. I-lyke mane*r* dyuersite of diet shold kepedyñ be in the dyue*r*site of age, and of tyme and of region and of custumes. Anothyr mane*r*e of diet couena⁴bill is to yonge men *and* anothyr to olde men; to yonge men gret diet and moisti, to holde men suttill diet and hote. In veer, diet in tempure, In heruste, hote mettis and moisti, In wyntyr, gret diet hote and drye, In somyr, suttill diet, colde and moysty. In the region of the Northe, grete diet and hote; In the region of the South, suttill diete and temporate. Thay that bene wonnyd moche to

[4] 78 b L.

4 8

12

16

20

24

28

32

36

³ the the, MS.

trauaill, sholde vse grete diet, *and* stronge to defie; Thay that *with work,*
bene wonnyd moche to reste, Sotyll diet is beste, *and* lyght to
defye. More-ouer hit Is to witte, that thay men wyche haue the *with complexion,*
4 complexcion hote and stronge, and haue throgh al the body the
oue*r*tures large, that clerkys callyth Pores, sholde vse grete
mettis, and in grete quantite. But thay men wych haue the *and with the size of the*
body more scarry, and the oue*r*tures streyte, shulde vse Sotille *pores.*
8 diet and in lytill quantite, ffor larges oue*r*tures tokenyth the
kyndely hette to be of grete vertue, and therfore hit askyth gret
diet and grete sustenaunce; Streyte oue*r*tures tokenyth the contrary, and therfor he askyth diet contrary. Suche-like dyue*r*site
12 may a man fynde in dyue*r*ses stomakis, ffor to tham that haue
the stomake hote and stronge, hit is beste to vse grete diet *and* *Hot and strong*
stronge, for suche a stomake is like a grete fy*r*e that hath Powere *stomachs demand*
to braunte grete shydis and stokkis. But whan the stomake is *coarse diet.*
16 colde and febill, the diet sholde be Suttill and lyght, ffor Suche
a stomake is likenyd to the litill fire, that may brande but flex
or stree. And hit is to witte, that in tymes hit is foundyñ that
al the body of man is hote, and no3th for than the stomake is
20 colde. The tokenys of a good stomake ben lyghtnesse of body, *The tokens of a good*
good appetite to mette, clernysse of vndyrstondynge. The tokenys *stomach;*
of a bade stomake bene heyuynesse of body, Slewthe, the face *of a bad stomach.*
dyscolourid, heuynesse of eyen, ventuosite *and* swollynge [1]of [1] Fol. 69 *b.*
24 the wombe, Defaute of appetite, [2]or luste to ette oftymes, and [2] 79 L.
Sudaynly to Strech the armys and al the body.

Of the goue*r*naunce of the body of man aftyr slepe, helth *Capitulum*
to mayntene. Cap*itu*l*u*m Lxiij^m. *Lxiij*^m.

28   han a man rysyth fro slepe, he sholde a lytill walke and *When a man rises let him*
w hym dysporte, and his lymmes euynly to streche, for that *walk a little;*
enforchyt the body *and* conforthyth his hede, to keine that
the wapours that gonne vp into the hede in tyme of slepynge
32 may haue issue. In Some*r*e hit is good to wesse the extremyteis *then wash;*
wyth colde watyr to holde the kyndely hette wyth-In the body,
and that shal make haue talent to ette. aftyr that he sholde
rube[3] his gomes w*ith* lewys of trenne, whych bene of hote and *clean his teeth.*
36 of dry kynde, for that clenyth the tethe, amendyth the tonge,
cleryth the spekyng*e*, and yewyth good talent to mette, and
makyth good breth. Aftyr that man sholde vse suffumyga-

[3] rude *in MS.*

cionys of herbis accordynge to the tyme and to his complexcioñ, for that opynyth the closures of the brayne, the face hit clarifieth and the syght, and the latre a man wexit hore. Whan this Is done, a man sholde anoynte hym with good onymentis, aftyr the 4 Seysone. Suche oynementis shulde bene of good odure, for that longe tyme confortyth the body, and hit makyth lyght and delyuere; and the good odure confortyth the Spiritis, and makyth the herte oppyn and youse, and for the yoy of the herte 8 the blode rynnyth Into the waynys, throgh al the body. For the blode is the frende of kynde, as Phisciens Sayne. And aftyr a man sholde vse letewaries aftyr the tyme and his complexcioñ. Moche worth is the lytwary y-makyd of fuste and aloes, for that 12 fuste confortyth the stomake, and procuryth dygestioun, and hit is good agayñ the febilnesse of herte and of the brayne, Agayns the cardiacle and al the Passions of the herte and of the brayne, and whoso haue not wherof he may make the letwary, then 16 sethe he fuste in wynne, and drynke hit erly. Reubarbe the Pris of thre Penys or foure rescewe erly, hit Purgyth colre, and wythdrauyth the fleme out of the mouthe of [1] the stomake, and enechyth the kyndely hette, dryuyth away Ventuosite, and 20 makyth the mouth sauourie. Also fayre thynge, and honeste clothynge, kyndely delytyth manes herte.

Of the ryghtfull houris and tymes of ettynge and drynkynge. Capitulum Sexagessimum quartum. 24

yghtful houre of ettynge is, whan the stomake is purchet and clenset, and voyde of the mette, by appetyte and the desyre that a man hath to ette, and by Sutil and thyñ spetil that descendyth or comyth doune fro the Palete of the 28 mouth to the tonge. For who-so ettyth afor that the dygestion be fulfillid, hit helpyth not the naturale course, but ouer-chargyth hit. And by so myche the kyndely hette shall be of lytill vertu, and so shal abyde the mette longe congilet in the stomake, 32 wherof comyth dyuers sekenys. But who-so ettyth atte the ryght houre aforsayde, he fedyth the kyndely hette whych is the Instrument of nature to turne the mettis and the drynkis into fleshe, blode, and bonys; and therfor to kepe kynde hete, and 36 to voyde the stomake, good is hit afor mette Sumwhate to walke or ryde, But bettyr is to walke than ryde, that the kynde hette be y-confortid by the mevynge; and yf anythynge be y-lefte in

the stomake, hit may descende into the botvm of the stomake. *Let the food digest.*
For the botum of the stomake is more hottyr than the entre, and
that whych is in the boet shall descende also, and than may the
4 wombe more lyghtyr be Purgid. Goynge afor mette dryuth *Exercise before meals.*
away the ventositeis, redressith the body, and streyntheth, al the
body hit makyth delyu*er*e; hit confortyth the kyndely hette
and destrueth ille humours, and whan a man hath talent to ette,
8 he sholde ette anone; and yf he ¹Doth not, the stomake anoone ¹ Fol. 70.
shale be replete or fulfillit of Humours, that hit shal draw to
hym of the super*fl*uyteis ²of the body, and aftyr shal sty vp to ² 80 L.
the brayne fumositeis, and trvbill hit, and grew hit, and make
12 the hede akynge. Whan a man syttyth atte mette, and dyuers
man*er* mettis afor hym Is sette, he sholde chese that wyche his *Begin with what you like best.*
harte yewyth beste to. the brede be hit made of whete and
euenly y-lauenyt; Of nesshe mette he shall begynne ³that the *The bread, soft meat,*
16 issue of the stomake be not lette, the wyne good and triet,
the flesshe of the Seyson wel ordeynet; And aftyr, ette mettys
that more ben⁴ byndynge, and lasse solubles: and al tymes ette *then firmer meat.*
they mettis, wyche bene moiste, lyghtly to defy; and aftyr grete
20 mettis. For yf a man ette fryste grete mett*es* and sethyn lyght *Results of the wrong order.*
mettis, the lyght mettis shal be anoone defyet, and shal not
mowe descende to the bouellis, and therfor thay shal twrne by
corrupcion into evil humours. But yf the lyght mettis vndyr
24 be, whan hit is defiet, hit shal descende into the boeɫ, and
Sethyn the grete mettis in his tyme shall goone the same way
wythout lettynge. And hit is to witte that the stomake is more *Reasons for this.*
hote atte the botvm than aboute the mouthe, ffor the botvm is
28 fleshy and neyeth myche the lyu*er* and to the galle, and of this
hit rescew*ith* hette; but the entre of the stomake is synnowy
and more is aloynet fro the lyu*er* and the gale, and the synnowis
bene of colde kynde, and the flesshe of hote. Whan a man
32 sittyth atte mette he sholde wythdrawe his honde afor that he *Leave off with an appetite.*
be y-fillit, and durant the appetit he sholde cesse; ffor whoso
doth othyr-wyse, Sone he shal be seke and his body y-grewid,
and the corage hurte; whoso drynkyth watyr atte mette, or *Don't drink water at meals.*
36 anoone aftyr, he shall felde harme, for that quenchyth the hette
naturaɫ, destourbyth the dygestion, and the mettis tvrnyth into
corrupcion. But whoso nedyth that to done, drynke a lytill

³ that that *in MS.*   ⁴ bende, MS.

SECRETE.   R

¹ 80 b L.   and colde temprely, ¹and yf hit were medelit wyth wyne, hit
were the lasse to dredde.

Now hit is to witte of the gouernaunce of the body aftyr mette. Capitulum lxv^m.

Capitulum
Lxv^m.

Take a little gentle walk.

Then rest on a soft bed.

not before meals though.

When is it best to eat, mid-day or evensong?

In the day the wits are at work.

² Fol. 70 b.

³ 81 L.
In the night the natural heat is driven inwards.

W han a lord hath ettyn, good is to stonde awhyle and
softely to walke, noght vpon harde erthe ne Pament, but
vpon erthe nesshly y-st[r]awet or russhet, for that shal
make the mette aisely descende by litill and lytill, into the 8
botum of the stomake. Sethyn hit is good to reste and slepe in
a softe bedde, in clothis fresshe wel oduret, Fryst vpon the ryght
syde and aftyr vpon the lyfte syde, and on that syde of the,
slepe an ende to make, for that syde is moste colde and moste 12
nedyth to be ychafit. Slepynge afor mette drieth the moysture
of the body, and hit makyth lene, but slepyng aftyr mette nurris-
shet the body and streyntyth. For whyle that a man slepyth,
al the wittis restyth ; and than retretith the natural hette that 16
spredyth abrode throgh al the body, and to the v wittis. hit
servyth to the stomake and to the entrailł, and than thay gederith
hare streynth and vertu, wyche was amenuset and febelit whan
hit was attendynge to al the wittis and menynges of the body. 20
And therfor sum Philosofers sayne that hit were more holsome
to the body to ette atte euynsonge-tyme than atte myde-day.
For atte myde-day the v wittes bene in trauaille, and the corage
of man is by that y-trauaillit, also by slepynge, by thogh, and 24
by dyuers othyr thynges that a man hath to done, and in tymes
by hette Of the sone, wyche more shewyth his vertue atte that
tyme of the day : and therfore the natural hette atte myde-day
is lasse stronge, and the stomake is of lasse Powere to defy the 28
mette, but atte evyne we scene ²al the contrary, ffor atte that
tyme the V wittys restyth Ham of Hare trauaillys, and the
dyssayses of the day bene Passid, and the nyght comyth, wych
is grauntid to reste ; ³and the colde of the nyght chasyth the 32
natural hette towarde the stomake and the entrailł ; and by so
mych hym helpyth the vertue dygestyfe that was destrubbit by
the hette of the Sone that drawyth to hym the kyndely hette of
the extremyteis of the body. For kyndly hette drawyth hete, 36
and colde hit destroubyth. And hit is to witte, that to kepe
covstoume is moche wourth to mayntene hele, so that hit be not
surfetouse ; and than hit sholde not be sodaynly chaungid that

wyche is custoumet, but slowly by lytill and by litill. Ther- *Do not change custom,* for he that is custumet to ette two tymes in the day, yf he wyth- drawe hym sodaynly, anone he may grevaunce take; and moche
4 may more dout that man wych was wonyt but ette onys, and aftyr that he ettyth two tymes in oone day. ffor the stomake *especially by increase of food.* shal be nuet to resceue more charge than hit was wonyt, Also hit is to witte that he that chaungith the houre of ettynge shall
8 fele greuaunce of kynde by reyson of both thes thynges, ffor custume is the seconde nature, and therfor who-so chaungyth *Custom is second nature.* custume hastely, he shall greuaunce recewe, like as the nature or complexciou were chaungid, and that wych is sayde of mettis
12 and drynkys, hit shal be vndyrstond in the same maner of othyr custume, as of slepynge, of trauaiH, of restynge, and of al othyr thyngis.

Of the foure Parties of the yere aftyr hare kyndes.
16   Capitulum. Lxvjᵐ.   *Capitulum Lxvjᵐ.*

AL the olde Phylosofers the yere dynysedyn in fowre Parties, wyche ben callid Veere, Somer, Herrust, and *Four seasons,* Wyntyr. Thes iiij^e tymes hath like Propyrteis to the foure
20 elementes, and to the foure complexciones, of the wyche I haue aforsaydyne. The compotistres sayne, that Veere begyn- nyth at the feste wych we callyth in kalenders, Cathedra *spring,* sancti Petri, and duryth into the feste of Seynte Vrbane. Than
24 begynnyth Somyr, and duryth into the feste of Seynte Sym- *summer,* phoriane. Than begynnyth herust, and duryth into the feste *autumn, I 81 b L.* of Seynte Clement. And fro that duryth wyntyr into the feste *winter.* of seynte Petyr aforsayde. The tyme of weere is hote and
28 moisti, like as the eyre is, And therfor in that tyme, al thynnges *Properties of spring.* begynnyth to renoue and wix newe, and returne Into estate. the tempestis begynnyth ham to wythdrawe, The snowes demet- tyth ham in the montayns, the ryuers rynnyth Into hillis, The
32 wellis spryngyth vp, The humours of tren and herbis styeth vp fro the rotis into the bowes, the seedis rysyth vp, The cornes growyth, The medys wixeñ grene, the flowris coloureth the erthe, the tren clothyn ham wyth lewis, botonyth and spourgyth,
36 the bestis engenderyth, And al quyke thynges takyth agayne thare vertues. The byrdys syngyth, the nyghtyngall shewyth his organe notis, al the Erthe rescewyth his anournement and his beute, and is like to a fayre yong man that arrayth hym

well of al maner of anournement to showe hym-Selfe atte the
weddynge. And for-als-moche as this tyme is hote and moysty,
the blode of man whych is of like complexcion, growyth in this
seyson more than in any othyr tyme of the yere, and spredyth
hym throgh al the lymes of the body. In this tyme hit is good
to ette temporate mettes, as chykenes, letus¹ sauage, that is
y-callid scariole, and mylke of a goote, and drynke good wyne
and in tempure. Noo tyme is more couenable to lete blode,
namely of the body, Purgacioun of the wombe, company of
women, bathes, Swetes, Pocions or drynchis of Spycirie, medicyns laxatifs sholde bene vsyd in this tyme. For al that is
voyde by blode-lettynge, or by othyr medycyne, this tyme
restoryth hastely by his hette and by his moysture.

margin: The complexion of spring.
margin: Meats.
margin: ¹ betus MS.
margin: A good time for purging in these ways.

[Of Somer. Capitulum Lxvij^m.]

²Somer Begynnyth in the feste of Scynte Vrbane, and
Duryth into the feste of Scynte Symphoriane. ³In this
tyme the dayes vyxen longe, and the nyghtis shorte. In
al regions the hettes bene encreschid, the turmentes of the eeyre
swagyth, the see wixit calme, the Serpentis growyth, the wynes
growyth, the cornes wixit rippe, And than the world semyth a
spowse ful woxen of body. and Parfite age, in ful vertue of
natural hete. The tyme of Somyr is hote and dry, and therfor
than regnyth reede colere, that hath the same condycion, and
for that, a man sholde enchu hotte mettis and dry, wych engendryth reede colere. A man Sholde ette mettis of colde and
moisti complexcion, that the nature ne Passe not ryght ful
temprure, as flesh of Velis, Vynegre, hemroll, and Potage of
oot-mell, gourdes and Poumgrenes, and Suche othyr mettis.
Also drynke grene wyne, clere, sharpe, and sparklynge in
tempure. Also a man may vse mettis in tempure, that is to
witte, that thay be not ouer colde ne ouer hote, and for that the
naturale hete of man is more febill in somere, than in othyr
tyme, hit nedyth a man do more abstynence in that tyme than
in wyntyr, whan the stomake is more hote, by the reyson than
in colde tyme the colde chasyth the naturall hete, and the othyr
lymes wyche bene wyth-In the body, Company of women,
mevynge of body, and grete trauaill, Swotes, and bathes, a man
shold scarsly and seldyn vse, lettynge of blode none vse, but
yf grete nede be.

margin: Capitulum Lxviij^m.
margin: ² Fol. 71.
margin: Summer begins.
margin: ³ 82 L.
margin: The properties of summer.
margin: Meats.
margin: Use these but seldom.

[Of Herust.] Capitulum Lxviij^m.

HErust begynnyth atte the feste of Seynte Symphoriane, and duryth Into the feste of Seynte Clement. Than wixen the dayes more shorte than thay weryñ, and the nyght more longyr. But like as in Veere fallyth equinoccium, that is to Say, evnesse of day and nyght, So hit is in heruste, but in veere, the dayes longyth fro equinoccium forth, and the nyghtes shortith. In herust fallyth the contrary. In this tyme the eeyre wixeth colde *and* dry, the wynde of the Northe oftymes turnyth, Wellis wythdrawen ham, grene thynges fadyth, Frutes fallyth, the Eeyre lesyth his beute, the byrdys shechyñ hote regions, the bestis desyryth hare receptis, Serpentes gone to hare dichis. Than semyth the worlde as a woman of grete age, than nowe wox a colde and hade nede to be hote clothyde, for that the yowuthe is Passyde, and age neghyth. Wherfor hit is no mervaile yf beute she hath loste. This tyme is dry and colde by kynde, and than rengnyth blake coler, that is ¹callid malencoly; therfor hit nedyth to vse in this tymes hote mettys *and* moiste, as chykenys well refeted, lambes of oone yere, Pardriches, culueres, good Swete wyne. *and* ripe, that wel nurshyth the body, fygis, datis, and reysyns. To enchue hit nedyth al mettis that engendryth malencoly, of the wyche y shall say yow aftyr this. To trauaille and to company w*ith* women, a man may more, w*ith*out perill, than in somer. Bathis and Purgacionys a man may vse in this tyme for nede. If a man haue nede to vomyte, lete hit be done atte myde-day, whan the Son*n*e is moste hote, for atte that houre the Superfluyteis bene gaderit. Medycinal Purgacions sholde bene y-makyd in this tyme, of thynges that Purgyth malencolie, as is agarik and Suche other*is*. Agarik Purgyth fleme *and* malencoly.

Autumn begins.

Properties of autumn.

¹ 82*b* L.

Meats.

What may be done in this time.

[Of Wyntyr.]

Yntyr begynnyth atte the feste of Seynt Clement, And duryth into the feste of Seynte Petyr, as is afor-sayde. In this tyme the dayes ben woundyr shorte, and the nyghtes longe, for that the Son*n*e louyth hym ²fro oure regiou*n*. And there-for the colde is moche, the wyndys Bene Sharpe, the stormys of the eeyre hidous and horribill, the tren bene dispoylid of thare lewis, al the grene is fadid, outake the Pynes, lorreis, olyues, and few othyr treñ.

Capitulum Lxix^m.

Winter begins.

² Fol. 71 *b*.

Many bestes ham hydyt in caues of montayns, to fle and enchue colde and mostnesse, the eere becommyth derke and foule, bestis that no recepte haue, tremblyth, empeyryth, and mournyth for the colde, and moistnesse, wych is perissynge and contrarie to the lyfe, and therfor al that dede is, anoone wixet colde. In this tyme the world semyth like an olde katte, al ouercome wyth age and trauaill, that lyue ne myght, for she is al disspoylit of beute and of Streynth and vertue. Wyntyr is a colde tyme and moiste, therfor hit is good to vse hote mettis, as fleshe of motton, fat capons, and flesh y-rostid, wych is more hottyr than in seau, or sode in watyr, figes, reisynes, nottes, and good wyne reede, stronge, and clere: letuaries bene good in this tyme, good fyre of colle, and of dry wode, than bene in seyson. But fire with smoke in none seyson nath Place couenable, but oonly ¹in helle. Trauaill of body, and company of women, a man may vse wyth-out surfaite, and more than in somer, herust, or weere. In none tyme of the yere a man may not ette so myche as in the Wyntyr, for the grete colde of heyre, makyth the naturall hette reboute and retourne to the stomake, and the entraill, and therfor the dygestion is the bettyr and more vertuose in wyntyr than in any othyr tyme: but in Veere, and in somer, the wombe and the stomake is more colde, for in that tyme for the hette of the tyme, the natural hete spredyth throgh al the body, and by so myche the stomake wexit the coldre, and the digestion destourbet, and the humours turnyth into corrupcion. And hit is to witte, that als longe as the natural hette duryth in ryght tempure by euenesse of the foure humores, the helth of man shal be y-keppit; for in two maneres fautyth the nature of man; One manere by grete age, and that is y-callit dethe natural; ffor nature wolde that euery thynge wyche is y-makyd of the foure Elementes Wyche bene contraryous, ne may al tymes endure: That othyr maner is by ill kepynge, Wherof commyth sekenys and Sornesse, Wyche ledyn to deth. Suche deth is callid deth of auenture, out of kynde, ffor-why, the nature myght more longyr endure, yf hit had be wel gouernyd, as hit sholde haue bene.

Of thyngis that makyth the body fat, moisti, *and* wel dysposyd. Capitulum Lxx^m.

He body of man and al that is y-makyd of the foure elementis, bene gouernyd aftyr the mevynges of heuyn, and aftyr the same mevynges the tyme dyuersyth, and therfor in dyuers tymes hit behouyth to haue dyuers kepyngis. Noght for than, sum thyngis that in euery day of the yere hath his effecte more and lasse, as slepynge nurshith the body euery tyme of the yere, and myche wakynge makyth the body lene, and hit destrueth. Therfore, gracious lorde, like as wryttyn y fynde, I shall you say shortely What thynges makyth the body fat, moiste, *and* well dysposid; and what thynges done the contrary. The body makyth fat, moiste, and wel ¹disposyd, good mettis *and* drynkis accordynge to manys complexcion aftyr the tyme of the yere and the houre of the day y-custumet or vset as is afor-sayde; aboue al thynge reste of body, gladnys of herte, yoyful fellochippe or company, mettis hote and moiste, drynkes of good Wyne *and* rype, swete mylke, *and* hote drynke makyd wyth Hoony, tendyr brede makyd of the floure of Whete, Slepe mesurable aftyr mette vpon a nessh ²Bedde and in a place tempure, colde Bathis in Watyr temprure colde; and Shorte tyme sitte in bathe that the nature ne be nat enfebelit; Vsynge of honementys aftyr the tyme *and* complexcione, fflaurynge of Swete odures accordynge to the tyme. In wyntyr the hodure of hote thynges, as is aloynge *and* suche otheris; In somer odure of colde thynges, as of rose *and* vyolet: a vomyte in euery monthe atte alerleste, for vomyte Purgyth the stomake of ill humours aboue, as a medecyne laxatyfe benethe; and whan the ill humours bene Putte away, the kyndly hette shal be y-confortid, to defie the mette. To this thynges hit vaillyth moche to haue richesse *and* glory, victorie vpon enemys, and haue asperaunce and truste in the Pepill, wyche bene vndyr youre gouernaunce. Delite in honeste Play, and hit beholde, as to see horsyn rynne, yonglyngges to skyrme, bestis to chase in venurie, and abow al thynge, fayre thynges oft-tymes to beholde, Fayre Workys to make *and* dyuyse, delytabill songes to hyre and synge, good bokys to rede and study, wyth lefe *and* welbelowid Pepill lagh and Play, to solace in dyuers instrumentes of musike, as harpis and Suche otheres, clothynge of

All things increase and decrease with the times,

yet some are always good.

¹ 835 L.

This is the diet you should follow—

² Fol. 72.

sweet odours,

vomits,

good fortune,

good sport,

good books and music.

248   *Things that make the Body lean.*

                dyuers clothis, goode and fayre *and* of dyuers colours, *and* ofte-
All these are tymes ham chauuge. Thes bene the thynges Wyche confortyth
good for you. the herte, the body makyt fatte, hole, and wel dysposyd.

            Of thynges that done the contrarye. Capitulum Lxxj^m. 4
                Hes bene the thynges wych done the contrary to the
These things t thynges aforsayde; lytill mette that is not nurshynge,
are always
more or less   lytill drynke, namely of febill, moche trauaill *and* grete
bad. Iourneis make, to be longe agayne the Son*n*e in hote weddyr, 8
                Slepe afor mete, goynge vpon hard Pament, bathynge in salte
                watyr, or in watyr in wych there is brymstone, moche vsynge
[1 84 L.] [1] of salt mettis, ouer-old wyne moch to drynke, to haue wombe
                moche soluble, moche bledynge or dyuers tymes; and abow al 12
                thynge enfebelyth the body *and* destructh the Spyrytis, Wak-
                ynge moche, ouer myche thoght, company of women ouer myche
                to vse, grete drede, moche doutynge, oftymes to be wrothe, and
                wrath longe tyme holde, goodis of fortune gretly to covete, of 16
Avoid them hatredyn *and* vengeaunce oftymes to thynke, For the lesynge of
if possible. goodys gerte Sorrow make, fowle thynges and vnsemely to be-
                holde, Songis of dolure to hyre, Euyl thynkes to hyre, or
                myschaunces to remembyr. 20

                Fro al manere of myschefe, almyghty god de-fende oure lyge
                lorde, kynge henry the Fyfte, *and* James the Botillere, Erle of
                Ormonde, his lyeutenaunt of Irlande, Whyche this boke to
                translate me comaundet, And graunt ham, grete god, and al 24
                hare Subiectis, in the Sewyn Vertues, grace al tymes to growe.
                Amen. **Laus deo clementissimo.**

                    I-thankyd be god, that is so Hende,
                    That of this Worke hath maket an ende. 28

APPENDIX.

LIST OF CHAPTERS OF THE VERSION IN ASHMOLE 396, BODLEIAN LIBRARY.

[1]Here begynneth the Chapiters of the comendacioun of the prohemy of the Doctour in comendacioun of Aristotle.

Of the prologe of Iohn[2] that transulated this booke.
Of the epistle of Aristotle sent at the peticioun of kyng alexandre.
Of kynges largesse & scarsenes and of other vertues apropred to thaym).
Of Aristotle doctrine in vices and vertues.
Of the fynall intencioun that kynges oweth to have.
Of the harmes that foloweth flesshly appetite.
Of Prudence.
Of kynges Sapience.
Of kynges Religioun.
Of kynges Providence.
Of kynges arraye and ornamentes.
Of kynges contynence.
Of kynges consuetude.
Of kynges Iustice.
Of fynall intencioun.
Of kynges Chastite.
Of kynges solas and discrecioun.
Of kynges Reverence.
Of kynges worthynesse.
Of kynges lykenesse and symylytude.
Of kynges aides and subvencioun.
Of kynges Mercy.
Of the trewe kepyng of feith.
Of promovyng of Study.
Of kepyng of the body.
Of an houre to be chosen).
Of the profite of Astronomye and of kynges helthe.
Of conservacioun of helthe and in how many maners.
[3]Of a epistle of vnestimable pris for-to kepe helthe, and a rule to lyve by.
Of the maner of slepynge.
Of observance of Custume.
Of the .4. tymes and sesons of the yere.
Of theire qualitees and dyversitees.
Of prime temps veere.
Of the Somare.
Of hervest.
Of the Wyntere.
Of the knowyng of the .4. principall membres.

---

[1] fol. 2.
[2] In the margin, in a later hand:—"This John did translate it into Caldee & Arabicke, vide fol. 4to, ut sequitur; for Phillip translated it into Latin ut apparet, fol. 1m." [3] fol. 2 b.

Of siknesse of the hede and his remedies.
Of the Infirmitees of the coddes and thaire remedies.
Of Sikenesse of the brest with his remedies.
Of knowyng of Metes.
Of knowyng of waters.
Of knowyng of wynes.
Of that wher-thurgh the body waxeth fatte.
Of that that maketh it lene and voydeth it.
Of disposicioun of vaynes.
Of makyng of hony for medycynes.
Of the first medycyne.
Of the Seconde.
Of the Thirde.
Of the Fourthe.
Of the Fyveth.
Of the Sixt.
Of the Seventh.
Of the Eyght.
Of the most last and fynall medycyne.
Of blode-lettyng and of houres accordyng therto.

Of knowlechyng of the qualitees of men.
Of thayre heeres.
[1]Of theyre Eighen).
Of theyre Browes.
Of theire Nooses.
Of Movthe.
Of Faace.
Of Templis.
Of Voyces.
Of Movyng of thaire bodies.
Of the Throote.
Of the Woombe.
Of the bakkes.
Of the shuldres.
Of Armys.
Of Palmys.
Of thaire knees.
Of the plantes of Fete.
Of Cheres in goyng.
Of the qualite and stature of man.
Of Iustice.
Of the goodes that cometh therof.
Of the Sercle and of an Example of Iustice.
Of lawe of kynges and of mone.
Of a prohemy of a worthy doctoure.
Of the comendacioun of Aristotle.

[*Follows:*—**G**od almyghty kepe oure kynge to the glorye of trew cristen men in bileve / . . .]

[1] fol. 3.

GLOSSARY.

BY T. HENDERSON, M.A.

ABAYST, *pp.* abashed, 114.
Abbate, *v.* bring low, humble, 160; soften, mitigate, lighten, 188.
Abblastre, *s.* arbalaster, crossbowman, 215.
Abbregge, *v.* abridge, 63.
Abide, -ite, *v.* abide, wait, 26; tr. wait for, 105.
Aboue(n), -yn, -ven, *prep.* and *adv.* above, 67, 90, 92, 247.
Aboundon, *s.* complete control, absolute disposal, 102. (*N.E.D.* Abandon.)
Abouyn, *v.* pass above, 66. (Not in *N.E.D.*)
Abow(e), -owen, -own, *prep.* and *adv.* above, 88, 89, 90, 94, 135, 163, &c.
Abregge, *v.* abridge, shorten, 9, 199; lessen, mitigate, 13, 15. Abreggyng, *s.* shortening, 14. Abreg(g)ement, *s.* abridgment, 63, 67.
Abroune, *a.* auburn, 233. (Earlier than *N.E.D.*)
Accident, *a.* accidental, 23, 29, 32, 103. (Earlier than *N.E.D.*)
Accompte, *s.* account, computation, 214; *v.* reckon, compute, 204.
Accordant, *a.* harmonious, 98, 103.
Accusement, *s.* accusation, 187.
Ache, *s.* parsley, smallage, 77.
A-cremet, *a.* shivering, 74. Cf. mod. dial. *creem*, to shiver. *N.E.D.*
Acuement, *s.* sharpness (tr. *acuitas*), 98. (Not in *N.E.D.*)
Adrede, *a.* adread, afraid, 215, 229, 230.
Adresse, *v.* set right, reform (tr. *corrigere*), 103; delight, please, 100 (tr. *letificat*).
Adulteour, *s.* adulterer, 191.
Adventure, *also* Auenture, *s.* chance, hap, fortune; risk, peril, jeopardy,
20, 55, 57, 69, 110; mishap, mischance, misfortune, 12, 32, 37, 59, 134, 138, 139, 170, 196. Of a. = perchance, 138; accidental, by accident, 29, 246. By a. = by chance, 99.
Aduerser, *s.* adversary, 111.
Aferd(e), *a.* afraid, 15, 19.
Affiance, *s.* faith, trust, confidence, 62.
Afforce, *v.* strengthen, 80 (tr. *corroborat*); *reflex.* exert oneself, do one's best, strive, 57; force, compel, 213. *See* Aforse, Efforce, Enforce, *s. vv.*
Afoor(e), Afor(e), *prep.* and *adv.* before (in all senses), *passim.* Afor that, *adv.* before, 192. Hence Aforhand, -honde, *adv.* beforehand, 196. Aforsay, *v.* say before, 243. Aforspekynge, *s.* preface, 47.
Aforse, *v.* = Afforce: *reflex.* strive, try, 27; *tr.* exert, exercise, use strenuously, 178.
After, -ir, -yr, *prep.* and *adv.* after (in all senses), *passim.* After, After that = according as, 6, 16, 91, 111.
Afyre, *adv.* afire, on fire, 153.
Agastnet, *pp.* terrified, 222. (Not in *N.E.D.* which has Agast, *v.* Agasted, *pp.*)
Agayn(e), -ns, -nes, -nys, Ageyn, Ajein, -yn (forms of Again and Against), *prep.* against, 41, 122, 132, 135, 152, 157, 163, 170, 173, 178, 198, 207, 224, 240; opposite to, facing, 79; towards, 154, 166; *adv.* again, 243; back, 62, 105, 155, 168, 201, 213; on the other hand, 51. Hence A.-come, -cwm, *v.* return, 168, 175. A.-bowynge, *s.* 69. A.-bye, *v.* buy back, redeem, 55. A.-feghtynge, *s.* contention, strife, 88. A.-goyng, *a.* retrograde, 112. A.-led, -ynge,

Glossary.

a. relative, 93. A.-lete, *v.* prevent, avert, 74. A.-put, *v.* drive away, 87. A.-say, -sigge, *v.* contradict, gainsay, 42, 209. A.-stand(e), -stond, *v.* withstand, resist, 48, 57, 89, 111. A.-stryuynge, *s.* resistance, 54. A.-turnynge, *s.* revolution, 63. A.-ward, *adv.* contrariwise, 79.
Aggrauacion, *s.* 74. The word and context are nonsense.
Agone, *pp.* gone, 146.
Ahournyd, *pp.* adorned, 87, 95. (*N.E.D.* Anorn, Adorn.)
Aise, *s.* case, 165. Aisely, *adv.* easily, 242.
Aiuge, *v.* adjudge, deem, 84.
Ake, *v.* ache, 31.
Al, *a.* and *adv.* = All, *q. v.*
A-land, *adv.* by land, 142.
Alany, *s.* alum, 95.
Alatred, *s.* electuary, 70.
Alay, *v.* temper, 81; mitigate, 24, 26.
Albamet, *s.* 84. *See note.*
Albe that, *adv.* albeit, 142.
Alboth, *a.* both, 186, 198, 199, 207.
Alchitinum, *s.* 75. *See note.*
Alchymyng, *s.* 30. *See note.*
Aldaies, -day, *adv.* always, 22, 199.
Alegge, *v.* *See* Alleege.
Alerleste = aller-least, least of all. Atte a. = at least, 247.
Alevyn, *a.* eleven, 222.
Alibi Amei, 32. *See note.*
Aliene, *v. reflex.* depart, diverge, 7.
Alkenamy, *s.* alchemy, 42.
All(e), *a.* all; *adv.* although, albeit, 142. Al hool, *a.* entire, 97. All haly, holy, holely, *adv.* wholly, entirely, 81, 93, 94, 105. Al (o)only, *adv.* only, 61, 136. All so sone as, *adv.* as soon as, 83. If (yf) al(l) = even if, albeit, 42, 62, 65, 87. *Also* If alle that, 60. *See also* Albe, Alboth.
Alle-dayes, *adv.* always, 118.
Alleege, *v.* lighten, relax (taxes, &c.), 140; ease, relieve, 56, 109; cure, heal, 83; allay, appease (strife), 158.
Allegeaunce, *s.* relief (*from* tolls, &c.), 13.
Alloigne, *s.* 75. *See note.*
Allon, All-oon, *a.* alone, 88, 102, 192.
Allyght, *v.* light, kindle, 127. (Not in *N.E.D.*)
Allyke, *a.* like, 217.

Almaill, *a.* animal, 95.
Almayne, *s.* Germany, 136.
Almesse, *s.* alms, 65.
Aloigenement, *s.* tr. *elongatione*, distance, 65 (= eloignment, F. éloignement. *N.E.D.* Eloignment).
Alon, *a.* alone, 191, 195.
Al only, oonly, *adv.* only, 61, 136.
Aloynet, *a.* remote, distant, 241.
Aloynge, *s.* aloes ?, 247.
Als, *adv.* as, 47, 64, 68, 75, 146, 205. Als mekyl as, alsmoch(e) as, *adv.* as much as, 48, 65, 87; in as much as, 190.
Al-so, *adv.* so, 106; as, 147, 158, 163.
Alsson that, *adv.* as soon as, 195.
Altherbeste = aller-best, best of all, 147.
Al-trew, *a.* faithful, 133.
Altyme, -s, *adv.* always, 121, 138, 149, 156, 169, 187, 201, 202.
Alyenyng, *s.* separation, divergency, 24. *See* Aliene.
Alyke, *a.* like, 230.
Amanere, *s.* manner, 219.
Amende, *v.* 99. A meaningless misunderstanding of *mendicare* = beg.
Amenuse, *s.* lessen, diminish, 140, 212, 232, 242.
Amesurid, *pp.* proportioned, 225.
Amonest(e), *v.* admonish, 101, 140, 142, 188, 202.
Amonisshe, -ysshe, *v.* admonish, 35, 37.
Amount, *v.* mount, rise, ascend, 62; amount to, 143.
Ampte, *s.* ant, 74.
Amyddis, -ys, *adv.* in the midst, 215; *prep.* amidst, 198.
Amyse, -ysse, *adv.* amiss, 140, 158, 187.
An, *prep.* An hande = in hand, 143, 171 ; *conj.* and, 129.
And, *conj.* if, 6, 21, 23, 25, 26, 144, 176.
Androsinoun, *s.* androsæmum, 91. *See note.*
Aneche, *v.* increase, 213, 214. *Also* Eneche, 240. (Not in *N.E.D.*)
Anent(e), *prep.* towards, 123, 136, 167; against, 203; with regard to, 216.
Angelec, -il(l), *s.* angel, 104, 198, 212.
Angry, *v.* become angry, 228. (Much earlier than *N.E.D.*)
Angwysche, *s.* anguish, misery, 199.
Anheyrre, *v.* adhere, cleave, 192.
Anhonged, *pp.* hanged, 182.

Glossary. 253

Anisoun, *s.* 77. *See note.*
Anny, *a.* any, 193.
Anoon as, *adv.* as soon as, 26.
Anournement, -ournement, *s.* adornment, 146, 243, 244. *N.E.D.* Anornament, Anourement.
Antecessour, *s.* ancestor, 61.
Antidotum, *s.* antidote, 81.
Apay, *v.* satisfy, content, please, 212.
Apercewe, *v.* perceive, 153.
Apetyd, *s.* appetite, 72.
Apparaill, *v.* get, gather, amass, 138.
Apparayle, *s.* apparel, 13.
Apparceve, *v.* perceive, 195.
Appay, *v.* satisfy, 178, 186.
Appercewe, *v.* perceive, 201.
Appereld, *pp.* prepared, provided, 111.
Apperoue, *v.* approve, 66.
Appert, *a.* 'apert,' open, manifest, 164.
Appetyde, *s.* appetite, 220.
Approcede, *v.* proceed, go on, 187. (Not in *N.E.D.*)
Appryse, *s.* instruction, information, 123.
Apropird, -red, -ryd, *pp.* assigned, allotted, 90; appropriate, proper (to), 249.
Aprowe, *v.* approve, 192.
Aptyd, *s.* appetite, 72.
Ar, *pron.* (= har), their, 129.
Ar(e) (*also* Ar(e) that), *adv.* ere, 163, 168, 173, 187, 195.
Arabie, -ye, *s.* Arab, Arabian, 41, 42.
Araby(e), *s.* Arabia, 41.
Arayne, *s.* a spider; used attrib., 98.
Arblastere, *s.* arbalaster, crossbowman, 37.
Arcul, *s.* a measure, 85. *See note.* (Not in *N.E.D.*)
Areson, *v.* question, examine, 100.
Armour, *s.* ordnance, cannon, 110.
Arne, *v.* are, 7, 12, 17, 210, 212, 220, 225.
Arrest, *v.* halt, stop, 215; make to stop, 99.
Arsmaton, Asmon, *s.* asthma?, 28.
Arsmetyk, *s.* arithmetic, 103.
Arwe, *s.* arrow, 110, 111.
Ask(e), *v.* seek, 42; need, require, 56, 71.
Askis, *s. pl.* ashes, 154.
Askynge, *s.* request, 42.
Aslake, *v.* subside, 28.
Asperaunce, *s.* hope, 247. (Not in *N.E.D.*, but = Esperance).

Aspi, -y, *v.* examine, inquire into, 189, 211.
Aspie, *s.* spy, 37, 215.
Assamyd, *pp.* ashamed, 202.
Assaut(e), assault, 122, 144, 156, 160, 163, 174.
Assay, *s.* trial, experience, 61, 64.
Assemble, *s.* assembly, 32, 57.
Assert, *v.* 'ascertain,' make certain, assure, 156.
Asseth, *s.* satisfaction. Make asseth to = satisfy, 42; do (thine) asseth = satisfy (thee), 168.
Assiduell, *s.* constant, persistent, 64. (Much earlier than *N.E.D.*)
Assiege, -ige, *v.* besiege, 174, 177, 178, 198.
Assyd, *adv.* aside, 128.
Astronomyour, *s.* astronomer, 216.
Ateigne, *v.* attain, reach, 117.
Atempre, *v.* and *a.* Atemprely, *adv. See* Attempre, Attemprely.
Atouchable, *a.* (A.-stryngh, 98, translates *vis tactiva*) tactual. Perhaps a *touchable*, with same meaning.
Atretably, *adv.* duly, 113.
Attemper, -re, *v.* temper, combine in just proportion, 68, 83; make just estimate of, 114; regulate, govern, 55, 187.
Attemperally, *adv.* temperately, moderately, 67.
Attemperat (-orat), *a.* tempered, in just proportion, 29. Attemperatly, *adv.* temperately, in moderation, 25, 29, 33.
Attemp(a)ra(u)nce, -rou(n)ce, *s.* even balance, just proportion, moderation. 22, 53, 67, 103, 114.
At(t)empre, *a.* temperate (heat, &c.), 73, 75, 78; moderate, 52; well-proportioned, evenly attempered, 114.
At(t)emprely, *adv.* moderately, in moderation, 71, 80, 81, 83.
Attene, *v.* reach, attain, 112.
Atte ones, -onys, Attones, *adv.* at once, at one time, simultaneously, 25, 182; immediately, 33.
Atteynt, *v.* convict, 128.
Attitle, *v.* (with *to*) name (after), 90. (Only example in *N.E.D.* is 1393.)
Atto(u)rne, -urne, *v.* assign, appropriate, 42, 90, 91.
Auance, *s.* one who has been advanced,

Glossary

107. (*N.E.D.* Advance, *s.* 10.) Auauncement, *s.* 63.
Auaunce, *v.* advance, promote, 19, 124, 130, 137, 144; redress, succour, relieve, 207.
Auauncement, *s.* advancement, preferment, 36, 144, 179.
Auaunt, *v.* vaunt, 132, 153.
Aua(u)ntage, *s.* special advantage, privilege (tr. *prerogatiua*), 63; interest, profit, 132.
Avay, *adv.* away, 162.
Avayille, *v.* avail, 179.
Auctoricement, *s.* aggrandisement, 177. (Very early instance of *N.E.D.* Authorizement.)
Auctorite(c), *s.* authority, 193, 201, 206.
Avele, *v.* lower, 197. (*N.E.D.* Avale.)
Auenaunt, *a.* becoming, seemly, 140, 189.
Auence, Aueng, *s.* avens, herb bennet (*Geum urbanum*), 77.
Auenterous, *a.* accidental, by misadventure, 78.
Auenture, *s. See* Adventure.
Auere, *s.* wealth, possession, estate, 132, 175.
Auerous, 104; Auers, 51, *a.* greedy, avaricious; *s.* miser, 52.
Avie, *v.* send away, dismiss, 37. (*N.E.D.* Avye.)
Avise, -yse, *v. reflex.* take thought or counsel, consider (Fr. *s'aviser*), 143, 154, 155, 209.
Avised, -ysed, *a.* To be a. = (1) consider, reflect, 131, 143; (2) purpose, intend, 69. (*N.E.D.* Advised, I.)
Avisement, *s.* reflection, deliberation, 12.
Auisioun, Auysioun, *s.* vision, 91. (*N.E.D.* Avision.)
Auugille, *s.* angel, 3, 35.
Auoutry, *s.* adultery, 136.
Autentike, *a.* authentic, 201.
Auter, *s.* altar, 200.
Autorie, *s.* authority, 158. (Not in *N.E.D.*)
Avyce, *s.* advice, 184.
Auyse, *v.,* Auysed, *a. See* Avise, -d.
Avysely, *adv.* wisely, prudently, judiciously, 138, 157.
Auysement, *s.* prudence, judgment, discretion, 118.
Avysete, *a.* discreet, wary, judicious, 189, 209.

Auysioun, *s.* vision, 91. *See* Auisioun.
Awaill, -a(y)le, *v.* avail, 123, 160, 203, 205, 215.
Awantynge, *s.* vaunting, 158.
Awayte, *s.* ambush, lying in wait, 114 (tr. *insidias*).
Awe, *v.* ought, 58, 61, 63, 79, 87, 92.
Awen, *a.* own, 101.
Awow, *s.* 'avow,' vow, 133.
Awyse, *v. reflex.* take counsel, reflect, 156. *See* Avise.
Axcesse, *s.* ague, intermittent fever, 31. (*N.E.D.* Access, iv. 10.)
Ax(e), *v.* ask, 5; require, need, 19.
Axynge, *s.* question, 11.
Ayen(c), *adv.* again, 23.
Ayen-takyng, *s.* taking back, 9.
Ayennes, -ens, *prep.* against, 5, 8, 16, 133; towards, 11.
Ayeyn(e), -nnes, *adv.* again, 136, 144, 199; *prep.* against, 131, 173. Ayeyne-come, *v.* come back, return, 136.
Aym, *v. tr.* conjecture, forecast, 150. (*N.E.D.* Aim, *v.* 3.)
Ayse, *s.* ease, 172, 189, 199.

Bachelerie, *s.* knighthood, 129.
Bachyller, *s.* knight, 144.
Baillie, *s.* bailliwick, 153.
Bake, *pp.* baked, 25.
Balaunce, *s.* balance. Put in b. = risk, endanger, 173.
Balch, *v.* belch, 71.
Ballo(c)kis, -ys, *s.* testicles, 31, 77.
Bandoun, *s.* disposal, will, pleasure, 64.
Baratous, *a.* contentious, quarrelsome, 38.
Barayne, *a.* barren, 197.
Barbarys, *s. pl.* barbarians, 41.
Barbrion, *s.* barbarian, 179.
Barratoure, *s.* wrangler, quarrelsome fellow, 234.
Bat(t)ail(l)e, -ayl(le), *s.* battle array, 178; division of army, 215; battle, 37, 38, 56, 110, 129, 154, 156, 173, 203, 215; strife, contention, 10, 54; *v.* battle, fight, 203.
Be, *pp.* been, 162, 176; *prep.* by, 48, 49, 94, 169, 215.
Beand, *pp.* being, 82.
Behete, -tte, *v.* promise, 157, 191, 215.
Behight, *v.* promised (*p. t.*), 92.
Behold(e), *v.* behold, see; consider, regard, 51, 130.

Glossary. 255

Beholdyng, s. aspect, appearance, 106.
Behoste, s. promise, 197, 210. (= N.E.D. Behote, s.)
Behote, v. p. t. promised, 130; pp. promised, 157.
Behouabill, a. suitable, appropriate, 207.
Be-ladde, v. treated, used (p. t.), 136.
Belew(e), s. belief, faith, creed, 165, 200; v. believe, 165, 187.
Belk, v. belch, 68.
Bem, s. beam, ray, 41.
Bemurely, 182, so MS. = Benurely, q. v.
Ben(e), v. be, 132, 138, 150, 182, 241, &c.; pp. been, 53, 150.
Benefacte, s. good deed, 205.
Ben(n)ure, a. kind, gentle, 189, 224, 231, 236. Benur(e)ly, adv. kindly, gently, 134, 188. Benurtee, s. kindness, gentleness, 189. (N. E. D. Bonair, -ly, -ty.)
Bere, s. bear, 35; v. bear, 12, 134.
Bereue, -we, v. deprive of, 134; take away, detract from, 132.
Berre, v. bear, 170, 215. Berrere, s. bearer, 213.
Berrynge, s. bearing, mien, 141; (child)-bearing, 153; pp. 213.
Besely, Besil(l)i, -ily, adv. quickly, eagerly, 179; earnestly, 49, 57, 182; vehemently. 166; carefully, diligently, 86, 211, 217.
Bessie, v. reflex., strive, endeavour, 174. Bessid, p. pl. 168.
Bestayle, s. 'bestial' (collective), animals, 111.
Beste, s. beast, 14, 35, 181, 211, 216, 246.
Bestfull, a. (beast-ful), animal. Saule b. = tr. anima animalis, 53. (Not in N.E.D.)
Bestly, a. bestial, beastly, 5, 10.
Besy, a. busy, eager, solicitous, anxious, 107, 206. Besy(e), v. reflex. busy, employ, occupy, 49, 106, 210.
Besynes(se), s. care, carefulness, 52; charge, management, 52; affair, concern; solicitude, care, 102; anxiety, worry, 49, 80.
Be-take, pp. taken. Cryste b., 136, = taken to Christ.
Betene, v. beat, throb? 30.
Bethe, v. be, 139.
Bette, pp. beaten, 106.
Better, a. bitter (tr. amara), 52.

Be-tyde, v. befall, 139; befell (p. t.), 129; pp. befallen, 139, 157.
Beute, Bewte, s. beauty, 27, 28, 243, 245, 246.
Beyne, pp. been, 164.
Bicome, v. become, 13.
Bid, v. pray, 169.
Bienvoillaunce, s. goodwill, friendship, 183. Cf. Woillance. (Not in N.E.D.)
Bigge, v. build, 82.
Bigger, s. builder, 59 (tr. edificantibus); buyer, 16.
Biholde, v. look at, behold, 30.
Bihote, v. promise, 37.
Bihove, v. behove, 6, 28, 31, 36.
Bihoueful, a. necessary, 39.
Bild, v. build, 33.
Biloue, v. belove, 10.
Bireve, v. bereave, deprive of, 37.
Bistere, v. bestir, stir, move, 5.
Bisynes(se), s. diligence, 34, 36.
Bitakyn, v. betoken, 112.
Bithinke, v. bethink, 10.
Blaas, Blaste, s. blast, 153.
Bleddre, s. bladder, 31.
Bleghtly, adv. blithely, 56 (tr. libenter).
Blesfull, adv. blissful, innocent, 212.
Blestly, adv. gladly, willingly, 134.
Blete, s. blite (herb), 83.
Bloodlate, s. blood-letting, 73.
Blow, v. blossom, bloom, 141.
Blynde, v. blind, 159; p. t. blinded, 162.
Blyne, a. blind, 167.
Bobaunce, s. boasting, 172, 176.
Bocche, v. swell, 227. (See N.E.D. Botch, s.[1] and Boss, s. and v.)
Boef, s. ox, 78.
Boel(l)e, s. bowel, 241.
Bok, s. book, 195.
Boklere, s. buckler, 190.
Bole, s. bull, 35.
Boln(e), v. swell, 23, 68.
Bolnynge, s. swelling, 69, 80.
Bonand, a. kind, tender, 57.
Bonere, a. kind, courteous, 211. Bonerte, s. kindness, courtesy, gentleness, 123, 176, 233. (N.E.D. Bonair, -ty.)
Bonny, a. bony, 226.
Bonyte, s. goodness, excellence, 132.
Boore, s. boar, 35.
Bordelle, s. brothel, 190.
Borowe, s. borough, 17.
Borthom, s. burden. Bear b. = be of

weight, consequence, 172. *See* Burthyn.
Both, *a.* two, 198. Both othir, each other, 192.
Boton, *v.* bud, 243.
Bouell(e), *s.* bowel, 241.
Bounte(e), *s.* goodness, excellence, 134, 160, 167, 186.
Bourdyng, *s.* jesting, 118.
Bourgynge, *s.* burgeoning, budding, 142.
Bow(e), *v. tr.* bend, curve, 161; incline, turn, direct, 10, 54, 74, 100, 114; *reflex.* incline, 58; *intr.* incline, bend, 115; incline, tend, 115; yield, submit (to), 41; turn aside, swerve, decline, 93, 102; with *from*, be averse (to), refrain (from), 99, 103.
Bowe, *s.* bough, 243.
Bowsty, *a.* rude, violent, 229.
Boystous, *a.* rough, rude, violent, 38, 104.
Brande, *v.* burn, 203, 205, 215, 229, 230, 239; burnt (*p. t.*), 204.
Brandoun, *s.* brand, 111. (Much earlier than *N.E.D.*)
Brandynge, *s.* burning, 153, 167; *pp.* 190.
Brant(e), *pp.* 204; *p. t.*, 204, burnt.
Braon(e), *s.* brawn, muscle, 222, 223, 230.
Braunt, *v.* burnt (*p. t.*), 204.
Braunte, *v.* burn, 239.
Brede, *s.* bread, 178, 247; breadth, 94, 151, 163.
Brednysse, *s.* breadth, 235. (Not in *N.E.D.*)
Brenne, *v.* burn, 12, 23, 68, 111.
Brente, *v.* burn, 153, 164; burnt (*p. t.*), 133, 163.
Brether, *s. pl.* brothers, brethren, 93.
Brethereth, *s.* brotherhood, 192.
Brewe, *s.* brow, 228.
Bridde, *s.* bird, 73.
Bronde, *s.* brand, 215.
Brut, *s.* bruit, fame, 121.
Brydde, *s.* bird, 73.
Bryghtyr, *adv.* more brightly, 167.
Brynnand, *pp.* and *a.* burning, fervent, 49, 91.
Brynnynge, *s.* ardour, burning desire, 102.
Bryse, *v.* bruise, 85.
Bryth, *s.* birth, 216.
Bugle, *s.* buffalo, 178.

Burthyn, *s.* burden. Bear b. = be of consequence, 179. *See* Borthom.
Busshemonte, *s.* bushment, ambush, ambuscade, 215.
But, *conj.* unless, 6, 62, 64, 69, 179.
But if, yf, yef, unless, 12, 25, 28, 64, 139, 144, 148, 171, 180, 192, 195, 215, 233.
Butte, *s.* end, 228, 234.
By, *v.* be, 148.
By cause to, *phr.* in order to, 64.
Bycome, *v.* become, 93, 185.
Byfall, *v.* happen, occur, 100, 114; beseem, befit, 100.
Byforepassyd, *a.* bygone, 60.
Bygge, *v.* build, 93.
Byhald, -hold(e), *v.* keep, observe, follow, 69; hold, include, comprise, 93; regard, behold, see, 53, 59, 76, 98, 107, 113. Byholdant debonerly (*astrol.*) = looking benignly, in good aspect, 112.
Byhote, *v.* command, 63.
Byhoue, *v.* behove, 49, 55, 77, 86.
Byleue, *s.* belief, faith, 105.
By-negh, -th, -neth(e), *adv.* beneath, 88, 94.
Byrry, *v.* bury, 153.
Byse, *a.* busy, earnest, 65.
Bysek, *v.* beseech, 65.
Bysely, *adv.* earnestly, 169.
Byth, *v.* be, are, 134, 137, &c. &c.
Bythoghte, *v.* bethought (*p. t.*), 105.
Bytoght, *v.* committed, handed over, delivered (*p. t.*), 106. (See *N.E.D.*, Beteach.)
Bytokenynge, *s.* meaning, signification, 106.
Bytokne, *v.* betoken, 117.

Caas, *s.* chance, hap, accident, 78.
Cabeli, *s.* 85. *See note.*
Campany, *s.* 'champaign,' level ground, 129.
Can(e), *v.* know, learn, 137, 196, 216, 217; *with* to *and* inf., 131.
Candrede, *s.* hundred, district containing originally 100 townships, 184. (*N.E.D.* Cantred.)
Capytre, *s.* chapter, 135.
Cardiacle, *s.* an affection of the heart (heartburn or palpitation), 240.
Cariele, *s.* 85. *See note.*
Carle, *s.* fellow, 179.
Carlok, *s.* charlock, 27.

Glossary. 257

Carroble, *s.* 85. *See note.*
Cas(se), *s.* case, 193, 194.
Cast, *s.* device, contrivance, plan, 34, 38.
Cast(e), *v.* vomit, 26, 30, 31, 74, 152; throw off, shed, discharge, 28; throw, 106, 111; set, place, put, 14; *reflex.* (with *to*) strive (after), aim (at), 107; with *inf.* set oneself (to), make it one's business (to), 28, 38.
Castel(l)e, Castle, *s.* castle, 19, 111, 137, 174; tower borne on elephant's back, 216.
Catele, *s.* chattels, 172.
Cauee, *s.* cave, 95.
Cawtele, *s.* trick, stratagem, 35. (*N.E.D.* Cautel.)
Centiloge, *s.* "Centiloquium," a work attributed to Ptolemy, consisting of 100 aphorisms of astrology, 216. (*N.E.D.* Centiloquy.)
Cerculer, *s.* circle, circular figure, 94.
Certeyn, *a.* certain, 105. Certeynesse, *s.* certainty, 91, 93. (Very early instance.)
Cese, *v.* cease, 11.
Ceyte, *s.* seat, 94.
Chafe, *v.* heat, 25, 26; rub, 69 (*margin*).
Chalange, *v.* chide, rebuke, 49.
Chambir, *s.* chamber. Ch. worke = fornication, 'chambering,' 30.
Chambret, *s.* small chamber, 82.
Chamer, *s.* treasury, 186. (*N.E.D.* Chamber, I. 5.)
Chanoun, *s.* canon (*attrib.*), 193.
Chapiter, -re, *s.* chapter, 50, 249.
Charce, *a.* thin, scanty, sparse, 223.
Chare, *s.* chair, 154.
Charge, *s.* tax, burden, 13, 56; load, weight, 243. (Bear charge = be of importance, weight, consequence, 211.) *v.* bid, command, 160, 162; load, burden, 25; attach weight or importance to, regard, estimate (*N.E.D.* Charge, 20, a.), 176; also with *of* = reck of, care for, 176.
Charle, *s.* churl, 172.
Charnell, *a.* carnal, 194.
Chaste, -en, *v.* chastise, 160, 167.
Chastese, *v.* chastise, 161.
Chastise, *v.* rebuke, 113.
Chaunche, *s.* mischance, misadventure, 215.
Cheef(e), *s.* best or principal part, 9; *a.* chief, 47.
SECRETE.

Chef, *s.* chief point, main thing, 112.
Chefe, *v.* succeed, prosper, 61.
Cheff, *s.* head, category, 147.
Cheitifty, *s.* ('caitiffty'), captivity, 54.
Cheken, -yn, *s.* chicken, 28, 73.
Chelde, *s.* shield, 190.
Chere, *s.* face, 114, 230; expression, mien, 157, 189; manner, gait, 250; welcome, hospitality, entertainment, 163.
Cherte, *s.* love, affection, 34.
Chese, *s.* cheese, 178; *v.* choose, 9, 15, 17, 66, 107, 135, 151, 152, 214; pick out, recognise, 15.
Cheue, *v.* succeed, prosper, 112.
Cheyne, *s.* chain, 199.
Cheyre, *s.* chair, 160.
Chill, *s.* child, 194.
Chippe, *s.* fragment (of wood), 68; gesture ?, 235.
Chorl(le), *s.* churl, peasant, 12; *a.* churlish, 220.
Chose, *pp.* chosen, 149, 214.
Chyer, *s.* face, 233; *see* Chere.
Chyfe, *a.* chief, 122.
Chyldyr, *s.* (*pl.*) children, 144.
Chynchry, *s.* stinginess, 128. (*N.E.D.* Chinchery.)
Clanly, *adv.* constantly, 91.
Claundrynge, *pp.* (slandering), blaspheming, 205.
Cled, *pp.* clad, clothed, 55, 73.
Clen, *a.* clean, 63, 86.
Clepe, *v.* call, summon, 106, 107; name, 66, 73, 83, 84, 88.
Cler(e), *a.* clear, 7, 70, 84.
Clergeable, *a.* learned, 122.
Clergi(e), -y, *s.* learning, 3, 144, 217.
Clernes, -ys, *s.* clearness, 9, 122.
Clerte, *s.* brightness, lustre, glóry, 8.
Cleth(e), *v.* clothe, 69. Clethinge, -ynge, *s.* clothing, 55, 69.
Closure, 240; Closynge, 69. *s.* (*N.E.D.* Closure), term applied to the fontanels of the skull. *See* Shettynges.
Coddes, *s. pl.* testicles, 250.
Cold(e), *v.* become cold, 74; make cold, 25.
Colectyf, *a.* collective, 93. (Earlier than *N.E.D.*)
Colere, *s.* choler, 73, 74, 244.
Colle, *s.* coal, 196, 246.
Collodioun, *s.* 92. (For c. = Fertilodioun ?) *See note and margin.*

S

Colre, *s.* choler, 28, 219, 240.
Colurge, *s.* colure, 86.
Come, *v.* become, 60, 71.
Comend, *pp.* commended, 193.
Comfort, *v.* strengthen, confirm, 5.
Command, *pp.* coming, to come, future, 61.
Company, *s.* fellowship, harmony, 219; *v.* keep company, 29, *reflex.* 139. Companyed, 164 = travelling in company.
Compass, *v.* understand, grasp, comprehend, 21.
Compaygnable, *a.* companionable, 234.
Compayne, *v.* accompany, 121.
Compotistre, *s.* computer, 243.
Comprend, *v.* comprehend, 49.
Comyn, *a.* common, 147, 178. Comyne, -s, *s.* commons, community, 137, 142.
Comyte, *s.* county, 164.
Conable (= Couenable), *a.* useful, 104; fitting, suitable, 42.
Concauacion, *s.* cavity, 95. (*N.E.D.*'s earliest is 1623.)
Concewe, *v.* conceive, 193, 197.
Condit(e), *s.* conduit, 23.
Confit(e), -fyt, *a.* preserved, confected (tr. *confectus*), 81, 83. (Earlier than *N.E.D.*)
Conforte, *v.* strengthen, 241; cheer, encourage, 215.
Confortyf, *a.* comfortive, strengthening, reviving, cordial, 77.
Confurtabill, *a.* comfortable, comforting, cheering, encouraging, 215.
Coniurisoun, *s.* conjurement, conjuration (tr. *attestatio*), 50.
Connynge, *s.* knowledge, wisdom, 121, 138.
Conquere, *v.* get, gain, win, acquire, 130, 135, 140, 149, 209.
Consail, -ll(e), -eille, -eyll(e), *s.* council, 184; *v.* counsel, 127, 209; *s.* counsel, advice, 47, 64, 100, 127, 196, 209.
Consaillour, -eiller, -yller, *s.* counsellor, 46, 100, 107, 209, 213, 216.
Conseyle, *v.* conceal, 166.
Constabil, *s.* constable, bailiff, 213.
Constory, *s.* consistory, council-chamber, 58.
Constreyne, *v.* draw together (tr. *constringit*), 70.
Consuetude, *s.* custom, 249.
Contenaunce, *s.* demeanour, behaviour, 141, 178, 195; gesture, attitude, 235.
Conten(e), -eyne, *v. reflex.* behave, conduct, comfort, 54, 59; *tr.* contain, 5.
Content, *v.* contain, 42; *reflex.* refrain, abstain, 58; *pp.* contained, 49, 67, 98.
Contenu, *v.* continue, remain, 83.
Contrariouste, *s.* contrariety, diversity, 69. (*N.E.D.* Contrariosity.)
Contre(e), -ey, *s.* country, 56, 110, 171, 173, 178.
Contreue, -eve, *v.* contrive, 137, 178, 196.
Contyna(u)nce, -ence, *s.* behaviour, conduct, 69, 249; gesture, 234.
Contynow, -ue, *v. reflex.* behave, conduct, comport, 171, 174; continue, abide, 133, 166.
Convenabille, *a.* becoming, 11.
Couveyte, *v.* covet, 122.
Conynge, *s.* science, knowledge, 41, 47, 48, 53.
Cooke, *s.* cock, 221.
Coppyt, *a.* 234 = coped (*N.E.D.*). 'having the top or upper surface sloping down on each side like a coping'; or possibly = copped (*N.E.D. s. v.* and Cop, *s.*²), having a knob or protuberance.
Corage, *s.* heart, mind, soul, spirit, 16, 54, 102, 138, 147, 187, 241; heartiness, good-will, 17; courage.
Coragious, -aious, *a.* courageous, 111, 115, 228, 230.
Corn(e), *s.* seed, 60, 73; corn, grain, 17, 61.
Coronet, -yd, *pp.* crowned, 137, 179.
Corssife, *a.* stout, fleshy, 225. (*N.E.D.* Corsy.)
Corsyd, *a.* accursed, wicked, 183.
Corteyse, *a.* courteous, 211.
Corumpe, *v.* corrupt, 79, 91. Corypcioun, *s.* corruption, 58.
Cossine, *s.* kinsman, relative, 191.
Costage, *s.* cost, expense, 214.
Costeer, *s.* "a sitter beside," 139.
Costom(e), *s.* custom, 72; *v.* be wont, 110. Costomed, *a.* wont, accustomed, 68, 83, 111. Costumabli, *adv.* customarily, 144.
Cosyn(ne), *s.* kinsman, 163, 165.
Couenabill, -ble, -yable, *a.* convenient, suitable, appropriate, 67, 69, 82, 188, 238; useful, advantageous, 150.

Glossary. 259

Couerant, *a.* covering, enclosing, *i. e.* outer, exterior, 95.
Couertoure, *s.* covering, 212.
Coue(y)te, *v.* covet, 57. Couetable, *a.* 113. Coueytous, *a.* 57. Coue(y)tyse, *s.* covetousness, 113, 132, 210.
Covme, *v.* come, 199.
Couaunt, *s.* covenant, 175.
Countenance, *s.* behaviour, comportment, 12.
Coursid, *a.* cursed, accursed, wicked, 151.
Courteisly, *adv.* courteously, 211.
Couth(e), *v.* could, 128; knew, 174, 200; learnt, 217.
Couwardy, Covardy, -wardy, *s.* cowardice, 175, 211, 215, 224.
Covstoume, *s.* custom, 242.
Cowardnes, *s.* cowardice, 14. Cowardys, *a.* cowardly, 190.
Cowete, *v.* covet, 132. Cowetyse, *s.* covetousness, 156, 210.
Cowna(u)nte, *s.* covenant, 144, 200.
Cowth(e), *v.* knew, 145.
Creacion, *s.* creature, 114.
Crop(p)e, *s.* top or "head" of tree or herb, topmost or upper branch, 27, 73, 80.
Crowel, Cruwel, Crwel, *a.* cruel, 138, 174, 199. Cruwlte, *s.* cruelty, 181.
Cryspe, *a.* curly, 230; *v.* curl, 236.
Cucurbit, *s.* 73. *See note.*
Culuer(e), *s.* dove, 212, 245.
Cumpas, *s.* compass, 223.
Cun, Cvne, *v.* 'con,' learn, 137, 144. Cun or con thank(s), 188 = express or offer thanks. (*N.E.D.* Con, *v*¹ 4. a.)
Cvnnynge, *s.* wisdom, 148, 149.
Cuntre, *s.* country, 13.
Cure, *s.* care, anxiety, 139, 141, 158. Have (take) no c. = not to care, have no liking or desire (constr. with *of* or *to* and inf.), 158, 178, 179, 190; (with *that* ...) 172.
Curious, *a.* zealous, 107. Curio(u)site, -yte, *s.* anxiety, 58, 92.
Curlyour, *s.* curlew? 221.
Cursly, *adv.* cursedly, wickedly, 166.
Curtasye, *s.* courtesy, 59. Curtays, -eyse, *a.* courteous, 103, 212.
Custume, *s.* custom, 243, 249. Of c. = customarily, 139.
Cust(o)umet, -ent, *a.* accustomed, customary, 243.

Cytteseyne, *s.* citizen, 177.
Dalwe, *v.* delved (*p.t.*), 175.
Damagelees, *a.* without loss, 204. (Not in *N.E.D.*)
Dambre, *s.* dammar, a kind of resin, 85. (*N.E.D.* Dammar.)
Damoysele, 73; Damycelle, 191; -sell, 190; *s.* damsel.
Dampnabill, *a.* damnable, 132.
Dampne, *v.* condemn, 55, 169.
Darseim, *s.* 85. *See note.*
Daunger, *s.* danger. En daunger anent (a person) = within his power, at his mercy, 133. (*N.E.D.* Danger, *s.* I.)
Daunt, *v.* tame, 225, 230.
Daw, *v.* dawn, 153.
Dayen. A thre-dayen iornay = three days' journey, 200.
Deboner(e), *a.* courteous, gentle, kind, 39, 103.
Debonerly, *adv.* courteously, kindly, 103; benignly, 112.
Debonertee, *s.* gentleness, kindness, 48.
Debonure, *a.* kind, courteous, gentle, 64.
Deceit, Desceyt, Disceyt, Dysceyte, Disseyt, *s.* deceit, 19, 62, 168, 175.
Deceive, Discewe, Dissewe, Disseyve, *v.* deceive, 37, 188.
Deceyua(u)nt, *a.* deceptive, deceitful, 113, 116, 212. (*N.E.D.* has only 1393.)
Deceyuoure, Dysceioure, -ceyuoure, *s.* deceiver, 227, 233, 234.
Declyne, *v.* incline, tend (to), 230; turn away (from), 205.
Decresce, *v.* decrease, 196.
Decrewe, *v.* decree, 185.
Decyuant, *a.* deceitful, 116.
Ded(d), Dede, *s.* deed, 57, 129, 194, 211. D.-doynge = action, practice, 11, 165.
Dede, *s.* death, 47; *a.* dead, 20, 59.
Ded(e)ly, *a.* mortal = human, 5, 154, 177; that will perish, 49; deadly (poison), 64, 91, (sin), 159, 194; mortal (enemy), 210; deathly?, 223; *adv.* in deadly manner, mortally, 158.
Deed, *s.* death, 64. Take d. = die, 64; *a.* dead, 13, 29.
Defaut(e), *s.* lack, want, defect, deficiency, 67, 102, 129, 232, 237, 239; indigence, poverty, 137, 169; error fault, sin, 19, 138; absence, 5.

Glossary.

Defende, v. ward off, 206.
Defie, -fye, Dillie, -y, Difye, v. digest, 23, 25, 26. 68, 70, 71, 75, 80, 239, 242.
Defuyle, v. defile, 196.
Defy(e), v. digest. *See* Defie.
Defyne, v. decide, come to a conclusion, 156.
Dele, v. give, distribute, 41 ; deal (blows), 164.
Delfull, a. doleful, 169. Delfully, adv. 168.
Delicate, a. subtle, 22.
Delice, s. pleasure, delight, 54.
Delilege, s. 85. *See note.*
Delitable, a. pleasant, 67.
Delin(e)re, v. set free, 112 ; save, preserve, 101.
Delyce, s. pleasure, delight, 54, 57, 67.
Delycious, a. delicate, 226.
Delye, a. small, delicate, subtle (opp. to "greet," = gross), 88. (*N.E.D.* Delie.)
Delytabill, -ble, a. delightful, pleasant, 70, 76, 247.
Delyver, v. release, set free, 56 ; save, preserve, 80. 93, 161, 199 ; hand over, give, 66.
Delyuer(e), a. active, nimble, 212, 220, 221, 237, 240.
Delyuerannce, s. freedom (in evacuation), 220.
Delyuerit, pp. 227.
Delyuernesse, s. activity, nimbleness, 146, 227 ; ability, dexterity, 236.
Delyure, v. save, preserve, 80 ; give, 87.
Deme, v. judge, pronounce judgment on, 19, 140 ; abs. 167 ; decide, determine (a question), 185 ; decree, pronounce (that . . .), 185 ; deem, think, 63, 152; decide, come to decision, 34, 36 ; determine (between two theories), 154.
Demene, v. (= *N.E.D.* Demean, v.¹) *reflex.*, (also "be demeaned," 167, 210), behave, conduct, comport (oneself), 130, 138, 169 ; keep up, maintain, 199 ; (= *N.E.D.* Demean, v.²) make "mean," humble, lower, debase, 150 (very early instance).
Demelte, v. *reflex.* melt, dissolve, 243.
Demynge, s. judgment, opinion, 101.
Denunce, v. denounce, 185.
Denys, s. pl., tr. *decani*, captains of ten, 109. *See* Doien.

Departe, -perte, v. divide, 42, 72, 84, 88, 175, 207; sever, sunder, 159, 192 ; discern, distinguish, 149. Departynge, s. division, 65. Departid, -pertyd, pp. 115, 207, 223.
Depeynte, v. paint, 217.
Depnys, s. depth, 127. Deppyr, a. deeper, 169 ; adv. more deeply, 209.
Depute, s. deputy, 14, 133.
Dere, v. harm, 78.
Derke, a. dark, 5, 9. Derkly, adv. 5.
Derlynge, s. darling, 122.
Desceyt, s. deceit, 62.
Descreue, v. describe, 171.
Descase, s. distress, misery, 60.
Despend(e), -sc. *See* Dispend, -ce.
Despice, -ie, Dyspyce, -se, v. despise, 45, 61, 136, 151, 161. 209.
Despite, -yte, Dispite, s. contempt, 16, 34, 37, 56, 91, 179, 187, 200, 211.
Despitous, -pytous, Dispitous, a. contemptuous, 114 ; terrible, 35, 109.
Destourb(e), &c. *See* Distourbe. Destourbaunce, s. disturbance, 141.
Destreyn(e), v. strain out, express, extract by pressing or straining, 85 ; constrain, compel, oblige, 62. (*N.E. D.* Distrain, I. 5 and I. 4.)
Destroube, &c. *See* Distourbe.
Destru(e). -uye, -we. v. destroy, 101, 110, 131, 134, 135, 160, 163, 164.
Destruere, -uour, s. destroyer, 52, 213.
Destynour, s. fore-ordainer, predestinator, 65.
Det(te), s. debt, 168, 193, 194. Of d. = under obligation, 49.
Deuys, s. consideration, reflection, 101.
Deuyse, v. examine, scan, scrutinize, 178. (*N.E.D.* Devise, v. 12.)
Dewe, a. due, 35, 36.
Dewre, v. dure, endure, last, 27.
Deyn, s. *decanus*, captain of ten, 109. *See* Doien.
Deyne, v. deign, 173.
Dictamm, s. dittany, 76.
Diffame, v. defame, 11.
Diffence, s. defence, 36. Diffend, v. defend, 13.
Diffie, -y, Difye, v. *See* Defie, Defye.
Dighte, -yd, pp. dight, decked, attired ; 73 ; prepared, 83, 85.
Dilatable = Delytable, a. delightful, pleasant, 57.
Dingnite, s. dignity, 192.

Glossary. 261

Discewe, Disceyt. *See* Deceive, Deceit.
Disceyuable, 84; Disceyuous, 217, *a.* deceitful. (Deceivous not in *N.E.D.*)
Disclose, *v.* unclose, open, 142.
Discomfort, *v.* dishearten, discourage, 37.
Disconuenyent, *a.* dissimilar, 90.
Discordeynet, *a.* ill-regulated, 238.
Discrese, *v.* decrease, 28.
Discrewe, *v.* discern, 214.
Disese, Dyses(s)e, Dyssayse, -es(s)e, *s.* distress, trouble, 6, 7, 60, 103, 140, 142; hurt, 172; disease, 16; pain, 31; *v.* trouble, 26; harm, hurt, 160, 181.
Dishordeynyt, *a.* ill-regulated, 224. (*N.E.D.* Disordeine, -deny.)
Disobeyshaunce, *s.* disobedience, 6.
Dispence, -se, Despense, *s.* expense, 8, 103; *v.* (with), = grant special remission, relaxation, or exemption (to), 57. (*Cf. N.E.D.* Dispense, *v.* III. 9.)
Dispende, Despende, *v.* spend, 6, 8, 50, 156; *intr.* 128, 131, 187.
Dispysable, *a.* contemptible, 103.
Dissesoun, *a.* unseasonable, 16.
Dissolacion, desolation, *s.* 192.
Distinccon, *s.* division, section, 42.
Dist(o)urb(e). *Also* Destourbe, -towrbe, -troube, -trub(b)e, Dystorube, -trowbe, *v.* disturb, disorder, confuse, 101, 140, 147, 160, 178, 179, 209, 218, 241, 242, 246.
Distruour, *s.* destroyer, 52.
Do, *v.* put, 30; do on = put'on, don, 24; do away = put away, 89; do out = drive away, 52; cause (to be ..), 3; do to write = cause to be written, 61; do to witte = cause to know, 123, 131, *and see* 122; did assemble = caused to assemble,174; do crie, ponysshe, slee, wype = cause to be proclaimed, punished, slain, wiped, 17, 59, 82, 152.
Doghty, *a.* doughty, 175. Doghtynesse, *s.* 172.
Doien, *s. decanus*, captain of ten, 214. Also Deyn, Dyen. (*N.E.D.* Doyen.)
Dom(e), Doom, *s.* judgment, opinion, 99; doom, sentence, 158; jurisdiction, 208.
Don(e), Donne, Doon, *v.* do, 3, 26, 132, 139, 176, 187, 188, 195, 197, 209, 217, 231; cause, 61; *pp.* done, 58.
Doomesman, -ysman, *s.* 'doomsman,' judge, 94.
Dotdrat, *a.* doddered, 169.
Douceoure, *s.* gentleness, amiability, 189. (*N.E.D.* Douceur.)
Douly, *adv.* duly, 136.
Doume, *a.* dumb, 89.
Doun, *v.* do, 133.
Doungate, *s.* downgoing, setting (of sun), 89.
Doure, *v.* dure, live, 199.
Doutable, *a.* doubtful, 55.
Doute, *v.* fear, 38, 50, 55, 77, 78, 136, 140, 171, 197; *reflex.* 5; *s.* doubt, 49, 52, 63, 87, 206.
Dowe, *a.* due, 127.
Dowe, -wue, *s.* dove, 3.
Dowsett, *a.* 'dulcet,' sweet, sweetened, 29.
Dowtance, *s.* doubt, 156.
Dowt(e), *s.* fear, 6, 32; *v.* fear, 11, 14, 128, 152, 178; *s.* doubt, 8.
Doyne, *pp.* done, 135.
Draght, *s.* draught, curve drawn, 223.
Dragme, *s.* drachm, dram, 85.
Dred, *pp.* dreaded, 11, 12, 59.
Dred(e), *s.* dread, fear, 92, 170, 230.
Dred(e)ful(le), *a.* timid, 221, 223, 230. Dredfulnesse, *s.* 228, 230.
Dredy, *a.* timid, 38.
Drery, *a.* sad, gloomy, 76.
Dress(e), *v.* direct, guide, 92, 121, 138, 156; regulate, set right, 49; array, marshal, 52, 111, 197.
Dreyne, *v.* drown. Dreynte, *p.t.* 174.
Drobyld, *pp.* troubled, 100.
Dromyder, *s.* dromedary, 111.
Drond, *pp.* drowned, 193.
Dronk(e)lew(e), *a.* drunken, 36, 107, 116, 213, 234. (*N.E.D.* Drunkelew.)
Dronken, *a.* drunken, 218.
Dronkenshipe, 15, Dronknesse, 218, *s.* drunkenness.
Dront, *pp.* drowned, 193.
Dropping, *pp.* dripping, 192.
Drowe, *v.* drove, *p.t.*, 166, 180.
Druerie, *s.* pleasure, delight, solace, 160. (*N.E.D.* Druery.)
Drynche, *s.* drink, draught, potion, 244.
Du, *a.* due, 139; *v.* do.
Dud, *v.* did, 191.
Durant, *pp.* D.- the appetite = while it lasts, 241. Hence *prep.* during.

Dure, *v. intr.* last, 132, 160, 178, 213; endure, suffer, 237.
Dures(se), Duris, *s.* harshness, severity, 128, 151, 158.
Durke, *a.* dark, 176.
Dute, *s.* 139; *v.* 147, doubt.
Dyd, *v. (p.t.)* did. D. out = drove away, 52.
Dyen, *s. decanus*, captain of ten, 109.
Dyfformyd, *a.* deformed, 232.
Dylyuer, *a.* active, 220.
Dynte, *s.* dint, stroke, 161, 162.
Dyonysion, *s.* 31. *See note.*
Dyrke, *a.* dark, 74.
Dysceioure, -cewe, -ceyte, ceyuoure. *See* Deceyoure, Deceive, Deceit.
Dysceynous, *a.* deceiving, deceitful, 217.
Dyscomfite, *s.* discomfiture, 216.
Dyscorde, *s.* discord, strife, 235; *v.* dissent, disagree, 165; be at variance, 149. Dyscordaunt, *a.* quarrelsome, 235. Dysco(u)rdour, *s.* quarreller, wrangler, 115.
Dyscrewe, *v.* describe, 160.
Dyses(s)e. *See* Disese.
Dysharmyd (Disarmyd, 215), *a.* unarmed, 173. (Very early instances of *N.E.D.* Disarmed.)
Dyshoneste, *s.* dishonesty, 158, 187; *a.* dishonest, 172, 187.
Dysir, *s.* desire, 112.
Dysmesure, *a.* transgressing or exceeding due measure (*démesuré*), 102.
Dysobeiaunt, *a.* disobedient, 122.
Dyspite, -yce, -se, -yte. *See* Despice, -te.
Dyssayse, -es(s)e. *See* Disese.
Dystyncted, *pp.* 227 (very early instance).
Dyners(e), *v.* vary, 218, 238, 247.
Dyuyde, -yse, *v.* divide, 159, 243.

Echynge, *s.* tr. *species*, 94.
Edifie, *v.* build, 200.
Ee(i)re, -yre, *s.* air, 236, 237, 244, 245, 246.
Effocntim, *s.* euphrasy, 76. *See note.*
Efforce, *v.* strengthen (tr. *corroborare*), 85.
Eft, *adv.* afterwards, 82, 85, 106.
Egestioun, *s.* excretion, evacuation, 87. (Perhaps earlier than *N.E.D.*)
Egge, *s.* edge, 164. Egge tole = edge tool, 29.

Egh, *s.* eye, 222; *pl.* Eghen, -yn(e), 107, 128, 222.
Eght, *a.* eighth, 45. Eghte, *a.* eight, 84.
Egle, -yll, *s.* eagle, 15, 228.
Egre, *a.* sharp, sour, 73; eager, 229. Egrenesse, -yrnesse, *s.* sharpness, sourness, 98, 208.
Eighen, -yn, *s. pl.* eyes, 68, 128, 223.
Eighlidde, *s.* eyelid, 223.
Eir(e), *s.* air, 48, 142.
Eisili, *adv.* easily, gradually, 238.
Elcorenge, *s.* 84. *See note.*
Eld(e), *s.* age, 73, 80; old age, 42, 47, 58, 74, 75. Eldand, *pp.* growing old, 42.
Eldryn, *s. pl.* elders, 166.
Eldys, apparently *tr.* viventibus, living things, 95.
Elegantria, *s.* 84. *See note.*
Elles, -is, -ys, *adv.* else, otherwise, 4, 42, 48.
Emblemysh, *v.* blemish, mar, injure, 135, 139.
Emblissh(e), *v.* embellish, 35.
Emlege, *s.* 82, 85. *See note.*
Emparlement, 24; Emparlyng, 13, *s.* parley, talk, conference.
Empeirement, *s.* impairment, 187.
Emperie, *s.* empire, 122, 150, 151.
Emperien, *a.* celestial, empyrean, 47 (very early instance).
Empeyre, *v.* make worse, impair, 56, 189, 220; become impaired, 246. Empeyrement, *s.* damage, 196, 213.
Emplastre, *s.* plaster, 83.
Empouer, *v.* impoverish, 178. (*N.E.D.* Empover.)
Emyron, *v.* (so MS. for) environ, 153, 208.
Emyste, *a.* (= neathmost), lower (lip), 225, 228.
Enarmed, -et, -it, *pp.* armed, 139, 203, 216.
Encence, *s.* incense, 33.
Encherch, *v.* inquire into, 189. *See* Enserche.
Encheson, -oun, -eyson, *s.* cause, occasion, 64, 93, 113, 144, 145, 190. (*N.E.D.* Enchenson.)
Enchou, -chu(e), *v.* avoid, eschew, 131, 132, 135, 145, 158, 162, 187, 210, 215; with *inf.*, 140, 144.
Encombre, *v.* oppress, burden, 183.
Encrece, -sce, -sche, -se, *v.* increase, 86, 140, 209, 210, 244.

Glossary. 263

Endaunger, 133. *See* Daunger.
Endeyne, *s.* indignation, 179 (not in *N.E.D.*); *v.* deign, condescend, 166, 172, 190. Nendeyneth, 171, = ne endeyneth.
Endeynet, *adv.* condescendingly, 177.
Endeynous, *a.* disdainful? 228.
Endite, -itt, *v.* indite, write, 35.
Endly, *a.* final, 43, 53.
Endyngnacion, *s.* indignation, 189.
Endyte, *v.* indite, write, 106.
Endyth, *pp.* ended, 159.
Eneche, *v.* increase, 240. *See* Aneche. (Not in *N.E.D.*)
Enemyly, *a.* hostile, 167.
Enfebel, *v.* enfeeble, 148.
Enfeblissh, *v.* make feeble, enfeeble, 6, 26; become feeble, 26.
Enfleccioun, *s.* infliction, 6.
Enforce, *v.* (with *reflex.*) do one's best, be eager, strive, try, 6, 13, 22. *See* Afforce, Efforce.
Enforche, *v.* strengthen, 239.
Enformacion, *s.* instruction, 150.
Enforme, -fourme, *v.* mould, train (character, &c.), 6, 50, 57, 108, 110.
Engele, *v.* cool, 72, 95; *intr.* 86.
Engenderour, *s.* begetter, generator, 99.
Engend(e)rure, *s.* generation, birth, 45, 60, 64, 99.
Engendre, *s.* a person engendered, tr. *genitus*, 99.
Engendrynge, *s.* birth, 100.
Engrose, *v.* make gross (tr. *reddere grossiorem*), 80. (Early ex. in this sense.)
Engrotury, *s.* gluttony, 103. (This and two foll. not in *N.E.D.*)
Engrute, *v.* surfeit, glut, gorge (with food), 76. (Fr. *englouttir*.)
Engrutynge, *s.* gluttony, 44.
Engyn(e), *s.* intelligence, intellect, genius, 122, 127, 234; artifice, contrivance, device, 201; engine of war, 37, 174, 215.
Engynous, *a.* clever, crafty, cunning, 115, 116.
Enhanse, -aunce, -se, -hawse, *v.* exalt, enhance, 36, 144, 171; raise, 187.
Enheigh, -heye, -hye, *v.* exalt, extol, 47, 55, 57, 59, 86, 91.
Enioye, *v. intr.* rejoice, 70.
Enlargisshe, *v.* bestow bountifully, 7. (*N.E.D.* Enlargisse.)

Enlumyne, *v.* illumine, 7.
Ennoye, *v.* hurt, injure, 80; trouble, vex, 58.
Ennoynt, *v.* anoint, 180.
Ennue, *v.* injure, hurt, 140. *See* Ennoye.
Enny, *a.* any, 192.
Enorche, *v.* ? nourish (*see forms* Norche, &c.), 141.
Enourne, *v.* adorn, 56, 106, 140. (*N.E.D.* Anorn, Enorn.)
Enoynt, *v.* anoint, 70, 76, 83, 162.
Enpeche, *v.* hinder, 31. (*N.E.D.* Impeach.)
Enquere, *v.* inquire, ask, 108; inquire into, 137, 211; inquire after, seek, search for, 36, 49, 107; enquere of = examine into, inquire into, 17, 51, 60.
Ensample, *s.* example, 137; *v.* liken, compare, 60.
Ensens, *v.* incense, 81, 83.
Enserche, *v.* examine, 47, 197; study, 66; inquire into, 137.
Entencioun, *s.* intent, purpose, 10.
Entendant, *a.* diligent, careful, 103.
Entende, *v.* (*with* to) aim at, design, purpose, 36.
Entendement, *s.* meaning, purpose, 35; understanding, 9.
Entent(e), *s.* intent, purpose, 47, 102, 110, 151, 163, 178, 186; attention, care, 105, 110. Take (put, 103, do, 56) e. to, 60, give attention to, Give e. to (of), listen intelligently to, 105, 107; give care, heed, to, 108; busy oneself with, 110. Take (put, 47) e. to (*inf.*), take care to, 63.
Enterpretacioun, -cyso(u)n, *s.* interpretation, 42, 106, 114.
Entierly, *adv.* with whole heart, earnestly, fervently, 128, 199. (*N.E.D.* Entirely, 4. b.)
Entre, *s.* entrance, 241; admittance, 179.
Entremedele, *v.* intermix, intersperse, 123; interfere with, 206.
Entremyt(te), *v.* (with *of*), meddle with, take part in, 171; *reflex.* 171, 188. (*N.E.D.* Entermete.)
Entremyttere, *s.* busybody, interferer, intermeddler, meddler, 220.
Entrikyd, *a.* intricate?, 91.
Entrikynge, *s.* stratagem, trick (*circumventio*), 111. (*See N.E.D.* Entrike.)

Entrykour, *s.* deceiver, trickster (*circumventor*), 111.
Entyere, *a.* unfeigned, sincere, 169. (*N.E.D.* Entire, 10.)
Enuemynd, *pp.* envenomed, poisoned, 111.
Enuiroun, *v.* environ, 94.
Enuyous, *a.* envious, 114, 233, 234.
Enuyron, *v.* surround, 149, 153, 188, 208.
Eny, *a.* any, 6.
Equere, *v.* (*for* enquere), ask, inquire, 49.
Equinoccium, *s.* the equinox, 245.
Er, *v.* are, 41, 56, 57, 58, 111; *adv.* ere, 71.
Ere, *s.* air, 88; ear, 36.
Erste, *adv.* first, 209.
Ert, *v.* art, 2. *p. s.* 58, 64.
Eschaufe, *v.* heat, 58, 75.
Eschaunge, *s.* change, variation, 238.
Eschauntement, *s.* enchantment (tr. *incantamentum*), 42, 89.
Eschewe, *v.* escape, 6, 67; avoid, 69, 111.
Ese, *s.* ease, 152.
Espaunte, *v.* terrify, 179, 197. *Cf.* Espontous. (Not in *N.E.D.*)
Esperience, *s.* experience, 83.
Esperite, -iryte, *s.* spirit, 60, 62.
Esplaite, *s.* success, 203.
Esplete, *s.* end, issue, 157; *v.* bring to happy or prosperous end, alleviate, relieve, 158.
Esploit, *s.* success (good or bad), 136, 204; *v.* alleviate, relieve, 139.
Espolid, *v.* spoiled, despoiled (*p.t.*), 133.
Espontous, *a.* terrible, 111.
Esprit, *s.* spirit, 106.
Espyse, *v. for* despise, 110.
Essampill, -ple, *s.* example, 123, 158, 181.
Estable, *v.* appoint, create, 208; *a.* stable, steady, 187.
Estate, *s.* good or normal condition, 238, 243; also, good estate = good 'condition,' 23. *N.E.D.* I. *d.*
Estatue, *s.* statute, 136, 149.
Estature, *s.* stature, 233, 235.
Estoure, -owre, *s.* battle, war, tumult, 134, 144, 197.
Estra(u)nge, *a.* foreign, 173; strange, 187, 209. Estraunger, *s.* stranger, 163.
Estudy, *s.* study, 144.
Esy, *a.* (of food) light, digestible, 23.

Ethir, -re, *a.* each, 207. *See also* Euery ethre, *s. v.* Eueriche.
Ette, *v.* eat, 152; *pp.* Ettyn, 180; Ettynge, *s.* eating, 186, 237, 243.
Etyl(l), *v.* "ettle," desire, 108, 112.
Euche, *a.* each, every, 211.
Euen(e), -yne, *a.* equal, impartial (justice), 6, 14; equal, 28, 74, 88, 103; *adv.* impartially, 103.
Euenesse, -ys, Evnesse, *s.* evenness, 128; even balance, 246; equality, 245.
Euenhe(e)d(e), *s.* equal justice, impartiality, 62, 105; even balance, well-balanced state, 67.
Euenly, -ynly, *adv.* equally, 88, 241; temperately, 187; tranquilly, calmly; impartially, 128.
Eueriche, -y, -yche, -ylke, *a.* each, every, 62, 88, 90, 128, 137, 147, 195, 209; *indef. pron.* each, each individual (*foll. by of*), 146, 147, 209, 214; euery . . . othir = each . . . the other, 195. E. ethir, -re = each other, 191; each man, 238; also with *pl.*, each, 233.
Euerlaste, *v.* endure, last, for ever, 63.
Euyn(e), *a.* -ly, *adv. See* Euen, -ly.
Excercitacioun, *s.* (intended to tr. *excreationes*), 69.
Exody, *s.* Exodus, 203.
Expaund, *v.* expand, spread abroad, 140 (earlier than *N.E.D.*).
Expendour, *s.* spender, 108.
Expertly, *adv.* by experience, 87.
Expone, -oune, -owne, *v.* expound, explain, set forth, 6, 42, 87, 159.
Exrohand, *s.* rhubarb, 70. *See note.*
Exspeciall, *a.* special. In e. = in a special degree, especially, 193, 195.
Extent, *v.* extend, 148.
Eye, *s.* egg, 45, 88.
Eygh, *s.* eye, 145.
Eyr(e), *s.* air, 4, 16, 73, 88, 129.
Eyren, -rn, *s. pl.* eggs, 73, 78, 88.
Eyte, *v.* eat, 75.
Eyyn, *s. pl.* eyes, 229.

Facion(e), *s.* (a man's) make, 219, 226, 232.
Faco(u)nde, -uunde, *s.* eloquence, 41, 56, 140; skill, ability, 42, 219.
Fader, -yr, *s.* father, 104, 150.
Faghte, *v.* fought (*p.t.*), 197.

Glossary. 265

Faille, *v.* lose, 136; be unsuccessful, fail, 130.
Fairhede, *s.* beauty, fairness, 73.
Fall(e), *v.* befit, beseem, 55, 58, 70; fall out, happen, 99, 100, 143, 157, 161, 245; *pp.* fallen, 143, 161, 166.
False, *v.* make false, forswear, 18.
Fam, *s.* fame, repute, 195.
Famulier, *a.* familiar, 15. Famulyarite, *s.* homeliness, 10.
Fand, *v., p.t.* found, 48, 49, 99, 106.
Fantome, *s.* disdain, derision (*tr.* derisionis), 118.
Farre, *a.* far. On farre, 106, = afar off.
Farred, -et(e), *s.* forehead, 222, 223, 229.
Faste, *a.* fast (in prison), 175; *v.* confirm, strengthen, establish, 56.
Fatte, *v.* fat, fatten, 75, 82.
Faute, *s.* fault, sin, 201; *v. tr.* lack, 232, 233; *intr.* fail, 246.
Faylle, *v.* miss (a mark), 130.
Fayrhe(e)d(e), *s.* fairness, beauty, 69, 87; splendour, magnificence, 55.
Faytour, *s.* ? 'factor' (*N.E.D.* I. 2.), partisan, adherent, 97.
Feb(e)le, *v.* enfeeble, 44, 76, 79, 242.
Febille, *a.* feeble, 22.
Fecche, *v.* fetch, 16.
Fecicien, *s.* physician, 152.
Feder, *s.* feather, 221.
Feer, *s.* fire, 68.
Fcete, *s.* feat, 37.
Felawschippe, *v.* with *reflex.* join company, become companions, 104.
Felde, *s.* field, 151; *v.* feel, 142, 241; felt (*p.t.*), 217.
Feldman, *s.* countryman, rustic, 73.
Fele, *v.* feel, 58, 93, 95; felit, *p.t.* 183.
Fell, *a.* cruel, savage, 104.
Felle, *v.* feel, 131.
Fellon, *s.* villain, wretch, 168, 169.
Fel(l)ow, *s.* companion, equal, 189; tie, link, bond, 218.
Felonous, *a.* malicious, cruel, 233.
Femynyne, *a.* effeminate, 14.
Fenyd, *pp.* feigned, 55.
Ferd, *a.* timid, 35.
Fer, Fere, Ferre, *a.* and *adv.* far, 106, 157, 165, 173, 187, 208, 231. Fro ferre = from afar, long before, 157.
Ferforth, *adv.* = so far, to such an extent (that), 194. *N.E.D.* Far-forth.
Ferth(e), *a.* fourth, 45, 82.

Ferthyre, *a.* further, 161.
Fesisyen, *s.* physician, 44, 77.
Feste, *s.* feast, 73, 153, 243.
Festene, -tne, *v.* strengthen, make strong, 68; fix, implant, 34.
Fetare, *s.* feature, 190.
Fette, *s.* fect (*pl.*), 232, 235; *v.* fetch, 208; *pp.* fetched, 17.
Feure, *s.* fever, 78.
Fewtee, *s.* fealty, 183.
Fey, *s.* faith, 105.
Feynt(e), *a.* feigned, 11; faint, 139, 190.
Feyntise, -yse, *s.* faintness, cowardice, 111, 170.
Fic(c)he, *v.* fix, 195, 230.
Ficicien, *s.* physician, 152.
Filit, *v.* felt, experienced (*p.t.*), 183.
Fille, *v.* fell, befell (*p.t.*), 3, 34, 104.
Filth(e)hede, Filthet, *s.* filthiness, 138, 187, 212.
Fir, *s.* fire, 47, 84.
Fisiciane, -ien, *s.* physician, 20, 195.
Fisike, *a.* Arte f. = medicine, 144.
Fisnomye, *s.* physiognomy, 38.
Fixe, *a.* fixed, 21.
Flaure, *v.* smell, 247. (*N.E.D.* Flair.)
Flawme, *v.* flame, 112.
Fle, Flegh, *v.* flee, 20, 57.
Flee, *v.* fly (*volare*), 202.
Fleis, *s.* fleece, 163.
Fleme, *s.* phlegm, 245.
Fleme, *v.* banish, 9, 163. Flemer, *s.* banisher, 9.
Flesch, -ssh(e), *s.* flesh, 78, 117. F.-lyking = copulation, 74.
Fleschy, -shy, -(s)shly, -sly, *a.* fleshy, 70, 226, 228, 241; carnal, 192, 226, 228. F.-likynge, 73; *see prec.*
Fleshely, *adv.* carnally, 192.
Fleshnes, *s.* fleshiness, 117.
Flessh, *v.* flinch, 170. (*N.E.D.* Flecche.)
Fleu(e)me, -wme, *s.* phlegm, 24, 33, 70, 81.
Flevmatike, -etyke, *a.* phlegmatic, 86, 219.
Flex, *s.* flax, 239.
Fleynge, *ppl.* flying, winged, 153.
Flixe, *s.* flux, 31.
Flod(e), *s.* liquid, fluid, 68; river, stream, 74, 101; flood, deluge, 193.
Florsche, -ysshe, *v.* flower, bloom, 90, 108; flourish, 153; wave, brandish (sword), 152.
Flostrynge, *s.* excitement, elation; *or*

Glossary.

swagger, bluster, 129. (*N.E.D.* Flustering.)
Flow, *v.* fled (*p.t.*), 163, 174, 182.
Flume, *s.* phlegm, 80.
Focche, *v.* fetch, 111.
Folarge, Fole large, Folle large, *a.* extravagant, 52, 131; *s.* spendthrift, 131.
Folargesse, -yse, Fole(e) largesse, *s.* extravagance, 52, 128, 130, 131, 134.
Fole, *a.* foolish, 149; *s.* fool, 198, 235.
Foltisch, -ysch, *a.* foolish, 104, 110.
Foltynesse, *s.* foolishness, 114.
Folwe, *v.* follow, 60, 63, 90, 111, 117.
Foly, *s.* folly, 53, 117, 159; *a.* foolish, 54, 139.
Folych(e), *adv.* foolishly, 131, 175, 185.
Fond, *v.* found (*p.t.*), 4. Fonden, *pp.* found, 107.
Fool(e), *a.* foolish, 35, 218.
Fool(e) large, *a.* extravagant, 7, 8; *s.* extravagance, 8.
Fool largesse, *s.* extravagance, 8.
Fooly. *s.* folly, 235; *a.* foolish, 134.
For, 4; For that, 127, 193, 217; For as, 209, *adv.* because. For-alsmoche (mekyll, myche) -as (-that, 160, 196), *phr.* 65, 148, 198, 203, 216. For-thy = because, 92, 129; *also* for-thy that, 84, 122, 133, 150. For-why = because, 127, 128, 131, 138, 153, 159, 171, 172, 211; *also* for-why that, because, seeing that, 127, 149, 153. 169, 172.
Force, *s.* force. Of force = of need, needs, of necessity, necessarily, 65.
Forcible, *a.* powerful, mighty, 178.
Forclose, *v.* shut off, cut off, 136.
Foreyn, Foryne, *a.* outward (opp. to inward), 50 (tr. *extrinseca*), 147; external, 147; foreign, 135, 176; ? inferior, 60 (tr. *inferiores*), 88 (tr. *inferiorem*; *s.* ? foreigner, 57, 140.
Foreynte, *s.* 88 (tr. *inferioribus*, opp. to soueraynteʒ, *superioribus*). (This word, its apparent meaning, and the corresponding meanings of *foreyn*, are not in *N.E.D*.)
Forfete, *v.* commit fault or crime, 13.
Forgo, *v.* lose, 137.
Forgynge, *s.* smith-work, 100.
Forme, *s.* 33.
Forne fadre, *s.* forefather, 18.
Forsake, *pp.* forsaken, 143.
Forsey, *pp.* foreseen, 65.

Forte, *a.* brave, 155.
Forth, *adv.* onwards (time), 245.
Forthbere, *v.* advance, promote, 55.
Forþer, *v.* further, aid, assist, 63.
For-thy. *See* For.
Forwarde, *s.* first place, front, van, 148. (*N.E.D.* Foreward.)
Forwe, = four, 214.
For-why. *See* For.
Forwyt, *s.* foresight, prudence, 61.
Foryate, *v.* forgat, forgot (*p.t.*), 155.
Foryawe, *v.* forgave (*p.t.*), 181.
Foryet(e), -the, *v.* forget, 11, 136, 143, 211. 218; Foryetene, *pp.* forgotten.
Foryeue, -w(e), *v.* forgive, 181, 191; Foryewyn, *inf.* 189. Foryeue, *pp.* forgiven, 181.
Foryne, *a.* foreign, 135.
Founden, -yn, *pp.* found, 48, 87, 88.
Fourhede, *s.* ' fourhood,' ' fourness.' In f. = in *quaternario*; embrace f. = *complectuntur quaternarium*, 109.
Fourme, *s.* form, 48, 49, 90, 113, 218; *v.* form, make, fashion, 191.
Fourmer, *s.* former, creator, 191.
Fououre, *s.* favour, 182.
Fowle, *a.* foul, 35.
Frame, *prep.* from, 132.
Frauncesse, -ches(e), -is(e), -yse, *s.* liberality, generosity, 130, 131, 132, 136, 142, 144, 235.
Fre, *a.* free, open-handed, generous, 130, 227; liberal (sciences, &c.), 63, 144, 150.
Fredome, *s.* liberality, generosity, 128, 130.
Frekelit, *pp.* freckled, spotted, 195.
Frenesye, *s.* frenzy, 92.
Frenys, *s.* liberality, generosity, 130.
Frete, *v.* rub, 24.
Fro, *prep.* from, 91, 132, 140.
Frosshyn, *s. pl.* frogs, 79. (*N.E.D.* Frosh.)
Frote, *v.* rub, 24, 69. (*N.E.D.* Frot.)
Frouncet, -set, *a.* wrinkled, 222, 224.
Frusshe, *s.* frog, 227. (*N.E.D.* Frosh.)
Frust(e), *a.* and *adv.* first, 191, 193.
Frutur, *s.* fritter, pancake, 74.
Fryst(e), *adv.* first, 158, 201, 209; *a.* 128.
Ful(e), *a.* foolish, 131, 211.
Fulfille, -ylle, *v.* finish, complete, achieve, carry out, 8, 71, 83, 87, 88, 123, 158, 177, 201, 204, 211, 240; fill, 75, 199, 241; satisfy, satiate, 139.

194; make up for, supply (a want), 5, 49; make perfect or complete, 38.
Fullastyng, *s.* long life, 98.
Fulle-large, *a.* extravagant, 220. *Cf.* Fol(le) (Fool(e)), -large.
Fundemente, *s.* foundation, 175.
Furste, *a.* first, 191.
Fuste, *s.* aloes (but see *N.E.D.* Fust, *s.*²), 240. *See note.*
Fylthed, *s.* filthiness, 190.
Fynable, 10; Fynal, 48; *a.* final.
Fyne, *s.* make f. with = make one's peace with, by composition, or money payment, 204. (*N.E.D.* Fine, s¹. III. 8. *a.*) *a.* pure, 197. (*N.E.D.* Fine, *a.* 3.)
Fyr, *s.* fire, 68, 72, 84.
Fysnomye, *s.* physiognomy, 38.
Fyveth, *a.* fifth, 250.
Fywe, *a.* five, 197, 198.

Gader, -ir, *v.* gather, 29, 35, 82.
Galde, *s.* Chaldee, 207.
Gale, *s.* gall, 241.
Galengal, -an, *s.* galingale, 85. *See note.*
Galerne, *s.* the west, 153. Littré (*s. v.*). *Favonius* et vulgairement *galerne.*— Vent entre le nord et l'ouest. *See note.*
Gar, *v.* make. Gart, *p.t.* 105.
Gastefull, *a.* timid, 221.
Gasten, *v.* frighten, 215.
Gastnys, *s.* terror, 129.
ʒate, *s.* going-out, end, 98.
Gedder, -yr, Geder, -ir, *v.* gather, 29, 42, 128, 137, 174, 213.
Gefe, *v.* give, 47.
Gemeals, *s.* constellation Gemini, 99.
Genlogi, *s.* genealogy, 135 (*margin*).
Gentcrie, *s.* nobility, 153.
Gentile, *s.* gentleman, 15, 144; *cf.* 133.
Gentrie, *s.* courtesy, 163.
Gerner, *s.* garner, granary, 142.
Gerte, *a.* great, large, 235, 248.
Gestes, *s. pl.* 'gesta Romanorum,' 178.
Gete, *s.* goat, 27.
Gete, *v.* get, 176.
Geten(e), 10, Gette, 158, Get(t)yn, 53, 98, 102, 150; *pp.* got, gotten. Also Gette, *p.t.* 176. Gettyn, *inf.* 206.
Geue, *v.* give, 56, 99 and *passim.*
Geuer, *s.* giver, 88. Geuyn, *pp.* given, 83.

Gewmatry, *s.* geometry, 42.
Gide, *s.* and *v.* guide, 121, 127, 184, 194.
Gildyn, *a.* golden, 153. Gilti, *a.* guilty, 169.
Giloure, *s.* beguiler, deceiver, 233.
Glad, *v.* gladden, 69, 140.
Glysinynge, *pp.* glistening, 223.
Gome, *s.* gum, 69, 228.
Gon(n)e, Goone, *v. inf.* go, 199, 200, 201, 215.
Gonne, *s.* gun, 37.
Goodly, *adv.* well, 137. Goodnes, *s.* prosperity, 199.
Goot, *s.* goat, 35.
Goschauke, *s.* goshawk, 230.
Gostely, *a.* ghostly, spiritual, 191.
Got, *s.* goat, 35.
Goten, *pp.* gotten, got, 197.
Gouernaill(c), -ayll, *s.* governance, government, 53, 100, 107, 108, 109, 130.
Gouernoure, *s.* government, 122.
Gounour, *s.* governor, 94.
Goute, *s.* gout (tr. *gutam*), 77.
Gracis, *s. pl.* thanks, 5.
Gravnde-syrc, Graunt-sire, *s.* grandsire, 129, 171.
Graunge, *s.* grange, barn, 142.
Grecans, -ys, *s.* Greeks, 122, 129.
Grece, *s.* grease, 75.
Gree, *s.* step, degree, 112. *But see note.*
Greet, *a.* great, 28, 82; (of food), gross, 78.
Grefhound, *s.* greyhound, 174.
Gregeis, -eys, *s.* Greeks, 47, 83. Gregeys, a Greek, 77.
Grene, *a.* (of wine) immature, 244.
Grennes(se), *s.* greenness, sappiness, 29, 30 (tr. *pinguedo*).
Grestis, *a.* greatest, 204.
Gret(e), *a.* great, 3, 4, 100, 170; (of food) gross, 23, 68.
Grete, *s.* greeting, salutation (a nonsense version drawn from *salutantibus respondere*, 53).
Gretly, *adv.* greatly, 4, 33, 57.
Gretnesse, -nys, *s.* amount, size, quantity, 77, 228.
Grotte, *a.* great, 191. Gretter(e), -yr greater, 69; more grettyr, 186, 200. Grettist, -yste, greatest, 3, 35, 213.
Greuance, -aunce, *s.* hurt, harm, 243; severity, 196.

Greuant, *a.* painful, 115.
Greue, -ve, *s.* mischief, harm, 17; *v.* grieve, harm, 23, 70.
Grew, *a.* Greek, 49. *Cf.* Gru.
Grew(e), *v.* grow, 57, 74, 86, 103; grieve, hurt, 170, 241.
Grewos, *a.* grievous, 160.
Greyne, *s.* grain, seed, 77, 85.
Gromell, *s.* gromwell, 77.
Grounde, -own(d)e, *s.* base, bottom, 35, 70, 102; ground, 174, 204; fundamental principle, 111.
Gru(e), *a.* as *s.* the Greek language, 154, 219.
Grysnesse, *s.* horror, fear, 153.
Guerdon, *v.* reward, 53.
Gurche, *v.* grudge, 188.
Guy, *v.* guide, 138.
Gyf(e), -ffe, *v.* give, 63, 99, 108.
Gyffand, *pp. pr.* giving forth, 82.
Gyfnesse, *pps.* for ʒifernesse = greediness, but apparently transl. of *uidere facit*, 91.
Gyldyn, *a.* golden, 148.
Gyloure, *s.* beguiler, deceiver, 227.
Gyltelcs, *a.* guiltless, 169.
Gyse, *s.* 'guise,' 'wise,' manner, 158.

Haatredyn, *s.* hatred, 53. *See* Hatredyn.
Haberion, *s.* habergeon, hauberk, 110.
Habound(e), *v.* 4, 33, 39; Habundance, *s.* 17, 33; Habundant, *a.* 100; Habundantly, *adv.* 7; for abound, &c.
Hafe, *v.* have, 173.
Halde, *v.* hold, 90. Haldyn, *pp.* held, deemed, esteemed, 56.
Hale, *a.* hale, sound, 42; good, sound (advice, &c.), 47.
Half, *s.* behalf, 60.
Halfe, *v.* have, 71.
Halowe, *s.* saint, 41.
Haly, *a.* holy, 41, 66; *adv.* wholly, 93; generally, 104.
Halynes, *s.* holiness, 41.
Ham(e), *v.* am, 122, 176.
Ham(e), *pron.* them, 137, 161, 187.
Hamely, *a.* tame, domesticated (tr. *domesticus*), 104.
Han, *v.* have, 13.
Happe, *s.* chance, risk, 29; *v.* happen, 34, 35, 138.
Hard(e), *a.* stingy, niggardly, 130, 131.
Harde, -dyn, *pp.* heard, 199, 206, 233, 234.

Hardi, Hardy, *a.* bold, brave, 138, 139, 163, 171, 187, 211, 233.
Hardynesse, *s.* fortitude, bravery, 37, 110, 170.
Har(e), *poss. a.* their, 129, 132, 137, 144.
Harne, *s.* brain, 98, 112. *Cf.* Hernys.
Haske, *v.* ask, seek, 159.
Haste, 180, = hast thou.
Hast(e), *v. reflex.* hasten, 198.
Hastely, -tly, *a.* hasty, 138 (226?); *adv.* hastily, 55.
Hasty, *v.* hasten, quicken, 105.
Hastyf, *a.* hasty, 55, 115.
Haterell, *s.* neck, 80. (*N.E.D.* Hattrel.)
Hatredyn, *s.* hatred, 91, 135, 161, 248.
Haue, -ve, *v. reflex.* behave, comport (oneself), 138; bear a relation (to), 161.
Haule, *s.* hail, 198.
Haunge, *s.* haunch, 222.
Havyn, *s.* haven. H.-toune, 184, port.
Hauyng(e), *s.* wealth, property, 34, 94, 102, 104, 107, 108.
Haw(e), *v.* have, 144, 163, 169, 172.
Hawle, *s.* hail, 198.
He, *a.* high, 61.
Hechil, *s.* 'heckle,' comb for flax, 190.
Hedyr, *adv.* hither, 177.
Heelfull, *a.* healthful, 79, 80.
Heer(e), *s.* hair, 46, 221, 225, 250.
Hegh, *a.* high, 41, 55, 110. Heghnesse, *s.* highness, height, 41, 94.
Heght(e), *s.* height, 55, 163.
Hei, *a.* high, 231; *compar.* Heiere, 215.
Heiere, *s.* air, 219.
Heigh, *a.* high, 61. Heigh(e)nes(se), *s.* highness, 49, 92.
Hele, *s.* health, 29, 42, 66, 75, 92; benefit, profit, 61, 144; heel, 117; *v.* heal, 138, 161, 199.
Hel(e)ful(l), *a.* healthful, wholesome, 63, 78, 81, 92.
Helle, *s.* hill, 80, 110.
Helpeliche, *a.* helpful, 16, 23.
Hem, *pron.* them, 52.
Hemrolle, *s.* lobster, 244.
Henchekyn, *s.* hen-chicken, 73.
Hende, *a.* kind, 248.
Henemy, *s.* enemy, 204.
Henny, *v.* whinny, neigh, 89.
Henyouse, *a.* heinous, 160.
Hepe, *s.* heap, 136.
Her, *pron.* their, 13, 29, 52, &c.
Herbere, *v.* harbour, shelter, 99. (*N.E.D.* Harbour.)

Herbe(r)gage, *s.* shelter, 65; encampment, 110. (*N.E.D.* Harbergage.)
Herbrowe, *v.* harbour, shelter, 34, 216.
Herd, *a.* hard, difficult, 51.
Here, *s.* hair, 155, 221, 224. Here as, 219; *adv.* where; *cf.* Ther-as. *v.* hear, 58; *pron.* their, 11, 57; her, 64.
Heremyte, *s.* hermit, 169.
Herfore, *adv.* therefore, 81.
Herly, *a.* early, 178.
Hernoys, *s. membr. virile,* 81.
Hernys, *s.* brains, 85. *Cf.* Harne.
Hert(e), *s.* heart; courage, 37, 162; hearty affection, 36.
Herthely, *a.* earthly, 153.
Her(r)ust(e), Heruest, *s.* 'harvest,' autumn, 27, 28, 127, 238, 243, 249.
Herytaunce, *s.* heritage, inheritance, 159.
Hest, *s.* promise, 18, 19.
Hesyn, *pron.* (his'n), his, 211. *Cf.* Hissyn.
Het, *a.* hot, 71; *v.* eat, 152.
Hete, *v.* promise, 110. Hetynge, *s.* promise, 110.
Het(t)e, *s.* heat, 23, 75, 231, 242; *v.* heat, make hot, 80; become hot, 26.
Heued, *s.* head, 44, 69, 73, 97, 114.
Heuery, *a.* every, 163.
Heuye, *v.* make heavy, 80; be burdensome, 60.
Hew, *s.* head, 69 (margin).
Hewyn, *s.* heaven, 143, 169, 171.
Hey, *a.* high, 146, 231; *pron.* they.
Heyet, *pp.* exalted, 143.
Heyghen *for* eyghen, eyes, 225.
Heyght(e), *s.* height, 115, 153.
Heyly, *adv.* in a high degree, greatly, 170, 182, 193; loftily, 171.
Heynesse, -nys(se), *s.* highness, height, high estate, 127, 149, 151, 153, 169, 212.
Heyr(e), *s.* heir, 7, 134; air, 73, 74, 246; *v.* hear, 212.
Hide, *pp.* hidden, 93.
Hidlynges; in h. = in secret, 171.
Hidous, *a.* hideous, 245.
Hie, *a.* high, 97.
Hight, *v.* was called, 38.
Hir(e), *pron.* their, 11, 34, 62, 99.
His, *v.* is, 205.
Hissyn, *pron.* (his'n), his, 162. *Cf.* Hesyn.
Hit(te), *pron.* it, 137, 205.

Hodure, *s.* odour, 247.
Hoge, *a.* huge, 64.
Holdand, -ynge, *a.* (of food), binding, 70.
Hold(e) (Hollde, 148; Halde, 90), *v.* deem, consider, 47, 172; retain, remember, 234; (of food) bind, 70; *reflex.* refrain, 58; restrict, confine, limit (to), 72. Holde moche of = set store by, 151, 211; (without *of*), 156. Holde, *s.* stronghold, castle, 37; *a.* old, 238. Holde, -en, -yn (Haldyn, 56), *pp.* kept, observed, 52, 105; held, constrained, bound, obliged, under obligation, 5, 41, 49, 58; deemed, 99, 105, 138, 171, 187; made whole, healed, 220.
Hole, *v.* hold, 99.
Hol(l)e, *a.* whole, entire, 198; safe and sound, 174; whole, without defect, 233.
Hollow(e), *s.* saint, 121. *See* Halowe.
Holsome, *a.* wholesome, 32, 33.
Holte, *v.* hold, 207, 222.
Holy, *adv.* wholly, entirely, completely, 73, 81.
Homclynes, *s.* familiarity, 10, 13.
Homyste, *a.* upper (lip), 228. For *superl.* omest, = overmost, uppermost.
Honde, *s.* hand. Honde-crafte, *s.* handicraft, 217.
Honemente, *s.* ointment, 247.
Honest(e), *a.* seemly, 24, 240. Honestely, *a.* honourable, 58; *adv.* befittingly, 163.
Honged, *pp.* hanged, 198.
Honourablyte, *a.* honourable, 107.
Honurabilite, *a.* honourableness, 103.
Hooke, *s.* oak, 161.
Hoole, *s.* hole, 28; *a.* 'whole,' sound, healthy, 32, 41, 77; solid, 95; unbroken, 97.
Hooly, *a.* holy, 145, 162; *adv.* wholly, 63, 206.
Hoony, *s.* honey, 247.
Hoot(e), *a.* hot, 23, 33, 80.
Hore, *a.* hoary, grey-haired, 240; *v.* become grey, 24, 69.
Horibilyte, *s.* horribleness, 114.
Horsyn, *s. pl.* horses, 154, 155, 219, 230.
Hostynge, *s.* expedition, 204.
Houe, *v.* (owe), ought, 188.
Housbon(d), *s.* husband, 193.
Howe, *v.* (owe), ought, 156.

Howge, Hugy, *a.* huge, 111, 129, 174.
Hugely, *adv.* extremely, 216.
Hyd, *v.* hide, 55. Hyd(d)(e), *pp.* hidden, 84, 87, 105.
Hydoure, *s.* dread, terror, 216.
Hydousnesse, *s.* hideousness, 80.
Hydows, *a.* hideous, 153.
Hyest, *a.* highest, 94.
Hyght, *pp.* plighted, pledged, 62.
Hyneye, *v.* whinny, neigh, 97.
Hynes(se), *s.* highness, 101, 106.
Hynge, *v.* hang, 89.
Hyr(e), *v.* hear, 129, 139, 166, 225, &c.
Hyre, *s.* air, 129.
Hyt, *pron.* it, 48.

Iangelour, Ianglere, -oure, *s.* talkative fellow, 103, 115, 221.
Ianlynge, *s.* talkativeness, 211.
I-asked, 194; -blamyd, 172; -blyssyd, 159; -caghte, 195; -chafet, 229; -chargid, 122; -conquerid, 183; -deseruyd, 152; *pps.* asked; blamed; blessed; caught; chafed, heated; charged, commanded; conquered; deserved.
Ieneracioun, *s.* generation, 191.
Ientric, *s.* courtesy, nobility, 191.
Iere, *s.* year, 169.
Ieue, Iewe, *s.* Jew, 165.
If (Yf) al(l), *adv.* even if, although, albeit, 42, 62, 65, 87; if alle that, 60.
I-had, *pp.* had, 130.
I-haue, *v.* have, 215.
I-lernyd, 122; -likenet, -yd, 229, 230; -logid, 204; *pps.* learned, likened, lodged = encamped.
Ilk, Ilk a, Ilka, Ilke, *a.* each, every, 50, 57, 58, 70, 76, 77, 82, 87, 88, 90, 91, 92; Ilk (Ylk) oon, Ylkon, *indef. pron.* 42, 50, 58, 95.
I-lyke, *a.* like, 229, 238.
I-maked, *pp.* made, 191.
Inconvenient, *s.* inconvenience, 22.'
Infirmatyf, *a.* mistake for *informatyf,* 96. (The Lat. is *uis informatiua.*)
Inhabite, *pp.* inhabited, 164.
Inli, -ly, *a.* inland, (and therefore) remote, 203, 204. I.-streynthe = Mydstreynthe, 204.
Inlightyd, *v.* lightened (*illustrauit*), 96.
Innocent, *s.* an innocent, 53, 168.
Inobedience, *s.* disobedience, 50. Inobedient, -yent, *a.* 205, 233.
I-norshit, *pp.* nourished, 195.

Instaunce, *s.* urgency, earnestness, 184, 195, (frequent).
Into, *prep.* until, till, 140, 143, 156. Toke into his prysoner, 162, = took prisoner.
Inwijs, *a.* wise, prudent, 8.
Iogoloure, *s.* juggler, trickster, 234.
I-ordeynet, -yd, *pp.* ordained, 214, 216.
Iornay, -ey, *s.* day, 155; journey, 163, 200.
Iowell, *s.* jewellery, 162.
Iowse, *s.* juice, 84.
Ioynant, *a.* adjoining, 110.
Ioynture, *s.* joint, 70, 80, 225.
I-provid, -wid, 195, 218; -putte, 182; *pp.* proved, put.
Iren, -yn, *s.* iron, 95, 203.
I-richit, *pp.* enriched, 186.
Irous, *a.* passionate, wrathful, 115, 116.
I-sette, 241; -shewit, 209; -sprotid, 233; -stabelid, 170; -styrryd, 194; -thankyd, 248; *pps.*shewn; spotted; established, confirmed; stirred; thanked.
Issue, *s.* outlet, 68, 201, 241; outgoing (of money), 103.
Iude, *s.* Judea, 140.
Iue, *s.* Jew, 139, 165, 166, 167.
Iuster, *s.* jouster, 215.
Iustificacio(u)n, *s.* punishment, 18, 211.
Iustifie, *v.* sentence, condemn, 13; discipline, 22.
Iuwys, *s.* juice, 83.
Iuyn, *s.* June, 72, 81.
Iwe, *s.* Jew, 139, 165.
I-write, 128; -wyrshupped, 214; *pps.* written; worshipped = honoured.

Kalengera, *s.* 85. See *note.*
Kan, *v.* (= can), know, 17.
Karle, *s.* fellow, carle, 221.
Kastyng(e), *s.* vomiting, 75, 77.
Kaytefnesse, -ifnes, *s.* captivity, 11, 96.
Kede, *s.* kid, 32.
Keine, *v.* ('can'), know, 239.
Kele, *v.* cool, 26.
Kembe, *v.* comb, 24, 69.
Kende, *s.* kind, 90.
Kend(e)ly, *a.* kindly, natural, 71, 91.
Kenne, *v.* know, 42, 83, 86.
Kennynge, *s.* knowledge. Fleschly k. = carnal knowledge, 64.
Kennysman, *s.* kinsman, 106.
Kepe, *s.* thought, heed, care, 130, 155, 158, 218.
Keper, *s.* keeper, guard, 9, 215.

Kepynge, -ppynge, *s.* heed, care, 109; guard, watch, 215; preservation, 19, 69, 196.
Kerne, *s.* army of (Irish) kernes, 133; *v.* seed, 141.
Keste, *v.* cast (*p.t.*), 152, 198, 203.
Kid, *pp.* known, 19.
Kind(e), *s.* nature,
Kitte, *v.* cut, 192.
Know(e), *pp.* known, 18, 65, 143, 144.
Knowlech(e), *s.* knowledge, 208, 212; *v.* acknowledge, 186; know, 250.
Koghe, *s.* cough, 77.
Kokke, *s.* cock, 221.
Konne, *v.* learn, know, 21, 64.
Konnyng(e), *s.* knowledge, wisdom, 8, 9, 11; *a.* learned, wise, 19.
Kouth(e), Kowth, *v.* could, 34; knew, 122.
Kyde, *s.* kid, 27.
Kyen, *a.* of cows, tr. *bubali*, 78.
Kynde, *s.* nature, 7, 83, 135, 152, 216, &c. *a.*, natural, 106, 240.
Kynd(e)ly, *a.* natural, 15, 91, 181, 215; *adv.* naturally, 114.

Laat, *a.* slow, 223.
Lachesse, *s.* cowardice, 82 (due to tr. of *trepiditatem* as if *trepiditatem* assumed as the opp. of *intrepiditatem*).
Lad(d), *v.* led (*p.t.*), 154, 174, 217.
Laffull, *a.* lawful, 194.
Lagh, *v.* laugh, 58, 187, 247.
Laitynge, *s.* lightning, 141.
Lambren, *s. pl.* lambs, 74.
Lanceaunt, *a.* cutting like a lance, 111.
Lanceour, *s.* lancer, 215.
Lange de boef, *s.* (tr. *lingua bovina*), 84. See note.
Languyre, *v.* languish, 236.
Lap, *v.* wrap, 91. See Vmbylappe.
Larg(e), *a.* liberal, generous, open-handed, 7, 51, 130, 131. Largely, *adv.* 128, 130, 171. Largenes, *s.* 7.
Larges(se), *s.* liberality, generosity, 7, 50, 51, 58, 131.
Largete, *s.* largesse, liberality, 9.
Lasse, *adv.* less, 242. Lasse than, = unless, 132, 133, 137.
Lasson, *s.* lesson, 128.
Lastand, *a.* lasting, enduring, 57, 61. Lastandly, *adv.* immutably, 60.
Lat(e), *v.* let, 58, 67, 69, 73, 102.
Latly, *a.* slow (tr. *tardus*), 117; *adv.* slowly, 55; sparingly, 73 (tr. *parce*), 114.
Latnesse, *s.* slowness, 89.
Lutre, *a. compar.* more slowly. Also, More latre, 220.
Latyr, *adv.* later, latter, 135. Neuer the latyr, = nevertheless, 196, 218, 232.
Laue, *s.* law, 128, 135, 149.
Lawe, Lawgh, *a.* low, 88, 101. Lawnesse, *s.* lowness, 112.
Layne, *v.* conceal, hide, keep secret, 87, 100, 105.
Leaute, *s.* loyalty, 190.
Lechelorus, *a.* lecherous, 217.
Lecheour, -urer(e), -urre(re), *s.* lecher, 193, 230, 234.
Leddre, Leder(e), Leedir, -yr, *s.* leader, 108, 109, 214.
Leef tenaunte, *s.* lieutenant, deputy, 35.
Leel, *a.* loyal, faithful, 115.
Leet, *v.* let, 71, 100.
Lefe, *a.* dear, 247.
Leffe, *v.* leave, 106.
Leful(le), *a.* lawful, right, 39, 49, 104.
Lege, *a.* liege, 183, 184, 185.
Legeaunce, *s.* allegiance, 186.
Leghe, *s.* leaf, 80.
Leghere, *s.* liar, 115.
Legistre, *s.* lawmaker, legislator, 153.
Lei, *a.* low, 234.
Lekyn, *v.* liken, 108.
Lele, *a.* legal, tr. *legalis*, 96; faithful, loyal, 36, 106, 107, 109.
Lene, *v.* make lean, 2.
Lenger, *a.* and *adv.* longer, 19, 62, 67, 74.
Lengh(e), *s.* length, 72, 94, 115.
Lenghth, *v.* become long, lengthen, 74.
Lennesse, *s.* leanness, 115.
Lepre, *s.* leprosy, 76, 81.
Lere, *v.* teach, 53, 57, 83, 99, 100; learn, 59, 61, 63.
Lese, -sse, *v.* lose, 29, 128, 132, 136, 142, 190.
Lesse, *v.* lessen, make less, diminish, reduce, 55; become less, 69; *a.* less. L. world (werld) = microcosm, 88, 104.
Lest, *a.* least, 41.
Lesynge, *s.* 'leasing,' lying, falsehood, a lie, 10, 53, 54, 135, 157, 211; losing, loss, 248.
Lete, *v.* let, 18, 29; leave, 174.
Lete of, *v.* cease, let be, 'hold!' 182.

Glossary.

Letewary, s. electuary, 240.
Letil, v. make little, diminish, 107.
Let(te), v. hinder, obstruct, 29, 80, 160, 206; with *inf.*, prevent, 5, 31; leave, 174; *pp.* obstructed, 241.
Lett(e)rid(d), -yd, a. learned, 41, 63, 149.
Lett(e)rure, s. learning, 19, 47, 63, 122, 148.
Lettyn, 174, left (*p.t.*).
Lettynge, s. hindrance, obstruction, 16, 241.
Letuary, s. electuary, 246.
Letuce, -us(e), s. lettuce, 27, 73, 244.
Letwary, s. electuary, 240.
Leuand, *pp.* living, 59.
Leue, -ve, s. leave, permission, 6; leaf, 27; v. leave off, cease, 33, 70, 141; with *of*, cease from, 18; depart from, leave, 14; with *of*, pass from (a subject, 133, 160, 161; desert, abandon, 105; give up, forsake, 53; fail, neglect to, 49, 142; live, 47, 59, 67; believe, 132; leaf, form leaves, 27.
Leuefull, a. lawful, 194.
Leuenynge, s. levin, lightning, 59.
Leuer, *adv.* liever, rather, 171, 173, 177.
Lewe, s. leaf, 141, 245; leave, permission, 200, 201; v. leave, 181; forsake, give up, avoid, eschew, 135; cease, 141; depart from, 150, 163.
Lewte, s. loyalty, fidelity, 3, 19, 143, 175.
Lewted, s. loyalty, 144.
Ley, s. law, 105.
Leyser, s. leisure, 25.
Leythe, s. length, 163.
Liegeaunce, s. allegiance, 185.
Liflode, s. livelihood, food, subsistence, 67, 74.
Ligeaunce, s. allegiance, 6.
Ligey, s. liege, liege subject, 47.
Liggyne, a. (lying), flat, smooth, 224.
Light, v. make famous, illustrious, 63; enlighten, 206.
Lijf, s. life, 14, 19. Lijk, a. like, 38.
Like, Lyke, v. please, 105; *impers.* 34, 70, 101; *prep.* according to, 131, 137; l.- as, *adv.* even as, just as, 146, 147, 150, 159, 160, 183, 217, 247; according as, 140; as if, 127, 152, 229.
Likynge, Lykynge, s. pleasure, 73;

will, pleasure, 48; fleshly l. = copulation, 22, 74; a. pleasant, 82, 83, 114.
Litille, a. & *adv.* L.- & l.-, gradually, 26, 33. By l. and by l., 238, 243.
L.- kyng, s. the wren, '*regulus*,' 35.
L.- world = microcosm, 35.
Litterure, s. learning, 41.
Lof, s. love, 136.
Logge, v. lodge, encamp, 37.
Lokyn, *pp.* shut, enclosed, 71.
Lombe, s. lamb (*attrib.*), 78.
Lond(e), s. land, 34, 203, 213.
Long, *adv.* Wheron it was long, 34, = to what it was due or owing; *cf.* 'along of.'
Long(e), v. belong, appertain, 8, 16, 18, 21, 23, 142, 143, 150, 158, 172; befit, beseem, 5, 9, 11, 19, 134; become long, lengthen, 245; make long, prolong, 202.
Longe, s. lung, 77, 79.
Lo(o)re, s. instruction, 24, 38.
Lorchuppe, s. lordship, 135.
Lordand, a. ruling, reigning, 54.
Lorrei, s. laurel, 245.
Lose, s. name, fame, repute, 53, 54 (always 'good lose').
Losenge, v. flatter, 175, 177.
Losengeoure, -gere, s. flatterer, 129, 187, 188, 228.
Losengerie, -grie, -gry, s. flattery, 157, 187.
Loset, *pp.* lauded, renowned, famous, 160, 190.
Loste, s. loss, 151; lust, 181.
Losynge, v. flatter, 129, 176.
Losynger(e), s. flatterer, 129, 157, 175.
Losyng(e)rie, s. flattery, 175.
Lothe, v. loathe, 136.
Lou(e)able, a. laudable, praiseworthy, 53, 54, 56, 111.
Loue, s. love, 4, 59, 218; v. love, 66, 103, 140, 145, 167, 233; praise, 56, 57, 59, 63, 84; lower, make low, 245.
Louand, *pp. pr.* loving, 60.
Loue-drede, s. 12.
Louely, *adv.* (lowly), humbly, 163.
Loufand, *pp. pr.*, loving, 113.
Lough, a. low, 39.
Louynge, s. praise, 51, 56, 57, 63, 84, 106.
Lowable, a. laudable, praiseworthy, 54.

Glossary. 273

Lowe, s. love, 127, 135, 145, 167, 235; a. low, 189, 231; v. love, 122, 140, 145, 163, 171, 174, 189; make low, humble, 4.
Lowynge, s. praise, 140.
Luchrus, a. lecherous, 226.
Lust, v. impers., please, 20.
Lyckenys, s. likeness, 138.
Ly(e), s. flame, 222, 229, 230.
Lyege, a. liege, 185.
Lyer(e), s. liar, 115, 234.
Lyf(e), s. life, 67; v. live, 67, 237.
Lyflode, s. food, sustenance, 67.
Lyft(e), v., p.t., lifted, 105, 166.
Lyfte, a. left (side, &c.), 143, 214, 242.
Lyge, a. liege, 248.
Lygh, s. light, 148.
Lyght, s. light, 134, 205; a. easy, 130, 220, 222; delicate (meat), 241; v. lighten, reduce, 214; shine, 205; alighted (p.t.), 165, 168, 177.
Lyght(e)ly, adv. easily, 128, 210, 220, 231.
Lyk(e), Lykynge. See Like, -ing.
Lyme, -mme, s. limb, 22, 126, 230.
Lyn, s. linen, 82; line, lineage, 110.
Lynage, s. lineage, line, family, 105, 140.
Lyne, s. line, 91.
Lytel, -il, v. make little, reduce, 85, 102.
Lytill, 139; L.-world, = microcosm, 212; Lytillie, 146, adv. little.
Lytwary, s. electuary, 240.
Lyu, s. life ?, 99.
Lyue, -ve, s. life, 200, 202; v. live, 14. Lyuand, pp. living, 67.
Lyue-day, s. day of life, 139.
Lyueloker, a. livelier, 237.
Lyuene, s. living, life, 132.
Lyuer, -ure, -ver, -vir, s. the liver, 25, 31, 70, 80, 81, 241.
Lyuer, -uyere, s. liver, one who lives, 57, 139, 206.
Lyuere, s. livery, 133.
Lyvyng(e), -wynge, s. living, subsistence, 11, 134, 144.
Lywe, s. life, 137, 195; v. live, 237.

Maʒafege, s. 84. See note.
Mageste, -iste, s. majesty, 61, 136.
Makyd, pp. and p.t. made, 161, 162.
Mulancoly, s. black choler, 74.
Male, s. wallet, 105, 165.

Male, a. evil. Male talent = ill-will, 12, 175.
Malencolie, -y, s. black choler, 92, 245. Malencolien, -ik, a. melancholic, 86, 87, 220.
Mallerde, s. mallard, 74.
Manaunt, a. possessing, holding, wielding; able, strong, 155.
Maner(e), s. measure, moderation, 81; way, manner, 60, 210; pl. character, 140, 210, 220; kind, 61, 98, 105. Al maner (law, &c.), 136, 147; thes maner thynges, 134; dyuers maner mettis, 241.
Manerly, a. moral (tr. moralia), 62.
Mangole, s. mangonel, engine for battering walls, 111.
Maugrie, s. banquet, 153.
Manisand, a. menacing, 59.
Manyer, a. compar. more (in number), more numerous, 214.
Marcha(u)nd(e), -aunt(e), s. merchant, 13, 14, 57, 139, 140.
Marchaundise, s. merchandise, 13, 57.
Margarite, s. pearl, 41, 95.
Margh, adv. more, 42.
Marice, -is, -iʒ, Marriʒ, s. womb, matrix, 96, 114, 152, 232.
Massie, a. massy, massive, 221.
Mastyk, s. mastic, 31.
Mater(e), -ier(e), -ir(e), -y(e)r, s. matter, material, 10, 53, 74; matter, subject, 123, 133, 161, 191, 201, 215.
Matifoun, s. See note.
Matture, s. matter, 123.
Maynage, s. household, 136.
Maynteigne, -ene, v. maintain, 88, 139, 236. Mayntenyth, pp. 139, 144.
Mayntenaunce, s. 37.
Maynye, s. train, retinue, 141.
Mayster, s. master, 3, 34.
Maystow = mayst thou, 141.
Maystre, v. master, overpower, get the mastery, 68.
Maystri(e), s. mastery, 7, 138, 151, 198.
Mecche, s. (match), wick, 237.
Meddelite, pp. mingled, mixed, 222.
Mede, s. mead, meadow, 27, 243; meed, reward, 36, 168, 205; mead (drink), 29; v. reward, 107.
Medelit, pp. mingled, mixed, 220, 236, 242.
Medessin, -esyne, s. medicine, 195.
Medill, -le, v. 187; interfere, 209.

SECRETE. T

Medlid, *pp.* mingled, tempered, 6, 30, 39.
Medwe, *s.* meadow, 73.
Meene, Mein, *s.* mean, average, 51; *a.* 234.
Meite, *s.* meat, 74.
Meke, *a.* meek, 3; *v.* make meek, humble, 48; Mekly, *adv.* 41.
Mekel, -yl(l), *a.* and *adv.* much, 47, 48, 67.
Meld, *v.* mingle, engage (in battle), 129.
Mele, *s.* meal (food), 22.
Mell(e), *v.* mix, 85, 95, 97, 99, 118, 233. Mellit, -yd, *pp.*
Melyon, *a.* of millet. Greynes melyons = *grana milii*, 77.
Men(e), -ee, *a.* mean, 'nethyr grete ne smale,' average, 32, 39, 78, 114, 229.
Men(e)ly, *adv.* meanly, averagely, 39, 227, 234; modestly, 171.
Meney, *s.* train, retinue, following, 129.
Mengyd, *pp.* mixed, 114.
Mennyth, *v.* 3 *p.* admonishes (tr. *monet*), 194.
Meoule, *s.* 85, 'medulla.' *See note.*
Merabole, *s.* 85. *See note.*
Merciabil(l)e, *a.* merciful, 138, 225. Merciably, -cyably, *adv.* 60, 191.
Meritori, *a.* meritorious, 193.
Merroure, *s.* mirror, example, 151.
Meruail, -wele, *s.* marvel, wonder, 81, 201; *v.* 172; *reflex.* 153, 172. Mervellous, -ueylous, *a.* 82, 89, 100, 129. Mervelosly, -eilously, *adv.* 81, 129.
Merytorye, *a.* meritorious, 159.
Meseyes, *s.* 'misease,' trouble, misery.
Mespryce, *s.* mispraise, dispraise, 157.
Messa(n)ger, *s.* messenger, 213.
Mester(e), -ir, *s.* 64, need, 77, 82, 173, 175, 209. *Also* Mistir, Myster, *q. v.*
Mesurabill, *a.* moderate, mean, average, 229, 247. Mesurably, *adv.* moderately, temperately, 7, 67.
Mesure, -wre, *s.* and *v.* measure, 64, 157, 158, 238. Mesurly, *adv.* temperately, moderately, 67.
Met(te), *s.* meat, 152, 168.
Meuabill, *a.* fickle, changeable, 225.
Meue, -ve, *v.* move, 16, 190.
Meuemente, 187, Mevynge, 218, *s.* movement, 247.
Meure, *a.* ripe, 85.
Mewe, *v.* move, 198, 231.

Mewynge, *s.* movement, 216.
Meyne(e), *s.* retinue, train, following, 37, 58, 62.
Meyster, *s.* master, 106.
Mikel, *adv.* much, 41.
Mistir, *s.* need, 75. *See* Mester.
Mo, *a.* more, 66.
Moche, *a.* and *adv.*, 139, 151, 237, 247. Mochedell, *adv.* 'much-deal,' very, 230.
Moder, -ir, -re, -yr, *s.* mother, 54, 104, 152, 192.
Moiste, *v.* moisten, 75.
Moisti, -y, *a.* moist, 231, 238, 243.
Mone, 250, *for* mene, = men.
Monken, *a.* monastic, monkish, 193.
Monstrison, *s.* parade, review, 139.
Moo, *a.* more, 91.
Moote, *s.* mote, speck, particle, 89.
Mor(e), *a.* greater. Britane the m. = England, 184.
More, *s.* moor, 129.
Morwe, -owe, *s.* 'morrow,' morning, 32, 76, 77.
Morwyn, *s.* morning, 81.
Moste, *v.* must, 65, 131, 134, 144.
Mostnesse, *s.* moistness, damp, 246.
Motoun, -tton, *s.* mutton, 29, 74; sheep, 246; constellation 'Aries,' the Ram, 29.
Mountant, *s.* ascendant, 112.
Mow(e), *v.* may, can, 4, 15, 37, 58, 60, 61, 64, 226; be able, *prec.* by auxiliary (*shall* in every case), *e. g.* shall mowe (come, &c.), 32, 69, 163, 174, 188, 194, 199, 236, 241; (with *to*), 160.
Moyste, -ie, *v.* moisten, 82, 141.
Moysti, -y, *a.* moist, 127, 219, 237.
Mug-wode, *s.* mugweed, 31.
Muschet, *a.* musked (tr. *muscata*), 85.
Mych(e), *a.* and *adv.* much, 127, 129, 133, 150, 170, 240, 241, 247. *See* Moche.
Myde, = mid. In myde = *prep.* a-midst, 168.
Mydouernone, *s.* mid-afternoon (3 p.m.), 74.
Mydstreynthe, *s.* central stronghold, 204.
Mygh, *v.* might, 217.
Myghtful(l), *a.* mighty, powerful, 55, 117.
Mykyl(l), *a.* and *adv.* much, 74, 75.
Mylle, *s.* millet, 32.

Glossary. 275

Mylte, *s.* spleen, 23, 31.
Myn, *s.* 87.
Mynde, *s.* memory, 103, 163, 167, 211, 212; have m. = remember. 150, 154, 156, 167; *v.* remember, 154; *reflex.* 148.
Myne, *s.* mine, 89, 90; *v.* mine, 87.
Mynoure, *s.* miner, sapper, 37.
Myrt, *s.* myrtle, 81.
Mysattemperance, *s.* distemperature, uneven balance, 81.
Mysauentrous, *a.* deformed, 114.
Mysayse, *s.* uneasiness, anxiety, 172.
Mysbelewyn(g)e, *a.* misbelieving, heathen, 160, 199.
Mys-don, *v.* act wrongly, sin, 195.
Myse, *s.* misease, 134.
Mysericord, *s.* mercy, pity, 149.
Mys-fall, *v.* be unseemly, 52.
Mys-hope, *s.* despair, 110.
Mys-lade, *pp.* misled, 142.
Myspayed, *pp.* displeased, 142.
Mys-preyse, *v.* mispraise, dispraise, 157.
Mys-say(ne), *v.* speak against, gainsay, impugn, 155, 161, 181.
Myssais(se), -ayse, *s.* discomfort, misery, hardship, 137, 166, 169, 192, 199.
Mys-seme, *v.* be unseemly, 52; without to, 62.
Mys-speke, *v.* (with *of*) malign, 59.
Myster(e), *s.* need, 67, 73, 101, 106, 108, 109, 110, 114; *v.* need, 110; *impers.* 104. *See* Mester.
Mysturn, *v.* pervert to wrong use, 199.
Myth, *s.* might, strength, 66.

Nad(e), *for* ne had, had not, 153, 176, 178.
Nam(e)ly, *adv.* especially, 225, &c. (*frequent*).
Nas *for* ne was, was not, 198.
Nath(e) *for* ne hath, has not, 140, 158, 200.
Natheles, *adv.* nevertheless, 147.
Naue *for* ne haue, have not, 132.
Nawle, *s.* navel, 222.
Nedder, *s.* adder, 73, 74.
Neddy, *a.* needy, 137.
Ned(d)e, *s.* need, 5, 12. Wyth n. = with difficulty, scarcely, 152 (for Unethe); *v.* need, 131; be necessary, 154; *impers.* 87, 107, 155, 212.

Nedfull, *a.* needful, necessary, 5, 12, 13, 33, 147, 214; needy, necessitous, 52, 61, 131.
Nees, *s.* nose, 46, 115.
Negh, *a.* nigh, 86, 188; *adv.* nearly, almost, 41, 105; *v.* draw nigh, 74, 194, 245.
Nel *for* ne will, will not, 157, 162, 213.
Neme, *v.* name, 88.
Nendeyneth *for* ne endeyneth, deigneth not, 171.
Nese, *s.* nose, 97.
Nesh(e), Nesse, Nesshe, *a.* soft, 73, 139, 226, 227, 231; *v.* soften, make effeminate, 190.
Nesshly, *adv.* softly, 242.
Nest, *a.* nighest, next, 96.
Nethe. With n. *for* unethe, *q. v.* = scarcely, 180; (*cf. s. v.* Ned(d)e.)
Nethir, -yr, *conj.* nor, 153, 181, 189, 222. Nethyr . . . ne = neither . . . nor, 172, 194, 209, 229, 235.
Neuen, *v.* name, 102.
Neuer the latyr, *adv.* nevertheless, 196, 218, 232.
Newe, *v.* make (become?) new, 73.
Neye, Neygh, *a.* nigh, near, 163, 208; *v.* be nigh, near (to), 241; draw near, 175.
Neynge, *s.* neighing, 208.
No, *conj.* nor, 47, 63, 64, 82.
Nobeldi, *s.* nobility, 179.
Nobeley, -bleye, *s.* nobleness, nobility, noble nature, 52, 58, 113.
Nobelesse, -lles(se), *s.* nobleness, 147, 171, 181, 207.
Nobill(e), *a.* noble, 4, 204.
Nobilte, *s.* excellence, 203.
Noble, *s.* nobility, rank, 199.
Noght (Noȝth) *for* than (that, 209, 225), *phr.* nevertheless, 217, 239, 247.
Nolde = ne would, would not, 236.
Nombre, -yr, *s.* number, 60, 129, 178.
Nome, *s.* name, 88.
Non(e), Noo, Noon(e), *a.* no, 26, 118, 211, &c.; *indef. pron.* none, 211.
Noose, *s.* nose, 228.
Noose-thurl(le), *s.* nostril, 228, 234.
Norchynge, *s.* feeder, exciter, inflamer, *tr. fomes (veneris)*, 139.
Norisshe, Norryshe, Norsche, -she, -sshe, -ysche, *v.* nourish, feed, maintain, 20, 32, 60, 68, 71, 153; cherish, 37; promote, increase, 74, 81; rear,

Glossary.

nurture, 13, 142, 166; grow, 82.
Norschight, *pp*. 60.
Norshynge, -isshynge, *s*. nourishment, food, sustenance, 60, 80.
Norissha(u)nt, *a*. nourishing, 23, 93.
Nose-thrilles, -sterles, -strylles, -thurl-is, *s*. nostrils, 30, 76, 115, 208.
Notabilitee, *s*. notable instance, 201.
Note, *s*. nut, 29, 32, 78.
Nobelces, -les. *adv*. nevertheless, 59, 60, 62, 65, 79, 99, 107, 113.
Nother, *conj*. neither, 64, 104.
Notte, *s*. nut, 75, 85, 246.
Noughti, *a*. naughty, 14.
Noumbrable, *a*. mineral, 104. *See note*.
Noun certayn, 176, ? non-certain, uncertainty ?.
Nourtoure, *s*. nurture, 122.
Noy(e), *v*. hurt, harm, 32, 71, 76.
Noyand, -ant, -ynge, *a*. hurtful, injurious, 71, 79; mischievous, 104; malign, adverse (planet), 86.
Noyous, *a*. hurtful, injurious, 70, 71, 97; irksome, disagreeable, 81, 108.
Noysance, *s*. vexation, trouble, care, 112.
Nue, *v*. (Nuyth, 3 *p. s*.; Nuet, *pp*.) annoy, vex, grieve, hurt, harm, 152, 165, 243.
Nuons, *a*. noyous, noxious, hurtful, 212.
Nurche, -she, -ishe, -isshe, -yshe, *v*. bring up, rear, 166, 225; strengthen, nourish, 242, 245, 247, 248.
Nusant, *a*. adverse, malign (stars), 86.
Nve, *s*. trouble, vexation, worry, 140; *v*. annoy, 139; hurt, harm, 143, 160.
Nvons, *a*. noyous, hurtful, 143.
Nygh, *s*. night, 245.
Nyght, *v*. become night, 153.
Nynore, *a*. nine-year, 136. (Or can it be error for mynore = minor ?)
Nyowely, *adv*. newly, 193.
Nynesse, *s*. nighness, closeness, 235.
Nys = (ne is), is not, 140, 151, 180, 187, 188, 196, 224.

O. *prep*. of, 185, 221.
Obeiance, Obeissaunce, Obeyaunce, Obeysaunce, -shaunce, *s*. obedience, 6, 128, 131, 140, 176.
Obeisaunt, -ssant, -yaunt(e), -ysant, -yshaunt, Obieiaunt, *a*. obedient, 4, 48, 92, 93, 123, 135.

Obeisse, *v*. obey, 57; also *reflex*., 50.
Odeur, -ure, *s*. odour, 208, 240.
Oduret, *pp*. scented, 242.
Of-betyn, 79. *See note*.
Oft(e)-sithes, -sythes, *adv*. oft-times, 50, 60, 90, 110, 111.
Oghte, *v*. ought, 65; aught, anything, 134.
Oldennys(s)e, *s*. antiquity, 193. Old-nysse, *s*. old age, 134.
Oliphaunt, Ol(l)yfa(u)nt, *s*. elephant, 35, 111, 212, 216.
Olt, *v*. = holds, 3. *p*. 143.
Omange, *prep*. among, 59.
On, *a*. one, 3, 6, 34, 47, 82, 153, 192, 195. *Also* Oo, Oon(e).
Ondyth, *v*. ? undoeth, 139.
Oneste, *a*. honest, 192.
Onkynge, *a*. dethroned, 162.
Onlase, *v*. unlace, 173.
On(ne)wyse, *a*. unwise, 148, 157.
Onoynt, *v*. anoint, 75.
Onreuli, *a*. unruly, 160.
Ons, *adv*. once, 190.
Onsely, *a*. unhappy, 163.
Ontreueli, *adv*. untruly, 192.
Onyment, *s*. ointment, 75, 240.
Onys, *adv*. once, 15, 33, 56, 82.
Oo, *a*. one, 20, 34.
Oold, *a*. old, 36.
Oon(e), *a*. and *indef. pron*. one, 20, 47, 75, 147, 203, &c.; *a*. alone, 41, 47. That oon(e) . . . that othyr, 144, 165, 175, 207, 209, 228.
Oonly, *adv*. only, 133, 147.
Oonys, *adv*. once, 75.
Oot-mell, *s*. oat-meal, 244.
Oppyn(e), *a*. open, 136, 203, 240; *v*. open (the heart), 141.
Oppynly, *adv*. openly, manifestly, 136, 185.
Or, Or that, *adv*. ere, before, 20, 22, 24, 26, 80, 91.
Orche-3erd, *s*. orchard, 108.
Ordayne, *v*. arrange, array, marshal, 215. *See* Ordeyne.
Ordaynly, *adv*. in orderly manner, 129.
Orde, *s*. order, 83.
Ordeyn(e), *v*. set in order, govern, regulate, 10, 22, 138, 216; prepare, get ready, 152, 174; appoint, institute, enact, 13, 17, 193; prescribe, 20, 21; take 'order,' provide, take measures (with *for*), 17, 56; with *infinitive*, 38; appoint, choose, 63, 180; orduin,

decree (that), 13, 56, 155, 200; *reflex*. set oneself (to), 5.
Ordinant, *a*. able to keep order, 109.
Ordina(u)nce, -yna(u)nce, *s.* government, constitution, 4, 56, 62; 'order,' measures (for, against, of), 12, 13; demeanour, behaviour, 11; position, arrangement, 21; orderly arrangement, 37.
Ordyner, *s.* ordainer, 193.
Oribilite, *s.* horribleness, 233.
Orible, *a.* horrible, 110, 111, 215, 231.
Origenale, -al(l), *s.* fossil, 95, 104; cause, source, 111.
Orribill, *a.* horrible, 199, 235.
Ortrow, *s.* (= overtrow), confident belief, *cf.* Ouertrouth, -trow, 171.
Ost(e), *s.* host, 37, 46, 89.
Othyr(e), *a.* other, 138, 207, &c.; *conj.* either, or, 138, 180, 208, 215. Othyrwhile, ... othyr ... while, = sometimes ... sometimes, 194.
Ouer, *prep.* besides, 123, 137, 141, 143, 237; above,111, 148; ouer al, especially, 215; *adv.* too, 223.
Ouer-charge, *v.* overload, 25, 223, 240.
Ouer-do, *v.* overdo, carry to excess. Hence Ouerdoon, *pp.* excessive, 53; Overdoynge, *s.* excess, 53.
Ouer-drownynge, *s.* inundation, 59.
Ouer-lede, *v.* make subject, 135.
Ouer-lippe, *s.* upper lip, 228.
Ouer-passe, *v.* exceed, 52; go to excess, exceed, 67; *tr.* 108; transgress, 11, 131, 136, 139, 147; pass over, 141.
Ouerset, *v.* postpone, defer, 162; overrule, 129; *pp.* beset, 182.
Ouer-taken, *ppl.* ensnared, 192.
Ouer-trade, *v.* trod upon (*pret.*), 168.
Ouertrouth, *s.* overconfidence, overweeningness, 187.
Ouertrow, *v.* be too confident, 169.
Ouerture, *s.* opening, pore (in body), 239.
Ouerwel, *adv.* too much, 199.
Oughwhere, *adv.* anywhere, 12.
Ounly, *adv.* only, 143.
Oure, *s.* hour, 44, 45, 70.
Outake, *prep.* (= out-taken), except, 24, 245.
Oute, *a.* external (tr. *extraneum*), 68.
Outerly, *adv.* utterly (tr. *penitus*), 68.
Out-gone, *v.* go out, 201.
Out-kastyng, *s.* vomiting, 75.

Out-passynge, *s.* evacuation, excretion, 67, 76; departure, 96.
Outrage, *s.* excess, 81, 121; *a.* excessive, 8; *v.* exceed, go to excess, 22.
Outrageous, *a.* excessive, 9.
Outragously, *adv.* excessively, to excess, 67.
Out-rase, *v.* pluck out, 128.
Outre, *adv.* completely, entirely, 123.
Out-sayd, *pp.* uttered, 206.
Ouyr, *adv.* over, 11, 25.
Owe, *v.* ought, 8, 9, 15, 137, 141; owe, 207.
Owen, -yn(e), *a.* own, 96, 168, 191.
Oynement, *s.* ointment, 24, 33, 70, 82, 83.

Paisyble, *a.* calm, tranquil, 73.
Pament, *s.* payment, 133; pavement, 161, 242, 248.
Papelardry, *s.* hypocrisy, 136.
Parage, *s.* peerage, rank, 172, 187, 190.
Parcemyn, *s.* parchment, 217.
Parcenere, *s.* partaker, 219.
Parceue, -w(e), -eyve, *v.* perceive, 7, 26, 122, 136, 141, 209, 212.
Pardriche, *s.* partridge, 245.
Parfit(e), *a.* perfect, 21, 212. Parfitely, *adv.* 187. Parfyness(e), *s.* perfectness, perfection, 148.
Parlement, *s.* conference, 11.
Partable, *a.* divisible, 88.
Partie, -y(e), *s.* part, 11, 42, 64, 71, 88.
Partifelewe, *s.* (part-fellow), sharer, 219.
Passant, *a.* transient, 57. Passyng, *a.* surpassing, 21; *adv.* exceedingly, 181.
Pastour, *s.* shepherd, 94; pasture, 73.
Paueillon, *s.* pavilion, 129.
Payet, *pp.* appayed, satisfied, contented, 186.
Payne, *s.* punishment, 128, 155, 167; *v.* hym payneth = he tries, 154. *Cf.* Peyne.
Paynge, *s.* paying, 133.
Pees, *s.* peace, 83, 123, 164.
Peise, *v.* appease, 217.
Penne, *s.* feather, 221.
Pensyfe, *a.* pensive, thoughtful, 138; cogitative, 98 (*virtus cogitativa*).
Perceaunt, *a.* piercing, sharp, 111.
Perchemyn, *s.* parchment, 113.
Pere, *s.* peer, equal, 160; 187.

278   *Glossary.*

Pereill, -ell, -eyle, -ill, *s.* peril, 16, 21, 171, 194. Perelos, -ouse, *a.* 160, 213.
Perentele, *s.* 'parentail,' kindred, kinship, 163.
Pereugale, *a.* equal, 64.
Perfit(e)ly, *adv.* perfectly, 6, 51. Perfitnesse, 211.
Periodie, *a.* periodic, 102.
Perissynge, *a.* destructive, 246.
Perlesy, *s.* palsy, 76.
Perrerer, *s.* 'perrier,' an engine for throwing stones, 111.
Persand, *a.* keen, acute, 47, 48.
Persaynant, *a.* thoughtful, 103.
Persayue, *v.* perceive, 51.
Pers(c)hyd, *pp.* perished, destroyed, 59, 64, 169.
Perseyne, *v.* perceive, 54.
Pershaunt, *a.* sharp, pointed, 228.
Perneylosse, *a.* perilous, 132.
Peryode, *s.* period, 83; *see note.*
Pesablely, -eabely, -ebly, -ibly, *adv.* peacefully, peaceably, 4, 48, 57, 127.
Pesabilyte, *s.* peaceableness (tr. *mansuetudinem*), 114.
Pesable, *a.* (peisable), weighed, measured, 93. P. right = *insticia ponderata.*
Peyne, *v.* pain, 176; *reflex.* take pains, strive, endeavour, 32, 105, 108, 111.
Peyse, *v.* poise, balance, 17; *reflex.* reflect, 199; appease, 220 (*cf.* Peise).
Philesofre, *s.* philosopher, 3, 34. Philosophable, *a.* philosophic (tr. *philosophica*), 96. Philosophiant, *s.* philosopher, 88.
Phisnomye, -onomy, Physnomye, *s.* physiognomy, 20, 113, 219.
Piche, *v.* pitch (tent), 129, 215.
Piromancye, *s.* pyromancy, 42.
Pistill(e), -tle, *s.* epistle, 2, 127, 161.
Piteyous, -nouse, -yuous, Pitteuous, *a.* pitiful, compassionate, 12, 106, 138, 220. Pitously, *adv.* 17.
Plante, *s.* sole (of foot), 250.
Plantisoun, Pla(n)ntoun, *s.* plant, 92.
Plate, -tte, *a.* flat, 234.
Plauntoun, *s.* plant, 92.
Playn(e), *v. tr.* lament, 177; *reflex.* bewail, bemoan, 168, 172; *a.* smooth, level, flat, 79, 235, 236.
Plege, *s.* pledge, hostage, 175.
Plesaunce, *s.* will, pleasure, 11; delight, joy, 60.
Pleyne, *v. reflex.* bewail, bemoan, 103.

Pleynte, *s.* plaint, complaint, 168.
Plunche, *v.* plunge, 96.
Pollygony, *s.* polygonum, 30.
Polut, *a.* polluted, 194.
Ponticite, *s.* pungency, 98.
Ponysse, -ysshe, *v.* punish, 57, 59.
Poo, *s.* peacock, 104.
Porret, *s.* leek, 90.
Porteour, -er, -our, *s.* chamberlain, 97, 102, 179.
Portrewe, *v.* portray, 38.
Pouer(e), *s.* power, 51, 131, 169; *a.* poor, 60, 131, 140, 154, 173, 177.
Pouert, *s.* poverty, 52.
Pomme-garnet, Pomme-grene, *s.* pomegranate, 84, 244.
Poure, *a.* poor, 62.
Powdyr, *s.* dust, 154, 200.
Power(e), *a.* poor, 128, 169, 177.
Powerte, *s.* poverty, 131.
Poynte, *s.* point. In p. to = on the point of, 164.
Pray, Prei, *s.* prey, 162, 190; take in p. = rob, pillage, 183.
Preise, *v.* praise, 140.
Prere, *s.* 143. So MS. Probably for 'pere,' equal.
Prerogatif, *s.* special privilege, 19.
Preson, *s.* prison, 199.
Prest, *s.* priest, 160.
Prenable, *a.* approveable, worthy, 118.
Prene, *s.* proof, 67, 91; *v.* prove, 8, 20, 64, 87, 109.
Preuely, *adv.* privily, 42.
Preuyte, -eyte, *s.* secret, 42, 47, 50, 212.
Prewe, *s.* trial, proof, 216.
Preye, *v.* prey upon, rob, plunder, 183.
Preyer, *s.* prayer, 142.
Preyse, *v.* praise, 11, 140, 157, 176, 209, 235.
Pricche, *v.* prick, 31.
Prime temps, *s.* spring, 2, 27, 249.
Principaly, *a.* principal, chief, 44.
Pris, *s.* price, 240, 249.
Prise, *v.* praise, 140.
Prive, *a.* privy, intimate, 35.
Prodegaleous, *a.* prodigal, extravagant, 52.
Proesse, *s.* prowess, 180, 235; feat of arms, valiant deed, 205.
Profet, -ite, *s.* profit, 8.
Profete, *s.* prophet, 22, 66.
Prohemy, *s.* proem, preface, 249, 250.
Promove, *v.* promote, 249.

Propyr, *s.* private property, 130.
Prosse, *s.* prowess, 154.
Prou, *s.* profit, 213.
Proue, *s.* proof, trial, 209; *v.* prove, 155, 203.
Proute, *a.* proud, 235.
Providabill, *a.* profitable, 191.
Prow, *a.* brave, 115.
Prow(e), *s.* profit, benefit, 140, 157, 173, 177, 178, 180, 236; *v.* prove, 128, 136, 203, 213, 217.
Prowid, *pp.* proved, tried, 129, 144, 187.
Prowos, -ous, *a.* brave, 91, 176.
Prowte, *a.* proud, 133, 160, 205.
Pruesse, *s.* prowess, 91.
Prute, *a.* proud, 154.
Pryncypales, *s.* chief member, 85.
Pryue, *s.* genitals, 85; *a.* secret, private, privy, 44, 48, 88, 107, 134, 207, 212; confidential, privy, 58, 140, 213; timid, retiring, 212. In pryuee, iii, = privately.
Pryueli, -y, *adv.* privately, secretly, 57, 187.
Pryuyte, *s.* secret, 212.
Prywey, *a.* privy, 167.
Pulegye, Pulyol, *s.* mint, pennyroyal, 76. *See note.*
Purchace, -s(e), *s.* winning, gaining, 53, 213; *v.* get, gain, win, procure, 51, 67, 91, 96, 135, 150, 209, 210.
Purche, *v.* purge, 240.
Purches(e), *s.* gain, profit, 50; *v.* win, gain, 90.
Purpes, *s.* purpose, 177.
Purveaunce, -(e)yaunce, *s.* prudence, forethought, foresight, 12, 17, 61, 110, 155; provision, store, 17.
Purueyaunt, *a.* prudent, 138, 234.
Purvey(e), *v.* provide, furnish, 17, 32, 60, 61, 157; ordain, appoint, beforehand, 65; provide for, 92.
Pusaunce, *n.* puissance, 139.
Pusoun, *s.* poison, 195.
Pyment, *s.* a spiced drink, 75.
Pyne, *v.* (with *reflex.*), take pains, strive, 100.
Pystel, -ill, *s.* epistle, 122.
Pytous, *a.* pitiful, 55.

Quarel, *s.* 'quarrel,' bolt, dart, 110.
Quarre, *a.* square, 92, 228.
Quarreure, *s.* quadrature (*astrol.*), 112.
Quarteyne, *s.* a quartan fever, 32.
Quatreblee, *a.* quadruple, 82.

Queller, *s.* killer, slayer, 164.
Quenqueste, *s.* conquest, 171.
Queynte, *a.* crafty, cunning, 116.
Queyntise, -yse, *s.* cunning, craftiness, 101, 172, 229; cunning device, 50, 63, 216.
Queyntly, *adv.* cunningly, 167.
Quite, -yte, *v.* requite, repay, 18.
Quod, *v.* quoth, 165.
Quy(o)ke, *a.* lively, vivid, 223, 232, 236; living, alive, 208, 243.
Quylete, *s.* collection, 136. Fr. *cueillette.*
Quynche, *v.* quench, 205.
Quyrre, *s.* quiver, 110.
Quyte, *v.* requite, 18; *see* Quite.
Qweynte, *a.* cunning, crafty, 106, 107, 109.

Raane, *v.* ran (*p.t.*), 153.
Ra(a)se, Race, *v.* pluck, tear up, 91, 164.
Radir, -yr, *adv.* sooner, first, previously, 215; rather, 122, 183, 237.
Rambe, *s.* ram, 104.
Rappynge, *s.* striking, rattling, 97.
Rasynge, Raysyn, *s.* raisin, 74, 77.
Rauener, *a.* ravenous, 230.
Raunsone, *s.* ransom, 191.
Raveyne, *s.* 'raven,' rapine, 132.
Real, *a.* royal, 52, 56, 59, 63, 100.
Realte, *s.* royalty, 151.
Reame, *s.* realm, 210.
Rebell(e), *a.* rebellious, 35, 37, 108, 138. Rebelloure, *s.* rebel, 206.
Reboute, *v.* retire, withdraw, 246.
Rebuke, *v.* repulse, drive back, 204.
Reburgone, *v.* re-burgeon, revive, 59.
Rebutte, *v.* fall, 139.
Receit, *s.* receipt, 134.
Recepte, *s.* retreat, lair, 245, 246.
Recewe, *v.* receive, 243.
Receyte, *s.* receipt, reception, 96, 101; prescription, 84.
Rechand, *a.* effective, 106.
Reche, *v.* reck, 172; reach, stretch, 83.
Record(e), *s.* memory, 106; *v. reflex.* remember, 150.
Recreiet, *pp.* 'dead beat,' 165.
Redd(o)ur(e), *s.* rigour, strictness, harshness, 58, 59, 128, 160.
Rede, *a.* red, 229, 230; *v.* advise, 38.
Redresse, *v.* set right, put in proper order, 241; redress, remedy, correct, 158, 238.

Redy, *a.* ready, 234.
Reed(e), *a.* red, 29, 38, 92, 229; *v.* blush, 168.
Reeke, *s.* and *v.* smoke, 81.
Refeccioun, *s.* meal, repast, 25, 26; refreshment, 24.
Refete, *v.* cook, 245.
Refo(u)rm, *v.* restore, bring back, 204.
Refrayne, -eyne, *v.* curb, check, restrain, bridle, 5, 12, 147, 188; *reflex.* 22.
Refuyt, *s.* refuge, 192.
Regalite, *s.* kingship, 199.
Regnacioune, *s.* reign, 182.
Regne, Regnyne, *s.* reign, 3, 6; *v.* 3, 14, 148.
Reioiet, *v. reflex.* rejoiced (*p.t.*), 153.
Reissoun, *s.* reason, 194. Reissonable, *adv.* reasonably, 191.
Reisyne, *s.* raisin, 246.
Rekand, *pp.* smoking, 79.
Reke, *s.* 'reek,' smoke, 79, 84.
Reke, -kke, *v.* reck, 5, 157.
Reky, *a.* 'reeky,' smoky, 79.
Reles(se), *s.* relaxation, remission, 90; *r.* relax, lighten, remit, 57, 128, 139, 140; mitigate, soften, 53, 128, 134, 158.
Relewe, *r.* relieve, 143.
Religiousite, -ste, *s.* religiousness, piety, 43, 59.
Reme, *s.* realm, 8, 128, 132; *v.* remain? 157.
Remeable, *a.* moveable, 215.
Remember, *v. reflex.* remember, 175. Remembrid, -t, *ppl. a.* mindful, 127, 158.
Remena(u)nt, *s.* remnant, remainder, 83, 204.
Remene, *v.* recall, bring to mind, tr. *commemorare*, 56.
Remeue, -ewe, -oue, -owe, -ue, *v.* remove, 93, 102, 108, 109; refer, 147.
Renable, *a.* reasonable, 103.
Rengne, *v.* reign, 245.
Renne, *v.* run, 24, 33.
Ren(n)o(u)n(e), Renome, *s.* renown, 3, 47, 121, 123, 135, 137, 140, 144.
Renounet, *a.* renowned, 135.
Renoue, *v.* renew, 243.
Renunciatyf, *a.* renunciative (a meaningless misreading of *denunciativa*), 96.
'Repair, -ayre, *v.* return, 175, 179, 204, 237.

Reparaill, *v. tr. reparare*, 112. *See note.*
Repel(l)(e), *v.* recall (error), 12, 55, 138.
Rependant, *a.* repentant, penitent, 65.
Replevisshing, = replenishing, 29.
Repreef, -refe, *s.* reproof, censure, reproach, 14, 16, 22, 54.
Represent, *s.* representation, presentment, 98; *v.* 61, 62, 98.
Repreuable, *a.* deserving reproof, 66.
Repreue, *r.* reprove, 5; spoil, 9.
Reproue, -we, *s.* reproof, 130, 158; *v.* reprove, 188, 189. Reprowere, *s.* reprover, 189.
Resceive, -eue, -ewe, -nyue, *v.* receive, 71, 123, 132, 140, 162, 168, 172, 173, 243.
Resceyt, *s.* apprehension (tr. *apprehensio*), 114.
Resolue, *v.* melt, dissolve, 72.
Reson, -oun, *s.* reason, 21, 58. Resonable, *a.* reasonable, 71.
Resorte, *s.* escape, 153.
Ressayt, *s.* taking (of medicine), 82.
Ressayue, *v.* receive, 48, 58, 63, 77, 90, 96.
Resset, *s.* lair, retreat, 74.
Resseyt, *s.* receptacle, 114.
Retene, -tenue, *s.* retinue, 127, 204.
Retrete, *v.* return? 242; *pp.* drawn back, retracted, 222.
Reubarb(e), -bard, *s.* rhubarb, 70, 81, 85.
Reve, *v.* rob, bereave, deprive of, 38.
Reuenine, *s.* return, 175; (? reading).
Reuemeth, *s.* revenue, 134.
Reule, *s.* rule, 76, 113; *v.* govern, rule, 63; regulate, restrain, 70.
Reward(e), *s.* reward, 130, 158, 169, 205, 208; regard, respect, reference, 216; in rewarde of, 183, = in regard, respect, of; *v.* reward, 63, 144, 165, 171, 205, 213; regard, look at, 178, 190, 217, 222, 232; consider, reflect, 186; *intr.* look, 174, 230.
Rewe, *s.* rue (herb), 32.
Rewle, *s.* rule, 5, 11, 16.
Rewme, *s.* realm, 4, 5, 6, 7, 11, 16.
Reyne, *s.* rein, kidney, 31, 77, 222; *v.* reign, flourish, 38.
Reyn(n)e, *s.* rain, 16, 141.
Reyose, *v.* enjoy, 137.
Reyson, -onne, -oun(e), *s.* reason, 138, 147, 156, 158, 170, 188, 193, 243.
Reysonably, *adv.* 137.

Reysyn(ge), *s.* raisin, 28, 245.
Rialtee, *s.* royalty, 148.
Ric(c)hes(se) (*pl.* -essis, -ys, 6), Ricesse, *s.* riches, 10, 16, 60, 149.
Right as, *adv.* just as, 106.
Rightfull, Ry—, *a.* just, 105, 167, 169, 189, 207 ; right, proper, 240. Ryghtfully, *adv.* 167, 188. Ryghtfulnes(se), *s.* 167, 168, 172, 207.
Rightwis(e), -wys, Ryghtwys, Ryghwys, *a.* righteous, just, 5, 7, 57, 62, 66. Rightwisnes, Ryghtwysnes(se), *s.* justice, 3, 6, 33, 99.
Ripe, *v.* ripen, become ripe, 141.
Rist(e), *s.* rest, 75, 83 ; *v.* 83.
Riuale, *s.* bank, shore, 52. (The Latin is *amara littora paupertatis.*)
Roche, *s.* rock, 79.
Roelme, *s.* realm, 135.
Rogh(e), *a.* rough, 220, 225, 230, 235.
Roial, *a.* royal, 173, 200. Roialme, -elme, *s.* realm, 130, 132, 134, 135, 140, 142, 144, 148, 149, 198, 213.
Roialte, *s.* royalty, 151, 153.
Roob, *s.* robe, 151.
Rootte, *v.* rot, corrupt, 138.
Rosel, *s.* reed = Fr. *roseau*, 68.
Roset(t), *a.* compounded of roses, 31, 77.
Rote, *s.* root, 30, 53, 93, 135, 148 ; a measure, quarter of a Roman pound, 84, 85.
Roule, *v.* rule, 136.
Rousty, *a.* base, abominable, 136.
Rowte, *v.* 'rout,' snore, 23.
Royal, *s.* person of royal birth, 12.
Royalme, *s.* realm, 135.
Roynous, *a.* mangy, scabby, 31.
Rubbe, *v.* rob, 183.
Rull, *s.* rule, 193.
Ruly, *a.* able to rule, 136.
Rumour, *v.* murmur, 136.
Russhet, *a.* strewn with rushes, 242.
Ruthe, *s.* rut, rutting, rutting season, 225.
Ryall, *a.* royal, 148. Ryaltee, *s.* royalty, 148.
Rygh, *adv.* 'right,' very, 201.
Ryght, *a.* upright, erect, 233.
Ryghtful(l), Ryghtwys, -nes(se) ; *see* Rightful, Rightwis, &c.
Rymor, *s.* rhymer, poet, 157, 176.
Ryn(ne), *v.* run, 50, 70, 73, 89, 102, 151.
Ryue, *v.* rive, estrange, 93 ; ? 185.

Saad, *a.* sad (of colour), 232.
Saate, *v.* sat (*p.t.*), 168.
Sacrament, *s.* holy mystery, 50, 51.
Sadnesse, *s.* stability, seriousness, gravity, 15.
Sadyn, *pp.* said (to be), called, 201.
Sain, *v.* (3 *p. pl.*) say, 196.
Sak(k)e, *s.* sack, sack cloth, 198, 200.
Sal, *v.* shall, 61 ; Salt, 2 *p.* shalt, 111.
Sandell, *s.* 81. *See note.*
Sarpe, *a.* sharp, 155.
Sarteyn, *a.* certain, 193.
Sauacioun, *s.* salvation.
Sauage, *a.* wild, 244.
Sauand, *pl. pr.* saving, wholesome.
Saue but = but only, 188.
Sauely, *adv.* safely, 204.
Sauere, *s.* saver, preserver, 213.
Saucoure, -eure, -our, *s.* savour, 70, 187, 208.
Sauyoure, *s.* saviour, 161.
Sauf, *a.* safe, 26, 92.
Saule, *s.* soul, 50, 70 ; drunkenness, 73.
Saw(e), *s.* word, saying, 48, 65, 105 ; *v.* save, 142, 168 ; sow (tr. *seminare*), 53.
Sawen, *pp.* sown, 92.
Sawle, *s.* soul, 56, 70, 80, 96, 110, 112.
Sawlte, (probably) = swelled, 152.
Sawly, *a.* of the soul, spiritual, 96.
Sayd, *pp.* called, styled, 52, 80, 85, 92, 94. Saydyn, spoken, 207.
Sayne, *v.* say, *inf.*, 209.
Scap(p)e, (Skape, 15), *v.* escape, 153, 164, 198.
Scarcite, *s.* meanness, niggardliness, 130.
Scariole, *s.* 244 (Skariole, 73), lettuce. (Fr. *escarole*). *Lactuca Scariola*, the origin of garden lettuce. *See note.*
Scarry, *a.* lean, meagre, 239.
Scars(e), Skars, *a.* niggardly, mean, 7, 130 ; sparse, thin, 224. Scarsly, *adv.* 67, 157. Scarsenes, 249 ; Skarsnes, 7, 8 ; Scarsite, 131 ; Skarste, 8 ; *s.* niggardliness.
Schamefaste, *a.* modest, 229.
Scome, *s.* scum, 84.
Scomfite, *s.* discomfiture, 129 ; *v.* discomfit, 204 ; *pp.* discomfited, 129.
Scripture, *s.* writing, 4, 63.
Scryueyn, *s.* scribe, 46, 106.
Se, *v.* see, 21, 55.
Seau, *s.* pottage, 246.
Seche, *v.* seek, 28, 156, 202, 205.

Secre, *a.* secret, 84.
Secre(e), *s.* secret, 48, 50, 51.
Sede, *s.* seed, 77.
Seden, *pp.* said, 131.
See, *s.* seat, throne, 149.
Seek, *a.* sick. Seeknes(se), *s.* sickness, 22, 78.
Seete, *s.* seat, 174; *v.* set, seated (*p.t.*), 174.
Sege, Segee, *s.* siege, 162, 179.
Seke, *a.* sick, 198. Sekenesse, -nys, *s.* sickness, 202, 237, 240.
Seker, -ir, -yr, *a.* certain, assured, 48; safe, secure, 80, 111.
Sekerly, *adv.* safely, securely, 57.
Selde, Seldewannes, 157, Seldyn, 244, *adv.* seldom.
Seler, *s.* cellar, 61.
Self, -ue, *a.* same, 72, 78, 82, 83, 113.
Semand, *a.* seeming, 55.
Semblable, *a.* similar, 99.
Sembla(u)nt, *s.* appearance, outward show, 172, 236; likeness, 217, 232.
Seme, *v.* beseem, befit, be seemly, 55, 56, 58, 70, 106.
Semly, *adv.* in seemly manner, 73.
Semyng, *a.* seemly, 12.
Semynge, *s.* seeming, semblance, 11, 47.
Sen, *pp.* seen (to be), 55.
Sendall, *s.* 82. *See note.*
Send(e), *v.* sent (*p.t.*), 122, 150, 163, 181, 195; *pp.* sent, 183, 213.
Sene, *v.* see, 128; *s.* ('seeing'), sight, 168.
Senne, *v.* sin, 194.
Sentence, *s.* opinion, 156.
Septentrione, *s.* north, 28.
Septre, *s.* sceptre, 13, 148.
Sercle, *s.* circle, 63, 95, 96, 98, 145, 250.
Serement, *s.* oath, 143, 144, 185.
Sermon(de), *s.* speech, oration, 56; sermon, 183.
Serris, *s. pl.* seers, 196.
Sertayn, *a.* certain, 179, 196, 213.
Sertis, *adv.* certes, 236.
Seruage, *s.* servitude, 55.
Seruysable, *a.* kind, courteous, 115.
Sesaryn, *s.* 82. *See note.*
Sese, *v.* cease, 52, 74.
Set, *v.* set lytillie at, 146, set (settyn) lytill of, 139, 161, = set little store by; sette the lasse by, 139 = think less of.

Seth, *v.* 3 *p.* seeth, sees, 187.
Sethe, *v.* seethe, boil, 76, 85, 232, 240; digest, 71, 80; be digested (*decoqui*), 70.
Sethen, -yn, Sithen, Sythen; *adv.* since, seeing that, 49, 65, 152, 164; also, sithen that, 145, 152, 196, 236; then, next, after that, 128, 129, 152, 157, 201, 209, 217, 241, 242; since (the time that), 113, 148, 197; since that time, ever since, 146, 183.
Sett, *pp.* planted, 96. A shot at tr. of *planatina?*
Sette, *s.* seat, 174.
Settyn, *pp.* set, 161. *See* Set.
Setynge, *s.* position (tr. *situs*), 97.
Seuen, *v.* follow, 43, 54. *See* Sue.
Seuend, *a.* seventh, 45.
Seuerall, *a.* separate, distinct, 209.
Seuerally, *adv.* separately, 101.
Seuerance, *s.* distinction, difference, 180.
Seurte, *s.* surety, 132.
Sew(e), *v.* ensue, follow, 5, 77; pursue, 50; *see* Sue; shew, 166, 180.
Sewyn, *a.* seven, 153, 248.
Sextyl Mylee = *per miliaria sexaginta*, 110.
Sey(e), *v.* say, 71, 161. Seyere, *s.* sayer, 158.
Seyn, *pp.* seen, 199.
Seyne, *v.* see, 11; 3 *p. pl.* say, 7.
Seysone, -oun, *s.* season, 72, 74, 240.
Shaarpe, *v.* sharpen, 69.
Shadwe, *v.* shadow, shade, 79. Shadwy, *a.* shady, 78.
Sham(e)faste, *a.* modest, 194, 233.
Share, *s.* the 'fork' of the body, 31.
Sheche, *v.* seek, 245.
Shedow, *s.* shadow, shade, 176.
Sheede, *v.* shed, 61.
Shelde, *s.* shield, 206.
Shend, *v.* destroy, ruin, spoil, 70.
Shenshipe, -ype, *s.* destruction, 19, 110.
Shent(e), *pp.* killed, destroyed, undone, 105, 135, 160, 187, 195. *See* Shend.
Sheppe, *s.* sheep, 221.
Sherte, *s.* shirt, 71.
Shettynge, *s.* = closure of the brain, 24. *See* Closure.
Shewable, *a.* demonstrative (tr. *demonstratina*, 103; *judicialis*, 96).
Shildryme, *s.* 'shield-formation,' schiltrome, 174.
Sholde, -yn, *v.* should, 161.

Shorte, *v.* shorten, make short, 58, 89; become short, 245.
Shote, *s.* shot, 204; *v.* shoot, 111, 167.
Shrew, *s.* wicked person, 158. Shrewed(n)nesse, -etnesse, *s.* wickedness, 199.
Shul(le), -llyn, *v.* shall, 4, 11, 13, 14, 21, 205.
Shuldyn(e), *v.* should, 205, 216.
Shyde, *s.* piece of wood, 239.
Siege, *s.* seat, 200.
Sige, sigee, *s.* siege, 163, 174, 178.
Sigge, *v.* say, speak, 203, 209.
Signifiaunce, *s.* hidden meaning (tr. *enigma*), 50; token, sign, 135.
Sill, *v.* sell, 159.
Siller, *s.* cellar, 142.
Sire, *s.* lord, 217.
Sitee, *s.* city.
Sithen, *adv.* See Sethen.
Sixt, *a.* sixth, 250.
Skape, *v.* escape, 15.
Skariole, *s.* 73. See Scariole.
Skars, Skarsnes, Skarste. See Scars, &c.
Skole, *s.* school, 19.
Skowre, *v.* 'scour,' beat, 100.
Skr(e)(y)ueyn, *s.* scribe, 106.
Skyl, *s.* cause, 102.
Skyn, *s.* parchment, 49.
Skyrme, *v.* skirmish, 247.
Sla, *v.* 3 *p. s. pr. subj.* 61. Slaa, Slee, *v.* slay, 48, 162, 165; Slas, 88, Slees, 61, Sleth(e),18, Sleyth, 142, 143, 161, 3 *p. s.*; Slawe, 143, Slayn, 61, -nne, 160, 168, Slowen, 198, Yslayne, 162, *pp.* slain; Sleyne, 151, Slow(e), 61, 133, 153, 162, 163, 174, 175, 179, 197, *p. t.* slew.
Slaght, *v.* slaughter, 129, 142; also *attrib.* 129.
Slake, *a.* slack, loose, 221; *v.* become slack, flag, 110.
Slas, Slawe, Slayn(n)e, Sle, Slees. See Slaa.
Sleghte, *s.* 'sleight,' craft, cunning, 55.
Slekyn, *v.* extinguish, 79.
Slethe, *v.* See Slaa.
Sleuthe, -wthe, *s.* sloth, 68, 91, 228. Sleuthful(l), *a.* slothful, 104, 115.
Sleythe, *v.* See Slaa.
Slouthe, *s.* sloth, 14, 187; *v.* slight, 35.
Slow(e), Slowen. See Slaa.
Sluggy, *a.* sluggish, 23.

Slyme, *s.* clay, 191.
Smale (meat), *a.* delicate, light, *opp.* to grete = gross, 32.
Smertre, *adv. compar.* more smartly, more sharply, 180.
Smokke, *s.* fume (of wine), 218.
Smothe, *adv.* smoothly, softly, 177.
Snythe, *v.* blow (the nose), 189.
Sodan, -ayn(e), -eyn(e), *a.* sudden, 18, 157; Sodanly, -aynly, -eynly, Sud(a)ynly, *adv.* suddenly, 37, 110, 157, 162, 187, 196, 215.
Sode, *pp.* sodden, seethed, boiled, 246.
Softe, *adv.* softly, 187.
Soke, *v.* sucked (*p.t.*), 180.
Solempne, *a.* solemn, 194.
Solerne, *s.* the east, 153. (Littré, *s. v.* Solaire) Le vent d'Orient qui est dit en latin *solanus*, en français *solaire*. —Brise *solaire*, brise qui vient dans la direction des rayons du soleil. See *note*.
Soluble, Solyble, *a.* laxative, 27, 87.
Some, Somme, *s.* sum, total; in s. = altogether, 109; quantity, amount, 172, 173, 177.
Somyr, *s.* summer, 141; Somare, 249.
Sone, *adv.* soon, 7, 50, 57.
Sone, Sonne, *s.* sun, 4, 96; son, 5.
Sool(e), *a.* sole, only, 20, 34, 35.
Soore, *a.* sore, 205; *adv.* sorely, grievously, 236.
Sope, *s.* sop, 71.
Soper, *s.* supper, 71.
Sorefull, *a.* sorrowful, 199, 200, 217.
Sorfete, *s.* surfeit, excess, 238.
Sorsrie, *s.* sorcery, 199.
Sorte, *a*, short, 163; *v.* shorten, make short. Sorthyth, 3 *p. s.* 139. Sortely, *adv.* shortly, briefly, 178, 199, 200, 220.
Sorwe, *s.* sorrow, 60; sorwand, *pp. pr.* sorrowing. 106. Sorwfull, *a.* sorrowful, 105.
Sote, *s.* sot, 157; *v.* shoot, 176.
Sotel(le), -ille, -yl(l), *a.* subtle, acute, 3, 4, 106; delicate, light, opp. to gross (of meat), 68, 78. Sotely, -ily, *adv.* subtly, 51, 137. Sotilte, -ylte, *s.* subtlety, 127, 132, 134, 164, 212.
Soth(e), *s.* truth, 6, 38, 156, 161; *a.* true, 90, 99, 134. Soth(e)ly, *adv.* truly, 41, 65, 84.
Sothen, -yn, *pp.* sodden, 75, 76, 84, 114.

Soth(e)fast, *a.* truthful, 103, 116, 211, 234. Sothfastnesse, *s.* truthfulness, truth, 54, 88, 96.
Sothfull, *a.* true, reliable, 88.
Sotille, -yl(l), *a.* Sotilte, -ylte, *s.* Sotily, *adv.* See *under* Sotel.
Soudeour, -yor, *s.* hired soldier, 94, 208.
Soueran, -ayne, -eyne, *s.* sovereign, ruler, 189; *a.* principal, chief, 12, 147, 232; supreme, lofty, commanding, 17, 52, 97, 113, 207; sovereign (remedy), of supreme efficacy, 197.
Soueranly, -antly, -aynely, -eynely, *adv.* principally, chiefly, especially, 35, 135, 154; prevailingly, commandingly, 99.
Soule, *s.* sole (fish), 31.
Souleyn, *a.* sole, alone, 134.
Soun(e), *v.* sound, 73, 208.
Soune, *s.* son, 49.
Souple, *a.* supple, 70.
Soupyng, *s.* sop, 81.
Sowe, *v.* ensue, follow, 126.
Sowel, -wle, *s.* soul, 9, 91, 218.
Sowne, *s.* sound, 208, 215.
Spatill, *s.* spittle, 72.
Spece, *s.* species, 219.
Speche, *v.* speak, 146.
Spede, *s.* success, 112; *v.* speed, aid, help, succour, 56.
Spedynge, *s.* success, 112; *a.* successful, 235.
Spedfull(e), -phulle, *a.* expedient, useful, profitable, 4, 5, 15, 183; fluent, ready (of speech), 80.
Spere, *s.* sphere, 65, 86, 94, 95.
Spetil, *s.* spittle, 240.
Spice, *s.* species, kind, 208, 219. *See* Spece.
Spiritalte, *s.* spiritual quality (tr. *spiritualitas*), 97.
Spiritualy, *a.* spiritual, 47.
Spirynge, *s.* young shoot, sprout, 73.
Splekot, *pp.* speckled, 230.
Spor, *s.* spur, 165.
Spourge, *v.* sprout, shoot up, 243.
Spowse, *v.* espouse, 190.
Spowse-brige, *s.* 'spouse-breach,' adultery, 128.
Spraden, *pp.* spread, 208.
Sprak(e)lynge, *pp.* sparkling, 230, 244.
Spratle, *v.* scatter. Spratlit, *p.t.* 137.
Spryt, *s.* spirit, 66, 110.
Spyce, *s.* species, 87, 219; drug, 64. *See* Spece.

Spycirie, *s.* spicery, spices, 244.
Spyre, *s.* young shoot, 161. *Cf.* Spirynge.
Spyritte, *s.* spirit, 143.
Stab(e)le, -yle, *v.* establish, fix, place, 63, 92, 218; fix, appoint, settle, 60; appoint, set up (a person), 60, 92, 93, 97; ordain, enact (law, &c.), 113, 128, 178; confirm, strengthen, 140, 147, 148; promote, advance, 110. Stablyd, -yld, *pp.* fixed, appointed, 64; fixed (star), 66; steadfast, 100.
Stabely, -illi, *adv.* steadily, 170, 231.
Stabill, -le, -yl, *a.* lasting, enduring, 57; firm, stable, 62; stationary, 215.
Stablement, *s.* law, statute, 55.
Stablisse, *v.* establish, 54.
Stabylnes(se), -ilnes, *s.* stability, 112, 136, 176.
Stalworth(e), Stalworthy, *a.* strong, 71; firm, steadfast, 103; sound, healthy, 68, 69; strong (of meat or drink), 68, 80. Stalworthly, *adv.* stoutly, vigorously, 111; grievously, 52.
Staunch, *v.* subside, 90.
Stede (also Steyde, Stid), *s.* place, 4, 88, 106, 110, 112; throne, 56, 139.
Steepe-owt, *a.* projecting, 115.
Steigh, *v.* ascended (*p.t.*), 47. *See* Sty(e).
Stel(l)e, *s.* steel, 155, 197.
Stere, Sterne, Sterre, *s.* star, 42, 86, 196, 216, 217.
Ster(r)e, *v.* move, stir, 85, 115, 116; *reflex.* 98; stir, excite, stimulate, 14, 20, 69, 70, 73.
Steryn, *a.* stern, 174.
Sterynge, *s.* movement, motion, 66, 67, 73.
Stewe, *s.* bath, 69; *v.* bathe, 69; *reflex.* 69.
Stewynge, *s.* bathing, 69.
Steyde, *s.* place, 75. *See* Stede.
Sticke, *v.* stab, pierce, 153.
Stid, *s.* stead, place, 138. *See* Stede.
Stifly, *adv.* greatly, exceedingly, 153.
Stilli, *adv.* quietly, 141.
Stipticite, *s.* astringency, 98.
Stire, *v.* stir, move, 71, 79. *See* Ster(r)e, *v.*
Stirrand, *ppl.* as *a.* active, 104.
Stode, *s.* stud, 204.
Stodie, -y(e), *v.* study, 3, 7, 19, 21, 48, 98. Stody, *s.* study, 19, 47.

Stok(e), *s.* stalk, stem, 80, 98, 108.
Stokke, *s.* log, 239.
Stond(e), *v.* stand, 7, 20, 76, 79; consist, 7, 78; depend, rest, 20, 22.
Stoon, *s.* stone, 45, 87, 90; the disease, 77, 78.
Store, *v. reflex.* provide, supply, 150.
Storyer, *s.* historian, 100.
Stoup, *v.* droop, 234.
Stoure, Stowre, *s.* battle, 110, 134.
Stowp, *v.* droop, 233, 234.
Stowtesse, *s.* valour, bravery, 180.
Stowtly, *adv.* sturdily, bravely, 134.
Straak = struck (*p.t.*), 105.
Strache, *v.* stretch, 233.
Straght, *a.* straight, 233, 234, 235.
Strayt(e), *a.* strait, narrow, 23, 70.
Stree, *s.* straw, 239.
Streight, *v.* stretch, 69.
Strene, *v.* strain, 85.
Strengh, *s.* strength, 59, 96.
Strength(e), *v.* strengthen, 24, 28.
Streyght, *v.* stretch, 69.
Streynt(he), *s.* strength, 121, 134, 146, 170, 172, 179, 235, 246; stronghold, 174, 203, 204; *v.* strengthen, 241, 242.
Streyt(e), *a.* strait, narrow, 68, 129, 228, 234, 239; hard, difficult, 90. *See* Strayte.
Streythe, *v.* stretch, extend, 156.
Stronge, *a.* hard, difficult, 216, 239.
Stryf, *v.* strive, 41.
Stryngh(e), -ght, -gthe, -the, *s.* strength, 58, 60, 62, 67, 73, 82, 84, 87, 96, 105, 117.
Strynghe, -ghte, -gthe, *v.* strengthen, 44, 71, 82, 106.
Studia(u)nt, 21, 51, 63; Studyaunt, 19; Studier, 144, *s.* student.
Stuff, *v.* supply, equip, 37.
Sture, *s.* battle, 75. Apparently intended to translate *saturitas*, satiety.
Sturre, *v.* excite, stimulate, 80. *See* Stere, *v.*
Stuynge, *s.* bathing, 82.
Sty(e), *v.* ascend, 73, 80, 241, 243. Steigh, *p. t.* 47.
Stydde, *s.* stead, place, 146. *See* Stede.
Stydfaste, *a.* steadfast, steady, 146, 159, 201, 223.
Styfe stafe, *s.* so MS., but evidently = distaff, 190.
Stynche, *s.* stench, smell, 208.
Styngill, *s.* sting, 181.

Stynte, *v.* cease, 201; stopped (*p. t.*), 166.
Styr(re), *v.* stir up, excite, 56; stir, move (as medicine does), 87. *See* Stere.
Styrt, *v.* mount (on a horse), 105; mounted (*p. t.*), 106.
Su, *v.* follow, 209. Suante, *pr. pp.* following, 195. *See* Sue.
Suaille, 88. *See note.*
Subgite, -gyt, *s.* subject, 51, 55, 92, 100, 108.
Submyt, *v.* place in subjection, 146.
Subvencioun, *s.* aid, 249.
Sud(a)ynly, *adv.* suddenly, 162, 187.
Sue (Su, 209), *v.* pursue; (suyt, suet, *p. t.* 162, 179); accord, correspond, with, 218; follow, result from (Suys, 3 *p. s.* 51); act in accordance with, 93.
Sufferand, *a.* patient, 108. Sufferaunce, *s.* patience, 176; sufferance, 133; suffering, 169.
Sufferayne, *a.* = sovereign (remedy), 196.
Sufferynge, *a.* ? patient, 213.
Sufferyth, *pp.* suffered, 172.
Sufficlie, -ise, -ys(e), *v.* suffice, 69, 78, 178, 179.
Sufficiante, -ssent, *a.* sufficient, 53, 92.
Suffrayne, -reyn, *s.* sovereign, ruler, 159, 213; supreme.
Suffyceant, -ysant, *a.* sufficient, 79, 83, 113.
Suget(e), -tte, *s.* subject, 7, 15, 19, 130.
Sumdell, *adv.* 'some-deal,' somewhat, 225.
Sum-tym, *adv.* sometime, formerly, 195.
Suppos, *s.* opinion formed, decision made, 158.
Sure, *a.* safe, secure, 183.
Surfaite, -ayte, -ete, *s.* surfeit, excess, 23, 52, 67, 68, 186, 246; *v.* surfeit, 237; go to excess, 186.
Surfetouse, *a.* excessive, 242.
Surhabunde, *v.* superabound, 76, 81.
Surlen, *s. Perhaps* sirloin (but barely possible), 73. *See note.*
Surly, *adv.* securely, safely, 121.
Surmontant, *a.* in the ascendant (*astrol.*), 112.
Surmo(u)nt(e), *v. tr.* and *intr.* surpass, exceed, excel, 147, 186, 199; get the mastery, 32, 111.
Surte(e), *s.* security, surety, 53, 186.

Surenant, *s.* one who comes, a comer (tr. *aduenieus*), 103.
Suspec(c)ious, *a.* suspicious, 117, 235.
Suspecte, *a.* suspected, 157, 190.
Sustantyf, *a.* vegetative (*tr.* uegetiua), 96.
Sustenable, -tinable, *a.* vegetable, 90, 95.
Sustentement, *s.* support, 50.
Suster, *s.* sister, 194.
Sutely, Suttilly, *adv.* subtly, 131, 209.
Sut(t)il(l), -yl(e), *a.* subtle, 80, 127, 220, 240.
Sutillyte, *s.* delicacy, fineness, 117.
Swage, *v.* assuage, 244.
Sweche, *a.* such, 106, 107.
Swene, Swevne, *s.* dream, 157, 199.
Swerde, *s.* sword, 164, 167, 198. Swerde mene, 215, = swordsmen.
Swilk, *a.* such, 50.
Swote, *s.* sweat, 244.
Swyche, -yk, -ylk, *a.* such, 60, 89, 101, 107. Swylk lyk, *a.* suchlike, 97.
Syche, *v.* sigh, 232.
Syggynge, *s.* saying, 186.
Sygh, *s.* sight, 212; *v.* saw (*p.t.*), 19.
Sygyn, *s.* sign, 230.
Syke, *a.* sick, 81. Syknes(se), *s.* 67, 81, 92.
Sylle, *v.* sell, 169.
Symoun and aggrauacionn, 74. Meaningless perversion of misread or misunderstood Latin.
Symplenesse, *s.* foolishness, weakness, 104.
Synewy, *a.* sinewy, 226.
Syngne (*pl.* Syngnesse, 219), *s.* sign, 232.
Synguler, *a.* private, 132. Syngulerte, *s.* 233.
Synnevey, -owy, Synowy, *a.* sinewy, 222, 226, 236, 241.
Synnowe, *s.* sinew, 227, 241.
Synnyer, *s.* sinner, 201.
Syrepe, -upe, *s.* syrup, 33, 83.
Sythe, *s.* time, 60.
Sythen, *adv.* since, 113. *See* Sethen.
Syungne, *s.* sign, 222.

Taght(e), *pp.* taught, 104, 144.
Taiche, *s.* stain, blemish, 188. *See* Tecche.
Taillet, *pp.* shaped, 223, 227.
Take, *v.*; Take on = undertake, 174; hence, Takynge on = enterprise, 180; take in hande, an hande, on honde = attempt, undertake, 59, 143, 171, 179, 187. Take to hevynesse = *aegre ferre*, be vexed or grieved at, 172. Take, Takyn, *pp.* taken, 15, 24, 29, 70, 143, 174, 175.
Takenynge, *s.* tokening, 47.
Takynge, *s.* talking ?, 54; winning, gain, 132.
Talent(e), *s.* disposition, nature, character, 15, 177; inclination, appetite, 24, 132, 141, 187, 239, 241. Male talent(e) = ill will, 12, 175.
Talentid, *a.* disposed, addicted, given, 228.
Tastable, *a.* of the touch, pertaining to touch (*tr.* palpatiua), 98.
Taste, *s.* sense of touch, 208.
Tecch(e), *s.* stain, blemish, 103, 231, 232. Techyd, *pp.* Euyl-t. = vicious, 116.
Tecche, *v.* teach, 9, 83, 180. Techand, *pp. pr.* 42.
Tell(e), *v. t.* lytill of (by), = think lightly of, 172, 232.
Temprely, *adv.* temperately, 237, 242.
Temprure, -pure, *s.* temperance, moderation, 146, 244; even balance, 221, 244, 246; *a.* temperate, 247; *adv.* moderately, 247.
Termyne, *v.* determine, 42, 93.
Terre, *s.* tear, 199.
Tetle, *s.* (*pl.* tetlys), title, 42.
Tha, *for* that (*rel. pr.*), 160.
Thar(e), *pron.* their, 140, 193.
That on (oon), . . . that othir = the one . . . the other, 8, *freq.*
Thawrtouer, *a.* thwarting, 'cross,' 188.
Thay, *dem. a.* those, 153, 160, 172, 225.
Payme, *pron.* them, 58.
Thechynge, *s.* teaching, 149.
Thedroward, *adv.* thitherward, thither, 163.
Thedyr, *adv.* thither, 57, 140. Thedyrwarde, *adv.* thitherward, thither, 184.
Thee, Thegh, *s.* thigh, 106, 166, 177.
Thegh, *s.* custom (= Thewe), 211; *adv.* though, 141, 180, 181, 193, 200.
Ther al-aboute, *adv.* in all that quarter, 198.
Ther(e)-as, *adv.* where, in which, 34, 153, 166, 174, 195, 198, 199, 224, 231; when 166, 215; since, be-

Glossary. 287

cause, seeing that, 134; whereas, 193.
Ther-ayeynes, *adv.* contrariwise, 141.
Therin as, *adv.* wherein, 167.
Therse, *v.* ferment, (*for* therfe)? 70.
Thewe, *s.* thief, 138, 181; (always in *pl.*) character, disposition, 3, 94, 100, 216.
This, *pr.* and *a.* these, 135, 137, 139, 146, 147, 149. He þis, 102, = this man.
Tho, *dem. a.* and *pr.* those, 20, 84, 134, 140, 167, 173, 211, 231; þo, *adv.* then, 52.
Thogh, *s.* thought, 242.
Thole, *v.* endure, 65.
Thoner, *s.* thunder, 97.
Þore, *adv.* there, 109.
Thorugh, Þoruȝ, Þourgh, Throgh, Throght, Throw, Þurgh, *prep.* through, 14, 16, 17, 47, 57, 72, 142, 144, 152, 153, 174.
Thoure, *s.* tower, 215.
Thow, *a.* two, 164, 190.
Thralle, *s.* servile person, 224.
Threes, *adv.* thrice, 141.
Thretynge, *s.* threatening, 217.
Þreuth, Throuth, *s.* truth, 49, 211.
Threst, þrist, *s.* thirst, 83, 105. Thristy, *a.* thirsty, 56, 83.
Throgh, Throw, Þurgh, *prep.* See Thorugh = through.
Thryes, *adv.* thrice, 58.
Thurle, *v.* 'thrill,' penetrate, 203.
Thurste, *s.* thirst, 166; *v.* 159.
Thyn, *a.* thin, 240.
Thynke, *s.* thing, 214, 248.
Thythynges, -is, *s.* tidings, 160, 174.
Tirande, *s.* tyrant, 153.
To, *adv.* until, till, 61, 81, 83, 84, 85, 88, 92, 105.
To-brenne, *v.* burn, 68.
To-comynge, *a.* coming, future, 196.
To-frushyd, *pp.* broken, dashed, to pieces, 106.
To-for(e), *prep.* before, 153, 169.
To-giddyr, *adv.* together, 163.
To-growynge, *a.* growing close (to), 230.
Token, *v.* betoken, 221.
Tok(e)nynge, *s.* sign, token, 59; sign of the zodiac, 72, 73, 86, 106.
Tole, *s.* tool, 29.
Toode, *s.* toad, 152, 212.
Torment, *v.* tormented (*p.t.*), 52.

Tormenty, *s.* torment, 192.
Torn(e), *v.* turn, 62, 194; turn away, avert.
Toþer = other (of two), 51, 89.
Tow, *a.* two, 127.
Toward, *prep.* near, beside, 110.
Towch, *v.* touch, 148, 183.
Traldome, *s.* thraldom, 201.
Translate, *v.* carry off, transfer, 132, 200.
Traua(i)ll(e), *s.* labour, work, 151, 152, 158, 170, 242, 243; *v.* work, 76.
Trayson(e), Tresoun, Treyson, *s.* treason, 36, 164, 175, 204.
Trechour, -ure, *a.* treacherous, 115, 116, 235.
Tree, *s.* wood, 70, 77, 110.
Treely, *adv.* truly, 172.
Treetys, *s.* treatise, 118.
Tren, *a.* wooden, 177.
Tren(e), Trenne, *s. pl.* trees, 141, 239, 243.
Tresoun, *s.* See Trayson.
Treso(u)r(e), *s.* treasure, 16, 36, 60, 102.
Trespas(e), *s.* wrong-doing, 103; *v.* (with *to*), derogate, detract (from), 62.
Treste, *s.* and *v.* trust, 170, 198.
Tretabill, -ble, *a.* conciliatory (Fr. *traitable*), 103, 109, 211.
Tretand, = 'treating,' 103. Debonerly tretand = tr. *benigne pertractans*.
Trete, *v.* threaten, 178; treat, discuss, 13, 20.
Trete(e), -yce, *s.* treatise, 87, 90, 236.
Tretynge, *s.* threatening, threat, 152.
Trewe, *a.* true, 19, 58.
Treyson, *s.* See Trayson.
Triasendale, *s.* 33. *See note.*
Triet, *pp.* tried, 188, 241.
Triplycite, *s.* triplicity (*astron.*), 112.
Trist(e), *s.* trust, 46, 54, 76, 104; *v.* 64, 106.
Trobbyl, Troble, Trowbele, -ble, *v.* trouble, confuse, disorder (the brain), 72, 80; trouble, grieve, annoy, vex, 105, 139.
Trobely, -ille, *a.* clouded (of eyes), 30; cloudy, troubled, 28.
Trowbelid, -blit, *pp.* troubled, anxious, 217; (of the eyes or face) troubled, clouded, 228, 230. Trowbely, *adv.* in a troubled or clouded manner, 229.

Troue. *v.* think, believe, 193. *See* Trowe.
Trouth, *v.* troth, betroth, affiance, 190, 191.
Trowage, *s.* tribute, 57. *See* Truage.
Trow(e), *v.* believe, credit (a person), 58, 139, 187; believe, place faith in (a thing), 14; trust (with to), 52; believe (to be), think, 63.
Truage, *s.* tribute, 140, 174.
Trvbill, *v.* trouble, 241.
Trues, Truse (*pl.* Trues, 163), *s.* truce, 163, 164.
Trump (up), *v.* proclaim by trumpet, 163.
Truse, *v.* truss, 179; *s. see* Trues.
Tryacle, *s.* remedy, 20.
Tryed, 85; an attempt at L. *tritus*, bruised.
Tryst(e), *s.* trust, confidence, 110; *v.* trust, 64, 164, 178, 210.
Tuche, *v.* touch, 195.
Tunge, *s.* tongue, language, 33.
Turment, *s.* torment, torture, 169; disturbance, tumult, 244; *v.* torment, torture, 183, 206.
Turmentrie, *s.* torture, torment, 183.
Turmenty, *s.* torment, 169.
Turse, *v.* truss, pack up, 162.
Turtille, -tyll, -ture, *s.* turtle-dove, 35, 104, 212, 221.
Tuty, *s.* tutia, 95.
Twyes, *adv.* twice, 15, 58, 72.
Tyme, *s.* time; in tymes ... in tymes (181) = sometimes ... sometimes; weather, 93, 220; *pl.* 74; season, 27, 72, 74, 247.
Tympan, *s.* drum, 97.
Tyne, *v.* lose, 93.
Tynge, *s.* thing, 165.
Tyraunt, *a.* tyrannous, 212.
Tythynges, *s.* tidings, 129, 200.

Vaille, *v.* avail, 247.
Valure, *s.* valour, 190; esteem, estimation, 139.
Variance, *s.* variation, diversity, 72.
Varia(u)nt, *a.* fickle, changeable, 137, 221, 231.
Varne, *v.* warn. Varnyte, *pp.* 195.
Varyant, *a.* fickle, 230.
Vaut, *s.* vault, 153.
Vaylant, -llaunt, *a.* of avail, 125, 167.
Vche, vche a, *a.* each, 77, 94, 109.

Vedlak, *s.* (collective), the married, married people, 191.
Veer(e), *s.* spring, 27, 75, 82, 243, 246.
Vegetabilite, *s.* vegetable, plant, 90.
Veir, *s.* spring, 72.
Velanye, -eny, -eyny, *s.* villainy, 107, 136, 187.
Vele, *s.* calf, 244.
Venurie, *s.* venery, hunting, the chase, 247.
Venym, *s.* and *v.* poison, 64.
Ver, *s.* spring, 27.
Veraily, -aly, *adv.* truly, 136, 191.
Verious, *s.* verjuice, 33.
Verray, *a,* true, 52, 153, 169.
Vertu(e), Virtue, *s.* virtue, 147, 188, 189; valour, 110, 174; (mental) vigour, 134; efficacy, 91, 240; vigour, 244.
Vertues, -ose, *a.* virtuous, 134, 182, 189; strong, powerful; active (digestion), 246. Vertuosly, *adv.* bravely, valiantly, 162; virtuously, 236.
Vesyte, *v.* visit, 110.
Veye, *s.* way, manner, 214.
Veyr, *s.* spring, 73.
Viage, *s.* journey, 204.
Vicaire, -arie, -ary, *s.* captain of a thousand men, 109, 214.
Vickidly, 166, -nesse, 199; Viesly, 194; Vif, 192, 194; *for* wickedly, -ness, wisely, wife.
Villache, *s.* village, 184.
Vilte, *s.* vileness, abjectness (tr. *abiectionem*), 91.
Virchippe, *s.* 'worship,' honour, 181.
Virocis, *s.* 85. *See note.*
Visach, *s.* visage, face, 228.
Vise, *a.* wise, 182. More visyr, *compar.* 211.
Viside, *a.* 130 = avised (*q. v.*). Be avised = take counsel, deliberate.
Vitayle, *s.* (collective) provisions, stores, 109.
Vitnesse, 157; Vitte, 208; Vixe, *v.* 176 = witness, wit, wax (*v.* grow).
Vmbesege, *v.* besiege, 182.
Vmbethynke, *v. reflex.* bethink, reflect, 138, 150, 157. Hence Vmbethoght, *pp.* thoughtful, deliberate, prudent, 155, 157; *also* (as *adv.*) after reflection, 138.
Vmbylappe, *v.* enwrap, 49.
Vmlappe, *v.* embrace, comprise, 109.

Glossary. 289

Vnabilte, *s.* disability, infirmity, 67.
Vnawyssely, *adv.* inadvisedly, injudiciously, 138.
Vnce, *s.* ounce, 84, 85.
Vnconvenient, *a.* unseemly, unbecoming, 8.
Vnconynge, -cun(n)ynge, *s.* ignorance, 42, 211, 233, 234; *a.* ignorant, 156.
Vnconyngnesse, *s.* ignorance, 235.
Vndauntdid, *a.* unbroken, untamed (horse), 168.
Vndirlout, *pp.* placed in subjection, 54, 55.
Vndreset, *v.* place in subjection, 146.
Vnderstandant, *a.* 93. Vnderstandandly, *adv.* advisedly, 101.
Vnderstandynge, -stondynge, *s.* meaning, sense, signification, 42, 51; intelligence, 68, 134, 211.
Vnderstondant, *s.* man of understanding, 51.
Vnderstonde, *v.* listen to, hear, tr. *exaudire*, 48; understand, 211; Vnderstond(e), *pp.* understood, 5, 6, 83, 173, 201, 211.
Vndertake, *v.* rebuke, chide, 5.
Vndertakynge, *s.* enterprise, 111.
Vnethe, Vnneth(es), -is, *adv.* scarcely, 49, 68, 129, 136, 161, 180, 198.
Vnmyghty, *a.* unfit, 52.
Vnrule, *s.* misrule, 136.
Vnryght, *s.* wrong, grievance, 59. Vnryghtly, *a.* wrong, false, 161.
Vnto, *adv.* until, 72, 84; *prep.* till, 34.
Vnwyt, *s.* ignorance, 42.
Vnyette, *pp.* united, 143.
Volatille, *s.* bird, 98.
Volde *for* wolde, = would, 202.
Voucheous, *a.* braggart?, 235.
Voyde, *v.* empty, make empty, 240; *a.* empty, 240; vain, 154.
Vp, *prep.* upon, 123, 129, 166, 175, 184, 202.
Vpbere, *v.* advance, promote, 53. Vpberand, *ppl. pr.* assisting, relieving, 104.
Vpberer, *s.* supporter, 45, 99, 100, 101.
Vprere, *v.* upraise, elevate, 223, 227.
Vprys, *v.* uprise, 89.
Vpsprongyn, *pp.* risen, 99.
Vpspryngand, -ant, *s.* ascendant, 112.
Vpsteye, *v.* ascend, 95. Vpstiyng, -styand, *a.* ascendant, 86; *s.* 86.
Vset, Vssit, *pp.* used, 193, 247.
Vtreli, *adv.* utterly, 188.

SECRETE.

Vttre, *a.* outer, remoter, 71.
Vygerous, *a.* vigorous, 57.
Vylenys, *a.* villainous (misreading of L. *vilis*), 104.
Vyntyr *for* winter, *s.* 124.
Vyolenly, *adv.* violently, 194.
Vyrchipp(e), 132, 154, 171; Vysdome, 138; Vyse, 134, 140, 144, 188; Vysely, -ilie, 131, 137; *for* worship, honour, wisdom, wise, *s.* and *a.*, wisely.
Vysage, *s.* appearance, outward show, 157.
Vyue, *a.* five, 138.
Vyxe, *v.* wax, grow, 244.

Wa(c)che, *s.* (tr. *insidias*) lying in wait, ambush, 89, 111.
Wakand, *a.* (tr. *vigilans*), vigilant, 47.
Walue, *s.* value, 171.
Wancraunt, *a.* roving, libertine, 212.
Wanhoppe, *s.* despair, 145.
Wapour, *s.* vapour, 239.
War(e), *a.* aware, 22, 59, 132.
Warre, *a.* wary, cautious, 107.
Warmstore, Warny stoor, *s.* (= garniture), store, supply (*Cath. Angl.* Warnstore. *Stratmann*, Warnesture), 61, 65, 111. *v.* 57.
Wastoure, *s.* waster, spendthrift, 131.
Wat, *v.* know, wot, 65.
Wayk, *a.* weak, 68, 80, 104, 116. Wayknesse, *s.* 47.
Wayne, *a.* vain, 129. In wayne, 198.
Wayte, *s.* ambush, 37; *v.* watch for, 93.
Webbe hous, *s.* weaver's house, 99.
Weddowe, *s.* widow, 168.
Weddyr, Weder, *s.* weather, 174, 248 (*plur.* 16).
Wede, *s.* weed, 164.
Wedlak, -lok, *s.* wedlock, marriage, 192, 193, 194; used *attrib.* 194.
Weere, *s.* (= veere), spring, 246.
Weigh, *s.* the 'Balance,' Libra, 74.
Wel, *adv.* very, 71; *v. for* weld, = 'wield,' rule? 135.
Weldy, *a.* strong, mighty, 154.
Wele, *s.* well, 102.
Wele lorde, 53. (Meaningless. *See note.*)
Weleyghe, *s.* willow, 81.
Welle, *adv.* very, 4, 17, 20; well, 20, &c.
Wende, *s.* wind, 52; *v.* wend, go, 80, 110, 153.

U

Wene, *v.* ween, think, 167. Wende (*p.t.*), 157, 188, 217.
Weneth(e), *for* unethe, scarcely, 136, 187.
Wenge, *s.* wing, 110, 111.
Wengeaunce, 174; Wenym, 174, 195; *for* vengeance, venom.
Wepen, -yn, *s.* weapon, 184.
Wepyntaille, -tale, *s.* wapentake, 184.
Weraly, *adv.* truly, verily, 135.
Werhy, *adv.* whereby, 150.
Were, *s.* war, 158, 159, 177, 179.
Werke, *s.* work, 11, 22, 111, 145; *v.* 71.
Werkyng(e), *s.* pain (tr. *dolorem*), 76, 77; work, operation, 111.
Werld, *s.* world, 66.
Werldes, 113. *See note.*
Werre, *s.* war, 21, 129, 185; *v.* fight, 129; war against, attack, 156.
Werriour, Wer(r)yor, *s.* warrior, 154, 155, 197.
Werry, *a.* very, true, real, 146.
Wers, *s.* verse, 141.
Werse, *a.* worse, 26. Werst, worst, 7, 115.
Wertu, *s.* virtue, 131. Wertuʒ, *a.* virtuous, 131.
Wery, *a.* weary, 12.
Weryn, *v.* were, 150, 173, 179, 198.
Weryor, *s.* *See* Werriour.
Wesse, *v.* wash, 239.
Wete, *v.* know, 49, 61, 110, 113.
Wethyr, *s.* wether (*attrib.*), 163.
Wetith, *v. imperat.* know, 71.
Weyand, *a.* heavy, 71.
Weyne, *s.* vein, 229.
Whare-tyll, *adv.* to what end? why? 113.
Whe, *pron.* we, 191, 195.
Whedyr, *adv.* whither, 107; *conj.* whether, 163.
Whele, *s.* circle, turn, 214.
Whem, *pron.* whom, 88.
Whemen, *s.* (*pl.*) women, 195.
Wher, *v.* were, 193.
Wher-throgh, -thurgh, *adv.* through which, by means of which, whereby, 128, 175, 184, 250.
Whik, *a.* quick, living, alive, 59.
Whilk(e), *rel. pron.* which, 41, 42, 48, 103.
Whit, *a.* white, 88.
Whon, *adv.* when, 63.
Whore, *adv.* where, 89, 96.

Whych, 206; Whyt, 89; Whyth, 167; = which, white, with.
Wies, Wijs, *a.* wise, 4, 11, 12, 195. Wiesser, *compar.* 193. Wiesdom, *s.* wisdom, 195.
Wike, *s.* week, 203.
Wilke, *pron.* 'whilk,' which, 42.
Will, *s.* well, spring, source, 135.
Willed, *pp.* with a will, willing, 103.
Willy, *a.* voluntary, 96 (tr. *woluntaria*).
Wirchipfully, 182; Wirship, 193; Wirsshupe, 193. *See* Wors(c)hipe, &c.
Wirke, *s.* work, 93.
Wirkere, *s.* worker, 90.
Wirkynge, *s.* operation, 93, 106.
Wisser, *a. compar.* wiser, 193.
Wiste, *v.* knew (*p.t.*), 157.
Wite, *v.* know, 5. Witeth, *v. imperat.* 3.
Withdraw(e), Wythdraw(e), *v. reflex.* abstain, refrain, 13, 52, 56, 58, 75, 77, 113, 189, 218, 243; retire, withdraw, 196; *tr.* keep (hands, &c.) from, 52, 70, 241; *abs.* refrain, 8; draw (breath), 152.
With-holde, Wyth-holde, Withold(e), *v. reflex.* abstain, refrain, 52, 73, 116; *tr.* keep, retain (in memory), 9; keep, preserve, maintain, 78; keep (one's counsel), 98; keep, detain, 110; restrain, 113. Withhaldand, *pp. pr.* preventing, restraining, 93. Wyth-holde, *pp.* bound, confined, 161. With(h)oldynge, *s.* retention (in memory), 116; costiveness, 67.
Withouten, -yn; Wythouten, -yn; *prep.* without, 54, 58, 62, 63, 64, 70, 85, 100, 103.
Witt(e), *s.* wisdom, 34, 196, 207; a sense, 208, 242; *v.* know, 137, 143, 196. *Also* Wyt(te).
Wittynge, *s.* tidings, information, 163.
Wix, *v.* wax, grow, 196, 213, 226, 232. 243, 244, 245, 246. Wixen, *pp.* fullgrown, 161.
Woche, *rel. pron.* which, 143.
Wodd(e), Wode, *s.* wood, 97, 180, 196.
Wod(e), *a.* mad, 138, 225; Wodeman, *s.* madman, 121, 167. Wod(e)nesse, -nys, *s.* madness, 153, 167, 181, 188. *Also* Wood(e), &c.
Woillaunce, *s.* Good w., 123, = Bienvoillaunce, 183, (*q. v.*) = good will, = Fr. *bienveillance*. (*N.E.D.* Bienveillance.)

Wol(le), v. will, 8, 11, 21.
Wombe, s. stomach, belly, 70, 71, 74, 244, 248; fig. 74.
Wonde, s. and v. wound, 162, 180, 181, 190, 201; pp. wound, twisted, 161.
Wone, s. wont, habit, 26.
Woned, -nnet, -nnyd, a. wont, 167, 204, 220, 238, 239.
Wonne, v. dwell, live, 180.
Wonte, v. for wotte?, know, 165.
Wonyd, -yt, a. wont, 140, 153, 220, 224, 225, 243.
Wood(e), a. mad, 159, 229. Woodnesse, s. madness, 230. See Wod(e), &c.
Woot, v. wot, know, 49, 51.
Worche, v. work, 157, 206.
Worne, s. serpent, 202.
Wormode, s. wormwood, 30.
Wors(c)hipe, -ippe, -up, also Wirship, -sshuppe, Wyrchippe, Wyrsepe, -shupe, s. and v. honour, 6, 11, 15, 19, 49, 53, 58, 67, 99, 137, 163, 193, 201, 215.
Wors(c)hipfull(e), also Wyrchipphull, a. honourable, 8, 19, 34, 35, 53, 133, 212. Wors(c)hipfully, also Wirchiphully, adv. honourably, 8, 100, 182.
Worthely, a. worldly, 146, 150.
Wost(e), v. 2 p. s. knowest, wottest, 5, 166, 213.
Woundyr, adv. wonderfully, 245.
Wourte, s. wort, root, 175.
Wourth, a. worth, 196.
Wourthe, a. wroth, 220.
Wourthy, a. worthy, 197.
Wox, v. waxed, grew (p.t.), 182, 217, 237.
Woxen, pp. grown, 244.
Woyce, 140; Woyde, 129, for voice, void.
Wp, prep. upon, 123.
Wreth(e), s. wrath, anger, 135, 136, 188, 220; v. enrage, anger, 105, 199, 220, 224, 231.
Wrethfull, a. wrathful, 233.
Wretyn, pp. written, 59, 93.
Wriet, v. turned aside or awry, averted (p.t.), 152.
Write, -tte, pp. written, 122, 149, 165, 183, 203; s. writ, 145.
Wroght, pp.; as a. artificial (tr. artificialis), 83, 85.

Wrongwys, -gys, a. unjust, 'wrongous' (tr. iniuriosus), 115, 116.
Wrothe, -i, -y, a. wrathful, passionate, 157, 229.
Wrothynesse, s. wrathfulness, passionateness, 227.
Wry, v. avert, turn away, 152; wriet (p.t.).
Wyce, s. = vice, 205.
Wych(e), rel. pron. which, 206, 243.
Wyke, s. week, 204.
Wylowe, s. willow, 33.
Wyn(e), s. vine, 244; wine, 229, 244.
Wynne, v. come, resort, 57, 140.
Wyrche, v. work, 149. Wyrchynge, -kynge, s. working, operation, 80; doing, performance, 136.
Wyrchiply, adv. worthily, 164.
Wyrchippe, Wyrchipphull, Wyrsepe, -upe. See Wors(c)hip(e), &c.
Wys(e), Wysse, a. wise, 3, 11, 92, 129.
Wysdome, s. 148, 149. Wysly, adv. 54.
Wyste, s. fist, 156; knew (p.t.), 190, 196.
Wyt, s. wisdom, 57, 63, 66; a sense, 98.
Wyten, pp. known, 65.
Wyth, s. withy, 161.
Wythdrawe, -holde, -outen (-yn). See Withdraw, &c.
Wythout-take, prep. except, 185.
Wytte, s. a sense, 58; v. know, 143. See Witte.

Y, pron. I, 4, 5, 41, 142, 165, 167.
Yaf, v. gave, 4, 34.
Y-aforsayde, pp. aforesaid, 147.
ȝalow(e), ȝalwe, a. yellow, 80, 85. ȝalownes, s. yellowness, 114.
Yanglour, s. talkative fellow, 227, = Ianglour, q. v.
Yarde, s. rod, 161, 167, 208.
Yate, s. gate, 37, 159.
Yaue, Yaw(e), v. gave, 130, 134, 139, 167, 174, 185, 191, 199.
Yawyn, ppl. given, 173.
Y-blessyd, 148; -bore, 152; -broght, 210; -broke, 143; -byl[d?]id, 201; -callid, -it, 136, 149, 197, 246; -chafit, 242; -changed, 172; -clothyd, 139; -colorid, -urid, 229, 230; -confortid, 240, 247; -cronet, 199; -custumet, 247; pps. blessed; borne; brought; broken; built; called; chafed,

Glossary.

heated; changed; clothed; coloured; comforted, strengthened; crowned; accustomed.
Ydell, *a.* idle, vain, 64.
Y-do, -don, 162, 165, 181, 190; -drawe, 71; -dreddyd(e), 137, 183; -dressid, 165; *pps.* done; drawn; dreaded; dressed = fully prepared, ready.
Yede, *v.* went, 154, 168.
Yef, *adv.* if, 192, 193, 195, &c.: But yef = unless.
Yefe, *v.* give, 7, 35, 144.
Yefte, *s.* gift, 6, 20, 103, 130, 131, 134, 157, 195, 209, 210.
Yeld(e), ȝelde, *v.* yield, give, render, 5, 49, 57, 140; fulfil, 110; show, prove, 57.
Yene, *v.* yawn, 23.
Yer, ȝer, *s.* year, 145. ⁊ On *p.* 63, mistransl. of *annales*.
Yeue, -ve, *v.* give, 6, 35, 134, 149, 157, 236. Yeue, Yevene, Yeuyn, *pp.* given, 5, 34, 156, 158, 202.
Yeuer, *s.* giver, 157.
Yewe, *v.* give, 134, 157, 198; incline, 241; *reflex.* 138; *pp.* given, 142, 143. Yewyn, *inf.* 179; *ppl.* 190.
Yf(e), *adv.* if. Yf all, *adv.* even if, although, 42. But yf, *adv.* unless, 144.
Y-fillit, 241; -flesshide, 224; -founde, 137, 160; -freklet, 233; *pps.* filled; fleshed; found; freckled.
Yfte, *s.* gift, 173, 185.
Y-gaderid, 208; -gouernet, -yd, 207, 208; -greuid, -yd, -wid, 199, 238, 241; -hadd, 133, 163; -harde, 221, 235; *pps.* gathered; governed; grieved; had; heard.
Y-hillid, *pp.* flayed, 167.
Y-holde, 138, 175; -hyde, 136; *pps.* held, deemed; hidden.
Yieft, *s.* gift, 139.
ȝit, *adv.* yet, still, 41, 75.
Y-kepid, -ppit, 132, 246; -know, 123, 134; -kyde, 148; -ladd, 201; lauenyt, 241; *pps.* kept; known; cut?; led; leavened.
Yle, *s.* Hyle, 94. *See note.*
Y-lefte, 240; -lettyd, 174; *pps.* left; hindered.
Y-like, *a.* like, 169, 230, 233.
Y-likenet, -yd, *pp.* likened, 230.
Ylkon, -oon, *indef. pron. See* Ilk.
Y-lowet, 172; -lowid, 137, 170, 183, 189; -lyghted, -id, 214, 237; *pps.* lowered, degraded; loved; lightened, relieved.
Y-lyke, *a.* like, 149, 155; alike, 151, 211.
Y-lykenid, -yd, *pp.* likened, 228, 230.
Ymagynary, *a.* imaginative, tr. (virtutem) *imaginatiuam*, 97.
Ymagynacione, *s.* image, likeness, 217.
Y-makid, -yd, 143, 240, 245; -manerit(e), 226, 231; -markyd, 199; -mesurid, 233, 236; -meuet, 156, 189; *pps.* made; mannered; marked, limited; measured; moved.
Yn(ne), *adv.* and *prep.* in, 57, 70.
Ynde, *s.* India, 34.
Yndoys, *s. pl.* Indians, Hindoos.
Ynens, *prep.* against, towards, 86, 93, 105.
Ynogh, *adv.* enough, fairly, tolerably, 236.
Y-norshid, 166; -noryschid, 237; *pp.* nourished.
Ynow(e), *adv.* enow, enough, 6, 180, 186.
Y-nued, 170; -nurshit, 237; *pps.* (an)noyed, grieved; nourished.
Yofe, *v.* give, 36.
Yolde, ȝolden, *pp.* granted, given, rendered, 56; yielded, surrendered, 133.
Yolow, *a.* yellow, 222.
Yonge-man-hode, *s.* youthful manliness, 134.
Yonglynge, -gge, *s.* youngling, youth, 144, 217, 247.
ȝons, *adv.* at once, straightway, 100.
Yonte, Yonture, *s.* joint, jointure, 225, 227.
Youse, *a.* joyous, 240.
Yousty, *v.* joust, 144.
Yove, en(e), *pp.* given, 5, 12, 20.
Yowele, *s.* jewel, 146.
Yowuthe, *s.* youth, 245.
Yoy, *s.* joy, 138, 150, 240.
Yoyful, *a.* joyful, 247.
Y-passet, -passyd, -paste, *pp.* past, 157, 166.
Ypatetik, *s.* peripatetic, 47.
Ypocritly, *adv.* hypocritically, 9.
Y-praysid, 172; -prowide, -yd, 134, 148; -put, -tte, 162, 237; -queynte, 237; *pps.* praised; proved; put; quenched.
Yre, *s.* ire, wrath, 12.
Y-rostid, *pp.* roasted, 246.
Yrysshe, *a.* Irish, 166.

Ys, *pron.* = his, 57, 94; = is, 57.
Y-sayde, 178; -sette, -ssette, 162, 208, 237; -seueret, 223; -slayne, 162; -spokyn, 212; -spratelid, 233; *pps.* said; set; severed, separated; slain; spoken; scattered.
Yssue, *s.* outgoing (of money), 211.
Y-stabelid, 135, 196; -storid, 142; -strawet, 242; -swolle, 227; *pps.* established; stored; strewn; swollen.
Ytaile, *s.* Italian, 51.
Y-take, 158, 197; -temperit, 186; -temptid, 213; -thoght, 157; -thryste, 229; -translatid, 236; -trauaillit, -alid, 162, 242; -trowbelid, 173; *pps.* taken; tempered, temperate; tempted; thought; thrust; translated; fatigued, troubled, tormented; troubled, disordered.
Yvel, -ille, *a.* evil, 6, 10, 19, 38; *adv.* ill, 8; *s.* evil, 17, 38.
Y-vitaillid, 215; -wone, 133; -wonet, 213; *pps.* victualled; won; wont, accustomed.
Y-wourthe, *v.* be; let him y-w., = let him be, left him alone, 217.
Y-writ(te), 149, 176, 207; *pp.* written.
ȝyf, *adv.* if, 70.
ȝyt, *adv.* yet, 60; still, 70.

www.ingramcontent.com/pod-product-compliance
Lightning Source LLC
Chambersburg PA
CBHW021959220426
43663CB00007B/876